LIBRARY OF HEBREW BIBLE/
OLD TESTAMENT STUDIES

513

Formerly Journal for the Study of the Old Testament Supplement Series

BEHOLD YOUR KING

The Hope for the House of David
in the Book of Zechariah

Anthony R. Petterson

t&t clark

NEW YORK • LONDON

T & T Clark International, 80 Maiden Lane, New York, NY 10038

T & T Clark International, The Tower Building, 11 York Road, London SE1 7NX

T & T Clark International is a Continuum imprint.

Visit the T & T Clark blog at www.tandtclarkblog.com

Library of Congress Cataloging-in-Publication Data
Petterson, Anthony Robert.
  Behold your king : the hope for the House of David in the book of Zechariah / by Anthony Robert Petterson.
      p. cm. -- (The library of Hebrew Bible/Old Testament studies ; 513)
  Revision of the author's thesis (Ph. D.)--Queen's University of Belfast, 2006.
  Includes bibliographical references (p.   ) and index.
  ISBN-13: 978-0-567-09215-1 (hardcover : alk. paper)
  ISBN-10: 0-567-09215-1 (hardcover : alk. paper)
  1. Bible. O.T. Zechariah--Criticism, interpretation, etc. I. Title. II. Series.

  BS1665.52.P48 2009
  224'.9806--dc22

                    2009004448

06 07 08 09 10   10 9 8 7 6 5 4 3 2 1

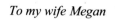

To my wife Megan

CONTENTS

ABBREVIATIONS

ABD	*Anchor Bible Dictionary*. Edited by D. N. Freedman. 6 vols. New York, 1992
ABR	*Australian Biblical Review*
ANE	*Ancient Near East*
ANES	Ancient Near Eastern Studies
AOTC	Abingdon Old Testament Commentaries
ATD	Das Alte Testament Deutsch
BDB	Brown, F., S. R. Driver, and C. A. Briggs. *The New Brown–Driver–Briggs-Gesenius Hebrew and English Lexicon*. Peabody, Mass.: Hendrickson, 1979
BHS	*Biblia Hebraica Stuttgartensia*
BibInt	*Biblical Interpretation: A Journal of Contemporary Approaches*
BibSac	*Bibliotheca Sacra*
BRev	*Bible Review*
BTB	*Biblical Theology Bulletin*
BZAW	Beihefte zur *ZAW*
ConBOT	Coniectanea biblica, Old Testament
CBQ	*Catholic Biblical Quarterly*
CRBS	*Currents in Research: Biblical Studies*
ESV	English Standard Version
EvQ	*Evangelical Quarterly*
FAT	Forschungen zum Alten Testament
FRLANT	Forschungen zur Religion und Literatur des Alten and Neuen Testaments
GTJ	*Grace Theological Journal*
HAR	*Hebrew Annual Review*
HeyJ	*Heythrop Journal*
IB	*Interpreter's Bible*. Edited by G. A. Buttrick et al. 12 vols. New York, 1951–57
IBRI	Interdisciplinary Biblical Research Institute
ICC	International Critical Commentary
IDB	*The Interpreter's Dictionary of the Bible*. Edited by G. A. Buttrick. 4 vols. Nashville, 1962
IEJ	*Israel Exploration Journal*
ITC	International Theological Commentary
IVP	Inter-Varsity Press / InterVarsity Press
JBL	*Journal of Biblical Literature*
JBQ	*Jewish Bible Quarterly*

JETS	*Journal of the Evangelical Theological Society*
JJS	*Journal of Jewish Studies*
JNES	*Journal of Near Eastern Studies*
JNSL	*Journal of Northwest Semitic Languages*
JSOT	*Journal for the Study of the Old Testament*
JSOTSup	Journal for the Study of the Old Testament: Supplement Series
JSS	*Journal of Semitic Studies*
MT	Masoretic text
NAB	New American Bible
NASB	New American Standard Bible
NCBC	*The New Century Bible Commentary*
NEB	*New English Bible*
NICOT	New International Commentary on the Old Testament
NIDOTTE	*New International Dictionary of Old Testament Theology and Exegesis*. Edited by W. A. VanGemeren. 5 vols. Grand Rapids, 1997
NIV	New International Version
NRSV	New Revised Standard Version
NSBT	New Studies in Biblical Theology
OTG	Old Testament Guides
OTL	Old Testament Library
RB	*Revue Biblique*
RHPR	*Revue d'histoire et de philosophie religieuses*
RTR	Reformed Theological Review
SBL	Society of Biblical Literature
SBS	Stuttgarter Bibelstudien
SCM	*Student Christian Movement*
SJT	*Scottish Journal of Theology*
TDOT	*Theological Dictionary of the Old Testament*. Edited by G. J. Botterweck and H. Ringgren. Translated by J. T. Willis, G. W. Bromiley, and D. E. Green. 8 vols. Grand Rapids, 1974–
TynBul	*Tyndale Bulletin*
TOTC	Tyndale Old Testament Commentaries
VT	*Vetus Testamentum*
VTSup	Vetus Testamentum, *Supplements*
WBC	Word Biblical Commentary
WMANT	Wissenschaftliche Monographien zum Alten und Neuen Testament
ZAW	*Zeitschrift für die alttestamentliche Wissenschaft*

ACKNOWLEDGMENTS

This book is a revised Ph.D. dissertation, completed in 2006 at the Queen's University of Belfast under the supervision of T. D. Alexander. Desi was a wonderful supervisor. Not only was his expertise and diligence of great benefit to me at every stage of my research, but he provided me with a wonderful model to imitate of serious scholarship that has at its heart a desire to benefit the church. I count it a privilege to have studied under him.

There were many others who provided encouragement and support along the way and it is with a great sense of gratitude that I acknowledge their kindness. I am very thankful to the trustees of the F. J. Church Scholarship who generously contributed to the costs of my study. Thanks must also go to the staff of Tyndale House, Cambridge, for the opportunity to spend a week or so each year using their research facilities. So too, the staff at the Irish Baptist College who co-ordinated the practical aspects of my study, and more recently the staff of Morling College Library. A word of appreciation is also in order for my Old Testament teachers Barry Webb and Graeme Goldsworthy, for the way that they helped to bring the Old Testament to life while I was an undergraduate student and their encouragement to do further study.

It was a real privilege to be actively involved in the life of Grosvenor Road Baptist Church in Dublin during our four years in Ireland. I am very thankful to God for the way that they ministered to my family and me. We have many fond memories of our time in the Emerald Isle. The Lord Jesus' words in Mark 10:29–30 have been so true for us. Special thanks must go to John Samuel who has been so understanding of the demands of this research and has always provided me the time and support to dedicate to it. Thanks also must be given to Frank and Damaris Rieger, Ingrid Harley, James Hely Hutchinson, Heather Maiden, Les Gill, Gary Millar, and Geoff Harper who have taken an interest in my research and provided various input along the way.

Since submitting my thesis, I have benefited from the feedback of Philip Johnston and James McKeown along with interactions with Michael Stead who completed his doctoral research on the intertexts of Zechariah. I have also received helpful feedback from the editorial staff of T&T Clark and students at Morling College, who have sat through my classes on Zechariah that have drawn heavily on my thesis. Any deficiencies in this book remain my own.

Last and by no means least I would like to acknowledge my family: my parents who have always encouraged me in my studies; my four children—Luke, Emma, Sophie and Hugh—who happily went to the other side of the world with me; and my wife Megan who selflessly served our family and spent too many lonely evenings while her husband kept company with Zechariah. This book is gratefully dedicated to her with all my love.

Soli Deo gloria.

Chapter 1

INTRODUCTION

1.1. *The Hope for the House of David in the Book of Zechariah*

Scholarship is radically divided over the nature of the hope for the house of David in the post-exilic period, particularly in relation to the expectations concerning the governor Zerubbabel and whether the Davidic monarchy would be reinstated in Jerusalem. Moreover, with the failure of Zerubbabel to take the throne, there is no agreement among scholars on the shape that the earlier hope for a Davidic king took. Was it heightened or reduced? Or did the earlier Davidic hope shift in a democratizing, priestly, or theocratic direction?

While the book of Zechariah is certainly not easy to interpret, it makes a vital contribution to this significant issue. The prophet Zechariah had an important part to play in articulating a future role for the house of David after the return of the exiles as they sought to rebuild their community life. However, one of the main reasons for the lack of consensus over the nature of the Davidic hope in Zechariah is that much research has tended to interpret the nature of the Davidic hope through the historical-critical framework laid down by Julius Wellhausen. Even though Wellhausen's assessment of the post-exilic period has been challenged by a number of scholars in recent years, his approach still seems to dominate the way that the Davidic hope is read in the book of Zechariah, even by those who reject his synthesis.

A fresh assessment of the nature of the Davidic hope in Zechariah is called for that adopts a more literary approach to the book and is willing to question some of the long-held conclusions of the Wellhausian approach. It is on these grounds that the present study aims to investigate the nature of the Davidic hope in the final form of the book of Zechariah in order to contribute to a deeper understanding of the topic. What will be demonstrated is that the canonical book of Zechariah presents a robust hope for a future king in the line of David who will be instrumental to Yahweh's restoration programme for his people and the world.

1.2. *Setting and Date of the Book of Zechariah*

The book of Zechariah can be divided into three parts: chs. 1–6, 7–8, and 9–14.[1] Zechariah 1–6 contains an introduction (1:1–6), the night visions of Zechariah (1:7–6:8), and a sign action (6:9–15). It is dated to the second year of Darius (520–519 B.C.E.) (1:1, 7), some twenty years after the initial return of exiles from Babylon. The visions largely concern the rebuilding of the community in Jerusalem with the reconstruction of the temple under Zerubbabel and the re-establishment of the cult under the high priest Joshua. Hope is held out that with evil removed, sin atoned for, and Yahweh present once more among his people, Israel will experience his blessing again and this will spill over to the nations.

Zechariah 7–8 is dated in the fourth year of Darius (518 B.C.E.) (7:1). This section functions as a bridge or transition between chs. 1–6 and 9–14.[2] The scholarly consensus is that the dates in chs. 1–8 are indicative of chs. 1–6 and 7–8 being written in the period closely preceding or not long after the completion of the temple.[3]

Zechariah 9–14 is clearly a different style of prophetic literature to chs. 1–8. It is undated and lacks reference to readily identifiable persons, including the prophet himself. There is no need to trace the scholarly proposals for its setting and date here as others have done this adequately.[4] Approaches to dating chs. 9–14 that depend on identifying

---

1. Most scholars divide the book at the end of ch. 8. Some see a further division at the end of ch. 11. More recently, E. W. Conrad, *Zechariah* (A New Biblical Commentary; Sheffield: Sheffield Academic Press, 1999); M. A. Sweeney, *The Twelve Prophets*. Vol. 2, *Micah, Nahum, Habakkuk, Zephaniah, Haggai, Zechariah, Malachi* (Berit Olam: Studies in Hebrew Narrative & Poetry; Collegeville: Liturgical Press, 2000); B. G. Webb, *The Message of Zechariah: Your Kingdom Come* (The Bible Speaks Today; Leicester: IVP, 2003); S. Frolov, "Is the Narrator also Among the Prophets? Reading Zechariah Without Presuppositions," *BibInt* 13 (2005): 13–40, divide the book into two parts (1:7–6:15 and 7:1–14:21) with an introduction (1:1–6) on the basis of the dates that head each section. For literary and thematic reasons, I follow M. J. Boda, *The NIV Application Commentary: Haggai, Zechariah* (Grand Rapids: Zondervan, 2004), in seeing 7:1–8:23 as a separate section, and divide the book into three sections: 1:1–6:15; 7:1–8:23; 9:1–14:21.

2. M. J. Boda, "From Fasts to Feasts: The Literary Function of Zechariah 7–8," *CBQ* 65 (2003): 390–407, rightly argues that this section is a "bridge" or "segue" between Zech 1–6 and 9–14. However, I disagree with his characterization of Zech 1–6 as a vision of "realized" restoration in the present and chs. 9–14 as "frustrated" and directed towards the future, and will argue that both sections address the present and future.

3. Boda, *Commentary*, 29–30.

4. See the treatments by H. G. Mitchell, "A Commentary on Haggai and Zechariah," in *A Critical and Exegetical Commentary on Haggai, Zechariah, Malachi and*

historical events and people within the prophecy have proven rather elusory.[5] More recently, some scholars have sought to determine a date through linguistic analysis, but this has yielded conflicting results.[6] Some scholars have given up seeking to place Zechariah into an historical context and deal with it purely from a literary point of view.[7] However, purely literary and ahistorical readings prove to be rather emaciated.[8] An approach is needed that deals with both historical and literary concerns, while realizing the limitations of each.[9]

I believe that there are good reasons for placing chs. 9–14 in a later period in the prophet's ministry, after the completion of the temple (9:8). Differences with chs. 1–8 can be accounted for by the different literary genre that the prophet adopts at a later time.[10] The continuation of themes that run through the book further supports this.[11]

Jonah (ed. S. R. Driver, A. Plummer, and C. A. Briggs; Edinburgh: T. & T. Clark, 1912), 1–357 (232–59); D. L. Petersen, "Zechariah, Book of (Zechariah 9–14)," *ABD* 6:1065–68; B. G. Curtis, *Up the Steep and Stony Road: The Book of Zechariah in Social Location Trajectory Analysis* (Academia Biblica 25; Atlanta: SBL, 2006), 118–23.

5. The conquest mentioned in 9:1–8 does not reflect any known conquest and the reference to Greece in 9:13 could be contemporary with Darius. See the penetrating critique of this approach by P. L. Redditt, *Haggai, Zechariah and Malachi* (NCBC; London: Marshall Pickering, 1995), 97–100.

6. A. E. Hill, "Dating Second Zechariah: A Linguistic Reexamination," *HAR* 6 (1982): 105–34, sees Zech 10–14 as linguistically similar to Zech 1–8 and dates it 515–475 B.C.E. Contrast this with S. L. Portnoy and D. L. Petersen, "Biblical Texts and Statistical Analysis: Zechariah and Beyond," *JBL* 103 (1984): 11–21, who see three distinct sections in Zechariah with different settings, though they do not suggest a date for chs. 9–11 or 12–14. Portnoy and Petersen critique and build on the work of Y. T. Radday and D. Wickmann, "The Unity of Zechariah Examined in the Light of Statistical Linguistics," *ZAW* 87 (1975): 30–55.

7. E.g. Conrad, *Zechariah*, 7: "I am not concerned with reading Zechariah as providing information about a world external to it."

8. See the critique of Conrad by F. I. Andersen, "Reading the Book of Zechariah: A Review Essay," *ANES* 37 (2000): 229–40. Andersen highlights the inconsistencies in Conrad's approach.

9. See the work of I. W. Provan, V. P. Long, and T. Longman III, *A Biblical History of Israel* (London: Westminster John Knox, 2003), 81, who contend "a happy marriage between literary and historical concerns is possible, desirable, and necessary."

10. I find the arguments of J. G. Baldwin, *Haggai, Zechariah, Malachi: An Introduction and Commentary* (TOTC; Leicester: IVP, 1972), 66–70; Webb, *Zechariah*, 43–46, for dating chs. 9–14 in the early post-exilic period and attribution to the prophet Zechariah compelling. Literary differences with chs. 1–8 can be explained in ways other than multiple authorship. While not agreeing with all his conclusions,

1.3. *Method and Justification*

The stimulation for this study came from the publication of W. H. Rose's monograph, *Zemah and Zerubbabel: Messianic Expectations in the Early Postexilic Period.*[12] Rose challenges the standard reconstruction of the nature of Davidic hope in the book of Zechariah and argues that Zechariah always looked to a future figure, beyond Zerubbabel, for the realization of the Davidic hope. Rose's thesis seems to my mind to be more in keeping with the bigger picture of the Davidic dynasty tradition in the Hebrew Bible than the standard scholarly reconstructions that see in Zechariah a diminished hope for any future Davidic king. However, while I find myself in agreement with Rose's wider thesis, I remain unsatisfied with the way that he deals with some of the intertextual issues, particularly the background of "Zemah" in the wider Hebrew Bible, as this has important implications for the nature of the Davidic hope. Furthermore, Rose only examines chs. 1–6. Can his broader thesis be sustained in relation to the whole book? It was these things that led to the desire to research the nature of the Davidic hope in the whole of the book of Zechariah.

While there have been a number of major studies on the Davidic hope in the Hebrew Bible that have sections dealing with Zechariah,[13] many

particularly the radically different social setting of chs. 9–14, Curtis, *Steep*, 231–80, has recently presented a case for Zecharian authorship of chs. 9–14.

11. B. S. Childs, *Introduction to the Old Testament as Scripture* (London: SCM Press, 1979), 482–83, notes themes that are common to the book, such as: the security of Jerusalem; the judgment and conversion of the nations; paradisal fertility; the gathering of the exiles; cleansing and the outpouring of the Spirit; and a messianic figure. Some, including R. D. Moseman, "Reading the Two Zechariahs as One," *Review and Expositor* 97 (2000): 487–98, have disputed the significance of this. Other scholars, among them A. Hartle, "The Literary Unity of Zechariah," *JETS* 35 (1992): 145–57, have noted similar literary features such as vocabulary and style that run through the book, but again others, such as M. Butterworth, *Structure and the Book of Zechariah* (Sheffield: JSOT, 1992), 272–75, have disputed the significance of this. M. C. Black, "The Rejected and Slain Messiah who is Coming with his Angels: The Messianic Exegesis of Zechariah 9–14 in the Passion Narratives" (Ph.D. diss., Emory University, 1990), 47, argues that what holds chs. 9–14 together is not literary structure, but a unity based on common themes and a common perspective. I believe that many of the themes and the perspective of chs. 9–14 run through the book as a whole.

12. W. H. Rose, *Zemah and Zerubbabel: Messianic Expectations in the Early Postexilic Period* (JSOTSup 304; Sheffield: Sheffield Academic Press, 2000).

13. E. W. Hengstenberg, *Christology of the Old Testament*, vol. 2 (Florida: Macdonald, 1854); J. Klausner, *The Messianic Idea in Israel from Its Beginnings to the Completion of the Mishnah* (London: George Allen & Unwin, 1956);

short studies that have sought to focus on aspects of the Davidic hope or give an overview of the hope for the house of David in the whole or part of the book of Zechariah,[14] and some major studies that have dealt

S. Mowinckel, *He That Cometh* (trans. G. W. Anderson; Oxford: Blackwell, 1956); W. Wifall, "David—Prototype of Israel's Future?," *BTB* 4 (1974): 94–107; J. Becker, *Messianic Expectation in the Old Testament* (Edinburgh: T. & T. Clark, 1980); C. A. Briggs, *Messianic Prophecy: The Prediction of the Fulfilment of Redemption Through the Messiah* (Peabody, Mass.: Hendrickson, 1988); G. van Groningren, *Messianic Revelation in the Old Testament* (Grand Rapids: Baker, 1990), 872–914; A. Laato, *Josiah and David Redivivus: The Historical Josiah and the Messianic Expectations of Exilic and Postexilic Times* (ConBOT 33; Stockholm: Almqvist & Wiksell, 1992), 234–301; S. L. Cook, *Prophecy and Apocalypticism: The Post-Exilic Social Setting* (Minneapolis: Fortress, 1995), 123–65; W. C. Kaiser Jr., *The Messiah in the Old Testament* (Grand Rapids: Zondervan, 1995), 211–27; K. E. Pomykala, *The Davidic Dynasty Tradition in Early Judaism: Its History and Significance for Messianism* (Atlanta: Scholars Press, 1995), 53–126; A. Laato, *A Star is Rising: The Historical Development of the Old Testament Royal Ideology and the Rise of the Jewish Messianic Expectations* (Atlanta: Scholars Press, 1997), 195–218; R. A. Mason, "The Messiah in the Postexilic Old Testament Literature," in *King and Messiah in Israel and the Ancient Near East: Proceedings of the Oxford Old Testament Seminar* (ed. J. Day; JSOTSup 270; Sheffield: Sheffield Academic Press, 1998), 338–64.

14. The following list does not include any of the commentaries on Zechariah that also deal with this question to a greater or lesser degree. Studies include: A. Bentzen, "Quelques remarques sur le mouvement messianique parmi les Juifs aux environs de l'an 520 avant Jésus-Christ," *RHPR* 10 (1930): 493–503; C. L. Feinberg, "Exegetical Studies in Zechariah," *BibSac* 103 (1946): 161–75; R. T. Siebeneck, "Messianism of Aggeus and Proto-Zacharias," *CBQ* 19 (1957): 312–28; J. G. Baldwin, "Ṣemaḥ as a Technical Term in the Prophets," *VT* 14 (1964): 93–97; K.-M. Beyse, *Serubbabel und die Königserwartungen der Propheten Haggai und Sacharja: Eine historische und traditionsgeschichtliche Untersuchung* (Stuttgart: Calwer, 1972); K. Seybold, "Die Königserwartung bei den Propheten Haggai und Sacharja," *Judaica* 28 (1972): 69–78; M. Barker, "The Two Figures in Zechariah," *HeyJ* 18 (1977): 38–46; W. J. Dumbrell, "Kingship and Temple in the Post-exilic Period," *RTR* 37 (1978): 33–42; R. A. Rosenberg, "The Slain Messiah in the Old Testament," *ZAW* 99 (1987): 259–61; P. G. Samaan, *Portraits of the Messiah in Zechariah* (Washington: Review and Herald Publishing Association, 1989); P. D. Hanson, "Messiahs and Messianic Figures in Proto-Apocalypticism," in *The Messiah* (ed. J. H. Charlesworth; Minneapolis: Fortress, 1992), 67–75; J. E. Tollington, *Tradition and Innovation in Haggai and Zechariah 1–8* (JSOTSup 150; Sheffield: JSOT, 1993); I. M. Duguid, "Messianic Themes in Zechariah 9–14," in *The Lord's Anointed: Interpretation of Old Testament Messianic Texts* (ed. P. E. Satterthwaite, R. S. Hess and G. J. Wenham; Carlisle: Paternoster, 1995), 265–80; C. L. Meyers and E. M. Meyers, "The Future Fortunes of the House of David: The Evidence of Second Zechariah," in *Fortunate the Eyes That See* (ed. A. B. Beck et al.; Grand Rapids: Eerdmans, 1995), 207–22; E. M. Meyers, "Messianism in First and Second

specifically with the Davidic hope in parts of the book of Zechariah (including the work of Rose, and more recently T. Pola, on chs. 1–6),[15] there is no major study that has sought to assess and integrate these findings in a study of the Davidic hope expressed in the whole canonical book of Zechariah. This is in large measure due to the historical-critical approach to the book that has dominated critical scholarship.

By comparing seven critical commentaries on Zechariah published since 1984, M. H. Floyd has demonstrated that while recent commentators are much less concerned with the reconstruction of original texts and descriptions of detailed redaction histories than earlier commentators, each still reflects the trends of historical criticism, and in turn informs a view of the post-exilic period largely defined by Julius Wellhausen (1844–1914), primarily in his *Prolegomena zur Geschichte Israels* (1878).[16] Wellhausen saw the post-exilic period as having four characteristics:

Zechariah and the 'End' of Biblical Prophecy," in *"Go to the Land I Will Show You"* (ed. J. E. Coleson and V. H. Matthews; Winona Lake: Eisenbrauns, 1996), 127–42; B. Uffenheimer, "Zerubbabel: The Messianic Hope of the Returnees," *JBQ* 24 (1996): 221–28; G. Herrick, "Conceptions of Davidic Hope in Ezekiel, Zechariah, Haggai, and the Chronicles" (1998 [cited 2008]), online: http://www.bible.org/page .asp?page_id=1565; M. J. Boda, "Oil, Crowns and Thrones: Prophet, Priest and King in Zechariah 1:7–6:15," *JHS* 3 (2001): Article 10; D. I. Block, "My Servant David: Ancient Israel's Vision of the Messiah," in *Israel's Messiah in the Bible and the Dead Sea Scrolls* (ed. R. S. Hess and M. D. Carroll R.; Grand Rapids: Baker Academic, 2003), 17–56; J. J. Collins, "The Eschatology of Zechariah," in *Knowing the End from the Beginning: The Prophetic, the Apocalyptic and their Relationships* (ed. L. L. Grabbe and R. D. Haak; JSPSup 46; London: T&T Clark International, 2003), 74–84; W. H. Rose, "Messianic Expectations in the Early Postexilic Period," in *Yahwism After the Exile: Perspectives on Israelite Religion in the Persian Era* (ed. R. Albertz and B. Becking; Assen: Royal Van Gorcum, 2003), 168–85; M. J. Boda, "Figuring the Future: The Prophets and the Messiah," in *The Messiah in the Old and New Testaments* (ed. S. E. Porter; Grand Rapids: Eerdmans, 2007), 35–74.

15.   H. J. Fuggian, "The Messianic Teachings of Zechariah 9–14" (Ph.D. diss., Southern Baptist Theological Seminary, 1951); P. Lamarche, *Zacharie IX–XIV: Structure Littéraire et Messianisme* (Etudes Bibliques; Paris: Lecoffre, 1961); L. V. Meyer, "The Messianic Metaphors in Deutero-Zechariah" (Ph.D. diss., University of Chicago, 1972); Black, "Messiah"; Rose, *Zemah*; V. M. Jauhiainen, "'Behold, I Am Coming': The Use of Zechariah in Revelation" (Ph.D. diss., University of Cambridge, 2003); T. Pola, *Das Priestertum bei Sacharja* (FAT 35; Tübingen: Mohr Siebeck, 2003); C. A. Ham, *The Coming King and the Rejected Shepherd: Matthew's Reading of Zechariah's Messianic Hope* (New Testament Monographs 4; Sheffield: Sheffield Phoenix, 2005).

16.   First published under the title *Geschichte Israels* and translated into English in 1885. See M. H. Floyd, "Zechariah and Changing Views of Second Temple

1) profound theological disappointment resulting from Judah's failure to regain national independence and restore the Davidic monarchy; 2) degeneration and loss of vitality resulting from the centralization of the cult of Yahweh in Jerusalem and its dissociation from local holy places; 3) loss of critical spirit resulting from the decline of prophecy; and 4) priestly legalism resulting from the theocratic authority given to Jerusalem's temple establishment by Judah's imperial overlords.[17]

Floyd believes that Zechariah's expectation of a future Davidic king has often been read and interpreted through this framework, and in turn has reinforced Wellhausen's synthesis. However, recent trends in Old Testament scholarship have raised questions concerning the traditional historical-critical approach to Zechariah, and Wellhausen's assumptions in particular. One of the challenges comes from the improved picture of Judaism of the Second Temple period that the Dead Sea Scrolls have given, showing that it is more richly diverse than Wellhausen ever imagined. For Floyd, this calls for a reassessment of documents such as Zechariah.[18]

At the same time, historical-critical approaches to Zechariah have come to something of an impasse. In 1979, B. S. Childs noted that,

> few Old Testament books reflect such a chaos of conflicting interpretations. If further evidence for the breakdown of method within the discipline is needed, the reader is challenged to compare the recent proposals made by Lamarche, Otzen, Hanson and Seybold. Although I am aware of the danger of offering still another approach, perhaps attention to the canonical shape of the book can aid rather than exacerbate the problem.[19]

Judaism in Recent Commentaries," *Religious Studies Review* 25 (1999): 257–63. The commentaries treated by Floyd are: D. L. Petersen, *Haggai and Zechariah 1–8: A Commentary* (OTL; London: SCM Press, 1985); C. L. Meyers and E. M. Meyers, *Haggai, Zechariah 1–8: A New Translation with Introduction and Commentary* (New York: Doubleday, 1987), and *Zechariah 9–14: A New Translation with Introduction and Commentary* (New York: Doubleday, 1993); H. G. Reventlow, *Die Propheten Haggai, Sacharja und Maleachi* (Göttingen: Vandenhoeck & Ruprecht, 1993); D. L. Petersen, *Zechariah 9–14 and Malachi: A Commentary* (OTL; London: SCM Press, 1995); Redditt, *Zechariah*; R. Hanhart, *Sacharja 1–8* (Biblisher Kommentar Altes Testament; Neukirchen–Vluyn: Neukirchener Verlag, 1998). W. O. McCready, "The 'Day of Small Things' vs. the Latter Days: Historical Fulfillment or Eschatological Hope?," in *Israel's Apostasy and Restoration* (ed. A. Gileadi; Grand Rapids: Baker, 1988), 223–36; and Cook, *Prophecy and Apocalypticism*, 123, also believe that the modern treatment of Zechariah has its roots in Wellhausen's views.

17. Floyd, "Changing Views," 260.
18. Ibid.
19. Childs, *Introduction*, 476.

Commentators since Childs have made similar comments, particularly concerning chs. 9–14. For instance, R. J. Coggins gives his assessment of the results of the historical-critical approach to these chapters: "all the supposed allusions to dates and historical situations are so vague and imprecise that there is little likelihood of general agreement, and as a result this approach to the material has been abandoned by many scholars."[20] In a similar vein, R. Rendtorff concludes that the allusions to contemporary history within chs. 9–14 remain largely incomprehensible and our insight into the post-exilic situation as a whole is still too incomplete.[21]

While there has been a shift towards more literary approaches to Zechariah, many commentators still seem reluctant to deal with all fourteen chapters of Zechariah as constituting a distinct prophetic book.[22] Even recent literary-critical approaches that read Zechariah as part of "the Twelve" often connect chs. 1–8 more closely with Haggai and chs. 9–14 with Malachi than with each other.[23] However, Floyd contends that even if little of the material in chs. 9–14 originated with the prophet Zechariah himself, this does not justify the continued treatment of the book of Zechariah as two separate works. He rightly says:

> The book's attainment of its canonical form is not only a literary phenomenon; it is also a historical event, and even a primarily historical approach must therefore deal at some point with the integration of 1–8 and 9–14 to form the book as a whole. Historical as well as literary commentators must eventually ask what concept provided a basis for bringing 9–14 and 1–8 together as a single prophetic book named for Zechariah and what sociocultural circumstances made such a concept viable.[24]

20. R. J. Coggins, *Haggai, Zechariah, Malachi* (OTG; Sheffield: JSOT, 1987), 63.

21. R. Rendtorff, *The Old Testament: An Introduction* (trans. J. Bowden; Philadelphia: Fortress, 1986), 241.

22. An observation also made by Floyd, "Changing Views," 262.

23. For instance, see the essays in J. D. Nogalski and M. A. Sweeney, eds., *Reading and Hearing the Book of the Twelve* (SBLSS 15; Atlanta: SBL, 2000); P. L. Redditt and A. Schart, eds., *Thematic Threads in the Book of the Twelve* (BZAW 25; Berlin: de Gruyter, 2003). E. Ben Zvi, "Twelve Prophetic Books or 'The Twelve': A Few Preliminary Considerations," in *Forming Prophetic Literature: Essays on Isaiah and the Twelve in Honour of John D. W. Watts* (ed. J. W. Watts and P. R. House; JSOTSup 235; Sheffield: Sheffield Academic Press, 1996), 125–56 (135–37), sounds a more cautious note on this enterprise, emphasizing the integrity of the individual books. Ben Zvi is right to focus on the individual books, but it is becoming more apparent that there is also value in determining how the books function within the Twelve. See, for instance, C. R. Seitz, *Prophecy and Hermeneutics: Toward a New Introduction to the Prophets* (Grand Rapids: Baker Academic, 2007).

24. Floyd, "Changing Views," 262.

Floyd believes that a literary-critical approach to the book of Zechariah holds much promise for developing a new view of the post-exilic age, and he concludes that the task still remains "to give a clear impression of what a predominantly literary-critical interpretation of Zechariah would contribute to an altogether post-Wellhausen view of the post-exilic period, or vice versa."[25]

Picking up this challenge, the present study aims to do this with special reference to the role of the house of David in the early post-exilic period. The "literary criticism" that Floyd refers to is not the classical sense of searching for evidence of multiple layers in texts, but refers to the analysis of literary artistry in the final form of the text. When this text is a prophetic book, literary criticism is concerned with issues of structure, rhetorical intent, use of vision reports, sign-actions, metaphor, poetry, narrative, and intertextuality (inner-biblical exegesis). I shall closely examine the final form of the book of Zechariah with these things in view to determine the nature of the Davidic hope that the book of Zechariah presents.

With the shift in Old Testament studies to the more synchronic approaches of canonical criticism and the new literary criticisms, there has been a growing interest in studying the final form of books of the Hebrew Bible. While some synchronic approaches are ahistorical, there is also legitimacy in studying the final form of a text to determine at least the historical perspective of the final editor, if not the original author.[26] My concerns are both synchronic and diachronic. They are synchronic in the sense that the final form of the book has come from a particular point

25. Ibid., 260.

26. The case for this has been well made by V. Philips Long, "The Art of Biblical History," in *Foundations of Contemporary Interpretation* (ed. M. Silva; Grand Rapids: Zondervan, 1996), 281–429, and "Historiography of the Old Testament," in *The Face of Old Testament Studies: A Survey of Contemporary Approaches* (ed. D. W. Baker and B. T. Arnold; Grand Rapids: Baker, 1999), 145–75. In the latter article, Philips Long makes the point that with the move from historical-critical studies that can silence the text "by dissection and fragmentation," modern literary studies may provide the "an opportunity to hear more clearly what the texts have to say, including what they may have to say about the historical past" (p. 162). See also J. Bimson, "Old Testament History and Sociology," in *Interpreting the Old Testament: A Guide for Exegesis* (ed. C. C. Broyles; Grand Rapids: Baker Academic, 2001), 125–55. J. M. Vincent, "L'apport de la recherche historique et ses limites pour la compréhension des visions nocturnes de Zacharie," *Biblica* 87 (2006): 22–41, argues that critical exegesis has been too obsessed by the quest to find the historical setting of Zechariah's night visions and that these readings are often circular and disappointing. While Vincent highlights some of the pitfalls of reconstructing history from biblical texts, he is ultimately overly sceptical about this.

in time and I shall focus on the final form to determine the hopes evinced by it. They are also diachronic, not because I will be seeking to uncover earlier redactional layers, but because the author of Zechariah uses biblical texts from earlier times. I shall seek to understand how they have been utilized and how they contribute to an understanding of the Davidic hope in the book.[27] This study will also be done in close dialogue with the diversity of scholarly interpretations.

There are two further reasons for studying the final form of the book. First, analyses of the hope for the house of David that depend on editorial stages involve more hypotheses and are therefore more tentative than those established from the final form of the text. Those who argue that the book of Zechariah has undergone revisions automatically assume that it is possible to reconstruct from the present book a comprehensive understanding of these earlier stages. However, there is no guarantee of this. Indeed, the final editor may have radically reversed the outlook of earlier stages. The whole enterprise of elucidating the pre-history of the text is very hypothetical and inherently unstable.[28]

Second, and closely related, there is a methodological weakness in interpretations of Zechariah that depend on ascribing various parts of the book to different authors at different times in order to understand the text. Apparent inconsistencies in the book become the basis for supposing different provenances of the parts against which the book is then interpreted. This argumentation runs the risk of being circular, with the conclusions proven by the nature of the hypotheses. Hence, an interpretation that explains the apparently diverging ideas in the text without the need to assign various parts to different authors and editorial stages is to be preferred, since it rests on a more secure basis, namely, the text as we actually have it.

Can a single picture of the hope for the house of David be found in the book? While it is true that the book of Zechariah poses many challenges

---

27. There are a number of studies that have identified the intertexts in Zechariah. These studies will be utilized in the present study and include: Tollington, *Tradition*; R. A. Mason, "The Use of Earlier Biblical Material in Zechariah 9–14: A Study in Inner Biblical Exegesis," in *Bringing out the Treasure: Inner Biblical Allusion in Zechariah 9–14* (ed. M. J. Boda and M. H. Floyd; JSOTSup 370; London: Sheffield Academic Press, 2003), 1–208. See also M. R. Stead, *The Intertextuality of Zechariah 1–8* (LHBOTS 506; New York: T&T Clark International, 2009).

28. Evidence for textual layers is often found on the basis of a reconstructed history. The reconstructed textual layers are then used as support for the same history. The circular nature of the historical-critical approach is well demonstrated by J. Barton, *Reading the Old Testament: Method in Biblical Study* (Philadelphia: Westminster, 1984). See particularly his comments on pp. 56–58.

to the interpreter, it is somewhat disingenuous to claim that it is unread-
able, or that the author intended it to be so.[29] Furthermore, the attempt to
read chs. 9–14 independent of chs. 1–8, or to break it up into smaller
units, or to see it as reflecting different ideologies, founders on the difficulty that both the editor(s) responsible for the final form of the book and
those responsible for its incorporation into the Hebrew canon clearly
considered it to be a coherent prophetic book. Moreover, it is the whole
work that they attribute to the prophet Zechariah.[30] This in itself should
caution against reading the different parts as setting forth different ideologies. Further, we would expect the final editor to produce a harmonious
work. While it is possible that he may fail to do this, it is methodologi-
cally sounder to attempt to understand the final form of the text on the
basis that it is coherent, rather than jump too quickly to the conclusion
that it is not. If the final form can be explained consistently as it stands,
then it is no longer necessary to make hypothetical reconstructions concerning the parts in order to understand it. This study will therefore seek
an integrated and coherent reading of the hope for the house of David in
the book of Zechariah. In doing this, other interpretations based on
hypothesized earlier editorial stages will certainly not be ignored, but
weighed carefully in the light of what is found. While the presentation
will be thematic, the foundation is a reading of the canonical book of
Zechariah against the background of its intertexts.

1.4. *Procedure*

This study seeks to determine the nature of the hope for the house of
David in the book of Zechariah.[31] Before examining the text of Zechariah
in detail, and in order to determine the texts most relevant for the present
study, the numerous scholarly reconstructions of the Davidic hope in the
book of Zechariah will be surveyed in a literature review (Chapter 2).
What will be seen is that there is a real lack of consensus, largely due to
differing views on the authorship and editorial history of the book. At the
same time, the themes and passages from Zechariah that bear directly on

---

29. E.g. M. C. Love, *The Evasive Text: Zechariah 1–8 and the Frustrated Reader*
(JSOTSup 296; Sheffield: Sheffield Academic Press, 1999); H. S. Pyper, "Reading
in the Dark: Zechariah, Daniel and the Difficulty of Scripture," *JSOT* 29 (2005):
485–504.
30. Sweeney, *Twelve*, 566, makes the apt comment: "it is clearly designed to be
read as a single work that depicts both the visions and oracles or pronouncements of
the prophet Zechariah."
31. Unless otherwise stated, biblical quotations are from the ESV.

this topic emerge from the literature review: the role of Joshua and Zerubbabel; the nature and identity of the Shoot; the king; the shepherd; and the pierced one.[32] Each of these themes shall be closely examined in Chapters 3–7 in order to elicit the nature of the Davidic hope in Zechariah.

In his recent monograph, B. G. Curtis comments: "It is not possible to exegete Zechariah correctly without granting a prominent role to a future Davidic figure."[33] Similarly, M. J. Boda recently states that "greater attention needs to be given to the theme of future leadership hope in our reading of the book of the Twelve."[34] The present study attempts to do this and to demonstrate that the book of Zechariah presents a strong hope for the house of David, and in particular, for a future Davidic king who will usher in Yahweh's kingdom. It is hoped that this study will contribute not only to discussion of the book of Zechariah and the Twelve, but to other areas of research, in particular the extent of Messianism in the post-exilic period. While many scholars since the late nineteenth century have seen Messianism as arising quite late in Israel's history, and in some cases as not even being evident in the Hebrew Bible,[35] this is presently being challenged by a number of scholars.[36] It is hoped that the results of this study will also feed into this discussion.

32.   I will argue that the term "Shoot" is used as a title by Zechariah—hence it is capitalized. Since the other terms are used in Zechariah more as descriptions, rather than titles, lower case is used.

33.   Curtis, *Steep*, 191.

34.   M. J. Boda, "Messengers of Hope in Haggai–Malachi," *JSOT* 32 (2007): 113–31 (131).

35.   For instance, J. J. Collins, *The Scepter and the Star: The Messiahs of the Dead Sea Scrolls and Other Ancient Literature* (ABRL; New York: Doubleday, 1995), 31–33; Pomykala, *The Davidic Dynasty Tradition*, 5. W. S. Green, "Introduction: Messiah in Judaism: Rethinking the Question," in *Judaisms and Their Messiahs at the Turn of the Christian Era* (ed. J. Neusner, W. S. Green and E. S. Frerichs; Cambridge: Cambridge University Press, 1987), 1–13 (10), concludes: "preoccupation with the messiah was not a uniform or definitive trait, nor a common reference point, of early Jewish writings or the Jews who produced them." Also, R. J. McKelvey, "Temple," in *New Dictionary of Biblical Theology* (ed. T. D. Alexander and B. S. Rosner; Nottingham: IVP, 2000), 806–11 (806), writes, "Jewish eschatology could thrive without the hope of a Messiah."

36.   See, for example, R. E. Clements, "The Messianic Hope in the Old Testament," *JSOT* 43 (1989): 3–19; Satterthwaite, Hess, and Wenham, eds., *The Lord's Anointed*; W. Horbury, *Jewish Messianism and the Cult of Christ* (London: SCM Press, 1998); J. H. Sailhamer, "The Messiah and the Hebrew Bible," *JETS* 44 (2001): 5–23; Block, "Servant," 17–56.

Chapter 2

A LACK OF CONSENSUS

2.1. *Introduction*

Scholarship is divided on the nature of the hope for the house of David in the book of Zechariah. Did Zechariah foster hopes for the monarchy to be restored, or were his hopes entirely eschatological? And what was the role of Zerubbabel in all of this? R. L. Smith formulates the questions in this way: "Did Zechariah identify Zerubbabel as the messianic king and expect the new age to begin in his lifetime? Or did he say that the time is coming when the branch or shoot of David (the Messiah) will come and be both priest and king?"[1]

The answers to these questions are complicated by the different views on authorship and editing of the book of Zechariah. The consensus among critical scholars since the middle of the nineteenth century is that the authorship of chs. 9–14 differs from that of chs. 1–8.[2] Consequently, many believe that chs. 1–8 evince a different view of the house of David to that of chs. 9–14, reflecting the hopes of a different author (or authors) and of a different period. Further, in chs. 1–8 many believe that Zechariah's original visions have been expanded by later oracles that have "corrected" Zechariah's views. The present chapter will survey the answers that scholars have given to the question of the fortunes of the house of David in order to highlight the main issues that will be examined in the present study.

It is possible to define broadly three scholarly views concerning the shape of the Davidic hope in the book of Zechariah: (a) Zerubbabel failed to restore the Davidic monarchy and the Davidic hope was recast; (b) there was no hope for the restoration of the Davidic dynasty in Zerubbabel's day or beyond him; (c) Zerubbabel was never seen as the promised future king, but there was a clear hope for the restoration of a Davidic king beyond him. The literature presenting each of these views will now be reviewed.

---

1. R. L. Smith, *Micah–Malachi* (WBC 32; Waco: Word, 1984), 218.
2. Childs, *Introduction*, 475.

2.2. *Scholarly Views of the Hope for the House of David in the Book of Zechariah*

2.2.1. *Zerubbabel as Failed Restorer of the Davidic Monarchy with the Davidic Hope Recast*

The dominant critical view since Wellhausen is that that chs. 1–8 initially envisaged Zerubbabel as the one who would restore the Davidic dynasty after its demise during the Babylonian exile. Zerubbabel was a grandson of Jehoiachin and therefore a rightful heir to the throne of King David. After the return from exile, Zerubbabel was appointed as governor and played a leading role in the reconstruction of the temple. P. R. Ackroyd argues that for the Persians the appointment of Zerubbabel, with his Davidic ancestry, was a means of restoring order, conciliating the Jewish community, and establishing a useful outpost on the route to Egypt.[3] For the Jewish community, many scholars hold that Zechariah saw Zerubbabel, initially at least, as the one who would fulfil the hopes of earlier prophets in restoring the Davidic monarchy and become the means by which God would usher in a new age.[4]

On this view, Zechariah drew from the terminology of the earlier prophets to describe this coming royal figure (e.g. the "Shoot" in Jer 23:5; 33:15; cf. Jer 30:9) and applied this directly to Zerubbabel. For instance, R. P. Carroll writes:

> Zechariah obviously believed in Zerubbabel's royal status, his role in completing the building of the temple and his designation as bearer of the prophetic title "branch." He was the one who would be the focus of the divine action when the kingdoms were overthrown and he would occupy the royal throne. The new age was about to dawn and Zerubbabel was the key figure in that new age.[5]

---

3. P. R. Ackroyd, *Exile and Restoration: A Study of Hebrew Thought of the Sixth Century B.C.* (London: SCM Press, 1968), 190.

4. Ibid., 190. Mitchell, "Zechariah," 104: "Zechariah follows Haggai in recognising Zerubbabel as the Messiah and the restorer of the Davidic dynasty." See also H. G. May, "A Key to the Interpretation of Zechariah's Visions," *JBL* 57 (1938): 173–84; G. Wanke, "Prophecy and Psalms in the Persian Period," in *The Cambridge History of Judaism* (ed. W. D. Davies and L. Finkelstein; Cambridge: Cambridge University Press, 1984), 1:162–88 (166–69, 180–83); J. J. M. Roberts, "The Old Testament's Contribution to Messianic Expectations," in Charlesworth, ed., *The Messiah*, 39–51 (50).

5. R. P. Carroll, *When Prophecy Failed: Reactions and Responses to Failure in the Old Testament Prophetic Traditions* (London: SCM Press, 1979), 163. Also, Ackroyd, *Exile*, 196: "The new age is to be ruled by a royal figure, and the member of the Davidic line appointed by the Persians is appropriately designated."

Similarly, S. Mowinckel says:

> Referring to his name Zerubbabel (the shoot from Babel), Zechariah announces that he is *semaḥ*, the Branch, the Rod, which has shot up again from the stump of David's fallen family tree, showing that life and the energies of life have been renewed... Zerubbabel will be king over the restored Jerusalem, and will gain power and renown.[6]

However, not all scholars agree on the magnitude of this expectation. J. Klausner argues:

> The remote expectations [of the earlier prophets] became near at hand—and their magnitude was reduced. The Messiah was brought nearer in time and was made less exalted: he was a contemporary of those holding the expectations and he did not engage in large undertakings; hence his chief virtue was his descent from the house of David.[7]

Either way, the failure of Zerubbabel to take the throne and usher in the new age posed something of a problem.[8] Scholars argue that the hope Zechariah initially held for the house of David underwent a radical revision and contend that this can be seen in two ways: first, in the editing of chs. 1–8 to reflect the new situation; and second, in the addition of chs. 9–14, which modified the prophet Zechariah's work.

Although Wellhausen was the first to propose that the text was edited after Zerubbabel's failure to take the throne, there were scholars before him who thought that Zechariah identified Zerubbabel as the Shoot and that the full-blown hopes fixed on him went unfulfilled.[9] For instance,

---

6. Mowinckel, *He That Cometh*, 120–21. Mowinckel rejects completely the interpretation that Zechariah spoke of an eschatological Messiah.

7. Klausner, *Messianic*, 196.

8. There is no record indicating why Zerubbabel disappeared off the scene. The most popular explanation is that Zerubbabel fell out of favour with the Persians. L. Waterman, "The Camouflaged Purge of Three Messianic Conspirators," *JNES* 13 (1954): 73–78 (73), contends that Haggai and Zechariah conspired to make Zerubbabel king and Zerubbabel became the victim of their political propaganda. A later hand changed the text of Zech 6 to "camouflage the purge of Zerubbabel."

9. It was Wellhausen who first proposed that some time after Zerubbabel's failure and after hopes for a revival of the house of David had faded, an editor sought to rehabilitate Zechariah's prophecy by providing for the changed circumstance. One significant way in which his prophecy was edited was by substituting the name of Joshua the high priest in the place of Zerubbabel in 6:11. This editorial work also explains why there is confusion about the number of crowns in the text. So, J. Wellhausen, "Zechariah, Book of," in *Encyclopaedia Biblica* (ed. T. K. Cheyne and J. Sutherland Black; London: A. & C. Black, 1903), 4:5390–95 (5392): "Zerubbabel is certainly meant here, and, if the received text names Joshua instead

S. Davidson, writing before Wellhausen, believed it "probable that
Zechariah thought of Zerubbabel as the Messiah about to inaugurate the
glorious period of prophetic anticipations. He applies the epithet *the
Branch* to him—a Messianic epithet taken from the former prophets."[10]
Davidson also believed that there is a strong messianic element in chs. 9–
14. However, he considered that chs. 9–14 were written earlier than chs.
1–8, and not by the prophet Zechariah.[11] For Davidson, the unfulfilled
hope for Zerubbabel to take the throne is reflected in Malachi, who "does
not even venture to mention one of David's descendants."[12]

For scholars who fall into this first category, chs. 1–8 reflect, to some
extent, to use Carroll's term, a "failure of prophecy."[13] The hope held out
for the house of David in the person of Zerubbabel was dashed and the
text was edited in order to come to terms with disappointed expectations
and the change within the post-exilic community. But what became of
this earlier hope for the house of David once Zerubbabel failed to take
the throne? Scholarly opinion can be categorized into five views: (1) the
hope for the house of David is shifted in a priestly direction; (2) the hope
for the house of David is democratized; (3) the hope for the house of
David is subsumed by the hope for Yahweh to be king; (4); the hope for
the house of David is abandoned; or (5) the hope for the house of David
is projected onto a future Davidic king.

---

of him (6 $_{11}$), this is only a correction, made for reasons easy to understand, which
breaks the context and destroys the sense and the reference of 'them both' in
v. 13." Those who follow Wellhausen include: A. Van Hoonacker, *Les Douze Petits
Prophètes: traduits et commentés* (Paris: Gabalda, 1906), 630–34; Mitchell, "Zechariah," 185–86; Bentzen, "Remarques," 496; Klausner, *Messianic*, 196; D. W. Thomas,
"The Book of Zechariah: Chapters 1–8 (Introduction and Exegesis)," *IB* 6:1053–113
(1080); W. Neil, "Zechariah, Book of," *IDB* 4:943–47 (945); T. H. Robinson and
F. Horst, *Die zwölf kleinen Propheten: Hosea bis Micha; Nahum bis Maleachi* (HAT
14; Tübingen: J. C. B. Mohr [Paul Siebeck], 1964), 238; T. Chary, *Aggée–Zacharie,
Malachie* (Sources Bibliques; Paris: Lecoffre, 1969), 49, 110; Beyse, *Serubbabel*,
89–91, 99, 102; Carroll, *Prophecy*, 166; Roberts, "Old Testament's Contribution,"
39–51 (50); F. Bianchi, "Le rôle de Zorobabel et de la dynastie davidique en Judée
du VI siècle au II siècle av. J.-C.," *Transeuphratène* 7 (1994): 153–65 (160–61);
Redditt, *Zechariah*, 66; Collins, "Eschatology," 74–84.
    10. S. Davidson, *An Introduction to the Old Testament*, vol. 3 (Covent Garden:
Williams & Norgate, 1863), 335.
    11. Ibid., 325.
    12. Ibid., 335. A similar view is presented earlier by W. Newcome, *An Attempt
Towards an Improved Version, a Metrical Arrangement, and an Explanation of the
Twelve Minor Prophets* (Dublin: Robert Marchbank, 1785), 182–202.
    13. Carroll, *Prophecy*.

2.2.1.1. The hope for the house of David is shifted in a priestly direction.
A number of scholars argue that with the failure of Zerubbabel to take the
throne, the Davidic hope shifted in a priestly direction. This seems to be
built on Wellhausen's historical reconstruction of the restoration period:

> At first a "son of David" had continued to stand at the head of the Bne
> haggola [sons of the exile], but this last relic of the old monarchy soon
> had to give way to a Persian governor, who was under the control of the
> satrap of trans-Euphratic Syria, and whose principal business was the
> collection of revenue. Thenceforward the sole national chief was Joshua,
> the high priest, on whom, accordingly, the political representation also of
> the community naturally devolved... [The hierocracy] took the form of a
> monarchy of the high priest, he having stepped into the place formerly
> occupied by the theocratic king.[14]

It is believed that this political shift also influenced the reshaping of the
Davidic hope in the book of Zechariah. H. G. Mitchell is representative
of this view:

> The present reading is a clumsy attempt, by an anxious scribe, to bring
> the prophet into harmony with history. Neither Zerubbabel nor any other
> descendant of David ever again ruled as king in Jerusalem, but, in process
> of time, the high priest became the head of the entire community. It is this
> condition of things, unforeseen by Zechariah, which the changes in the
> text were intended to justify.[15]

More recently, C. Stuhlmueller has argued that in 3:8 the high priest
Joshua is given a title formerly reserved for the Davidic royalty: "my
servant the Branch."[16] He believes that applying a title like this to the
priest either enhanced his role, or at least bestowed upon the priesthood
the role of tutor and guardian of the future royal Messiah. Either way,
Stuhlmueller argues that "the role of the messiah of the royal house of
David was eclipsed and another side of messianism is accented, that of
the priesthood... [I]t is a 'messianism without a messiah,' that is, without
human instrumentality and directed by Yahweh."[17]

---

14. J. Wellhausen, *Sketch of the History of Israel and Judah* (3d ed.; London:
A. & C. Black, 1891), 129.

15. Mitchell, "Zechariah," 186.

16. C. Stuhlmueller, *Rebuilding with Hope* (ITC; Grand Rapids: Eerdmans,
1988), 79.

17. Ibid., 80. He continues: "While priesthood was certainly being enhanced, it
was also being absorbed within the glorious presence of Yahweh in the temple and
its ritual." At the same time, Stuhlmueller also believes that the hope for a future
king shifts towards Yahweh alone being king, as in the next view.

2.2.1.2. The hope for the house of David is democratized. Another view is
that with the failure of Zerubbabel to take the throne, the hope for the
house of David is democratized. D. L. Petersen believes that in Zechariah's time, the fulfilment of the hopes that oracles such as Jer 23:5 held
out for the house of David rested with Zerubbabel alone as the returned
Davidic heir (cf. Hag 2:23).[18] He was the proleptic king, the one whom
Zechariah named as the Shoot of Jer 23:5 and 33:15. Zerubbabel's role is
stressed over against other functionaries, in particular the high priest.[19]

With the failure of Zerubbabel to fulfil these expectations, Petersen
argues that the Davidic hope is recast, and that this is seen particularly in
chs. 9–14. He believes that 9:9 does not foster any "standard royal or
messianic expectation, namely, the return of a real or ideal Davidide."[20]
On 12:7–8, which refers to the house of David, Petersen says "it is
inappropriate to think that the 'house of David' signifies members of the
Davidic lineage or aspirations for a renaissance of kingship associated
with them."[21] Petersen gives several reasons for his view: the infrequency
of the phrase "house of David" in post-exilic texts; the fact that there is
no reason to assume that other governors after Zerubbabel were Davidides; and the fact that none of the Davidides of 1 Chr 3 are remembered
as having exercised a political role. In these verses, he believes the
similes need to be "decoded," with the house of David being seen as a
symbol for the inhabitants of Jerusalem who will achieve the sort of
divine status that had been associated with the king in Israelite royal
ideology.[22] Petersen believes that the Davidic covenant is democratized,
as in Isa 55:3, and hence there is no hope held for a future Davidic king.[23]

A. M. Leske believes that while there was a tradition based on 2 Sam
7 that a descendant of David would be on the throne of David forever,
"as the exile dragged on, disillusionment in the kingship grew."[24]
This situation led to a limitation on the function of kings with greater
responsibility being given to the Zadokite priests. Zechariah 1–8 reflects

18. Petersen, *Zechariah 1–8*, 210.
19. Ibid., 276.
20. Petersen, *Zechariah 9–14*, 59. See also D. L. Petersen, "The Book of the
Twelve/The Minor Prophets (Hosea, Joel, Amos, Obadiah, Jonah, Micah, Nahum,
Habakkuk, Zephaniah, Haggai, Zechariah, Malachi)," in *The Hebrew Bible Today:
An Introduction to Critical Issues* (ed. S. L. McKenzie and M. P. Graham; Louisville: John Knox, 1998), 95–126 (123–24).
21. Petersen, *Zechariah 9–14*, 118.
22. Ibid., 119.
23. Ibid., 59.
24. A. M. Leske, "Context and Meaning of Zechariah 9:9," *CBQ* 62 (2000):
663–78 (665).

this with a dual leadership of the "two sons of oil" (4:14). Moving to chs. 9–14, Leske argues that "the 'king' in 9:9 should not be interpreted as a future messianic Davidide. Rather, in terms of Deutero-Isaiah's democratization of kingship in Isa 55:3–5, the 'king' is God's faithful people who are to present God's gracious rule through their faithfulness to covenant and their consequent witness to God's blessings before the nations."[25] Hence, while the earlier prophetic hope for a Davidic king is democratized, Leske states that in the end God will reign as the universal king. This overlaps with the next view.

2.2.1.3. *The hope for the house of David is subsumed by the hope for Yahweh to be king.* A third view holds that, with the failure of Zerubbabel to take the throne, the hope for the house of David is subsumed by the hope that Yahweh would be king. For instance, J. D. W. Watts believes chs. 1–8 identify Zerubbabel as the Branch and that it demonstrates that all the hope for the restoration of the Davidic dynasty was tied up in him.[26] Zechariah 9–14 reflects the failure of this hope to eventuate, with the messianic hope being pushed to the background and Yahweh himself being saviour and king.[27]

Hanson proposes a sociological reconstruction of the post-exilic community, one which sees it divided into two parties: "visionaries" who were dissident and dissatisfied followers of Second Isaiah along with a group of disenfranchised Levites, and "hierocrats" who had sold out to the Persian-supported government and included the prophets Haggai and Zechariah. Hanson maintains that chs. 1–8 (prophetic eschatology) supported the hierocrats, while chs. 9–14 (apocalyptic eschatology) is literature of the visionaries who vied for control of Israel's leadership in the early post-exilic period and challenged the pro-temple hierocratic party.[28]

P. D. Hanson believes that Zechariah (and Haggai) tied his prophecies to the specific details of the hierocratic program, which included "a specific high priest, Joshua, a specific David prince, Zerubbabel, a specific temple plan, that delineated in the book of Ezekiel."[29] Zechariah's message was effectively: build the temple and the kingdom of God would arrive. Zechariah drew on Ezekiel in portraying a messianism that

25. Ibid.
26. J. D. W. Watts, "Zechariah," in *The Broadman Bible Commentary.* Vol. 7, *Hosea–Malachi* (ed. C. J. Allen; London: Marshall, Morgan & Scott, 1972), 329–30.
27. Ibid., 309.
28. P. D. Hanson, *The Dawn of Apocalyptic: The Historical and Sociological Roots of Jewish Apocalyptic Eschatology* (rev. ed.; Philadelphia: Fortress, 1979), 227, 243, 247, 261, 283, 323.
29. Ibid., 245.

consisted of a diarchy between a Zadokite priest and a Davidic prince, and cast this in eschatological terms.[30] The immediate effect of Zechariah's prophecy was to rally both the hierocrats and the visionaries together. However, in the longer term, once the hierocratic temple program had been accomplished and Zerubbabel had mysteriously disappeared and the Davidides had fallen from power, the Zadokites either found it necessary or availed themselves of the opportunity to move the nation toward a hierocratic form of local rule.[31] The result was a movement back to a temple theology centring on the Torah. Hanson argues that once the visionary elements of chs. 1–8 had served their purpose, the hierocratic group discarded them. This, for Hanson, accounts for alterations in the text of chs. 1–8. For him, the prophet Zechariah contributed to setting the prophetic office on an ignominious path.[32]

Zechariah 9–14, Hanson proposes, was the literature of the visionaries who rejected all identification of present phenomena with the eschatological kingdom, "whether it be identification of Zerubbabel with the Messiah, the temple with the New Jerusalem, or the Zadokite priesthood with the end-time rulers."[33] Instead, they borrowed from the mythic Divine Warrior material to preserve the promise that Yahweh would one day save his people, in spite of the seemingly unambivalent message of history that the hierocrats had emerged as the victors. No longer is there a message that translates into historical events and persons; rather, we have an eschatological hope of restoration inaugurated by Yahweh's act.[34] Hanson sees a total absence of a Davidic messianism in the eschatology of the visionaries.[35] Moreover, Zech 9–14 actually is a polemic directed against the Davidic governor and the hierocratic temple party. Zechariah 9–14 has inverted the Davidic hope of Ezekiel with the Davidic shepherd coming under Yahweh's judgment. Hanson writes of 11:15–16 and 13:7–9:

> the time is ripe for a whole new examination of the Davidic house in the period of the Second Temple, but until such is completed, this writer feels that there is sufficient grounds tentatively to assume that the Judean governor, at least during part of the fifth century, was of the house of David. If this assumption is correct, the worthless shepherd in verses 15–16 is best interpreted as the Davidic governor.[36]

30. Hanson, "Messiahs," 69–70.
31. Ibid., 71.
32. Hanson, *Apocalyptic*, 247.
33. Ibid., 285.
34. Ibid., 333.
35. Ibid., 350 n. 39.
36. Ibid., 349–50.

The visionary passages of chs. 9–14 that speak of future leadership in Israel, Hanson says, speak about the faithful among the people.[37] The leadership is democratized, but the final hope is for Yahweh to be king.

Carroll argues that while the first part of Zechariah was edited to reflect the failure of Zerubbabel to bring about the hopes associated with the Messiah, Zech 9–14 was a later addition that reflects a development and transformation of the expectations concerning the coming king.[38] He believes that the Zechariah tradition was supplemented by various oracles—some that transformed the hopes concerning the future of the house of David (cf. 9:9; 12:7–9, 10–14; 13:1), and others that took the view that in the future Yahweh would be the king (cf. 14:9, 16, 17).[39]

P. L. Redditt claims that chs. 1–8 underwent three revisions, the final edition being prepared before the temple was completed.[40] Commenting on chs. 1–8, he writes:

> There can be no doubt that Zechariah saw Zerubbabel as the new David, the messiah in the typical Old Testament sense of the anointed king. Further, the mission of Zerubbabel to rebuild the Temple was eschatological in the sense that it would usher in a radically improved future here on earth, especially for Israel. It is difficult to find anything more specifically messianic than this. The fact that in 3:8 and 6:12 the term "Branch" designates the high priest Joshua suggests that a non-regal reinterpretation of Zechariah's hopes for Zerubbabel emerged in light of the rise to prominence of the high priest in the post-exilic community.[41]

While chs. 9–14 initially transmitted the hope that the Davidic monarchy would be restored and that the king would rule from Jerusalem, Redditt believes the redactor of these chapters considered the restitution of the monarchy problematic because of the sins of the shepherds, the ruling élite in Jerusalem, which included the Davidides. So, the redactor abandoned these hopes for the restoration of the monarchy in favour of the view that Yahweh would rule in the future.[42] There was no hope for the post-exilic continuation of the office of Davidic king.[43]

---

37. While Hanson does not say so explicitly, he implies that the visionary material reflects Isa 56–66 where the Davidic hope is democratized. See ibid., 331.

38. Carroll, *Prophecy*, 166.

39. Ibid., 168.

40. Redditt, *Zechariah*, xxvii–xxviii. See also P. L. Redditt, "Zerubbabel, Joshua, and the Night Visions of Zechariah," *CBQ* 54 (1992): 249–59 (254–58).

41. Redditt, *Zechariah*, 44.

42. Ibid., 144. Redditt argues (p. 103) that chs. 9–14 arose in different stages during the first half of the Persian period and was later redacted by a pro-Judahite reformer.

43. Ibid., 135.

K. J. A. Larkin argues that the Shoot in 3:8 refers to both Zerubbabel and a future Davidic king, and that Joshua and Zerubbabel in 4:14 are "anointed ones" and therefore messianic in some sense.[44] Furthermore, she believes Zerubbabel was probably identified as the Shoot in 6:12, but his name was later removed "to square the record with the facts of history."[45] Larkin understands 6:9–15 as identifying Joshua as the Shoot with a second priest standing beside his throne wearing two crowns, although she admits to finding this confusing. In chs. 9–14, she contends that the old kingship traditions are transferred to God himself, rather than a contemporary human figure.[46]

Arguing quite differently, M. A. Sweeney also thinks it likely that Zerubbabel was the figure to be crowned in an earlier version of 6:9–15, but was replaced by Joshua as the book of Zechariah went through its process of editing and recomposition.[47] He argues that the book of Zechariah presents an understanding of kingship similar to that of the final form of the book of Isaiah, which points first to a Davidic monarch, then to a Persian monarch, and ultimately to Yahweh as the monarch who delivers Jerusalem from its enemies.[48]

While rejecting the view that later scribes have corrected the text of Zechariah,[49] Boda understands צמח in 3:8 and 6:12 as referring to Zerubbabel, who will "rebuild the land" and restore the Davidic house promised by Jeremiah.[50] Similarly, 9:9 expresses the hope for the restoration of Davidic kingship in Jerusalem and "was directed originally to the Jewish community in Yehud during the tenure of Zerubbabel as governor and looked with great hope to the ultimate reunification of the tribes under Davidic leadership."[51] While Boda sees a strong expression of hope for restoration of the house of David with Zerubbabel in chs. 1–9, he understands the later chapters of Zechariah, particularly chs. 10–11, as coming from a later time and reflecting the situation after Zerubbabel had

---

44. K. J. A. Larkin, "Zechariah," in *The Oxford Bible Commentary* (ed. J. Barton and J. Muddiman; Oxford: Oxford University Press, 2001), 610–15.

45. Ibid., 612.

46. K. J. A. Larkin, *The Eschatology of Second Zechariah: A Study of the Formation of a Mantological Wisdom Anthology* (CBET 6; Kampen: Kok Pharos, 1994), 76.

47. Sweeney, *Twelve*, 629.

48. Ibid., 634, 664.

49. Boda, *Commentary*, 338–39.

50. Ibid., 262, 338–41. See also S. G. Dempster, *Dominion and Dynasty* (Leicester: IVP, 2003), 187, who says: "The most likely candidate [for the Branch] is Zerubbabel, for he was the one to be involved in temple construction."

51. Boda, *Commentary*, 422.

been rejected.[52] He believes that any "hope of a unified province under Davidic rule appears to have died with the demise of Zerubbabel's leadership."[53] While he acknowledges at one point that "the prophet does not appear to be sidelining the Davidic house," in the end he believes that the idyllic portrait of chs. 1–6 has been tempered by chs. 9–14, where "greater weight has been shifted onto YHWH."[54]

Hence, scholars in this third group offer a variety of explanations as to why and how, once Zerubbabel failed to restore the throne, the hope for a future king was transposed into a hope for Yahweh to be king.

2.2.1.4. *The hope for the house of David is abandoned.* A fourth view sees the hope for a future king beyond the failure of Zerubbabel as largely abandoned. H. G. Mitchell argues that Zech 9–14 was not written by Zechariah, but much later, from the late fourth century B.C.E. onwards.[55] Hence, the teaching of chs. 9–14 differs from chs. 1–8 with reference to the leader of the future kingdom. Whereas, in chs. 1–8, Zechariah recognizes Zerubbabel as the Messiah and the restorer of the Davidic dynasty, in chs. 9–14 one learns that the leader has not yet appeared, and will not appear until the country over which he will rule has been subdued for him (9:1–10). Mitchell contends that there are no other references to the Messiah in this section, as 11:4–17 is "anything but a Messianic prophecy, while in ch. 12 it is the whole house of David, and not any particular member of it, who is to be 'like God' and 'like the angel of Yahweh' before the people."[56]

R. A. Mason suggests that it was the priestly circles who later developed chs. 1–8. He offers a slightly different scenario in proposing that originally Zechariah envisaged a diarchy between Joshua and Zerubbabel. However, when for unknown reasons Zerubbabel faded from the scene, the priests subsumed under their own role both prophetic and royal functions and attributes.[57] Mason argues that the text of Zech 1–8 in

---

52. Ibid., 440, 467.
53. Boda, "Figuring," 61.
54. Ibid., 63, 65.
55. Mitchell, "Zechariah," 258–59, argues that Zech 9:1–10 was written shortly after the battle of Issus (333 B.C.E.); 9:11–11:3 dates from Ptolemy III (247–222 B.C.E.); 11:4–17 and 13:7–9 from the battle of Raphie (217 B.C.E.). He believes that someone then undertook to present the whole in a more optimistic light by adding 12:1–13:6 and ch. 14.
56. Ibid., 241.
57. R. A. Mason, *Preaching the Tradition: Homily and Hermeneutics After the Exile* (Cambridge: Cambridge University Press, 1990), 208–9. See also R. A. Mason,

its present form speaks not of Zerubbabel, but of a future messianic ruler who would "build the temple" in the sense of building up the community of Yahweh's people.[58] The "messianic" hope, which once may have been attached to Zerubbabel, was still held out as a distant hope, though the priests ensured that if the Messiah ever turned up, they would still keep their positions of power.[59]

While there is a future Davidic hope for Mason, its significance is greatly reduced. He proposes that what we have in chs. 9–14 is a deliberate reinterpretation of the traditional messianic and royal ideology in the light of the suffering servant figure of Isaiah.[60] He notes that the king in 9:9–10 is passive, with God himself the active agent of deliverance. He also sees 12:7–13:1 as limiting the role of the house of David.[61] Concerning 12:7–13:1, he says, "This sees a place for a Davidic family…but it is far from the 'messianic deliverer' kind of picture we normally think of. For all its difficulties, this passage may be seen to provide some support for a view of 9:9–10 as offering an alternative royal ideology."[62]

He concludes:

> In summary, then, we have to say how little influence the concept of a renewal of the Davidic line after the exile exercised in the extant post-exilic biblical literature. Apart from some possible hope of it expressed by Haggai, a hope somewhat diminished in the present form of Zechariah 1–8, it occurs, where it occurs at all, either to be reinterpreted and its fulfilment looked for in other ways, or to be severely modified, as in Zechariah 9–14. Otherwise it is ignored.[63]

"The Relation of Zech 9–14 to Proto-Zechariah," *ZAW* 88 (1976), 227–39 (235–36), and *The Books of Haggai, Zechariah, and Malachi* (Cambridge Bible Commentary; Cambridge: Cambridge University Press, 1977), 75.

58. Mason, "Messiah," 348.
59. Ibid., 349.
60. Ibid., 355. Mitchell, "Zechariah," 273, takes a similar view.
61. Mason, "Messiah," 356.
62. Ibid., 357.
63. Ibid., 364. Elsewhere, Mason, "Relation," 237, argues: "It is illegitimate to detect a Messianic figure elsewhere in deutero-Zechariah. Whatever be made of the promise concerning David in 12 8, it cannot be overlooked that the house of David needs to share in the general act of penitence which follows… Even if v. 8 is secondary in its present position, this does not suggest that the circle responsible for the final form of these oracles saw the house of David in a traditionally Messianic way. Nor can the 'pierced one' of v. 10 be pressed into service here… Nor is the 'shepherd' of 13 7 to be equated with the 'good shepherd'… No reference to human leadership of any kind is found in ch. 14."

2.2.1.5. *The hope for the house of David is recast for a future Davidic king.* Instead of seeing no future for the house of David beyond Zerubbabel, a fifth view envisages the hope for the house of David as being recast for a future Davidic king. Scholars are divided on whether Zechariah saw this hope being fulfilled in the immediate or distant future.

D. R. Jones argues with respect to 6:9–15 that Joshua was crowned so that the Davidic prince Zerubbabel might be established on his royal throne.[64] While he acknowledges that this never happened, Jones does not attempt to explain the implications of this. Instead, he sees a strong expression of the hope for the restoration of the monarchy in chs. 9–14, and comments: "Earlier the utmost Zechariah could say was, 'Behold the man, the Branch' (6:12). Perhaps this later prophet [of chs. 9–14] was the freer to speak because his hope was, politically, impossible."[65]

W. Neil notes that some scholars believe that there were two different authors within Zech 1–8:

> (*a*) an earlier writer whose oracles echo, albeit faintly, the themes of the classical Hebrew prophets, and whose eschatological hopes centered on Zerubbabel as the coming messianic king; and (*b*) a later writer, in the tradition of Ezekiel, who, after Zerubbabel's fall from power, transferred his hopes to a supernatural intervention of Yahweh, which he expresses in apocalyptic visions of the new age, involving the destruction of the Gentiles and the subsequent centrality of the priesthood and the cultus of the temple.[66]

For Neil, the failure of Zerubbabel to take the throne means that the hope for a future Davidic king is not to be found in chs. 1–8. However, he thinks that it is possible that 9:1–12 sees "the hand of Yahweh preparing the way for the establishment of the messianic kingdom."[67]

W. Rudolph believes that rather than the text of Zechariah being edited after the failure of Zerubbabel, the text is original to Zechariah

---

64. D. R. Jones, *Haggai, Zechariah, and Malachi: Introduction and Commentary* (Torch Bible Commentaries; London: SCM Press, 1962), 90.

65. Ibid., 131. Elsewhere, D. R. Jones, "A Fresh Interpretation of Zechariah IX–XI," *VT* 12 (1962): 241–59, understands the key to Zech 9–14 as the reunion of the tribes under one Davidic king. He argues that there was a prophet living in or near Damascus in the first half of the fifth century B.C.E. who devised Zech 9–11 after meditating on the meaning of 2 Sam 15–19. In 2 Samuel, Absalom rode on horses and chariots and threatened the unity of all the tribes under David. We are also told that David rode on an ass. Jones believes that the prophet responsible for Zech 9–11 drew on this to speak of a time when a new king of the line of David would come to unite his people with humility and power.

66. Neil, "Zechariah," 944.

67. Ibid., 946.

and reflects the fact that he has already experienced the disaster with Zerubbabel that prevented him from completing the temple.[68] With the failure of Zerubbabel to take the throne and fulfil the expectations of Haggai, Rudolph believes that Zechariah looked to one of Zerubbabel's sons to take the throne. In this regard, he contends that Zerubbabel's name ("Branch of Babel") is significant. While Zerubbabel was from the line of David, Rudolph explains that his name means that he was born in a foreign land. In 6:12, Zechariah looked for one who would be born from the line of David and in the holy land, and hence looked to one of Zerubbabel's sons as the Shoot.[69] The vision of 6:9–15 pictures Joshua standing by his side, and hence Zechariah believed that he would arrive very soon and complete the temple that had been begun by Zerubbabel (cf. 4:9). Furthermore, Rudolph argues that the two sons of oil in Zech 4:14 picture the joint rule of Joshua and Zerubbabel, but with the failure of Zerubbabel, the crowning of Joshua in ch. 6 becomes the guarantee that the Shoot will come and rule alongside Joshua.[70]

S. Amsler argues that the book of Zechariah gives evidence of an evolution of the hope for the house of David.[71] Initially, Zechariah had the audacity to designate Zerubbabel as the Davidic Messiah. With the changing circumstances of the community, the priesthood came to take a place within the Davidic hope. Amsler believes this is seen in 4:14 with Zerubbabel and Joshua as the two "sons of oil." Eventually, on the basis of Jer 33:14–26, the high priest is made the heir of all the promises to David.[72] In Zech 9–14, he finds the earlier Davidic hope attested again. Zechariah 9:9–10 and 12:8 speak of a coming messianic king who wins a victory, with the house of David again being established at the head of his people. He summarizes: "In the prolonged waiting for the Messiah of the earlier prophets, these oracles attest the vitality of the Davidic tradition, always ready to reappear in new formulations, right until the last witness of old testament prophecy."[73]

---

68. W. Rudolph, *Haggai–Sacharja 1–8–Sacharja 9–14–Maleachi* (KAT; Gütersloh: Gerd Mohn, 1976), 130.

69. Ibid.

70. Ibid., 131.

71. S. Amsler, "Aggée, Zacharie 1–8," in *Aggée, Zacharie, Malachie* (ed. S. Amsler, A. Lacocque and R. Vuilleumier; 2d ed.; Geneva: Labor et Fides, 1988), 91, believes Zech 3 is a late addition, and 6:9–15 has been revised. For a summary of Amsler's view of the hope for the house of David in Zechariah, see S. Amsler, *David, Roi et Messie: La Tradition Davidique dans l'Ancien Testament* (Neuchâtel: Delachaux & Niestlé, 1963), 58–61.

72. Amsler, *David*, 59.

73. Ibid., 61 (author's translation).

Similarly, T. Chary argues that Zechariah initially held high hopes for Zerubbabel: "This one is the 'Servant' (3, 8), a term which indicates a relation of preference, and he receives the name of 'Seed' which in 3, 8, as well as in 6, 12 one has the right to apply to Zerubbabel."[74] With these expectations for Zerubbabel not being met, he sees a shift in the hope for the future king within chs. 1–8 with the prophet taking the new reality into consideration: first to a joint rule of Davidic prince and priest (chs. 4 and 6) which then shifts to the priesthood alone.[75] In Zech 9–14, Chary sees a harmonization of two strands of messianism: impersonal and personal.[76] In the impersonal strand (9:1–8, 11–17; 10:3–11:3; 14), Yahweh acts alone, initially against the nations, while reuniting the divided and dispersed people, and then for the nations. The personal strand presents a peaceful king (9:9–10); a good shepherd (11:4–17); a great pierced one (12:1–13:6) and a shepherd struck with a sword (13:7–9). The action of the personal Messiah is essentially directed towards the community. He believes that the originality of chs. 9–14 is in the way that these two programmes are harmonized into one great project.

In her study of Zech 1–8, J. E. Tollington has an extended section on "leadership in the restoration community and messianism" where she argues that Zechariah had both a short-term and a longer-term vision for the house of David. His short-term vision concerned Joshua and Zerubbabel. Concerning Joshua, Zechariah enhances the status of the priesthood, but does not extend his authority beyond the temple and the cultic realm. Zerubbabel, on the other hand, was given the role of overseeing the temple reconstruction, but it is left open as to whether his authority for this task stems from his role as governor or because of his Davidic lineage. She concludes, "Zechariah was not an ardent proponent of the restoration of the monarchy, though it would be unwise to claim that he was totally against it in the early stages of his ministry."[77] So, Tollington is less enthusiastic about Zechariah's hope for Zerubbabel than some of the views that we have just seen, but still does not reject the possibility that Zechariah may have countenanced hopes for the restoration of the monarchy in him. In the longer-term, Tollington holds that Zechariah believed that the Davidic covenant still stood and that he had his hopes

---

74. Chary, *Zacharie*, 49 (author's translation).
75. Ibid.
76. Ibid., 144–45.
77. Tollington, *Tradition*, 179. A little earlier she says (p. 173): "Whoever inserted Zech. 6:13 into the latter prophecy failed to catch this eschatological vision of the prophet and interpreted the motif צמח in relation to Zerubbabel and the monarchic hopes that they still retained for him... Zech. 6:13 originated in the early part of the prophet's ministry and related to Zerubbabel."

set on the Branch to restore the fortunes of the house of David: "Therefore I suggest that Zechariah adopts the motif צמח to point away from
current historical figures towards a future leader for the community…
[This leader is] the ruler in the new age that Yahweh will inaugurate…
[צמח is] a future Davidic ruler who will be raised up by Yahweh and
on whom a new dynasty will be founded."[78] Until that time, Tollington
believes that Zechariah envisaged the diarchic rule of Joshua and
Zerubbabel, and that the Branch would come within the lifetime of these
two men. Hence, for Tollington, in the initial stages of Zerubbabel's
governorship there was a hope for Zerubbabel to take the throne, but this
was later transferred to a Davidic ruler beyond him.

S. L. Cook also believes the hope is recast for a future Davidide. He
questions the traditional understanding of the way that the book of
Zechariah has been edited. Noting those who have observed the many
links in subject material between chs. 1–8 and 9–14, Cook argues that
chs. 1–8 and 9–14 represent phases within one tradition-history, and that
there is in fact a continuity of tradition that runs from chs. 1–8, through
the redactional additions to these chapters, and into chs. 9–14.[79] He
argues that Zech 1–8, with its radical eschatology, dualism, and messianism, is clearly apocalyptic. For Cook, this means that the saving work of
God will not come through human history, but rather through the intervention of the transcendent into history.[80] Zechariah's radical eschatology reveals his lack of hope in history and that the historical processes
are going nowhere and will accomplish nothing.[81] This means that while
Zechariah may have looked to Zerubbabel with messianic hopes at an
early stage, Zechariah only ever saw him as a candidate for the Messiah,
and the Zechariah tradition soon placed its hopes in a future Davidide,
referred to as צמח.[82] This is similar to Tollington at this point, though
Cook downplays any sense of disappointed expectations with Zerubbabel.

Significantly, Cook questions those scholars who have followed Wellhausen in seeing Zechariah's original messianic hopes replaced with a
priestly theocracy. Instead, he argues: "the ongoing Zechariah tradition,
rather than abandoning its apocalyptic/messianic features, continued
along apocalyptic lines. Redaction points the visions toward the future,
not toward any pragmatic community control. Indeed, the redaction of

78. Ibid., 172.
79. Cook, *Apocalypticism*, 125.
80. Ibid., 127.
81. Ibid., 128.
82. Ibid., 132.

chs. 1–8 as well as the composition of chs. 9–14 continue Zechariah's messianic focus on a future Davidide."[83]

Furthermore, Cook argues against Wellhausen's view that with the demise of Zerubbabel there was an increase in the stakes of the priesthood. Instead, the "ongoing Zecharian hope for the future rule of a Davidide tempers the group's enthusiasm for an expanded priestly role in Yehudite society."[84] Cook also takes issue with those who see a diminished Davidic interest in Zech 9–14. For him, these chapters continue Zechariah's hope for a Davidic king with a description of God's restoration of the Davidic empire in 9:9–10; a description of the millennial blessings that will flow from the Messiah in ch. 10; the positive messianic portrait of the future Davidic house in ch. 12; and the description of the millennial purification and cleansing of the house of David in 13:1.[85]

B. Uffenheimer believes that 4:14 proclaims Joshua and Zerubbabel as anointed and sanctioned by God to inaugurate a new era: "Zechariah expresses the exalted feeling of messianism which permeated the Jewish community in those days."[86] However, he notes that the high hopes aroused by Zechariah were shattered by the reality of history, where Zerubbabel mysteriously vanished from the scene.[87] On account of this, 3:8 and 6:12 contain an "echo of disappointment," and yet they also project the Davidic hope into the future with an ideal king: "Here the prophet rejects a realization of messianic hopes, transferring the building of the Temple and the re-establishment of the Davidic throne to a future 'Shoot'."[88]

B. C. Ollenburger believes that Zech 9–14, like Zech 1–8, expects a future royal figure in the line of David.[89] However, he says "this expectation, clearly expressed in 9:9–10 and implicit in 10:4–5, becomes complicated in chaps. 11–13 and is entirely absent from chap. 14."[90]

Zechariah's presentation of the hope for the house of David is a problem for M. J. Selman. He notes that both Joshua and Zerubbabel "are associated with the messianic term Branch."[91] Furthermore, Zechariah's

---

83. Ibid., 133.
84. Ibid., 136.
85. Ibid., 137–38.
86. Uffenheimer, "Zerubbabel," 225.
87. Uffenheimer thinks it likely that Zerubbabel was removed from office on account of the suspicion that Zechariah and Haggai raised concerning him among the Persian officialdom.
88. Uffenheimer, "Zerubbabel," 226.
89. B. C. Ollenburger, "The Book of Zechariah," *NIB* 7:733–840 (742).
90. Ibid., 743.
91. M. J. Selman, "Zechariah: Theology of," *NIDOTTE* 4:1303–7 (1305).

prophecy implied that Zerubbabel would become king. However, he also observes that, "the priest assumes a range of royal characteristics in a way that is unprecedented in the rest of the OT." His problem is that "Zechariah also speaks of the future leadership of God's people, especially in his use of the term Branch, so that Joshua and Zerubbabel are symbols of things to come as well as contemporary leaders (e.g. 3:8)."[92]

A. Laato believes that it is reasonable to assume that Zechariah identified Zerubbabel as the messianic king under whose leadership the temple would be built and the cult re-established.[93] However, with the failure of Zerubbabel to become king, he considers that it is possible to identify in the messianic passages in chs. 1–8 "traces of later reinterpretations, perhaps due to the dissonance created by unfulfilled expectations."[94] He states:

> We may therefore suppose that even though Zechariah 1–8 in its present form appears to contain a distinction between the ideal figures of the future (the Branch and the Priest) and the figures of the historical present (Zerubbabel and Joshua), the prophet himself, at least at one point in time, connected his messianic hopes with these persons. On the other hand, in the present form of Zechariah 1–8 a typological relationship appears to exist between Zerubbabel and the coming Messiah.[95]

Furthermore, Laato holds that the high priest took on the role of symbolizing the Davidic dynasty during the post-exilic period and he was a living sign that Yahweh would keep his promise and re-establish the Davidic kingdom at some time in the future.[96]

He believes that Zech 9–14 continues to push the Davidic hope into the eschaton: "Yhwh will bring his Messiah to Jerusalem in order to bring about the final restoration promised in Zechariah 1–8."[97] At the same time, Zech 9–14 contains criticism of the contemporary members of the house of David who failed to bring about the hopes for restoration,

92. Ibid. Selman comments somewhat enigmatically concerning chs. 9–14 (ibid.): "Some of the passages about leadership have messianic overtones, though these are mainly allusions about a suffering messiah and apart from 9:9–10 are not associated with royalty."

93. Laato, *Star*, 200. See also Laato, *Josiah and David Redivivus*, 234–301.

94. Laato, *Star*, 201. Compare (p. 206): "Later the original core of Zech. 6:9–15 was reworked, apparently after the rebuilding of the Temple and the disappointment of fervent expectations concerning the reestablishment of the Davidic dynasty through Zerubbabel. By means of this reinterpretation, the messianic prophecy in vv 12–13 received a new setting."

95. Laato, *Star*, 202.

96. Ibid., 203.

97. Ibid., 211.

seen particularly in chs. 11.[98] Hence, Zech 9–14 both awaits the future Davidic king and maintains a critical attitude towards the house of David since it failed to fulfil the eschatological hopes of the prophets.

P. R. Andiñach argues that chs. 9–11, and then chs. 12–14, were added in order to update chs. 1–8.[99] Where Zech 1–8 supports Joshua and Zerubbabel and their descendants, Zech 9–14 severely criticizes the leadership of Jerusalem, with useless shepherds being called forth. He states, "the message is not only one of disaster and criticism; there will come a messiah, humble and poor, not to govern as did the wicked shepherds but to rule with justice and proclaim peace (9:9–10). Chapters 9–11 have updated the text and made it relevant to the current situation."[100]

Acknowledging a complex redaction history of the text of Zechariah, J. M. O'Brien argues that the final form of the book suggests that Zerubbabel is the one who will fulfil the promises concerning the Branch.[101] She states:

> In claiming that a Davidic heir would again participate in the leadership of the community, the author voiced the conviction that God's past promises to provide a Davidic leader were not nullified by contemporary politics. The priesthood, which had taken on greater importance during the crisis of the exile and during the rule of the Persians, would continue; but so too would the promise of the Davidic covenant.[102]

O'Brien does not say anything about the failure of Zerubbabel to take the throne. Furthermore, in her commentary she is unsure whether there is any reference in Zech 9–14 to the future Davidic king.[103] However, she still concludes: "From beginning to end, the book of Zechariah...stresses that Yahweh's promise to David has not ended and that God's care of the people will continue, as will the divine call to accountability."[104]

L.-S. Tiemeyer finds the proposal that Zerubbabel is the "Branch" in the final form of the text as problematic as the proposal that the Branch

98. Ibid., 211–14.

99. P. R. Andiñach, "Zechariah," in *The International Bible Commentary* (ed. W. R. Farmer; Collegeville: Liturgical, 1998), 1186–98.

100. Ibid., 1189.

101. J. M. O'Brien, *Nahum, Habakkuk, Zephaniah, Haggai, Zechariah, Malachi* (AOTC; Nashville: Abingdon, 2004), 206.

102. Ibid., 207.

103. O'Brien believes Zech 9:9 "may be intentionally ambiguous" (ibid., 240) that the pierced one of 12:10 "is not precisely identified" (p. 263), and that the description of the shepherd in 13:7 "provides little basis for a determination" (p. 273).

104. Ibid., 284.

is a future messianic figure.[105] Tiemeyer's solution is that while Zerub-babel was "the most likely candidate for the 'branch'…Zech 3:8b was added at a much later time when Zerubbabel was no longer an important presence in Judah. At that time, the expression 'branch' had ceased to refer to him as a person, and instead had come to carry messianic con-notations, expressing the people's hope for the coming of a future saviour."[106]

In summary, the first view of the nature of the hope for the house of David in the book of Zechariah holds that Zechariah initially envisaged Zerubbabel as the one who would restore the Davidic monarchy; when, however, he failed to re-establish the throne, Zechariah's prophecy was altered to reflect this changed situation. Although the prophet Zechariah identified Zerubbabel as the Shoot of David, it is argued that the final form of the book reflects a shift in the Davidic hope away from Zerub-babel. Scholars in this first group differ on whether the Davidic hope is: (1) transferred to the priesthood; (2) democratized; (3) subsumed by the hope for Yahweh to be king; (4) abandoned; (5) recast for a future Davidic king.

2.2.2. *No Hope for the Restoration of the House of David in Zerub-babel's Day or the Future*
A second group of scholars concludes that Zechariah never held any hope for the restoration of the house of David either in Zerubbabel or in a future Davidide. M. Barker argues that Zech 1–9 effectively sees no present or future for the house of David.[107] She contends that all we know of Zerubbabel is in 4:6–10, and this "begins [with] a criticism of his policies, continues with two verses which are virtually untranslatable, and concludes with an assurance about the building of the Temple."[108] She believes that there is no indication that the term "Branch" is a Davidic title, and that Zechariah applies it to the high priest Joshua in 3:8 and 6:12. Whereas Zerubbabel is said to build the temple in ch. 4, this task is taken over by Joshua in 6:9–15.[109] Barker understands the "two sons of oil" in 4:14 as two priestly figures, with Joshua "almost certainly"

105. L.-S. Tiemeyer, *Priestly Rites and Prophetic Rage: Post-Exilic Prophetic Critique of the Priesthood* (Tübingen: Mohr Siebeck, 2006), 31.
106. Ibid., 32.
107. Barker, "Two Figures," 38–46. Barker gives no justification for dealing with Zech 1–9 and in her article she in fact only deals with chs. 3–6.
108. Ibid., 39.
109. Ibid., 43.

one of these priests.[110] Hence, there is no hope expressed for a Davidic ruler in Zerubbabel's day or in the future. She writes,

> I do not believe that the returned exiles gained comfort and cohesion from their treasured past. They had to rewrite this past, in order to justify themselves to the others who had shared this same past, those others who never accepted those histories and the theology implicit in them. This, in a nutshell, is what was behind Zechariah's apologetic for the new High Priest.[111]

Another scholar seeing no hope expressed for a future Davidic king in the book of Zechariah is K. E. Pomykala.[112] Dealing first with Zech 1–8, he doubts Zerubbabel's Davidic lineage. Furthermore, he believes that צמח in 3:8 and 6:12 does not necessarily have Davidic connotations and that there is nothing to link it with the hope of Jeremiah. He also considers that Joshua is given the prerogatives of the pre-exilic monarchy and that none of the portraits of the ideal future in these chapters mention a re-established Davidic monarchy. He summarizes: "To sum up this survey of Zechariah 1–8, I believe that the evidence does not substantiate the claim that Zechariah 1–8 sets forth hope for a davidic messiah."[113] Similarly, in chs. 9–14, Pomykala discovers no evidence of a hope for a future Davidic king. He concludes, "To be sure, Zechariah 9–14 witnesses to royal themes (9:9) and addresses the problem of leadership in terms of shepherding (10:2–3; 11:4–17), a metaphor commonly used of kings. But there is no evidence of a hope for a davidic king or messiah."[114]

Coming from a very different angle, M. Bič argues that Zech 1–6 does present a hope for a future "Messiah." He believes the title "Shoot" does not refer to Zerubbabel, but to an eschatological messianic figure.[115] However, according to Bič, this Messiah will come from the line of the high priest, rather than from the house of David:

> The high priest took the responsibility for the community after the exile. He was now no longer a royal civil servant, but the spiritual head of the community and the model of the Messiah. Zerubbabel, although a David-ide, stood and stepped, in strange circumstances, into the background. His

110. Ibid., 45.
111. Ibid., 43.
112. Pomykala, *Dynasty*, 53–60, 112–26.
113. Ibid., 60.
114. Ibid., 125.
115. M. Bič, *Die Nachtgesichte des Sacharja: Eine Auslegung von Sacharja 1–6* (Biblische Studien 42; Neukirchen–Vluyn: Neukirchener Verlag, 1964), 38.

task was only an earthly and temporal one: the reconstruction of the temple. His further traces disappear in the darkness of the past. Zechariah sees the Messiah in the line of the High Priest.[116]

Therefore, Bič sees no hope for the restoration of the house of David in Zechariah's day or in the future. Zerubbabel, and by implication the house of David, move into the background, and then disappear.

W. J. Dumbrell also argues that in the book of Zechariah the hope expressed by earlier prophets for the house of David has faded. He sees the entire book coming from the prophet Zechariah over a period of slightly more than two years, with chs. 9–14 offering a theological commentary on the more historically oriented first section.[117] He contends that Zechariah leaned heavily on Ezekiel's prophecy and that Ezekiel saw "no certain future for political monarchy and could hardly have been a proponent of a post-exilic Davidic restoration."[118] He suggests that Ezek 40–48 actually envisages the abolition of the monarchy with the direct rule of Yahweh.[119] Hence while Zechariah drew on Ezekiel's hopes for a restored temple, he questions whether this entailed a revived messianism.

Dumbrell argues that Zech 1–8 pivots on the fourth vision in ch. 4, which is centred on the temple. In this section, Zerubbabel is viewed primarily as a temple builder rather than the future king, and political rule is shared in diarchy form with the high priest Joshua, who is accorded greater attention than Zerubbabel. Rather than expressing hopes for the restoration of the monarchy, the main emphasis of chs. 1–8 is on the re-establishment of Yahweh's rule, with Joshua and Zerubbabel as his agents. In chs. 9–14, he follows Hanson in seeing a "greatly diminished Davidic interest in these chapters, with many points of contact to Is. 40–66 in which messianism is absent."[120]

Floyd expresses a similar opinion. He does not see in Zechariah any hope for a restoration of the Davidic dynasty in the present or the future. For him, the reference to the Shoot in Zech 3:8 and 6:12 does not represent a hope for a future Davidic king, but simply "describes someone's 'growth' into a leadership role that is somehow analogous to David's."[121]

---

116. Ibid., 70 (author's translation).

117. W. J. Dumbrell, *The Faith of Israel* (Leicester: IVP, 1989), 193–94.

118. Dumbrell, "Kingship," 37.

119. Dumbrell cites G. A. Cooke, *The Book of Ezekiel* (2 vols.; ICC; New York: Scribner's, 1936), xxx, for this idea.

120. Dumbrell, "Kingship," 40.

121. M. H. Floyd, *Minor Prophets: Part 2* (FOTL 22; Grand Rapids: Eerdmans, 2000), 375.

To be sure, Joshua and Zerubbabel are important leaders and represent Yahweh's kingship on earth. However, Floyd believes that Zechariah has reconceived the role of the Davidic monarchy: the temple with the high priest at its head has become its surrogate.[122] Regarding 9:9–10, he finds it "difficult to imagine that this unit could describe the prospect of either a new Persian emperor or the restoration of the Davidic dynasty in Judah."[123] Instead, Yahweh's sanctuary in Jerusalem

> remains the crucial means of signifying his divine kingship, as the pattern and personnel of both imperial hegemony and local leadership undergo change (9:8; 14:9–11). In Zechariah the primary manifestation of God's kingship is not the appearance of some local leader, Davidic or otherwise, but rather the persistence of Jerusalem as Yahweh's royal sanctuary as the world situation undergoes even the most radical transformations.[124]

2.2.3. *No Hope for the Restoration of the Monarchy in Zerubbabel, But a Clear Hope for a Future King*

A third group of scholars argues that Zechariah never expressed hope for the Davidic monarchy to be restored in Zerubbabel, but that the hope for a Davidic king was always future. Variations on this view depend on the exact role that Zechariah envisioned for Zerubbabel, assuming that he would not be king. This view may be broken down into three strands: (1) those who understand Zerubbabel as the Shoot and the Davidic king as a future figure beyond him; (2) those who understand the Shoot as the future Davidic king; and (3) those who understand the Shoot as the future Davidic king in chs. 1–8, but see this hope muted in chs. 9–14.

2.2.3.1. *Zerubbabel as the Shoot and the Davidic king as a future figure beyond him.* While the view that Zerubbabel was the Shoot bears some similarity to the first view above, the difference here is that scholars do not understand the Shoot as the Messiah, even if he is "messianic" in some sense. Hence, there is no disappointment when Zerubbabel disappeared from the scene, as on this view Zechariah never proclaimed him as a Davidic king. So, R. T. Siebeneck believes that the messianism of chs. 1–8 encompasses both Zerubbabel and a future Davidic king at the same time.[125] He says, "Zorobabel is given a messianic title [Shoot] in so far as the messianic promises pertaining to the Davidic dynasty are renewed in him."[126] For Siebeneck, there is a localizing of the messianic

---

122. Ibid., 384.
123. Ibid., 454.
124. Ibid., 512.
125. Siebeneck, "Messianism," 312–28.
126. Ibid., 321.

age in history, as well as a projection into the future. While he thinks that Zechariah probably identified Zerubbabel as the Shoot, he does not believe that Zechariah saw him as the Messiah, but an important prelude to the messianic age. He concludes, "All these considerations converge to give us the conclusion that these two postexilic prophets [Haggai and Zech 1–8] are prolonging the royal messianism of their predecessors, not by identifying Zorobabel as the Messias, but by naming him as the one who continues the ancient promises. They see him as the prototype of the future Messias."[127]

P. C. Craigie also holds that while the Shoot in 3:8 and 6:12 refers to Zerubbabel, these references also point forward.[128] Although Zerubbabel is crowned along with Joshua in 6:12–13, this is only ever symbolic, as "it would have been impossible, and illegal, to crown a king and priest in the Persian colony of Judah."[129] Zechariah therefore looks to a more distant age in which his hopes will be fulfilled.

2.2.3.2. *The Shoot as the future Davidic king.* Earlier scholars often took the view that Zechariah looked to the eschatological horizon for the fulfilment of the promises to David. Luther and Calvin understood both Shoot references to be to Christ and not Zerubbabel.[130] Similarly, of 9:9 Calvin says: "By the word *king*, the Prophet intimates, that except they thought God unfaithful in his promises, they were to entertain hope, until the kingdom of David, then apparently fallen, arose again."[131] Calvin argues that Joshua and Zerubbabel function as "types" of the king to come who will be a priest, lead Yahweh's people, and build the temple.[132] E. W. Hengstenberg, T. V. Moore, C. A. Briggs, and C. van Orelli offer the same interpretation.[133]

While dealing only with chs. 9–14, P. Lamarche's monograph influenced several scholars who see the hope for the restoration of the house

---

127. Ibid., 327.

128. P. C. Craigie, *The Twelve Prophets* (Daily Study Bible; Philadelphia: Westminster, 1984), 174.

129. Ibid., 187.

130. M. Luther, *Lectures on the Minor Prophets III: Zechariah* (trans. H. C. Oswald; Luther's Works 20; Saint Louis: Concordia, 1973), 40, 69; J. Calvin, "Zechariah & Malachi," in *A Commentary on the Twelve Minor Prophets*, vol. 5 (Edinburgh: The Banner of Truth Trust, 1986), 96, 157.

131. Calvin, "Zechariah," 252.

132. Ibid., 92, 112.

133. C. von Orelli, *The Twelve Minor Prophets* (trans. J. S. Banks; Edinburgh: T. & T. Clark, 1893); T. V. Moore, *A Commentary on Zechariah* (Edinburgh: The Banner of Truth Trust, 1958); E. W. Hengstenberg, *Christology of the Old Testament* (trans. R. Keith; Grand Rapids: Kregel, 1970); Briggs, *Prediction*, 444–48.

of David encompassing Zerubbabel and a future messianic figure.[134] As well as making a case for the unity of chs. 9–14, key to Lamarche's argument is that the author of these chapters used four themes to portray the ultimate victory of the kingdom of God, the major theme being that the future Davidic king would usher in the day of Yahweh. Zechariah presents a single portrait of the coming king where the "king" (9:9–10), the shepherd (11:4–17 and 13:7–9), and Yahweh's representative (12:10–13:1) are one and the same person. Furthermore, Lamarche suggests that the messianism of Second Zechariah was developed as a commentary on the suffering servant of Isa 40–55.[135]

Adopting Lamarche's structure for chs. 9–14, Baldwin also proposes a chiastic structure for chs. 1–6 and 7–8.[136] She argues that hope for the house of David is expressed both in the contemporary situation with reference to Zerubbabel and Joshua and also for a future messianic figure. In terms of the contemporary situation, Baldwin sees Zerubbabel and Joshua as the two "sons of oil" who were together the means of bringing hope to the community:

> Through the high priest acquittal is pronounced and access to God's presence made possible; through the prince the Temple is completed and the lampstand allowed to shine out to the world. Two "messiahs" or anointed ones have their roles co-ordinated; neither is adequate without the other. They are equal in dignity and importance. After the death of Zerubbabel the high priest was to increase in temporal power, for the governors in Jerusalem declined in importance, but the promises to the house of David were not forgotten.[137]

134. Lamarche, *Zacharie IX–XIV*, 112–13. Lamarche proposes that Zech 9–14 was composed about 500–480 B.C.E. by a single author who arranged a group of twelve diverse pericopes into a chiastic structure.

135. Ibid., 124–47. More recently, D. C. Mitchell, *The Message of the Psalter: An Eschatological Programme in the Book of Psalms* (JSOTSup 252; Sheffield: Sheffield Academic Press, 1997), 199–242, has also discerned an eschatological programme in chs. 9–14. Mitchell's wider thesis is that the Psalter bears some similarity to the eschatological programme of the prophets. Similar to Lamarche, he finds the motif of the Davidic shepherd king to be key to this programme (p. 215): Israel is first gathered under this king (9:11–10:12), then the hostile nations gather against Jerusalem (12:3; 14:1). Israel's king then dies with Israel exiled (12:10–14; 14:7–9; cf. 11:4–17). After this, Israel regathers and the nations are divinely routed (14:2–15). The programme finishes with the nations ascending to worship at Sukkoth in Jerusalem (14:16–21). For Mitchell, the Davidic hope for a future king is central to the programme of chs. 9–14. Cf. Black, "Messiah".

136. Baldwin, *Zechariah*, 81, argues that the whole book was written by the prophet Zechariah.

137. Ibid., 125.

As to the future, Baldwin argues that when Zechariah speaks of the coming Shoot (3:8; 6:12), he is referring to a future figure. However, Joshua and Zerubbabel, as priest and prince, both had an important role to play in contributing to the work of the coming Shoot, while neither on his own adequately represented him.[138] For Baldwin, 6:12–13 refers to a future leader who will unify the offices of priest and king. Concerning the Shoot, Baldwin writes, "The old interpretation that Messiah is meant has not been displaced. Nowhere else in the Old Testament is it made so plain that the coming Davidic king will also be a priest. It is for this reason that the passage has occasioned so much questioning."[139]

In Zech 9–14, Baldwin also sees a clear foreshadowing of the messianic king in 9:9–10 with reminiscences of earlier biblical material (Gen 49:10–11; Ps 72:8; Mic 5:10). The descriptions of the character of the king parallel the descriptions of Isaiah's king (Isa 9:7; 11:4, 5; 32:1), and also of Yahweh's Servant (Isa 49:4; 50:8; 53:12).[140] She argues that when Zechariah uses the term "shepherd," he was drawing on the significance that Ezekiel had already attached to the term in bringing together the concepts of the coming Davidic king and the ideal shepherd (Ezek 34:23, 24). Similarly with the "pierced one" of Zech 12:10, Baldwin follows Lamarche in seeing a connection with Isa 53:5, where, upon the piercing and death of the messenger of the Lord, there is forgiveness of sins. However, she also observes that Zechariah does not explicitly identify this pierced one with either the Servant or the king.[141] For Baldwin, Zech 9–14 continues to centre hopes for the house of David beyond Zerubbabel.[142]

Many scholars interpret the hope held for the house of David along the same lines as Baldwin and Lamarche.[143] In Zech 1–8, they identify the

138.   Baldwin, "Semah," 93–97, and *Zechariah*, 135.
139.   Baldwin, *Zechariah*, 137.
140.   Ibid., 165–66.
141.   Ibid., 194.
142.   Duguid, "Messianic," 265–80, explores the different images for the future king in chs. 9–14 (the coming king, the good shepherd, the pierced Messiah).
143.   See E. B. Pusey, *Zechariah* (The Minor Prophets 8; London: James Nisbet & Co., 1907); M. F. Unger, *Unger's Bible Commentary: Zechariah* (Amsterdam: Drukkerij Holland, 1963); G. C. Luck, *Zechariah: A Study of the Prophetic Visions of Zechariah* (Chicago: Moody, 1969); R. E. Higginson, "Zechariah," in *The New Bible Commentary Revised* (ed. D. Guthrie and J. A. Motyer; London: IVP, 1970), 786–803; E. Achtemeier, *Nahum–Malachi* (Atlanta: John Knox, 1986); J. M. Boice, *The Minor Prophets: Micah–Malachi*, vol. 2 (Grand Rapids: Zondervan, 1986); H. Heater Jr., *Zechariah* (Grand Rapids: Zondervan, 1987); Samaan, *Portraits*; M. Bentley, *Building for God's Glory: Haggai and Zechariah Simply Explained*

Shoot as a future Davidic king, and Joshua and Zerubbabel as his types. In chs. 9–14, many see a development of this hope along the lines of Isaiah's suffering servant. For instance, B. Tidiman believes that the hope for the house of David did not die with Zerubbabel, but that Zechariah uses the technical term Shoot to refer to a future Davidic king beyond Zerubbabel: "The Shoot can therefore express the vitality of a plant that produces new shoots (Baldwin), and in the prophets becomes the technical term for the expectation of a future king coming from David."[144]

Tidiman believes Joshua and Zerubbabel are types of the future Davidic king. He also distinguishes two often distinct messianic designs within chs. 9–14: one waiting for a personal Messiah (king of peace, 9:9, 10; good shepherd, 11:4–17; pierced, 12:1–13:6; shepherd struck by the sword, 13:7–9) as opposed to another, impersonal Messiah (9:1–8, 11–17; 10:3–11:3; 14:1–21).[145]

Tidiman suggests that if there is tension between Zech 1–6 and 9–14 on the nature of the coming king, it is appropriately resolved by noting that in Zechariah, as at Isaiah, there is a duality that presents the future Davidic king as both triumphant (Isa 2; 9; 11) and marked by sufferings (Isa 50:4–11; 52:13–53:12). The optimistic aspect appears in Zech 1–6 where the people must rebuild in a difficult situation. In Zech 9–14, a dark note of suffering, inseparable to the final victory, is then introduced to prevent any easy and illusory optimism.[146]

Linking Zechariah's messianic hope with his eschatology, B. G. Webb argues that the book of Zechariah has a "now" and a "not yet" aspect to

---

(Welwyn Commentary Series; Darlington: Evangelical, 1989); van Groningren, *Messianic Revelation*, 872–914; W. C. Kaiser Jr., *Micah–Malachi* (The Preacher's Commentary 23; Nashville: Thomas Nelson, 1992), 211–27; Reventlow, *Sacharja*, 72; E. H. Merrill, *An Exegetical Commentary: Haggai, Zechariah, Malachi* (Chicago: Moody, 1994); G. Emmerson, *Nahum to Malachi* (The People's Bible Commentary; Oxford: The Bible Reading Fellowship, 1998); Herrick, *Davidic Hope*; J. L. Mackay, *Haggai, Zechariah & Malachi* (Focus on the Bible; Fearn: Christian Focus, 2003); J. W. Rogerson, "Zechariah," in *Eerdmans Commentary on the Bible* (ed. J. D. G. Dunn and J. W. Rogerson; Grand Rapids: Eerdmans, 2003), 721–29; V. M. Jauhiainen, "Turban and Crown Lost and Regained: Ezekiel 21:29–32 and Zechariah's Zemah," *JBL* 127 (2008): 501–11.

144. B. Tidiman, *Le Livre de Zacharie* (Vaux-sur-Seine: Edifac, 1996), 118 (author's translation).

145. Tidiman notes the synthesis of Chary, *Zacharie*, 144–45, where the impersonal messianism speaks of the eschatological action of Yahweh towards the nations while the personal Messiah represents Yahweh's action in favour of the community.

146. Tidiman, *Zacharie*, 57.

his hope for the house of David.[147] He suggests that we understand Zerubbabel against the background of Isaiah and Jeremiah and see in him a strong encouragement to those who were longing for the fulfilment of the promises that had been made concerning the house of David (Isa 11:1; Jer 23:5–6; 33:15–21). Webb also sees a strong link between the "now" of Zerubbabel and the "not yet" of the future Davidic king:

> We can see, therefore, that in the context of the book as a whole, Zerubbabel is not presented as the Messiah, if by that we mean the complete fulfilment of earlier prophecies about an ideal king. Zerubbabel is a very important figure, with a number of significant messianic qualities: he is a descendant of David, a leader chosen by God and empowered by his Spirit. His specific divine calling is to rebuild the temple. But after him, in a "day" not yet present but foreseen by Zechariah, will come another, greater person, an ideal shepherd-king, who will bring salvation... Zerubbabel, then, is *a* "messianic" figure, but not *the* Messiah. He is a forerunner of the Messiah, just as his temple is a forerunner of the magnificent "house of the LORD" in the last two verses of the book (14:20–21).[148]

T. E. McComiskey recognizes that some scholars believe that Zechariah considered Zerubbabel to be the promised future king, but thinks that the way that Zechariah uses the symbolism of the high priest in ch. 6 makes Zerubbabel an unlikely contender.[149] Instead, the prophet's symbolic act:

> expresses a hope that extends beyond the moment to a figure who more closely fits the symbol... It is possible that Zechariah believed the Branch would emerge from the community to complete the temple and establish the long-sought-rule rule [*sic*] of Yahweh, but this is not likely. The time of the appearance of the Branch is indefinite and does not seem to be part of the community's immediate expectation.[150]

As to Zerubbabel's role, McComiskey seems also to see Zechariah giving him a reduced role in the community compared to the high priest. He argues that Zerubbabel's Davidic associations do not seem to be significant for Zechariah.[151]

Rose concludes that there is a strong hope in Zech 1–8 for a future king and also suggests an answer to the question regarding the fate of the

---

147.   Webb, *Zechariah*, 39–42.

148.   Ibid., 42 (emphasis original).

149.   T. E. McComiskey, "Zechariah," in *The Minor Prophets: An Exegetical and Expository Commentary* (ed. T. E. McComiskey; 3 vols.; Grand Rapids: Baker, 2000), 3:1003–244 (1113).

150.   Ibid., 3:1114.

151.   Ibid., 3:1069, 1093.

actual Davidic line and the place that Zerubbabel had in all of this. He not only argues that the hopes surrounding Zerubbabel were diminished during Zechariah's time, but goes further in concluding that they were virtually non-existent. Dealing only with chs. 1–6, Rose argues that Zechariah's hopes for the house of David were entirely future.[152]

The unique aspect of Rose's thesis is to challenge the usual translation of the messianic designation (in Zech 3:8 and 6:12) as "Branch." He argues that צמח means "vegetation, greenery, growth."[153] Whereas Isaiah uses the words חטר and נצר ("shoot" and "branch" respectively) to express the idea that there was still hope for the restoration of the monarchy and for an active role for the Davidic dynasty in that restoration (e.g. Isa 6:13; 11:1), Rose argues that Zechariah uses the term צמח in contradistinction to say that any hopes held for a future ruler will only come through the intervention of God, with no room for the input of the house of David. He removes any idea of Davidic continuity from these passages.[154]

For Rose, Zerubbabel seems almost a redundant figure. The future for the house of David is entirely eschatological. In chs. 1–8, Rose argues that there is an absence of Davidic associations. Quoting W. McKane,[155] he writes:

> the oracle of Jer. 23.5 "does not introduce a prediction which will be effected by replacing one Judaean king with another within the framework of a continuing historical institution of monarchy." What is announced is not a matter of simple historical progression, "the future hope which is here proclaimed accepts as inevitable the downfall of the historical institution of Davidic monarchy and does not foresee or indicate any connection in terms of historical probabilities between the present circumstances and the future hope."[156]

Rose understands Zechariah as not announcing, encouraging, or instigating a restoration of the monarchy in the person of Zerubbabel in any way. Instead, "the prophet Zechariah pointed the people of Jerusalem to look to the future, when better things would come, including a ruler who would truly build the temple."[157]

---

152. Rose, *Zemah*. See also Rose, "Messianic," 168–85.

153. Rose, *Zemah*, 106.

154. See the review by T. Renz, "Review: W. H. Rose, *Zemah and Zerubbabel: Messianic Expectations in the Early Postexilic Period*," *VT* 53 (2003): 136.

155. W. McKane, *Jeremiah 1–25* (ICC; Edinburgh: T. & T. Clark, 1986), 560–61.

156. Rose, *Zemah*, 117.

157. Ibid., 140–41. Rose's interpretation of "Zemah" as a future figure is followed by Block, "Servant," 49, and Curtis, *Steep*, 136.

Finally, Pola believes that there was never any messianic hope connected with Zerubbabel.[158] However, the book of Zechariah attributes to
Zerubbabel and Joshua roles that are more important than those proposed
by Rose. As a Davidide, Zerubbabel functioned as a patron for the construction of the temple and had an important role in laying down its
foundation stone.[159] At the same time, in Joshua he sees a development of
the messianic hope in a priestly direction. For Pola, 3:8 and 6:9–15
present the high priest and his priesthood as displaying the characteristics of the coming Davidic king, so that the "'servant shoot' is already
present in the temple in the temple and its priesthood in a mystical
sense."[160]

2.2.3.3. *The Shoot as the future Davidic king in Zechariah 1–8, but this
hope muted in Zechariah 9–14.* Finally, I survey the view of C. and E.
Meyers, who offer a detailed account of the historical background
against which the Davidic hope of the book of Zechariah should be
understood. With the return of the nation from Babylon and operating
under Persian rule, they argue that a modified system of leadership was
called for because of the threat that a monarchy might have posed to the
Persians. Rather than the monarchy being restored, they argue that
Zechariah sees it in the best interests of the restoration community to
establish a diarchic rule consisting of governor and high priest. Consequently, Zech 1–8 focuses on the rebuilding of the temple in Jerusalem
because this is the key to the establishment of the priesthood as leaders
within the community and hence the community's continued autonomy
under Persian rule. They write, "Could Yehud countenance a temple
without a king? Could internal rule be legitimate, resting on the temple
and its leadership alone, without the historically predominant monarchic
component of national life? Zechariah provides an affirmative answer to
these questions."[161]

C. and E. Meyers believe that Zechariah does not identify Zerubbabel
as the Shoot who will bring about the return of kingship. Politically, that
would have been quite provocative. Rather, they note that within the
prophetic tradition, the root צמח occurs in the context of the future

158.   Pola, *Priestertum*, 276.
159.   Ibid., 277–78.
160.   T. Pola, "Form and Meaning in Zechariah 3," in Albertz and Becking, eds.,
Yahwism After the Exile, 156–67 (165). Cf. Pola, *Priestertum*, 255, 261.
161.   C. L. Meyers and E. M. Meyers, "Zechariah, Book of (Zechariah 1–8),"
ABD 6:1061–65 (1062).

expectation of a Davidic scion.[162] They argue that Zechariah employs this imagery "to point to a future time when kingship might well be re-established."[163] In the meantime, the oracle in 3:8 "is the first of three oracular attempts to temper support for an expanded priestly role and acceptance of a civilian governor with future hope for Davidic leadership."[164]

Therefore, C. and E. Meyers see Zech 1–8 as setting forth a diarchic leadership structure of a Davidic governor ruling jointly with the high priest, while downplaying any "burning embers of monarchist feelings" with respect to Zerubbabel.[165] They refute the conjecture that Zerubbabel's name was removed from the text of ch. 6 because of an abortive attempt to re-establish the monarchy, arguing instead, "Zerubbabel is no longer mentioned in the text because of the success of the prophet Zechariah in resolving the monarchic issue, by allowing a Davidic governor to stand as the symbol, but not the reality, of an ultimate or eschatological enthronement of a Davidic king."[166]

C. and E. Meyers believe that there is nothing to disprove that Zech 1–8 was virtually all written by Zechariah himself some time before 515 B.C.E.[167] On the other hand, they hold that Zech 9–14 was added well into the post-exilic period.[168] During this time, the messianism of Zech 9–14 is muted on account of the international situation that the restoration community now found themselves in.[169] With the house of David no longer playing a role in the administration of the restoration community, Zech 9–14 addresses the question of failed leadership. Regarding the promise of a future king in 9:9–10, they say:

> It is even possible that the editor or redactor of chap. 9 or even the compiler of the book of Zechariah has inserted these verses into the divine

---

162.   Meyers and Meyers, *Zechariah 1–8*, 203. They cite: Isa 4:2; Jer 23:5; 33:15; cf. Isa 11:1, 10.

163.   Ibid. Cf. Meyers, "Messianism," 129: "[In the oracle in Zech 6] the unmentioned Zerubbabel is relegated to be a symbol of the future, as the prophet suggests that a Davidic governor only anticipates a future Davidic king."

164.   Meyers and Meyers, *Zechariah 1–8*, 223–24.

165.   Meyers, "Messianism," 129–30.

166.   Meyers and Meyers, *Zechariah 1–8*, 370.

167.   Ibid., xliv–xlviii.

168.   Meyers and Meyers, "Fortunes," 207.

169.   Ibid., 222: "The increasing international turmoil during the Greco-Persian wars had its impact in Yehud. Persia's relatively loose control over the internal affairs of Yehud and international traffic was tightened, and military garrisons were stationed along strategic routes and in the major cities. In such a setting, the language of power, reflected in the metaphor of Divine Warrior, set the promise of restored autonomy for God's people into an eschatological framework."

warrior hymn in an attempt to make it more compatible with the earlier
materials of Zechariah... The pacifistic, quietistic tone of this passage is
so different from the rest of the material in Second Zechariah...[170]

They conclude that in the time of Zech 9–14 fewer and fewer realistic
hopes could be attached to a future king from the house of David: "The
Davidic line became more and more a symbol of future hope that was
quite remote from the present."[171] Hence, the hope for a future Davidic
king expressed in Zech 1–8 is muted in Zech 9–14.

2.3. *Summary*

It is clear from this literature review that there is at present a complete
lack of consensus on the nature of the Davidic hope in the book of
Zechariah. Childs's assessment still holds true: "few Old Testament
books reflect such a chaos of conflicting interpretations."[172] As we have
observed, one of the main reasons for this is the differing views on the
authorship and editing of the book and the ongoing influence of Wellhausen's framework. From this survey it is apparent that one's view of
the authorship and editorial history of the book of Zechariah to some
extent determines the nature of the Davidic hope seen in the book. For
instance, the overview has revealed that those who believe that the book
of Zechariah gives a negative view of the house of David (Davidic hope
abandoned or recast in a democratizing, priestly, or theocratic direction)
nearly all argue: (a) that the text has undergone an editorial process
whereby Zechariah's original prophecies have been reshaped; and (b)
that chs. 9–14 present a different picture from chs. 1–8. However, it
should also be noted that among those who are more positive about the
future fortunes of the house of David are scholars who separate Zech 1–8
from 9–14 and posit redactional changes.

    Clearly, if Zechariah's hope for the house of David is constructed
from hypothetical earlier stages in the text, and if Zech 9–14 is read over
and against chs. 1–8, then there is no end to the possible reconstructions

---

170.   Meyers, "Messianism," 135. Elsewhere, commenting on the same passage,
Meyers and Meyers, *Zechariah 9–14*, 126, state: "The future Davidide is relegated to
the eschatological future both here and in First Zechariah; yet the present reality
recedes here in a way that it does not in First Zechariah. Still, this prophecy accords
well with the earlier ones in First Zechariah; and the fact that they mesh so well may
be evidence of redaction or editorial skill, or of the author's intentional utilization of
themes and language of his immediate predecessor."
171.   Meyers, "Messianism," 142.
172.   Childs, *Introduction*, 476.

that can be made.[173] There are very few controls on the interpretation. Reading the final form of the book has the major benefit of avoiding speculation about earlier textual stages and redactional layers. But more significantly, it reflects the outlook of the final redactor, whose competence must not be underestimated. Whatever the earlier stages of the text, these must remain obscure, but in examining the final form we are standing on firmer ground.

In this survey of scholarly literature, a number of issues emerge as being significant for the study of the nature of the Davidic hope in the final form of the book of Zechariah. In relation to chs. 1–6, the key questions are, first, the identity of the Shoot of 3:8 and 6:12 and, second, the role that Zechariah envisaged for Joshua and Zerubbabel. What is the strength of the evidence for the view that Zechariah transferred the prerogatives and privileges of the pre-exilic Davidic monarch to the high priest? The answers to these questions will largely explain whether Zechariah envisaged the restoration of the monarchy in his day, or in the more distant future. In relation to Zech 9–14, I shall seek to determine whether the king of 9:9–10 and the pierced one of 12:10 are to be understood as references to the future Davidic king or to Yahweh as king. I shall also seek to identify the shepherds in chs. 11–13 and explain how the shepherd theme is worked out through these chapters. In addition, the issue of whether Zech 9–14 reverses earlier prophetic expectations, as many scholars hold, shall be addressed (key is the interpretation of ch. 11). Related to this is the question of whether the presentation of the king, shepherd, and pierced one is influenced by earlier prophetic writings, particularly the Servant of Isa 40–55, as some suggest.

I shall approach each of these questions through a close exegesis of the relevant passages of Zechariah and seek to answer them while interacting as much as possible with the diverse scholarly interpretations. From this position, the findings shall be drawn together to provide a picture of the Davidic hope in the book of Zechariah.

---

173.   This is not to imply that there will not be a variety of interpretations among those who adopt a more literary approach to the text, which is patently true, just that there is an additional restraint on the interpretations, namely, all interpreters are seeking to read the one text.

Chapter 3

JOSHUA AND ZERUBBABEL

3.1. *Introduction*

Two key leaders in the early post-exilic period were the high priest Joshua and the governor Zerubbabel. Joshua features by name in Zech 3 and 6, and Zerubbabel in Zech 4. As we saw in the previous chapter, many see the hope of the earlier prophets for a future king being directly related to either or both of these figures. However, these views largely arise from supposed redactional layers in the text that are difficult to substantiate. In contrast, the present chapter shall seek to determine how the final form of the book of Zechariah perceived their roles. What was the relationship between their roles and the hope for the house of David? Is there evidence that Zechariah saw either of them taking the throne and reinstituting the monarchy? If not, what role did each of them have?

The answers to these questions are closely connected to Zechariah's hope for a Shoot (3:8; 6:12). Because of the importance of the Shoot theme, the next chapter will be dedicated to it. Therefore, the findings of this chapter will not be conclusive and need to be supplemented by the next. The focus of the present chapter will be on the role of Joshua in Zech 3:1–7, and the role of Zerubbabel in ch. 4. The key functions that each exercised in the restoration community shall be seen: Joshua in restoring the cult, and Zerubbabel in rebuilding the temple. While each of them had a key role, it will be demonstrated that the hope of the earlier prophets for a future king from the house of David clearly extends beyond them.

3.2. *The Role of the High Priest Joshua*

Zechariah 3 deals with the role of the high priest in the early post-exilic period, and my focus shall be on the prerogatives he is given in 3:7. Is the high priest here given the responsibilities previously held by the pre-exilic king? Or does the book of Zechariah here give theological backing for a diarchal rule of high priest and Davidic governor? Or is something else on view? Answers to these questions will be sought through a close examination of the text of 3:1–7.

3.2.1. *Composition and Structure of Zechariah 3*

Scholars place the emphasis of Zech 3 in one of two areas. Some, like C. and E. Meyers, understand it as primarily addressing the political situation in Yehud and see it "reconceiving" the role of the high priest over and against the Persian-appointed governor. They write: "The issue of the high priest's position in contemporary Yehudite society was evidently one fraught with tension, so that it has worked upon the prophetic imagination of Zechariah and evoked this extraordinary portrayal of his understanding of God's will with respect to the priesthood."[1] On the other hand, Smith is representative of scholars who see the emphasis of ch. 3 as dealing with the theological problem of forgiveness and cleansing for the returned community: "The thrust of the fourth vision is the cleansing of the priests (v 4) and the land (v 9) of עָוֹן 'iniquity or guilt.' "[2]

These two issues are not unrelated, but the question of which is the chief concern of Zech 3, as we shall see, has some bearing on the issue of the prerogatives of the high priest. In reviewing several recent commentaries and the way that they deal with this chapter, Floyd asks the pertinent questions: "Is the cleansing of Joshua in the heavenly council integrally related to the administrative responsibilities assigned to him (v. 7), or does the reference to these responsibilities amount to changing the subject?" and "why is the advent of someone called 'Branch' promised here (v. 8b), and in what time frame will Yahweh 'bring' him forth, and to whom does the title refer in this particular case?"[3] These questions require careful consideration.

It soon becomes clear from the secondary literature that the interpretation of this chapter is largely related to views on its compositional history. If this chapter is understood to be primarily about the political role of Joshua, culminating in 3:7 with the new privileges and responsibilities that he will enjoy, then 3:8–10 is often seen as additional to the

---

1. Meyers and Meyers, *Zechariah 1–8*, 217. Similarly J. C. VanderKam, "Joshua the High Priest and the Interpretation of Zechariah 3," *CBQ* 53 (1991): 553–70 (570): "The crucial fact about the chapter is, however, that it accents the central and expanded roles of the high priest in postexilic Jewish society."
2. Smith, *Micah–Malachi*, 199. Cf. D. W. Rooke, *Zadok's Heirs: The Role and Development of the High Priesthood in Ancient Israel* (Oxford: Oxford University Press, 2000), 138–39; L.-S. Tiemeyer, "The Guilty Priesthood (Zech 3)," in *The Book of Zechariah and Its Influence* (ed. C. Tuckett; Aldershot: Ashgate, 2003), 1–19.
3. Floyd, "Changing Views," 257–58.

original text.[4] Redditt for instance believes that 3:1–7, 9 formed the original vision (a vision that itself was an addition to the original seven visions), and that this was secondarily expanded by 3:8, 10 which he argues are "intrusive and messianic."[5] This, of course, raises the question: Has the compositional history been devised to fit the presupposition that Zechariah neither expressed nor drew on any pre-existing hope for a future king from the house of David? In the present examination of this vision, we shall see that a hope for a future king is not only found in 3:8 and 10, but that there are good reasons for seeing the vision as a whole as conveying a strong hope for the house of David. Having said this, 3:1–7 will be examined in this chapter and 3:8–10 in the next for thematic reasons. This is not to imply anything about the compositional history of the text.

It is generally agreed that this vision pictures a heavenly court scene, similar to that found in the opening of the book of Job. The participants are: Joshua the high priest as the accused; the angel of Yahweh as Yahweh's spokesperson; the Satan as the prosecuting attorney; Yahweh as judge; the prophet Zechariah looking on and contributing at one point (3:5); and Joshua's associates (3:8). It is common to divide the chapter into two parts: part 1 is seen as a visionary section (3:1–5); part 2 deals with oracular material (3:6–10).[6] The divide between vision and oracle is not as clear as this, however, and a more thematic structure[7] will be followed:

4. E.g. J. W. Rothstein, *Die nachtgeschichte des Sacharja; studien zur sacharja-prophetie und zur jüdischen geschichte im ersten nachexilischen jahrhundert* (Leipzig: Hinrichs, 1910), 87–89; F. Horst, *Die zwölf kleinen Propheten: Nahum bis Maleachi* (HAT; Tübingen: Mohr, 1964), 210; O. Eissfeldt, *The Old Testament: An Introduction* (trans. P. R. Ackroyd; Oxford: Blackwell, 1965), 433; Chary, *Zacharie*, 73; H. Gese, "Anfang und Ende der Apokalyptik, dargestellt am Sacharjabuch," *Zeitschrift für Theologie und Kirche* 70 (1973): 20–49 (25); K. Seybold, *Bilder zum Tempelbau: Die Visionen des Propheten Sacharja* (SBS 70; Stuttgart: KBW, 1974), 109; Rudolph, *Sacharja*, 100; C. Jeremias, *Die Nachtgesichte des Sacharja. Untershuchungen zu ihrer Stellung im Zusammenhang der Visionsberichte im Alten Testament und zu ihrem Bildmaterial* (FRLANT 117; Göttingen: Vandenhoeck & Ruprecht, 1977), 202–3; A. S. van der Woude, "Zion as Primeval Stone in Zechariah 3 and 4," in *Text and Context* (ed. W. T. Claassen; JSOTSup 48; Sheffield: JSOT, 1988), 237–48 (237).

5. Redditt, "Night Visions," 254; cf. Redditt, *Zechariah*, 66.

6. E.g. Petersen, *Zechariah 1–8*, 186–214; VanderKam, "Joshua," 554.

7. Butterworth, *Structure*, 113, comments: "Structural, as well as form-critical considerations suggest that the primary division in the final writer's mind was vv. 1–7, 8–10." Butterworth also highlights the participle "standing" which appears six times in Zech 3:1–7 to form *inclusio*s that divide the passage logically into two

3:1–3   Joshua accused and defended
3:4–7   Joshua cleansed and commissioned
3:8–10   Signs of the coming Shoot

3.2.2. *Joshua Accused and Defended (Zechariah 3:1–3)*

[1] Then he showed me Joshua the high priest standing before the angel of
Yahweh and the Satan standing at his right hand to accuse him. [2] And
Yahweh said to the Satan, "Yahweh rebuke you, Satan! Yahweh rebuke
you! He who has chosen Jerusalem. Is not this man a brand plucked from
a fire?" [3] Now Joshua was clothed in filthy garments, standing before the
angel. (author's translation)

Zechariah is shown Joshua the high priest standing before the angel of
Yahweh, and the Satan standing at his right hand to accuse him.[8] The
figures of Joshua and the Satan require some comment. The repeated
description of Joshua as "high priest" is significant (cf. 3:8). While the
usage of the title in the pre-exilic period is debated, the role to which it
referred can be established from the relevant texts as referring to the head
of the priestly family.[9] What is clear from the Pentateuch is that the high
priest was responsible for ensuring the purity of the community through
the temple cult, and hence ensuring their access to Yahweh's presence.[10]
Against this background, the high priest is seen as the supreme inter-
mediary between the people and Yahweh.

In contrast, C. and E. Meyers find the background for this term in
Num 35:25, 28 and Josh 20:6, texts which they argue do not refer to a

---

sections (p. 114): "Verses 1–3 describe the scene and Yahweh's intention; vv. 4–7
describe the symbolic vindication of Joshua (and therefore Jerusalem)."

8.   The subject of the verb ויַרְאֵנִי in Zech 3:1 is not explicit, and could refer to
either the angel who not only explains various aspects of the visions to Zechariah,
but also "shows" him (cf. 1:9, 14), or else it could refer to Yahweh who also "shows"
(cf. 1:20 [MT 2:3]). Since there is no questioning and explanation by the angel in this
vision as there is in the others, it seems most likely to refer to Yahweh. See further
D. J. Clark and H. A. Hatton, *A Handbook on Haggai, Zechariah, and Malachi*
(United Bible Societies Handbook Series; New York: United Bible Societies,
2002), 119.

9.   For a discussion of the usage of the terms referring to the high priest, see I. M.
Duguid, *Ezekiel and the Leaders of Israel* (VTSup 56; Leiden: Brill, 1994), 59–61,
and J. W. Bailey, "The Usage in the Post Restoration Period of Terms Descriptive of
the Priest and High Priest," *JBL* 70 (1951): 217–25.

10. E.g. Exod 28:38; Lev 16:1–17; 23:26–32. The difficulty remains in finding a
consensus over the dating of these texts. However, even on the view that they are
from the post-exilic period, they would presumably reflect a theology of the priesthood that was contemporary with the book of Zechariah.

chief priest in Jerusalem, but regional priestly officials whose role was more administrative than sacerdotal. They claim that the use of the term in Zechariah "reflects an administrative nuance which existed apart from the priestly hierarchy of the Jerusalem temple, where it appears only when the chief priests are involved in the extrasacerdotal duties of collecting funds and instituting building projects."[11] This understanding of the role is read against the apparent increase in authority of the office in the post-exilic period.

However, given the context of this heavenly court scene, the filthy garments and cleansing, the wider and immediate context of return from exile which was Yahweh's judgment on Israel's sin (cf. 1:1–6, 16; 3:9), and the subsequent return to Jerusalem of both the exiles and Yahweh, it is surely the sacerdotal function of the high priest and his role in providing cleansing for the sin of the returned community that is chiefly on view.[12] Cleansing was a massive theological problem for the returned community of exiles, and what happened to Joshua was of paramount importance for their own destinies.[13] As the high priest, Joshua represented the remnant of God's people who had returned from exile.[14] Not only was he charged with the ultimate responsibility for dealing with their uncleanness, but also, what happened to Joshua was indicative of where the community itself stood before Yahweh. Webb comments: "the acceptability of the people with God depended critically on the acceptability of the high priest. He symbolically carried them into the presence of God as their representative and mediator."[15] This representative

11. Meyers and Meyers, *Zechariah 1–8*, 181; cf. Tollington, *Tradition*, 131.

12. The immediate context of return from exile is picked up on in the phrase "a brand plucked from the fire." Love, *Evasive*, 204, surveys the background to this phrase in the Hebrew Bible and rightly concludes: "The brand snatched from the fire is that saved from the destruction. The fire that it is snatched from is the exile."

13. This has been highlighted by D. F. O'Kennedy, "The Theological Portrayal of Forgiveness in Zechariah 1–8," *Scriptura* 84 (2003): 410–22. See also Tiemeyer, "Guilty Priesthood," 1–19.

14. Moore, *Zechariah*, 64; P. R. Ackroyd, "Zechariah," in *Peake's Commentary on the Bible* (ed. M. Black and H. H. Rowley; London: Thomas Nelson, 1962), 646–55 (648); Baldwin, *Zechariah*, 113; M. G. Kline, *Glory in Our Midst: A Biblical-Theological Reading of Zechariah's Night Visions* (Eugene: Wipf & Stock, 2001), 99.

15. Webb, *Zechariah*, 85. Note also P. P. Jenson, "The Levitical Sacrificial System," in *Sacrifice in the Bible* (ed. R. T. Beckwith and M. J. Selman; Carlisle: Paternoster, 1995), 25–40 (33): "The defilement of the anointed priest is so serious because he is the religious head of the community and represents the people, who are bound up in his guilt (Lv. 4:3)." Also, Tiemeyer, *Priestly*, 241, states: "only a cleansed high priest would bring atonement to the land and its people."

function of the high priest is also significant in the logical progression of the vision, as we shall see.

The Satan (הֹשָׂטָן) is not a proper name, but a descriptive title that literally means "the accuser." Hamilton notes that הֹשָׂטָן can also have the added nuance of either "adversary" or "slanderer" depending on the context.[16] In the context here of a heavenly court scene, it is his role as an accuser that is primarily on view as he takes the role of the prosecuting attorney against Joshua.[17] While many scholars are keen to point out that this figure should not be understood as the devil,[18] his opposition to Yahweh and his purposes should not be overlooked. Some level of antipathy is seen in the fact that even before the Satan can speak to accuse Joshua he is rebuked by Yahweh. He is not a benign opponent.

The basis of Yahweh's rebuke is that he has "chosen Jerusalem," and that Joshua is "a brand plucked from a fire" (3:2). The choice of Jerusalem is a theme of earlier parts of Zechariah (cf. 1:17; 2:12 [MT 2:16]), and it draws on Deuteronomic theology. McConville, commenting on the book of Deuteronomy, says:

> The motif of Yahweh's choosing then, not only illustrates the deuteronomic theme of sovereignty, but does so in the way in which we have seen that other motifs (the gift of the land, blessing) illustrate it. That is, it shows that Yahweh initiates a situation within which Israel is expected to respond. It belongs in a profound way, therefore, to the deuteronomic theology which is its background.[19]

This Deuteronomic theology has both conditionality (human response) and unconditionality (Yahweh's choice), which, rather than being contradictory, are fundamental to its rhetoric.[20] In the post-exilic situation, a more explicit example of how this works is found in Neh 1:9: "but if you return to me and keep my commandments and do them, though your dispersed be under the farthest skies, I will gather them from there and bring them to the place that I have chosen, to make my name dwell

---

16. V. P. Hamilton, "Satan," *ABD* 5:985–89 (985–86).

17. The title is also used in Job 1–2 of a figure who plays out a similar role in the heavenly court. See also Ps 109:6 where the title is used of one who falsely accuses in a trial.

18. E.g. Sweeney, *Twelve*, 595: "The reference to 'Satan'…is frequently misconstrued as the devil figure of later Christian and Jewish literature and theology." Cf. Conrad, *Zechariah*, 89.

19. J. G. McConville, *Law and Theology in Deuteronomy* (JSOTSup 33; Sheffield: JSOT, 1984), 32.

20. See further, J. G. Millar, *Now Choose Life: Theology and Ethics in Deuteronomy* (NSBT 6; Leicester: IVP, 1998), 55–66.

there." In Nehemiah, blessing results from obedience, but God's sovereign grace is prior, as evident in the language of "choice." It is this same Deuteronomic theology that underlies the use of the "choice" language in chs. 1–3. Here the exiles in the north and in Babylon are commanded to return to Jerusalem (2:6–7 [MT 2:10–11]), for Yahweh has again chosen Jerusalem (2:12 [MT 2:16]).

In Yahweh's rebuke of the Satan, we can presume from Joshua's presence in Jerusalem that he has obediently responded to the call of Yahweh to return. At the same time, the descriptions of Jerusalem as Yahweh's chosen city, and Joshua as "a brand plucked from a fire" (3:2) highlight Yahweh's sovereign grace in saving him from the judgment of exile.[21] So, both themes of Deuteronomic theology, namely, human response and Yahweh's sovereign choice, are present.

A major obstacle remains. Even though the Satan is silenced, Joshua is clothed with filthy garments (Zech 3:3). Scholars note that the word "filthy" can be used to describe excrement (e.g. Deut 23:14; 2 Kgs 18:27; Ezek 4:12) and therefore this description "designates an extreme condition of dirtiness."[22] It is not only the exile, but the sin that led to it that was the cause of defilement for both the people and the priesthood.

Hence, the opening of this vision with Joshua the high priest standing before the angel of Yahweh clothed in filthy garments and being accused by the Satan conveys a problem. Given the high priest's representative role, it suggests that the people, even though they have returned from the fire of exile, still stand condemned. The problem is heightened by previous mention of the return of Yahweh to Jerusalem (cf. Zech 1:16; 2:5, 10, 13 [MT 2:9, 14, 17]). How can Yahweh dwell in the midst of a defiled people and bless them? It is this problem that the vision moves to resolve.

3.2.3. *Joshua Cleansed and Commissioned (Zechariah 3:4–7)*

> [4] And he replied to the ones standing before him, saying, "Remove the filthy garments from him." And he said to him, "See, I have taken your iniquity from you, and I will clothe you with pure garments." [5] And I said, "Let them put a clean turban upon his head." So they put a clean turban on his head and clothed him in garments. And the angel of Yahweh was standing by.

---

21. The latter phrase also appears in Amos 4:11 with reference to Yahweh's rescue of Israel just as Lot and his family were snatched from the judgment of Sodom and Gomorrah (cf. Gen 19).

22. Meyers and Meyers, *Zechariah 1–8*, 187.

⁶ And the angel of Yahweh charged Joshua, ⁷ "Thus says Yahweh of hosts: If you walk in my ways and if you keep my requirements, then you shall rule my house and have charge of my courts, and I will give to you the right of access among these who are standing here." (author's translation)

The first stage in the resolution of this problem is in the cleansing of Joshua in 3:4–5. The angel commands that Joshua's filthy garments be removed, and then declares that his iniquity has been removed, and that he will be clothed with pure garments (3:4).[23] The prophet Zechariah requests that a clean turban be put on Joshua's head, and this is carried out along with the re-clothing in 3:5 with the angel standing by.

Many scholars note that the word for "turban" (צְנִיף) here is not the usual word for the high priest's headwear as found in Exod 28:39 (מִצְנֶפֶת). Some argue that it is a royal turban indicating that the high priest is assuming the role of the pre-exilic monarch.[24] While צְנִיף is associated with royalty in Isa 62:3, this probably indicates the dignity of the new clothing, rather than the office of the wearer since it is also worn by rich women in Isa 3:23, and by Job in Job 29:14, neither having royal associations.[25] Instead, the crown is the headwear that connotes royalty (cf. Zech 6:11).

The reclothing of the chief priest was part of an ordination rite in Exod 29 and Lev 8–9, and this may be on view here. However, Joshua is already called the high priest in Zech 3:1, and this suggests reinstatement rather than ordination.[26] Having been cleansed and clothed, Joshua is then commissioned by the angel of the Lord in 3:6–7.

23. See D. W. Thomas, "A Note on מחלצות in Zechariah 3.4," *JTS* 33 (1932): 279–80, who argues that the context calls for מחלצות to be understood in the sense of "clean, pure."

24. Chary, *Zacharie*, 77; Meyers and Meyers, *Zechariah 1–8*, 192.

25. Smith, *Micah–Malachi*, 200, notes that it comes from the root צנף which means "to wind around." He concludes: "[it] is used here as the mark of the new dignity conferred on the high priest… With his head covered the priest was properly clothed to approach Yahweh." Cf. N. L. A. Tidwell, "*waʾōmar* (Zech 3:5) and the Genre of Zechariah's Fourth Vision," *JBL* 94 (1975): 343–55 (344); Sweeney, *Twelve*, 597–98. VanderKam, "Joshua," 557, states that if there are royal associations, then they are no more than with מצנפת. Similarly, Boda, "Oil," 4.

26. E.g. Num 3:7, 8, 25, 31, 36; Neh 13:14; Ezek 44:15; 48:11. Sweeney, *Twelve*, 593, believes that it is an ordination on the basis of these Pentateuchal texts; however, Petersen, *Zechariah 1–8*, 199–200, argues that it is not an ordination because Joshua is already called the high priest in Zech 3:1, and there are: "(1) no washing rites, (2) no detailed list of a costume, and (3) no sacrifices" (p. 200). For Petersen, it is the purification of a high priest who does not have access to normal purification rituals. It seems best to use the language of "reinstatement," as does Merrill, *Zechariah*, 137.

Zechariah 3:7 has a key bearing on the wider question of the hope for the house of David in this period. Is this speaking of "a redefinition of the chief priest's range of authority and responsibility in the postexilic period"?[27] Is this verse reassigning the pre-exilic functions of the monarchy to the high priest so that the latter is now supreme ruler?

In terms of the syntax of this verse, scholars are divided over where in the conditional clause the protasis ends and the apodosis begins. There are two options; most translations adopt the first:

Protasis:	(A)	If you walk in my ways and if you keep my requirements,
Apodosis:	(B)	then you shall rule my house and have charge of my courts,
	(C)	and I will give to you the right of access among these who are standing here.

Alternatively, it could be taken as:

Protasis:	(A)	If you walk in my ways and if you keep my requirements,
	(B)	and if you shall rule my house and have charge of my courts,
Apodosis:	(C)	then I will give to you the right of access among these who are standing here.

The latter sees phrase B as a responsibility whereas the former sees it as a privilege. It is also possible that in the former option, phrase B is introducing a new situation for the high priest that will result from obedience. The syntax is complex, but on balance favours the first.[28] This will become clearer once the meaning of each of the phrases is elucidated.

Phrase A is simplest. "Walk in my ways" is a call to covenant fidelity in the language of Deuteronomy (cf. Deut 10:12–22; 28:9). "Keep my requirements" is parallel in structure, and some argue that it has more of a ritual sense as it is a phrase that frequently refers to priestly duties.[29] However, the phrase is also used in non-priestly contexts to refer again to

27. Meyers and Meyers, *Zechariah 1–8*, 220–21.
28. Rose, *Zemah*, 68–69, has a detailed discussion and prefers the second, arguing that the two וגם continue the protasis and accumulate further conditions. However, וגם more likely functions with a second וגם in the same phrase to indicate "both… and" as part of the apodosis. See BDB, 169, which also gives several examples, including Zech 8:6, where גם introduces the apodosis (e.g. Gen 13:16; Jer 31:36–37; 33:21, 26). The absence of וגם before phrase C can be explained on the basis that it is redundant since the apodosis has already been introduced.
29. E.g. Merrill, *Zechariah*, 137–38; Clark and Hatton, *Handbook*, 125; Boda, *Commentary*, 254.

the broader idea of covenant faithfulness.[30] While priestly duties may be in the background, covenant faithfulness seems to be the idea that is uppermost. Both of these stipulations are prefaced by אם, which indicates the protasis of a conditional clause.

Interpretations of phrase B hinge on the meaning of the verb דין. Some scholars take it to mean "execute judgment" so that what is on view is the high priest replacing the king in the administration of justice in the post-exilic community, with a corresponding shift from the palace to the temple as the seat of justice. For instance, C. and E. Meyers argue:

> With the removal of the king as chief judicial officer, the likelihood…is that the priesthood filled this gap in social organization and that the temple precinct rather than the palace became the seat of justice. The chief officer of the temple…thus bore the final responsibility for the execution of justice and so regained a function held by the monarchy during the era of the Davidic kingdom…[31]

Rose identifies two problems with this view. First, "my house" does not refer to the community but to the temple building.[32] Second, "my house" is the object and not the locus of the verb דין; that is, Joshua will rule *over*, not *in* my house.[33] He summarizes: "If one wants to keep the semantic feature of jurisdiction of דין, and interpret ביתי as the temple, the only appropriate way to read this clause is as indicating jurisdiction over matters of temple and cult."[34]

---

30. E.g. Gen 26:5; Lev 18:30; Num 9:19, 23; Deut 11:1; Josh 22:3; 1 Kgs 2:3; Mal 3:14.

31. Meyers and Meyers, *Zechariah 1–8*, 195. Cf. R. A. Mason, "The Prophets of the Restoration," in *Israel's Prophetic Tradition* (ed. R. Coggins, A. Phillips, and M. Knibb; Cambridge: Cambridge University Press, 1982), 137–54 (147); Stuhlmueller, *Rebuilding*, 78–79.

32. Rose, *Zemah*, 71 n. 82, cites those who have understood "my house" (ביתי) as referring to the Jewish community: F. Hitzig, *Die zwölf kleinen Propheten erklärt* (Leipzig: Hirzel, 1881), 344–45; L. G. Rignell, *Die Nachtgesichte des Sacharja* (Lund: Gleerup, 1950), 120; P. Marinkovic, "What Does Zechariah 1–8 Tell us about the Second Temple?," in *Second Temple Studies*. Vol. 2, *Temple Community in the Persian Period* (ed. T. C. Eskenazi and K. H. Richards; JSOTSup 175; Sheffield: JSOT, 1994), 88–103. Against this interpretation, Rose, *Zemah*, 71 n. 82, cites Jeremias, *Nachtgesichte*, 214 n. 48, who observes that in Zechariah, בית only refers to people when specified by יהודה or ישראל (Zech 8:13, 15, 19), otherwise it refers to a house (Zech 5:4; 6:10), or to the temple (Zech 1:16; 4:9; 5:11; 7:3; 8:9). In addition, several commentators rightly observe that the parallel reference to the "courts" in the next clause means that it must refer to the temple building here (e.g. Rudolph, *Sacharja*, 93; Petersen, *Zechariah 1–8*, 205; Hanhart, *Sacharja 1–8*, 190).

33. Rose, *Zemah*, 72.

34. Ibid., 72.

A second approach takes דין more broadly, arguing that its use with the verb שמר indicates not just the administration of justice, but more the ultimate responsibility for the administration and management of the temple, a role previously held by the king (e.g. 1 Kgs 2:27; 2 Kgs 16:10–18; 22:3–20). Representing this view, Sweeney says that this phrase "must refer to the special role of the high priest as the chief supervisor of YHWH's Temple and courts."[35]

With both of these views it is almost universal to see here an extension of the powers of the high priest.[36] For instance, Pola recently concludes: "There is no doubt about the intention of v. 7: The high priest gains duties which belonged formerly to royal privilege."[37] As has been seen, this view can be traced back to Wellhausen.[38]

This issue is not insignificant. If it is the case that the prerogatives of the Davidic king are here being given to the high priest, this may indicate that the hope for any future king to come and recover the rights of the throne were fading.[39] While overstating the case, Tollington notes this connection when she says: "This interpretation [the transfer of former royal prerogatives to the senior priest] necessitates that no hopes were being fostered for a restored monarchy in the figure of Zerubbabel, and it would imply a significant rise in Joshua's status."[40]

It must be asked, however, whether scholars have read too much into the text. Mitchell notes: "The declaration here made, therefore, amounts to a charter granting to Joshua and his successors a sole and complete control in matters of religion never before enjoyed by the head of the hierarchy at Jerusalem... In fact, it is an advance upon the program of Ezekiel ([ch.] 45) in the direction of the priestly legislation of the

---

35. Sweeney, *Twelve*, 600. See also Chary, *Zacharie*, 81; K. Elliger, *Das Buch der zwölf kleinen Propheten* (ATD 25; Göttingen: Vandenhoeck & Ruprecht, 1982), 120–21; Amsler, "Zacharie," 78; VanderKam, "Joshua," 559.

36. Clark and Hatton, *Handbook*, 126, are typical: "full responsibility for the Temple and its worship is promised to the high priest. This was an increase in his privileges, since before the exile it was the king who had ultimate responsibility over at least the physical aspects of the Temple." See also, Bič, *Nachtgesichte*, 70; Baldwin, *Zechariah*, 115; Mason, *Zechariah*, 51; Achtemeier, *Nahum–Malachi*, 122; Merrill, *Zechariah*, 135; Tidiman, *Zacharie*, 116; Rose, *Zemah*, 83; Larkin, "Zechariah," 612; J. C. VanderKam, *From Joshua to Caiaphas: High Priests after the Exile* (Minneapolis: Fortress, 2004), 29.

37. Pola, "Form," 164; also Pola, *Priestertum*, 198–203.

38. See Chapter 2, §2.2.1.1.

39. This is not the case for Pola, however, who sees Zechariah holding high hopes for a future king.

40. Tollington, *Tradition*, 159. However, this is not Tollington's view.

Pentateuch."[41] While the dating of the sources in the Pentateuch is open to debate, and this clearly has a bearing on whether this control by the high priest was "never before enjoyed," and while I do not believe that Mitchell has proven his conclusion of an unprecedented charter being given to Joshua, he does helpfully observe that there is some connection between what is said here in Zechariah with Ezekiel and the Pentateuch. Indeed, there are several passages that speak of Levitical priests and the high priest dispensing justice.

Deuteronomy 17:9–12 makes provision for difficult legal cases to be heard at the central sanctuary by the Levitical priests and judges. There are three significant issues here: first, the seat of justice is "the place that the Lord your God will choose" (17:8), so the priesthood ruling in the temple is not a novel idea; second, the chief priest seems to be on view in 17:12, being defined by the use of the article;[42] and third, the very next section in Deuteronomy deals with kingship by which we can imply that the juridical activity of the priesthood was never in lieu of that exercised by the king.

The juridical activity of the priesthood is also seen in Deut 19:17, where a malicious witness is to be brought before Yahweh by being brought before the priests and the judges who are in office. Similar juridical activity is seen in 21:5, where it is said of the Levitical priests that "by their word every dispute and every assault shall be settled."

In Ezek 44:15, the pre-exilic Levitical priests are described as the ones who "kept the charge of my sanctuary when the people of Israel went astray from me." In context, this reference to the activities of the Levitical priests in the pre-exilic period does not make clear what was involved when they "kept the charge of my sanctuary." However, if Ezekiel is envisioning a restoration of the past, then the wider context demonstrates that as well as offering sacrifices (Ezek 44:15, 27) it also included judicial activity (44:24): "In a dispute, they shall act as judges, and they shall judge it according to my judgments." In any case, the future reference to the judicial activity of the Levitical priests is certainly not a replacement of the king's prerogatives in the absence of a king, as Ezekiel still has a Davidic prince on view (cf. 44:3; 45:7; 46:2).[43]

41. Mitchell, "Zechariah," 154–55.

42. Bailey, "Priest," 217; J. A. Thompson, *Deuteronomy* (TOTC; Leicester: IVP, 1974), 203.

43. It seems that Ezekiel's preference for the language of "prince" instead of "king" is simply to highlight the distinction between the future ruler and recent occupants of the office. See further D. I. Block, "Bringing Back David: Ezekiel's Messianic Hope," in Satterthwaite, Hess, and Wenham, eds., *The Lord's Anointed*, 167–88 (176).

While from a later time than Zechariah, Chronicles presents the pre-exilic priesthood as having a role that included a judicial function. In 2 Chr 19:8–11, under King Jehoshaphat, Levitical priests were included in the appeal court in Jerusalem to judge difficult cases that local courts referred to them. Significantly, 2 Chr 19:11 states: "And behold, Amariah the chief priest is over you in all matters of the LORD; and Zebadiah the son of Ishmael, the governor of the house of Judah, in all the king's matters, and the Levites will serve you as officers."

Again we see the juridical activity of the priests, operating alongside that of the governor. Interestingly, Petersen argues that what Zechariah claims here is quite innovative, not because the responsibility for judging at the temple is shifted from the king to the high priest, but because it shifts from the priests as a class onto the high priest.[44] He acknowledges that the priests had a key judicial responsibility in the pre-exilic period, but it is the key role of the high priest that is novel. However, the presence of what seems to be a chief priest in Deut 17:12 (cf. 2 Chr 19:11), as has just been noted, tends to negate the claim that Zechariah is being all that innovative. Tollington also allows for the possibility that what is happening here is a reinstatement of the rightful authority of the priesthood in the person of Joshua the high priest. While this authority may have diminished towards the end of the monarchy, it had never been retracted. She says:

> It does not indicate an enhancement of Joshua's status in fact, but requires him to assume a more significant role in practice, and thus it is compatible with hopes for a restored monarchy or with recognition of the overall authority of a civil governor. This emphasis on *the return to the situation which pertained in the earlier days of Israel's faith and history* appears to be the more probable alternative…[45]

Hence, if דרך is understood in the limited sense of juridical activity, or in the broader sense of juridical activity plus the administration and management of the temple, then there is no evidence that 3:7 envisages anything more than a restoration of the prerogatives enjoyed by the high priest before the exile. The texts that have been reviewed here provide no evidence for any extension of power, much less that the high priest is being given the prerogatives of the pre-exilic monarch.

---

44. Petersen, *Zechariah 1–8*, 205–6. This view is also represented by Tollington, *Tradition*, 161. Rose, *Zemah*, 82, misunderstands Tollington's view when he cites her has saying that she affirms a transfer of former royal prerogatives to the senior priest. She clearly says (p. 161 n. 2): "Thus it is wrong to suggest that a royal function was being transferred to Joshua."

45. Tollington, *Tradition*, 160 (emphasis added).

This is also seen in the next phrase, where the courts over which Joshua will "have charge" (שׁמר) are the courts of the temple.[46] While later than Zechariah, 1 Chr 23:28–32 lists a broad range of activities of the priesthood that are summarized as "keeping charge (שׁמר) of the tent of meeting and the sanctuary." These include "having the care of the courts and the chambers, the cleansing of all that is holy, and any work for the service of the house of God." Again, this strongly suggests that having charge of the temple courts is not a new function being given to Joshua at this point, but rather the reinstatement of Joshua to a role that the priesthood enjoyed before the exile. It was a role that had a juridical component, but its main focus was the maintenance of the cult.

Once more, there are no grounds for interpreting 3:7 as a devolvement of the political representation of the community from the monarchy to the high priesthood. This view, going back to Wellhausen, reads more into ch. 3 than is actually present.[47] A few scholars have begun to question the scholarly consensus. P. R. Bedford claims and warns:

> There is no evidence to support the contention that when Zerubbabel disappeared from the scene, the high priest assumed the sole leadership position. If there were a diarchy, why did not Zerubbabel's successor as governor participate in it? Why would authority necessarily devolve upon the high priest?
>
> One needs to beware of understanding the role of the cult and the high priesthood in the early Achaemenid Persian period in terms of what is known of their role in the Hellenistic period.[48]

Similarly, in a paper on the relationship between the high priest and the monarchy, D. W. Rooke concludes:

> The relationship between the monarchy and the high priesthood is therefore an uneven one. The monarch can fulfil priestly duties because of the nature of his kingship, but equally because of the nature of his priesthood the high priest cannot be a king, nor should he ever be confused with a messianic figure. Kingship may well be priesthood in a certain sense, but priesthood, even high priesthood, is certainly not kingship.[49]

46. 'My house" and "my courts" are also used in conjunction in 1 Chr 28:6 (cf. Pss 65:4; 84:10).

47. Commentators before Wellhausen understand what is promised here as a return to the situation before the exile. E.g. M. Dods, *The Post-Exilian Prophets: Haggai, Zechariah, Malachi* (Handbooks for Bible Classes; Edinburgh: T. & T. Clark, 1879), 77; Moore, *Zechariah*, 66; Hengstenberg, *Christology*, 278.

48. P. R. Bedford, *Temple Restoration in Early Achaemenid Judah* (Leiden: Brill, 2001), 204.

49. D. W. Rooke, "Kingship as Priesthood: The Relationship between the High Priesthood and the Monarchy," in Day, ed., *King and Messiah in Israel*, 187–208 (208). Also Rooke, *Zadok*, 144, 51.

Furthermore, one would expect chs. 9–14 to reflect this transition to priestly rule, yet the priesthood is not even mentioned in this section of Zechariah. Hence, there is no evidence that 3:7 envisages the high priest being given the responsibilities of the pre-exilic monarch.

We are still left with phrase C, which is literally: "and I will give you goings among these standing ones." This phrase is also open to a number of interpretations that depend on prior presuppositions and conclusions. For instance, C. and E. Meyers believe:

> Just as the prophet is God's messenger, communicating God's judgment concerning Israel to the people and especially to the king as the official ultimately responsible for the carrying out of justice, so now the priest must execute justice and thus needs to have access to divine will… So we are left with the sense that the end of 3:7 in fact does accord Joshua an unprecedented position.[50]

On the other hand, Rose concludes his discussion of this phrase by stating that "there is no evidence left to support the view that Joshua was given the privilege of access to the heavenly court, a privilege which prophets enjoyed."[51]

The debate over the meaning of this phrase centres around the difficult word מהלכים. Rose notes that the early versions unanimously translate it as "those who go/walk," and modern interpreters usually take it as a plural of the noun מהלך and translate it as "access."[52] He argues that scholars who understand it as "access" do so on unsubstantiated assumptions, namely, that מהלך can mean something like "entrance," and then "(right to) access."[53] He contends that it is best understood as a Piel participle of הלך, the whole phrase thus being translated, "I will provide for you persons who go between these attendants."[54] However, as Rose himself acknowledges, his proposal is not without problems in that here the Piel participle does not follow the usual doubling that is found in

50. Meyers and Meyers, *Zechariah 1–8*, 197. VanderKam, *Caiaphas*, 29, has more recently argued that here the high priest is being given access into the traditional area of the prophets.

51. Rose, *Zemah*, 79.

52. Ibid., 74.

53. A further problem highlighted by ibid., 75–76, is that no one has really given a satisfactory explanation of why the plural form מהלכים is used.

54. Rose follows W. Beuken, *Haggai–Sacharja 1–8: Studien zur Überlieferungsgeschichte der frühnachexilischen Prophetie* (SSN 10; Assen: Van Gorcum, 1967), 293–96, and H.-G. Schöttler, *Gott inmitten seines Volkes: Die Neuordnung des Gottesvolkes nack Sacharja 1–6* (Trierer theologische Studien 43; Trier: Paulinus, 1987), 337–39, in seeing not so much a promise of direct access for Joshua, but of figures who will serve as mediators between Joshua and the divine council.

every other occurrence in the Hebrew Bible.[55] Further, Rose seems to overlook the obvious fact that in this vision at least, Joshua is already in the heavenly court. Rose's view that Joshua was never given the privilege of access to the heavenly court because this was the privilege of prophets alone is not supported by the evidence of the vision itself. The context must be taken into account when determining meaning.[56]

Butterworth notes the symmetry in word usage here, and this may account for the unusual usage of מהלכים:

p		If you will walk (הלך) in my ways
	q	and if you will keep my charge (שמר משמרתיך)
		r	then also you will judge my house
	q	and you will also keep (שמר) my courts
p		and I will also give you access (?) (מהלכים)[57]

This highlights a play on words, where if Joshua walks in the way of the Lord, he will be given what is literally, "walkings among the standing ones" (corresponding to the second "p" phrase above). Given this wordplay, it seems perfectly reasonably to understand it as "access" to the divine presence.

The question of the identity of "these who are standing here" remains. Joshua's associates can be eliminated, as they are described as "your associates *sitting* before you" (3:8). But there are others who are described as "standing" and these are Joshua and the Satan (3:1), and the angel of Yahweh (3:5). These are the ones standing in the divine council, but what is important for us to note is that this divine council is in Yahweh's presence. At this point we must recall again that the role of the high priest was to mediate on behalf of God's people, and that a key part of this was entering into Yahweh's presence in the holy of holies in the temple on the Day of Atonement each year. Sweeney comments:

> The term [מהלכים] appears only here in relation to this specialized meaning, but it appears to refer to the exclusive right of the high priest to enter the Holy of Holies in the Jerusalem Temple to appear before YHWH as the representative of the Jewish community to make atonement for the people's sins on Yom Kippur or the Day of Atonement (see Leviticus 16).[58]

Hence, rather than see this promise as taking over the prerogative of the prophet and giving the high priest a privilege that even the king did not

55. Ps 104:3, 10; Prov 6:11; Eccl 4:15.
56. Contra Boda, *Commentary*, 255, who follows Rose and argues: "the high priest is not being offered access to the heavenly council, but rather to individuals who already enjoy such access, most likely prophets (cf. Zech. 7:3)."
57. Butterworth, *Structure*, 116.
58. Sweeney, *Twelve*, 599.

directly enjoy in the pre-exilic period, in the context of the vision it seems to be saying something different altogether: Joshua has been cleansed and he is now being commissioned for his role in the new temple whereby he will represent the people in Yahweh's presence.

Given the meaning of these phrases, the syntax of 3:7 is best understood as:[59]

Protasis:	(A)	If you walk in my ways and if you keep my requirements,
Apodosis:	(B)	then you shall both rule my house and have charge of my courts,
	(C)	and I will give to you the right of access among these who are standing here.

The message of the vision of 3:1–7 is that if Joshua walks in the way of Yahweh and keeps his requirements, then once the new temple is constructed, he will have the privilege that the priesthood and high priest enjoyed before the exile, of exercising judicial responsibility, administering the cult, and having the special privilege of access to Yahweh's presence.[60] This was all-important for the returned community as it offered hope of cleansing once the temple had been constructed. In the shadow of the exile, this vision of the cleansing and commissioning of Joshua was Yahweh's solution to the problem of sin and defilement.

In summary, it has been common for scholars to interpret 3:1–7 as an elevation of the status of the high priest in the absence of a king and in the absence of hope for any future king. However, the text and its background do not support this interpretation. Those who adopt this interpretation are perhaps guilty of reading the role and position of the high priest in the later Hellenistic period back into the text.[61] Instead, 3:1–7 envisages Joshua the high priest being reinstated to the role that the high priest enjoyed before the judgment of exile. There is nothing here to suggest that hope for the house of David has diminished in any way. On the contrary, the restoration of the priesthood heightens the expectation for a coming king, as shall be seen.

59. Ibid., 600. Tiemeyer, *Priestly*, 252, views this phrase as part of the apodosis.
60. While offering a different interpretation of the text, M. Segal, "The Responsibilities and Rewards of Joshua the High Priest According to Zechariah 3:7," *JBL* 126 (2007): 717–34, comes to the same conclusions regarding Joshua's responsibilities.
61. This is made explicit by Merrill, *Zechariah*, 138: "This anticipates a quasi-political role of the high priest that gained increasing reality with the decline of postexilic secular authority. By the beginning of the Ptolemaic era (c. 300 B.C.) both political and religious power became centered in one man, the high priest."

3.3. *The Role of Zerubbabel*

3.3.1. *Zerubbabel outside Zechariah*

Zerubbabel is an enigmatic figure. Outside of the book of Zechariah, he is mentioned in Haggai, Ezra, Nehemiah, and 1 Chronicles. Haggai refers to him as the governor (פחה) of Judah (Hag 1:1, 14; 2:1, 21). However, it is difficult to know exactly how this title was understood.[62] He is also referred to as the son of Shealtiel, which speaks of his Davidic lineage (Hag 1:1, 14; 2:1, 23; cf. 1 Chr 3:17).[63] In Ezra and Nehemiah, Zerubbabel is listed among the returnees from Babylon who rebuilt the altar and re-laid the foundation of the temple (Ezra 2:2; 3:2, 8; Neh 12:1).[64] An important part of the background for understanding the role of Zerubbabel in Zechariah is found in the conclusion of Haggai, where Yahweh promises to make Zerubbabel like his signet ring: "On that day, declares the LORD of hosts, I will take you, O Zerubbabel my servant, the son of Shealtiel, declares the LORD, and make you like a signet ring, for I have chosen you, declares the LORD of hosts" (Hag 2:23).

The exact significance of Zerubbabel being made Yahweh's signet ring is debated. Some scholars hold that this is a declaration that Haggai saw Zerubbabel as the future promised king, or heir to the throne.[65] Others maintain that Zerubbabel is simply being given authority to rule and lead Yahweh's people.[66] Other scholars are less specific and understand Haggai's statement as simply indicating that Zerubbabel is the new

---

62. פחה could also refer to officials other than provincial governors. See the discussions in S. E. McEvenue, "The Political Structure in Judah from Cyrus to Nehemiah," *CBQ* 43 (1981): 353–64; Petersen, *Zechariah 1–8*, 23–27; Meyers and Meyers, *Zechariah 1–8*, 13–16.

63. For a discussion of the differing paternities of Zerubbabel given in Haggai and 1 Chronicles, see Boda, *Commentary*, 34–35. Cf. G. N. Knoppers, *1 Chronicles 1–9: A New Translation with Introduction and Commentary* (AB 12; New York: Doubleday, 2003), 328.

64. For a thorough treatment of Zerubbabel in Ezra–Nehemiah, see S. Japhet, "Sheshbazzar and Zerubbabel," *ZAW* 94 (1982): 66–98.

65. See Mitchell, "Zechariah," 78; Petersen, *Zechariah 1–8*, 104; Hanson, "Messiahs," 68–69; Redditt, *Zechariah*, 32; Uffenheimer, "Zerubbabel," 224; Laato, *Star*, 196; Sweeney, *Twelve*, 554; S. Sykes, *Time and Space in Haggai–Zechariah 1–8: A Bakhtinian Analysis of a Prophetic Chronicle* (Studies in Biblical Literature 24; New York: Peter Lang, 2002), 35.

66. See Meyers and Meyers, *Zechariah 1–8*, 68–70; L. B. Hinton, *Micah, Nahum, Habakkuk, Zephaniah, Haggai, Zechariah, and Malachi* (Basic Bible Commentary 16; Nashville: Abingdon, 1988), 83; Tollington, *Tradition*, 144; Merrill, *Zechariah*, 57.

earthly representative of Yahweh's kingship.[67] Others suggest that he is promised divine protection and special honour.[68]

The background to Haggai's statement is almost certainly Jer 22:24–25, where Yahweh announces his judgment on the Davidide Coniah (Jehoiachin): "As I live, declares the LORD, though Coniah the son of Jehoiakim, king of Judah, were the signet ring on my right hand, yet I would tear you off and give you into the hand of those who seek your life, into the hand of those of whom you are afraid, even into the hand of Nebuchadnezzar king of Babylon and into the hand of the Chaldeans." Here Coniah is likened to a signet ring, or seal, on Yahweh's right hand. The signet ring was an important possession for a king. It was a symbol of authority and was used to authenticate legal documents and royal pronouncements.[69] Now Yahweh declares that he would tear off this ring. In the context of Jeremiah, this action is a direct result of Coniah's evil (cf. Jer 22:17). Yahweh will cast off and disown his anointed (cf. Ps 89:38–45). Furthermore, Jeremiah states: "Thus says the LORD: 'Write this man down as childless, a man who shall not succeed in his days, for none of his offspring shall succeed in sitting on the throne of David and ruling again in Judah'" (Jer 22:30).

Coniah and his seed shall be cut off from the promise to David. Against this background, many scholars understand Hag 2:23 to be reversing Jeremiah's curse on the descendants of Coniah with the promise that Zerubbabel will take up the throne.[70] One of the problems for this interpretation is, as scholars admit, that these hopes for Zerubbabel "never came literally true."[71] This raises the important but neglected question: Why was the book of Haggai preserved if his prophecy never came true? However, it need not be a problem if Haggai is not actually stating this much. It may be, as Mason suggests, that "there is no reason to see in Hag 2:23 anything other than a belief that the Davidic dynastic line would be renewed in Jerusalem and would be a feature of the new, postexilic age of God's rule as it was of the earlier, pre-exilic one."[72]

---

67. Floyd, *Minor Prophets*, 258; R. Albertz, "The Thwarted Restoration," in Albertz and Becking, eds., *Yahwism After the Exile*, 1–17 (7).

68. Siebeneck, "Messianism," 317; Rose, *Zemah*, 249–50.

69. Gen 28:18; 41:42; 1 Kgs 21:8; Est 3:10; 8:2, 10. See further Clark and Hatton, *Handbook*, 63.

70. E.g. Redditt, *Zechariah*, 32: "There can be little doubt that Haggai had this very verse [Jer 22:30] in mind as he reversed the prophecy of Jeremiah."

71. Stuhlmueller, *Rebuilding*, 38. Cf. Smith, *Micah–Malachi*, 163: "[Haggai's] words were not fulfilled in the way or within the time he expected."

72. Mason, "Messiah," 342. Mason still believes that Haggai thought that Zerubbabel "would succeed to royal status."

While Coniah had been cast away, and Jeremiah's prophecy was true in that none of his direct offspring sat on the throne of David or ruled in Judah, Haggai proclaims that Zerubbabel, his grandson, was chosen once again. Through him, the Davidic line would be re-established in Judah, from whom the Shoot for David would come. Highlighting the paternity of Zerubbabel in Hag 2:23, against the background of Jer 22:30 which speaks of Coniah's "seed," also seems to indicate that the Davidic dynastic line is on view. Indeed, the wider context of Jeremiah indicates that Jeremiah saw a future for the house of David beyond this curse on Coniah (cf. Jer 23:5). Boda rightly concludes: "Haggai is not contradicting Jeremiah's prophecy but rather making a creative play on the prophecy and revealing a future for the Davidic line."[73] On the day when Yahweh shakes the heavens and the earth and overthrows his enemies, Zerubbabel will be seen to be Yahweh's signet ring. That is, Zerubbabel will be seen to have been instrumental in re-establishing the Davidic line in Jerusalem (and rebuilding the temple) after the disaster of Coniah. Zerubbabel will have renown on the day that Yahweh establishes his kingdom through the offspring of Zerubbabel. On this reading, Zerubbabel is not the promised king, but crucial for his coming.

This needs to be kept in mind in dealing with Zechariah, for many scholars read Zechariah believing that Haggai had pronounced him the future promised king. While it is possible to read Hag 2:23 in this way, it is by no means necessary, as has just been demonstrated, and it entails a number of problems. In fact, Zechariah provides important background for properly interpreting this passage from Haggai, as will be seen.[74]

3.3.2. *Zerubbabel in Zechariah 4*

Zerubbabel and his role among the returned exiles features prominently in ch. 4. Scholars do not dispute that Zerubbabel is here envisaged as the one who will complete the reconstruction of the temple. What is debated is whether he actually did this, and if so in what capacity, and whether Zechariah fostered hopes that with the completion of the temple the monarchy would be restored in him. A further issue in this chapter is the

---

73. Boda, *Commentary*, 165. Cf. Baldwin, *Zechariah*, 54–55: "This vivid figure attested the renewed election of the Davidic line, represented in Haggai's day by Zerubbabel." See also Coggins, *Zechariah*, 35; Curtis, *Steep*, 91.

74. Rose, *Zemah*, 208–47, dedicates a chapter of his monograph to Hag 2:20–23 and argues, most unconvincingly, that it has nothing at all to do with the office of kingship. Furthermore, Rose makes no reference at all to Jer 22:30, which is a glaring omission, but not surprising since it undermines his wider thesis that there is no continuity for the house of David with the coming of *Zemah*, as I will demonstrate in the next chapter. Compare also Rose, "Messianic," 168–85.

identity and role of the "two anointed ones" in 4:14. Do these refer to
Joshua and Zerubbabel as leaders of the restoration community? Does
Zechariah envisage a diarchy of leadership with this description?
Recently a number of scholars have argued that it is wrong to see these
two figures as "anointed," and Rose has concluded that the traditional
identification of these figures as the anointed leaders of the community
faces serious difficulties. Instead, he argues that they are heavenly
beings, attendants of the heavenly court.[75] Boda follows Rose in rejecting
the traditional interpretation, but argues that they are the prophets Haggai
and Zechariah.[76] This has implications for both the interpretation of the
chapter and our study of Zechariah's hopes for the house of David, and
their arguments must be carefully weighed up.[77]

3.3.3. *Composition and Structure of Zechariah 4*

Zechariah 4 comprises a fifth vision, one that is structured around a
question and answer dialogue between an angel and Zechariah, with both
participants being introduced in 4:1. Some scholars have seen 4:6–10a as
an addition to the original text, interrupting the flow of the vision and its
explanation.[78] More recently, scholars have begun to question this assessment and argue that this section is an integral part of the whole vision,
being connected thematically with what precedes and follows.[79] Floyd
rightly makes the point that while the two oracles in this section may
have originated in different contexts: "It does not necessarily follow,

75. Rose, *Zemah*, 206–7.
76. Boda, *Commentary*, 275. Kline, *Glory*, 164–66, while not limiting them to
Haggai and Zechariah, also holds that they are prophetic figures.
77. Block, "Servant," 36, cites Rose's study for his assessment that "this text
[Zech 4:14] is irrelevant to the present discussion." Contrast this with van Groningren, *Messianic*, 887: "This passage (Zech. 4) is to be considered one of the most
dominant messianic passages in the Old Testament."
78. Van der Woude, "Zion," 238: "Since Wellhausen the literary unity of ch. 4
has been contested by almost all commentators. The text of the original vision is said
to cover vv. 1–6aα and 10b–14 (excluding v. 12) only. The remaining verses are
held to be a small collection of prophetic sayings added later to the main text."
Petersen, *Zechariah 1–8*, 224, is representative of how this affects the interpretation
of the chapter: "What follows this introduction [Zech 4:6a] is an oracle *dealing with
quite another issue*, the status of Zerubbabel in temple-building ceremonies and
what that means for the postexilic polity" (emphasis added).
79. See van der Woude, "Zion," 238; Merrill, *Zechariah*, 158–59. Kline, *Glory*,
139: "Some have speculated that the middle section of Zechariah 4 (vv. 6b–10a) is
misplaced because, allegedly, it is not connected with what precedes. Actually, this
word of the Lord addresses itself to the very heart of the preceding symbolism."
Similarly, Baldwin, *Zechariah*, 125; Meyers and Meyers, *Zechariah 1–8*, 268.

however, that they should be read as texts independent from the vision report, or as texts independent from one another... They should thus not be treated as anomalous glosses but read as integral parts of 4:1–14."[80]

From a literary point of view, if this text is read as it is written, namely as a dialogue, then it is perfectly natural to expect repetition, disruptions and asides, while at the same time detecting a coherent thread that runs through it all. Reading it in this way, the first word of Yahweh to Zerubbabel (4:6–7) is an integral part of the dialogue between the angel and Zechariah, forming an answer to Zechariah's question and providing the setting for the menorah vision (4:1–5). The second word (4:8–10a) is a message that comes to Zechariah for the community based on what he has seen and heard from the angel (4:1–7).[81] This second word interrupts the dialogue between the angel and Zechariah, but it continues the theme. The text then moves back to the dialogue between Zechariah and the angel to relate the overall explanation given in these two words of the Lord (4:6–10a) to the various components of the menorah vision, particularly the two olive trees (4:10b–14). This reading makes sense of the repeated questions in 4:11–12: the angel seems to be dismayed (4:13) because for him the vision has already been explained in the two words of Yahweh (4:6–10a), and in his comment in 4:10.

The chapter can be structured as follows:

4:1–5	*The Vision Report*
4:1	Introduction
4:2–3	The vision of the menorah, bowl, lamps, pipes, and olive trees
4:4	Question: Zechariah to the angel about the vision
4:5a	Counter-question: The angel to Zechariah
4:5b	Zechariah's reply
4:6–10a	*Two Words of Yahweh Explaining the Overall Vision*
4:6–7	A word of Yahweh from the angel to Zechariah for Zerubbabel
4:8–10a	A word of Yahweh to Zechariah for the community
4:10b–14	*Further Details of the Vision Identified*
4:10b	Answer: The angel to Zechariah concerning the seven
4:11	Question: Zechariah to the angel about the olive trees
4:12	Question: Zechariah to the angel about the branches of the olive trees
4:13	Counter-question: The angel to Zechariah
4:14	Answer: The angel to Zechariah about the two sons of oil

80. Floyd, *Minor Prophets*, 381. See also M. H. Floyd, "Cosmos and History in Zechariah's View of the Restoration (Zechariah 1:7–6:15)," in *Problems in Biblical Theology* (ed. H. T. C. Sun and K. L. Eades; Grand Rapids: Eerdmans, 1997), 125–44 (140–41).

81. See further Floyd, *Minor Prophets*, 381.

3.3.4. *The Vision Report (Zechariah 4:1–5)*

[1] The angel who spoke with me returned, and he woke me, as a man who is awoken from his sleep. [2] And he said to me, "What do you see?" I said, "Look, I see a menorah—all of it gold, and a bowl on top of it, and seven lamps on it, and seven streams to each of the lamps which are on top of it. [3] And two olive trees by it, one on the right of the bowl, and one on its left." [4] And I answered and said to the angel who spoke with me, "What are these, my Lord?" [5] And the angel who spoke with me answered and said to me, "Do you not know what these are?" I said, "No, my Lord." (author's translation)

The details of this vision are complex. While the descriptions of the objects themselves are reasonably specific, their exact nature and relationship to one another is difficult to picture. There are five components mentioned in the vision: a menorah all of gold, a bowl on top of it, seven lamps upon it, seven pipes to each of the lamps on top of it,[82] and two olive trees by it. While it is natural to think of the menorah of the tabernacle (e.g. Exod 25:31–40; 37:17–24), the bowl, the pipes, and the olive trees set it apart. C. F. Keil suggests that these three additional elements form a contrast with the menorah of the tabernacle in that this menorah is continually supplied with oil without the intervention of humans (the priests).[83] This contrast certainly fits with the tenor of the vision, as we shall see.

---

82. The term מוצקות is difficult to translate as it only appears here in the Hebrew Bible. Archaeological discoveries of clay lamps have given rise to the translation "lips" (see, e.g., R. North, "Zechariah's Seven-Sprout Lampstand," *Biblica* 51 [1970]: 183–206; Petersen, *Zechariah 1–8*, 217–23; and Meyers and Meyers, *Zechariah 1–8*, 229–38, also have substantial discussions of this issue, with Petersen supplying possible pictures), but this is unlikely since the temple menorah better fits the context. The form מוצקות is the Hophal feminine plural passive participle form of the verb יצק ("pour, pour out, cast [metal]"), which is here functioning as a noun. It is literally seven "pourings" to each of the lamps. Given the overall context of supplying the lamps with oil from the trees through the bowl, it must refer to the oil pouring from the bowl to the lamps. The traditional reading, "pipes" or "channels," while problematic in some ways, supplies a mechanism by which the oil pours. "Seven... to each" (שבעה ושבעה) has a distributive sense. Yet it is difficult to know if it is one stream to each of the lamps, or seven streams to each of the seven lamps (49 in all). 2 Sam 21:20, which uses the same syntax, seems to suggest the latter (cf. Sweeney, *Twelve*, 605). On the other hand, the LXX translation has only seven. I have maintained the ambiguity in my translation.

83. C. F. Keil, "Zechariah," in *Biblical Commentary on the Old Testament: The Twelve Minor Prophets* (ed. C. F. Keil and F. Delitzsch; Grand Rapids: Eerdmans, 1949), 2:263–65 (265). Cf. Unger, *Zechariah*, 73.

Zechariah asks the angel for an explanation (4:4): "What are these?" (מה־אלה).[84] The angel responds with a counter-question that has the effect of delaying the response, heightening the tension, and thus highlighting the explanation that is given in the form of two oracles (4:6–10a).[85]

3.3.5. *Two Words of Yahweh Explaining the Overall Vision (Zechariah 4:6–10a)*

> [6] He answered and said to me, "This is the word of Yahweh to Zerubbabel: Not by might, and not by power, but by my Spirit, says Yahweh of hosts. [7] Who are you, great mountain? Before Zerubbabel you shall become level ground. He will bring forth the top stone amid shouts of 'Grace, grace to it!'
>
> [8] The word of Yahweh came to me, saying, [9] "The hands of Zerubbabel have laid the foundation of this house, and his hands will finish it, and you shall know that Yahweh of hosts has sent me to you. [10a] For whoever has despised the day of small things shall rejoice and see the chosen stone in the hand of Zerubbabel." (author's translation)

These two words of Yahweh concerning Zerubbabel can be understood as the overall explanation of the vision of 4:1–5.[86] In the first word (4:6–7), Zerubbabel is told that the temple building project will be accomplished by Yahweh's Spirit, rather than by his own ability and power,[87] and that all opposition to this project will be overcome. This explanation is consistent with the vision of the menorah that is continually supplied with oil. Whereas the menorah in the temple needed constant attending from the priests to remain alight, in Zechariah's vision the menorah is continually supplied with oil without the need for human attendants, and it is supplied directly with resources from outside itself. In the same way, Zerubbabel will be supplied with resources outside of himself to complete the reconstruction of the temple—Yahweh will provide his Spirit.

---

84. It is unclear whether "these" refers to the olive trees (Zech 4:3), the seven lamps (Zech 4:2), or the vision as a whole. The former seems most likely given that they are the items mentioned most recently, and that Zechariah explicitly mentions them when he repeats the question in Zech 4:12.

85. So, Butterworth, *Structure*, 119, who argues that the repeated question of the angel (Zech 4:5, 13) is a rhetorical device that heightens the tension in the narrative.

86. Cf. McComiskey, "Zechariah," 3:1085: "The angel responds (ʿānâ) to Zechariah's perplexity by giving the overall symbolism of the vision, not an explanation of each of its symbolic representations."

87. BDB, 298–99: "might" is commonly used to mean strength or ability, or even "an army" (e.g. Jer 32:2), or "wealth" (e.g. Jer 15:13). BDB, 470–71: "power" refers to human strength or ability; one's own power rather than Yahweh's (e.g. Amos 2:14; Isa 10:13).

Zechariah is told, that before Zerubbabel, a great mountain will become a plain (Zech 4:7). Who, or what, is the "great mountain"? Some have sought to identify specific individuals in this reference, including Joshua,[88] or the Samaritan governor Tattenai (cf. Ezra 4–6),[89] yet both of these seem too specific not to be named explicitly.[90] Others have suggested that it refers to the mound of rubble that remained after the destruction of the first temple.[91] While this interpretation is possible, it seems more likely, given the personification of the mountain (מי־אתה), that it is being used metaphorically to refer to all the difficulties that Zerubbabel faced in his building project.[92]

All difficulties shall be overcome and there will be shouts of joy when Zerubbabel brings forth the "top stone" (את־האבן הראשה). Again, there is a lack of consensus as to whether this was a stone that would commence the building process, or a stone that would complete the building.[93] A number of scholars argue for the former based on analogies with Mesopotamian building practices. In these a "former brick" was removed from the ruin of the earlier building to become a part of the new building, thereby conveying the idea of continuity of worship between the two buildings.[94] In Mesopotamia, this all happened in a special *kalû* ritual, and these scholars think that something similar occurred here.

88. Petersen, *Zechariah 1–8*, 240.

89. Rudolph, *Sacharja*, 113.

90. Other suggestions listed by Ackroyd, *Exile*, 173, include: a hostile political power such as Persia; political obstruction; the opposition of the "Samaritan" authorities; or the temptation to direct military action.

91. K. Galling, "Die Exilswende in der Sicht des Propheten Sacharja," *VT* 2 (1952): 18–36; A. Petitjean, *Les oracles du proto-Zacharie; Un programme de restauration pour la communauté juive après l'exil* (Études bibliques; Paris: Gabalda, 1969), 257–58; B. Halpern, "The Ritual Background of Zechariah's Temple Song," *CBQ* 40 (1978): 167–80 (170); A. Laato, "Zechariah 4:6b–10a and the Akkadian Royal Building Inscriptions," *ZAW* 106 (1994): 53–69 (66); Ollenburger, "Zechariah," 770; Sweeney, *Twelve*, 608; Pola, *Priestertum*, 117, 22; Boda, *Commentary*, 278.

92. So Baldwin, *Zechariah*, 121; Floyd, *Minor Prophets*, 381; Clark and Hatton, *Handbook*, 139; Mackay, *Zechariah*, 114; Webb, *Zechariah*, 91–92; O'Brien, *Zechariah*, 194. Merrill, *Zechariah*, 160, cites other usage of this metaphor in the Hebrew Bible (Isa 40:4; 41:15; 64:1, 3; Jer 4:24; 51:25–26; Mic 1:4; Nah 1:5; Hab 3:10; Zech 14:4–5).

93. For four different views, see E. J. C. Tigchelaar, *Prophets of Old and the Day of the End: Zechariah, the Book of Watchers, and Apocalyptic* (OtSt 35; Leiden: Brill, 1996), 32–33.

94. Petersen, *Zechariah 1–8*, 240–41; Meyers and Meyers, *Zechariah 1–8*, 247–48, 70–71; Laato, "Inscriptions," 53–69.

While there are some similarities between the account of the laying of the temple foundation in Ezra 3:8–13 and this Mesopotamian ritual, there are difficulties with the timing if the stone here is understood as a foundation stone.[95] Baldwin rightly observes that the context speaks against it being a foundation stone, as Zech 4:9 speaks of the foundation having already been laid by Zerubbabel.[96] Laato counters this by arguing that 4:6b–7 was an oracle composed before the temple foundation, and that 4:8–10a was composed after this ritual. However, this seems to be forcing the text into a compositional history for which there is no other evidence and assumes that the editor was unable or unwilling to resolve the difficulty in timing that combining these texts brought about. The final form of the text favours viewing this stone as a capstone and the event as marking the completion of the temple.[97]

Either way, Zerubbabel will have a key role in the reconstruction of the temple. The acclamation of "Grace, grace to it!" will testify to Yahweh's kindness in ensuring its construction, in a similar way to how this word began, "Not by might, and not by power, but by my Spirit, says Yahweh of hosts" (4:6).[98] Zerubbabel would certainly play a role, but the temple would only be completed by Yahweh's enabling.

A second word follows, a direct word from Yahweh (unmediated by the angel) concerning the prophet Zechariah's relationship with the community (4:8–10a).[99] If the first word does not make clear whether or not Zerubbabel would actually complete the project, this second word is unambiguous. Further, the completion of the temple by Zerubbabel will

95. The laying of the foundation was a past event (Ezra 3:8), whereas it would be future here.

96. Baldwin, *Zechariah*, 121–22, 52–53. Cf. Redditt, *Zechariah*, 69; Tidiman, *Zacharie*, 127.

97. Merrill, *Zechariah*, 161: "Zechariah describes the whole project from site preparation to finished structure. Historically, the former had been done (Ezra 3:10) over great opposition, but the building lay still unfinished as of 519 B.C., the date of the oracle." Other scholars who take it to be a completion stone include: Mitchell, "Zechariah," 192; M. Delcor, "Un Problème de Critique Textuelle et d'Exégèse," *RB* 58 (1951): 189–99; Redditt, *Zechariah*, 69; Clark and Hatton, *Handbook*, 140.

98. For a helpful survey of interpretations of the phrase חֵן חֵן לָהּ, see Clark and Hatton, *Handbook*, 140–41. While they acknowledge that the interpretation "Beautiful, beautiful!" has more scholarly support, they state that it could equally be "God has been very kind." I believe that the context favours the second.

99. Floyd, *Minor Prophets*, 382: "This interruption [vv. 8–10a] is signaled by the prophetic word formula in its first person, complete-clause form ('the word of Yahweh came to me," v. 8), which indicates that the prophet is here speaking for himself rather than continuing to narrate the speech of the angelic interpreter."

be confirmation that "Yahweh has sent me to you." A number of scholars take the "me" to refer to the angel who brings the word of Yahweh to Zechariah (cf. 4:6).[100] However, given that Zechariah is the closest refer- ent (4:8) and the same expression occurs in a similar context in 6:15 where it clearly refers to Zechariah,[101] it seems that the rebuilding of the temple is here linked to the authenticity of the prophet Zechariah's mes- sage (cf. 1:16; 2:9, 11; 8:9).[102]

This word finishes with a message to those who despised this work of temple reconstruction (4:10a). There has been much scholarly discussion about the object that Zerubbabel will hold in his hand (את־האבן הבדיל). The expression is a *hapax legomenon* and is traditionally taken to refer to a tin plummet (cf. LXX).[103] However, if the stone in 4:7 is understood as a completion stone rather than a commencement stone, then this verse probably refers to the same stone, namely, some sort of ceremonial com- pletion stone. In the context, the assurance that Zerubbabel will complete the temple is a message to those who have "despised the day of small things." This seems to refer to those who were pessimistic about the building project, or who thought it pitiful compared to the former temple (cf. Ezra 3:12; Hag 2:3). If this is the case, then it is further support for understanding the stone to be something that completes the temple, rather than a plummet. The people's despair was felt *during* the building pro- ject, and a plummet would hardly have removed their despair. However, if it is a completion stone, it explains why their despair would turn to joy.

The present time is described as "the day of small things." It is a phrase that provides insight into the way that Zechariah viewed the time in which he prophesied, and the events about which he spoke. Why did Zechariah speak of the reconstruction of the temple and the re-estab- lishment of the cult as "small things"? It seems most likely that this phrase refers to the slow and painful progress in these projects and the fact that, as they slowly advanced, the temple and the cult were still only a pale reflection of their former glory (cf. Ezra 6). It is also possible that Zechariah understood that these events were "small" in comparison to what lay in the future.[104]

Sweeney has recently argued that this second word is not about the reconstruction of the temple at all, but rather the re-establishment of the

---

100. E.g. Redditt, *Zechariah*, 70; McComiskey, "Zechariah," 3:1088.
101. Notice the absence of the angel of Yahweh.
102. So Ackroyd, *Exile*, 173, 175; Conrad, *Zechariah*, 107.
103. Petersen, *Zechariah 1–8*, 243–44. This is not the word used for plummet in Amos 7:7–8.
104. Webb, *Zechariah*, 96.

Davidic monarchy and the overthrow of Persian rule.[105] He notes that in Zech 4:9, Zerubbabel's hands will complete the building of the temple. Yet the fact that there is no evidence that Zerubbabel ever did complete it raises a problem (cf. Ezra 6; Zech 6). He argues that the verb "to complete" (בצע) in Zech 4:9 can be understood as "to cut off, gain by violence."[106] Hence, 4:6–10a "may originally have envisioned Zerubbabel's restoration of the Temple as a signal for the restoration of the house of David and the overthrow of Persian rule."[107] For Sweeney, the failure of the monarchy to be re-established is dealt with in chs. 9–14, where its establishment is projected into the future. Sweeney believes this also helps to clarify the nature of the stone in 4:10, in which he sees a reference to the separation process where metals are refined from their impurities. He argues that this image is the same as that of ch. 13, an image of the purification of the house of David and the people of Jerusalem. Hence, he argues that 4:10 originally envisioned Yahweh granting victory over the nations to Judah and the Davidic monarchy and purifying them, while in the final form of the book this hope is suspended to a more distant future.

While Sweeney's view is novel, and is to be commended in its concern to bring the whole of the book of Zechariah to bear on the question of the hope for the house of David, it is not the most natural reading of the text. While there is an ambiguity in the word "house" (cf. 2 Sam 7), it seems unlikely that it has the meaning of "dynasty" in this context where the idea of temple building is so dominant.[108] Sweeney also makes too much of the lack of any statement concerning Zerubbabel's completion of the temple. This is an argument from silence. Furthermore, while the term את־האבן הבדיל (4:10a) is difficult to translate, it seems inappropriate to interpret it by the purification image in ch. 13. The proposal to understand this as a completion stone (i.e. the same stone as in 4:7) has more merit. Therefore, it seems very unlikely that these verses express an explicit hope for the restoration of the monarchy, though the completion of the temple would implicitly raise such hopes. In this regard, M. G. Kline comments:

> Planned by king David, executed by king Solomon (cf. Ezra 5.11), the Jerusalem temple was clearly crown construction. The incorporation of the commission to build the temple in a covenant that was predominantly

105. Sweeney, *Twelve*, 609–12.
106. Ibid., 610.
107. Ibid., 612.
108. The phrase "his hands shall finish it" is difficult to interpret as a statement of the re-establishment of the monarchy.

a confirmation of the perpetuity of David's royal dynasty emphasizes the peculiarly royal nature of temple building (2 Sam. 7.13a; 1 Chron. 17.12; cf. Psalm 132). Such a commission indeed validated the appointed builder's right to the crown (cf. 1 Chron. 28:5–7).[109]

Kline makes an important connection between the construction of the temple and the ongoing hope for the house of David found in the Davidic covenant. In 2 Sam 7, the construction of the temple is the task for a Davidide and commissioned by Yahweh himself.[110] The same pattern is reflected here in Zech 4. However, while the construction of the temple may raise the hope for a king to be reinstated on the throne, there is no evidence in Zech 4 that Zechariah envisaged Zerubbabel as this king. All that is stated is that Zerubbabel will build the temple.

3.3.6. *Further Details of the Vision Identified (Zechariah 4:10b–14)*

[10b] These seven are the eyes of Yahweh that roam through the whole earth. [11] I answered and said to him, "What are these two olive trees on the right of the menorah and on its left?" [12] A second time I answered and said to him, "What are these two streams of the olive trees, which through two golden pipes are pouring out from them the gold[en oil]?" [13] He said to me, "Do you not know what these are?" I said, "No, my Lord." [14] He said, "These are the two sons of oil who stand by the Lord of the whole earth." (author's translation)

After the two words of Yahweh that gave an overall explanation of the vision (4:6–10a), the angel now identifies two components of the vision. However, there are still substantial elements of ambiguity. This was just as confusing for Zechariah, who asks repeatedly for an explanation (4:11–12).

The natural referent of "these seven" is the seven lamps on the menorah (Zech 4:2). The angel identifies these as "the eyes of Yahweh that roam through the whole earth." This phrase is also found in 2 Chr 16:9, where "the eyes of the LORD run to and fro throughout the earth, to give strong support to those whose heart is blameless towards him."[111] In 2 Chronicles, it is a statement of the omniscience and omnipotence of Yahweh towards his people. Similarly, in Zechariah, in coming so close to the

---

109.   Kline, *Glory*, 146.

110.   Pola, *Priestertum*, 277–78, argues that Zerubbabel as a Davidide functions as a patron for the building of the temple as he lays down the foundation stone.

111.   A similar usage is also found in Ezra 5:5. Petersen, *Zechariah 1–8*, 227, argues that in both texts, "the eyes of Yahweh signify benevolent divine presence." Boda, *Commentary*, 274, however, rightly notes that this statement of Yahweh's omniscience is also a warning to those who disobey him.

statements about the building of the temple, it seems to be saying that through the building of the temple and with Yahweh once again dwelling among his people, his sovereignty will be mediated to the world.[112]

While these seven lamps are a crucial part of the menorah, they are only one part of the whole and although the whole menorah is not specifically identified, it is appropriate to ask at this point what it symbolizes. Most scholars posit an identification, and Rose presents the various options and cites representatives of each view:

> (a) the lamp stand [*sic*] as a symbol representing the community of the people of God (or—more specifically—the Jewish community); and (b) the lampstand as a symbol representing YHWH (or one of his attributes, like his presence, or his omniscience and/or providence). A small number of scholars reject these two options and interpret the vision lampstand as either a symbol for the temple, or as a symbol for Zerubbabel.[113]

The grounds for understanding the menorah as a symbol for the presence of Yahweh are the identification of the seven lamps (4:2) as the seven eyes of Yahweh (4:10b), and the identification of the two olive trees by the menorah (4:3) as the two "anointed ones" who stand by the Lord of the whole earth (4:14). Rose rejects this identification of the menorah as Yahweh, arguing that it confuses genres of vision and allegory, and that in the genre of vision, there is no one-to-one correspondence between the pictured world and the real world.[114] Other scholars reject the view that the menorah symbolizes Yahweh for theological reasons, namely, that this would then make Yahweh dependent on resources outside of himself.[115] Rose prefers the association of the menorah with the community worshipping at the temple.

Another proposal for the identity of the menorah that Rose does not canvas is that the menorah represents the "community 'alight' with the presence of the all-seeing, all-knowing God, who dwells in their midst."[116] This is a combination of Rose's first two options. It resolves the problem of the dependence of the menorah on resources outside of itself; this is because, on this interpretation, while there is a special presence of Yahweh with the menorah, it does not necessitate the view that Yahweh's presence is limited to this.[117] However, it is difficult to understand exactly

---

112. Cf. Deut 11:12; Ps 24:15; Prov 5:21; 15:3; 22:12.
113. Rose, *Zemah*, 178–79.
114. Ibid., 181–82.
115. Baldwin, *Zechariah*, 123–24; Rudolph, *Sacharja*, 109.
116. Webb, *Zechariah*, 92–93. Cf. Keil, "Zechariah," 266.
117. Note the concept of Yahweh dwelling in the midst of his people in Zechariah (e.g. 1:3, 16, 17; 2:5, 10, 11; 8:3, 23; 9:8).

how identifying the menorah as the community alight with the presence
of Yahweh contributes to the overall meaning of the vision.

It is more likely that the menorah is not representing objects as such,
but rather the concept of Yahweh's presence in the temple and hence
among his people. The menorah described in Exodus has tree-like quali-
ties, possessing branches, blossoms, calyxes, and flowers (Exod 25:31–
40; 37:17–24). Longman notes the connection between trees and places
of worship (e.g. Gen 12:6; 13:18), and argues that this connection evokes
the imagery of the Garden of Eden. Eden represented the special
presence of God on earth, dwelling with humanity.[118] After the fall, this
special presence was associated with the tabernacle and then the temple,
and the gold menorah served as a reminder of this. Fire is also associated
with the presence of Yahweh in the Hebrew Bible (e.g. Gen 15:17;
19:18; 24:17; Ezek 1:13), and the burning menorah tree of the tabernacle
brings to mind the revelation of Yahweh to Moses at the bush that was
on fire but did not burn (Exod 3:2–6). Therefore, rather than trying to
identify the menorah with Yahweh, the community, or with a combination of both, it seems that Zechariah's vision of a constantly burning
menorah is a picture of Yahweh's presence in the temple. It is closely
related to the theme of the return of Yahweh to his people.[119] It is easy to
see how this vision would spur on Zerubbabel and the people to rebuild it.

However, there are still elements of the vision that remain unclear to
Zechariah, who returns to his question of 4:4, making it more explicit.
He first asks about the identity of the two olive trees (4:11) and then
repeats the question (4:12), providing more details about the original
vision and clarifying the relationship between the olive trees and the
menorah.[120] There are several difficult exegetical issues in this second
question. First, the word צנתרות is sometimes understood as referring to
part of the trees. Following the work of T. Kleven, Rose believes that it
is more likely related to the word צנור found in 2 Sam 5:8. Kleven
argues that צנור refers to some type of water-shaft, and hence Rose takes

---

118.   T. Longman III, *Immanuel in Our Place* (Phillipsburg: P. & R. Publishing,
2001), 21.

119.   Cf. Zech 1:16; 2:5, 10, 13 (MT 2:9, 14, 17).

120.   Many scholars have doubted the authenticity of Zech 4:12 (e.g. Petersen,
Zechariah 1–8, 234: "Verse 12 is, by almost universal agreement, understood to be
an addition to the original vision and its interpretation"). Rose, *Zemah*, 185–88, lists
the reasons given for this opinion, and, after very adequately refuting them, concludes (p. 188): "I take Zech. 4.12 as a verse that is original to the vision report, and
not a secondary addition. The function of the verse was most likely to make the
question in v. 11 more specific."

צנתרות to mean "pipes" or "tubes."[121] The fact that they are made of gold also indicates that they should be understood as part of the menorah and not the two trees.

Just as difficult to translate is שבלי הזיתים. There are two alternative translations of the root שבלת.[122] The first is "ear of grain."[123] The second is "flowing stream."[124] Rose prefers the first option and translates the phrase as "the two tops of the olive trees" on the basis that with the second usage it is difficult to imagine the nature of the syntactical relationship between שבלת and זיתים, and that the second usage only ever occurs in the singular whereas here it is plural.[125] However, against this is the fact that שבלת is elsewhere always used in connection with grain rather than olive crops.[126] Furthermore, Rose's translation is less favourable in that it introduces an additional element, otherwise unmentioned, into the vision. On balance, it seems best to translate the phrase as "streams of the olive trees" and see it as clarifying the relationship between the two olive trees and the oil, the point being that the olive trees directly provide the streams of oil.

A further issue is: What are the pipes actually conveying? It is literally "the gold" (הזהב) and most scholars, because of the context, see this as a reference to the olive oil that is coming from the trees, being described by its colour rather than its substance.[127] This seems likely.

While some of the details are hard to pin down, the overall picture that this repeated question provides is quite clear: the two olive trees provide oil for the menorah via two golden pipes, presumably emptying into the bowl, and from there fuelling each of the lamps.[128] To this repeated question the angel replies, seemingly in despair (4:13), "Do you not know

121. T. Kleven, "The Use of *ṣnr* in Ugaritic and 2 Samuel V 8: Hebrew Usage and Comparative Philology," *VT* 44 (1994): 195–204; Rose, *Zemah*, 183.

122. BDB, 987.

123. E.g. Gen 41:5; Ruth 2:2; Job 24:24; Isa 17:5.

124. E.g. Ps 69:3, 16; Isa 27:12.

125. Several scholars suggest that what is being described appears to have the same relationship to an olive tree that an ear does to a stalk of grain and therefore it may refer to the most outstretched branches or even the olives themselves considered collectively (e.g. Meyers and Meyers, *Zechariah 1–8*, 255–56; Amsler, "Zacharie," 89; Merrill, *Zechariah*, 154; Kline, *Glory*, 163), or "the fruit laden ends of the olive branches" (e.g. Smith, *Micah–Malachi*, 205).

126. So Boda, *Commentary*, 272.

127. See Meyers and Meyers, *Zechariah 1–8*, 257.

128. Note Floyd, *Minor Prophets*, 382: "The technicalities of this apparatus are unclear, but the main point seems to be that there is a close relationship between what the lampstand signifies and what the olive trees signify, by virtue of the fact that the olive trees supply the oil that is burned in the lamps."

what these are?" The implication is that Zechariah should have understood by now the significance of the two olive trees in his vision. He has
not, and admits this to the angel, who then replies somewhat cryptically:
"These are the two sons of oil who stand by the Lord of the whole earth."
This expression, "the two sons of oil," has traditionally been understood
to refer to Joshua and Zerubbabel, the two leaders of the post-exilic community, and in many cases is translated as "two anointed ones."[129] The
main argument for this is the fact that the overall literary context of ch. 3
and 4 deals with Joshua and Zerubbabel respectively and that the context
apparently makes it clear that anointing is being alluded to.[130] On this
reading, the message of ch. 4 is that amid all the difficulties of rebuilding
the community and the temple in Jerusalem, Yahweh will sustain his
people through Joshua and Zerubbabel, his Spirit-anointed leaders.[131]

This traditional interpretation has recently been challenged. Rose has
argued that the "two sons of oil" are most likely not human figures at all,
but heavenly beings, attendants of the heavenly court.[132] His argument is
detailed and runs for twenty pages of his monograph. Given its importance for our purposes, I shall summarize it before weighing it up.

First, Rose argues that the term used for "oil" in 4:14, יצהר, is not
synonymous with שמן (the more frequent word for "oil" in the Hebrew
Bible).[133] Further, he suggests that the distinction in meaning between the
two words is that יצהר refers to "'fresh oil,' the raw material, freshly
squeezed, before it is prepared," with שמן being the more general word
for oil, including oil as a final product used for anointing or fuel.[134] Rose

129.   Wellhausen, "Zechariah," 4:5392, understood them to be "Zerubbabel and
Joshua, the two anointed ones."

130.   E.g. Floyd, *Minor Prophets*, 383: "It is by now evident, however, that these
issues [concerning the meaning of the phrase 'sons of oil'] cannot be resolved on
philological grounds alone. It may thus prove fruitful to consider them in the light of
the overall literary context." Also Webb, *Zechariah*, 93: "Given all that has gone
before, they must be Joshua and Zerubbabel."

131.   See also Baldwin, *Zechariah*, 124; Rudolph, *Sacharja*, 107–8; Jeremias,
Nachtgesichte, 184; Mason, *Zechariah*, 48; van Groningren, *Messianic*, 886–87;
Merrill, *Zechariah*, 156.

132.   Rose, *Zemah*, 207.

133.   This is against L. Köhler, "Eine archaistische Wortgruppe," *ZAW* 46
(1928): 218–20, who concluded from their usage in 2 Kgs 18:32 and Deut 8:8 that
they were synonymous. Rose, *Zemah*, 190, states that while these phrases have the
same "reference" (i.e. olive trees), they do not have the same "sense" and therefore
cannot be understood as synonymous.

134.   Rose, *Zemah*, 191–92. Yet Rose concedes: "the evidence is lacking to be
absolutely certain about this nuance." A. S. van der Woude, "Die beiden Söhne des
Öls (Sach. 4:14): Messianische Gestalten?," in *Travels in the World of the Old*

uses this distinction to exclude the possibility that this could be oil used for anointing: "The usual interpretation of the Hebrew phrase בני היצהר as 'anointed ones' is flawed. יצהר is not synonymous with שמן, the usual word for oil, and the word used for anointing oil and oil used to burn a lamp. The phrase בני היצהר should be understood as referring to those who provide oil, that is, they are the oil suppliers."[135]

Turning to the phrase העמדים על־אדון, Rose argues on the basis of the use of the preposition על that it cannot mean "to serve" (i.e. "the two sons of oil who serve the Lord of the whole earth"). Rather, Rose notes that this phraseology is found in royal or heavenly court scenes where it refers to standing in the presence of Yahweh or the king.[136] Given this, and because of the difficulties that Rose perceives with understanding these two figures as Joshua and Zerubbabel (difficulties he presents in the next section), Rose prefers to see these two "sons of oil" as members of the heavenly court whose commission he later describes as "sustaining and supporting the community of the people of God which worships at the temple in Jerusalem."[137]

On the assumption, then, that these two figures are members of the heavenly court, Rose proceeds to dismiss the view that scholars hold "almost universally," namely, that the two sons of oil are Zerubbabel and Joshua.[138] He concedes that while generally only prophets were allowed access to the heavenly court, Zechariah may be being innovative here by giving a prince and a priest this privilege. However, as Rose concluded that Joshua was not given access to the heavenly court in the previous vision (3.7), he believes it is unlikely that Joshua and Zerubbabel are being given access here.[139]

Testament (ed. M. Heerma van Voss; Assen: Van Gorcum, 1974), 262–70 (265), also makes this distinction and concludes that the expression "sons of oil" should be interpreted as persons symbolizing the blessing of fertility, and therefore the ability to give blessing.

135. Rose, *Zemah*, 195.
136. Ibid., 198–99. Rose here cites the work of F. M. Cross, "The Council of Yahweh in Second Isaiah," *JNES* 12 (1953): 274–77 (274–75 n. 3); E. T. Mullen, *The Divine Council in Canaanite and Early Hebrew Literature* (Atlanta: Scholars Press, 1980), 256; A. S. van der Woude, "Serubbabel und die messianischen Erwarungen des Propheten Sacharja," in *Lebendige Forschung im Alten Testament* (ed. O. Kaiser; Berlin: de Gruyter, 1988), 138–56 (155 n. 58); A. Malamat, "The Secret Council and Prophetic Involvement in Mari and Israel," in *Prophetie und geschichtliche Wiklichkeit im alten Israel* (ed. R. Liwak and S. Wagner; Stuttgart: Kohlhammer, 1991), 233.
137. Rose, *Zemah*, 205.
138. Ibid., 200.
139. Ibid., 201.

Rose briefly states three further difficulties that he has with identifying the two sons of oil with Joshua and Zerubbabel. First, the priest and the prince are different offices, and this expression does not distinguish between them. Second, it is unlikely that the innovative idea of priest and prince being given access to the divine court would be expressed in this way. Third, the innovative idea of the prince and priest having equal standing (i.e. a diarchy) is also unlikely to have been expressed in this way.[140] Rose believes these difficulties are overcome if the two sons of oil are heavenly beings, attendants of the heavenly court.

Having rehearsed Rose's argument, it will now be evaluated. First, the distinction between יצהר as oil for freshly squeezed oil and שמן as oil for anointing seems to be a valid one, as other scholars have also observed.[141] Nonetheless, it should be noted that while יצהר is never used in contexts dealing with oil for anointing, neither is it used in contexts dealing with oil for burning lamps (as it is here). Accordingly, too much should not be made of this distinction.

Second, in determining who the "two sons of oil" could be, Rose overplays the notion that this is a heavenly court scene.[142] While it may be a heavenly court, we must be cautious about the conclusions drawn from this, especially since Joshua the high priest has just been pictured in the heavenly court in ch. 3.

Rose himself identifies a further problem with his interpretation of these figures as heavenly beings: "Admittedly, the failure to provide a satisfactory explanation of this important detail that there are specifically *two* sons of oil remains a problem in the interpretation I have proposed."[143] If these two are heavenly beings, there seems to be no apparent significance in their number. Rose acknowledges this difficulty with his interpretation but still prefers it, believing that it faces fewer difficulties than the Zerubbabel–Joshua identification.

---

140.   Ibid., 202.

141.   See Keil, "Zechariah," 268 n. 1; Petersen, *Zechariah 1–8*, 231; Kline, *Glory*, 164; Sykes, *Time and Space*, 45 n. 47.

142.   In a footnote, Rose, *Zemah*, 197 n. 60, dismisses the fact that the olive trees are described as standing "by" (על) the menorah in Zech 4:3 and 11, as "purely coincidental." However, this seems to go against the natural and more obvious reading of the passage, where the angel is identifying further details of the vision in response to Zechariah's repeated question about the vision (i.e. "What are these two olive trees on the right of the menorah and on its left?"). Zechariah had seen two olive trees "by" (על) the menorah (Zech 4:3, 11), and now he is being told what these represent, using the same language of the vision. It seems that Rose's view of the nature of the menorah has influenced his interpretation here (or vice versa).

143.   Ibid., 206.

There is another possibility for the identity of the "two sons of oil" that not only makes more sense of the expression, but also suits the context better than the Zerubbabel–Joshua identification and Rose's heavenly beings. This is that the "two sons of oil" are the prophets Haggai and Zechariah. Boda, building on Rose's work, has recently argued this.[144] He also bases his argument on the semantic distinction between יצהר and שמן, and Rose's conclusion that it was only the prophet who was allowed into the divine council of angelic beings. Perhaps key to this identification is the prominence of Haggai and Zechariah in this period and their crucial role in the rebuilding of the temple.[145] Boda notes that these two prophets are linked in Ezra 5.1–2 and 6.14–15 and are connected with the successful rebuilding of the temple. Furthermore, Zech 8:9 sees these prophets as instrumental in its construction: "Thus says the LORD of hosts: 'Let your hands be strong, you who in these days have been hearing these words from the mouth of the prophets who were present on the day that the foundation of the house of the LORD of hosts was laid, that the temple might be built'."

Boda also helpfully highlights the way that the Spirit is most often connected with the prophetic office in the Hebrew Bible.[146] The great prophet, Moses, is empowered by the Spirit, and through this same Spirit, seventy elders are enabled to prophesy (Num 11:24–29). Other prophets are also said to prophesy through the enabling of the Spirit,[147] and Zech 7:12 later makes the connection between the work of the prophet and the Spirit explicit: "They made their hearts diamond-hard lest they should hear the law and the words that the LORD of hosts had sent by his Spirit through the former prophets." Here the work of the Spirit is explicitly connected with the preaching of the prophets, meaning that Yahweh's word and Spirit are understood to work together.[148]

144. Boda, *Commentary*, 275. Cf. Kline, *Glory*, 164–66, who takes it as a reference to prophets, but does not think that the reference must be limited to the prophets Haggai and Zechariah.

145. Boda, *Commentary*, 275.

146. Ibid., 281–82. See also M. Turner, "Holy Spirit," in Alexander and Rosner, ed., *New Dictionary of Biblical Theology*, 551–58 (551): "the Spirit was understood in Judaism to be the 'Spirit of prophecy.' That is, the Spirit was considered to make God's will and wisdom known to his people, especially through the phenomenon of oracular speech called 'prophecy,' in which a message of the Lord was granted by the Spirit in a dream, vision or word."

147. E.g. Num 24:2; 2 Kgs 2:9, 15, 16; 2 Chr 15:1; Neh 9:30; Ezek 2:2; 11:5; Dan 4:18; Joel 2:28–29; Mic 3:8.

148. For this connection in Zechariah, see W. Eichrodt, *Theology of the Old Testament*, vol. 2 (trans. J. Baker; London: SCM Press, 1967), 64. While the menorah

Furthermore, priests and kings were generally those who were anointed with oil, while the prophets anointed and stood over the kings.[149] Kline comments: "The prophets, outstandingly the paradigm prophet Moses, were God's chief agents for anointing."[150] In the vision, the "two sons of oil" are oil providers, which better fits the office of prophet rather than priest or king.[151]

This connection between Yahweh's Spirit and prophecy throws light on several key elements of this vision. In the context of the chapter as a whole, the vision report of Zech 4:1–5 suggests that, since the menorah is supplied with oil without human instrumentation, it is a picture for Zechariah of how the temple will be reconstructed. While there are clearly humans involved, the main driving force will not be Zerubbabel, but Yahweh by his Spirit through his word proclaimed by the prophets. Hence, when Zerubbabel is told that he will build the temple, "Not by might, and not by power, but by my Spirit," given the link between Yahweh's Spirit and the role of the prophets, then this word from Yahweh also indicates that prophecy would be the main driving force behind the construction of the temple (cf. 8:9). Further evidence for the key role of the prophets is seen in 4:9 where the completion of the temple will be evidence that Zechariah is a true prophet of Yahweh (cf. 6:15).

This also may explain the difficulty that Zechariah has in understanding the identity of the two olive trees. Just as Moses and Jeremiah were hesitant to see the important role that they would play as prophets (Exod 4:10; Jer 1:6), in a similar way, Zechariah may underestimate the key role that he will play. He has to ask three times about the two olive trees that pour out the oil and fails to see himself in the vision.

While it is impossible to be certain about the identification of the "two sons of oil," since they are not explicitly identified, on balance, the interpretation that they are the prophets Haggai and Zechariah best suits the wider context of Zechariah and best explains the menorah vision itself. Zechariah is addressing the returned exiles who were living in the "day of small things" (Zech 4:10). With their return they were facing major challenges, challenges described metaphorically as a "great mountain" (Zech 4:7). The books of Ezra and Haggai give us a picture of both internal and external challenges that the community faced: financial

---

vision does not directly equate the oil with the Spirit, it is natural enough to equate these. Kings were anointed with oil, and also endowed with the Spirit by prophets.

149.   Contra Tigchelaar, *Prophets*, 42–43, who believes that they are the future king and messianic priest of Zech 6:13.

150.   M. G. Kline, *Images of the Spirit* (Grand Rapids: Baker, 1980), 87.

151.   In addition, Rev 11 interprets the two olive trees as prophets.

difficulties (Hag 1:6), challenges from outside enemies (Ezra 4:1–3) and challenges of low morale (Hag 1:14). Amid these difficulties, Yahweh had given this post-exilic community the task of restoring the temple and reconstructing their community life (Zech 1–2). Joshua is instituted as the high priest (Zech 3), which offers the hope of forgiveness and cleansing Against this background, as will be seen in the next chapter, Zechariah encourages them that the day of Yahweh is coming along with the Shoot (Zech 3). In the meantime, what will sustain the community as they rebuild? The answer of this fifth vision (Zech 4) is that it is Yahweh himself who will sustain them, by his Spirit, though his prophets. Hence, the central significance of 4:6 in this vision.[152] Not only will Zerubbabel complete his task by Yahweh's Spirit, but the Spirit, symbolized by oil in this vision, is also Yahweh's empowering presence among his people, sustaining them through these challenges.[153]

3.4. *Joshua and Zerubbabel and the Hope for the House of David*

Zechariah's treatment of Joshua and Zerubbabel raises a number of issues in relation to the hope for the house of David. Dealing with these chapters of Zechariah, Floyd believes that the institution of the temple has come to represent what the monarchy used to signify (i.e. the rule of Yahweh on earth), and that it is only by virtue of their association with the temple that Joshua and Zerubbabel together represent Yahweh's divine kingship.[154] He states:

> Since they are the human representatives of Yahweh's kingliness, the roles of Joshua and Zerubbabel are somewhat regal, and their status may thus perhaps be described as "messianic" in some sense. Because the temple was the central institution of the restored province of Judah, their joint responsibility for its operation and maintenance may perhaps be described as a "diarchy" of some sort... Zerubbabel's authority gains its sacramental significance primarily from the way in which it serves to confirm the authority of the high priest; and this complementary role, rather than his completely unmentioned Davidic ancestry or status as

152. Tidiman, *Zacharie*, 122–23. For an excellent discussion of how the various dimensions of biblical interpretation relate to each other, with Zech 4 as an illustration, see A. Wolters, "Confessional Criticism and the Night Visions of Zechariah," in *Renewing Biblical Interpretation* (ed. C. Bartholomew, C. Greene, and K. Möller; Grand Rapids: Zondervan, 2000), 90–117.

153. The "former prophets," as Zechariah calls them, also spoke of the exile as a death situation, and stated that Yahweh would once again give his people life by his Spirit (e.g. Ezek 37:5–6).

154. Floyd, *Minor Prophets*, 384.

governor, is what entitles him to bear the epithet ṣemaḥ ('branch," 3:8b;
→ 6:9–15). The temple with the high priest at its head, conceived as a
reincarnation of the old royal sanctuary, thus serves as surrogate for the
Davidic monarchy, and not the office held by Zerubbabel.[155]

Floyd's assessment brings into focus for us a number of pertinent issues:
In what sense are Joshua and Zerubbabel "messianic"? What is the
nature of their rule over the community? What are we to make of the lack
of any reference to Zerubbabel's Davidic ancestry, or that he is a
governor? And is the temple to be seen as a surrogate for the Davidic
monarchy?[156] I shall deal with these in turn.

We have seen that in the vision of Zech 4 the "two sons of oil" are oil
suppliers, and not recipients. Furthermore, the word for oil is not the
word that is usually associated with anointing. For these reasons, even if
the "two sons of oil" are to be identified as Joshua and Zerubbabel, then
it does not seem appropriate to see them as anointed or "messianic" in
any sense. The translation of "two sons of oil" as "two anointed ones" is
inappropriate. Furthermore, on balance, the identity of the "two sons of
oil" is more likely to be the prophets Haggai and Zechariah anyway.

Regarding the absence of reference to Zerubbabel's Davidic ancestry
and governorship in Zechariah, this feature can be, and has been, interpreted in opposite ways. Some have argued that reference to his status
is because Zechariah did not see him as heir to the throne.[157]
Equally, it could be argued that while Zechariah acknowledged Zerubbabel as heir to the throne, he played down Zerubbabel's status so that he
does not pose a threat to the Persians.[158] Clearly, this observation can be
made to fit whatever theory one holds about Zerubbabel's relationship to
the throne and cannot be determinative in any decision.

This raises the question of whether Zechariah expresses the hope that
the monarchy would be restored in Zerubbabel. While it has been noted
that the building of the temple raises the hopes for a king to be reinstated
on David's throne, particularly because of the hope held out by the

---

155.   Ibid., 383–84.

156.   The question of the identity of the "Branch" will be deal with in the next
chapter.

157.   Meyers and Meyers, *Zechariah 1–8*, 243: "For Zechariah the expectation
that Zerubbabel or any Davidide would ascend the throne and reestablish kingship is
one that is remote if not impossible. The monarchic hope can only be realized in
some future time. Zerubbabel's title and patronymic have been omitted because
Zechariah does not want to evoke hopes regarding Zerubbabel's role which he
would consider unrealistic." Cf. Pomykala, *Dynasty*, 56.

158.   For this background, see Watts, "Zechariah," 329; Petersen, *Zechariah 1–8*,
106.

covenant with David in 2 Sam 7, there is no evidence in Zech 4 that Zechariah envisaged Zerubbabel as this king. Zechariah obviously holds a high view of Zerubbabel and sees a significant role for him in the restoration community, especially as builder of the temple, but there is no suggestion to this point that he will be the one who will re-establish the monarchy in Jerusalem. In making this conclusion, caution is called for, since the significance of Zechariah's hopes for the Shoot has not yet been assessed. However, it has already been noted that it is not necessary to interpret Hag 2:20–23 as indicating that Zerubbabel would become king.[159]

What of the relationship between Joshua and Zerubbabel as leaders of the community? Is Joshua's status being elevated above that of Zerubbabel, as Floyd suggests? Or are they "placed on a par"?[160] It is common to speak of a "diarchy" of leadership, but this term is rarely explained and it seems to mean different things to different scholars. Rose concludes that there is no evidence in this passage for "a political organization called 'diarchy,' in which two leaders, a prince and a priest, stand at the head of the Jewish community."[161] If by "diarchy" is meant a joint rule by the governor and high priest which then collapses into the rule of the high priest after Zerubbabel disappears, Rose is right that this notion reads too much into the text.[162] It was established in the above treatment of Zech 3 that there is no basis to support the idea of Joshua being given the prerogatives of the pre-exilic monarch, and there is nothing to change this conclusion in Zech 4. If, on the other hand, "diarchy" only means that the governor and high priest have separate leadership roles within the life of the community, then chs. 3 and 4 both support this view. Moreover, if Joshua and Zerubbabel are the "sons of oil," then this is only describing them as leaders of the community and not necessarily indicating any priority in their roles.

Floyd's idea that in this post-exilic period the temple and high priest were to become a surrogate for the Davidic monarchy seems to depend again on the view that the high priest is taking over the prerogatives of the pre-exilic monarch, a view that lacks evidence from the text.

159. See Chapter 3, §3.3.1.
160. Meyers and Meyers, *Zechariah 1–8*, 259: "The priestly leader is placed on a par with the political administrator, an arrangement authorized by the Persian authorities." Cf. Petersen, *Zechariah 1–8*, 234: "the polity of the new community is to be diarchic rather than monarchic, its leadership comprising two individuals of equal status."
161. Rose, *Zemah*, 207.
162. Rose quotes J. L. Berquist, *Judaism in Persia's Shadow: A Social and Historical Approach* (Minneapolis: Fortress, 1995), 72, in support.

Furthermore, there is no indication that Zechariah envisaged a different role for the temple than it had exercised in the pre-exilic period. The idea that the temple with the high priest at its head served in the place of the monarchy in the post-exilic period also overlooks the fact that the king who ruled over Israel at this time was the Persian monarch Darius (1:1, 7; 7:1).

In summary, Zech 3–4 contains two visions that give encouragement to the returned exiles and their leaders. Zechariah 3 pictures Joshua the high priest being reinstated along with the priesthood to the temple duties that were undertaken before the exile. Through this, forgiveness and cleansing would be mediated to the community. The realm for these priestly duties was the temple, and the vision of Zech 4 indicates that Zerubbabel would reconstruct the temple in the power of Yahweh's Spirit through his prophets. Hence, amid the challenges that the community faced, Yahweh would be at work to rebuild the community. As we shall see in the next chapter, the reinstitution of Joshua as high priest in the temple heightens the expectation for a coming king from the house of David. Similarly, while there is no evidence in Zech 4 that Zechariah envisaged Zerubbabel as taking the throne, his role in rebuilding the temple raises the hope for a king to come, in line with the promise to David in 2 Sam 7.

Chapter 4

THE SHOOT

4.1. Introduction

A key aspect of the hope for the house of David in Zech 1–8 concerns the nature and identity of the Shoot (צמח), a figure that appears in 3:8 and 6:12. As the literature review in Chapter 2 has highlighted, the identity of the Shoot has been variously understood as Joshua, Zerubbabel, a future figure, or any of these figures at various stages in the transmission of the text. Similarly, there is no consensus on how this term is to be translated. "Branch" is most common.[1] "Sprout"[2] or "Shoot"[3] are other options.[4] More recently, the trend is simply to transliterate the Hebrew into a proper name "Zemah."[5] For reasons that will be explained shortly, "Shoot" best captures the ideas behind this term and this translation will be used unless quoting others.

In order to determine the nature and identity of the Shoot and its significance for the hope for the house of David I shall first consider the background to this term in the prophets, then turn to examine closely the texts in which it appears (Zech 3:8–10 and 6:9–15), before summarizing the nature of the hope for the house of David.

4.2. Background to the Term "Shoot" (צמח)

The background to the term צמח is to be found in the earlier prophets, particularly Isaiah, Jeremiah, and Ezekiel. Given that Zechariah refers to what he calls the "former prophets" (cf. Zech 1:4; 7:7, 12), it seems entirely appropriate to read his reference to this figure against this background.

---

1. E.g. KJV; RSV; ESV; NIV; NASB.
2. E.g. NAB in Zech 6:12.
3. E.g. NAB in Zech 3:8.
4. In French it is "le germe" or "Germe," and in German it is "Sproß."
5. So Rose, *Zemah*; Boda, *Commentary*.

The "former prophets" express a clear hope for a royal deliverer.[6] In particular, the eighth-century prophets provide a picture of the house of David being judged and yet preserved for the sake of Yahweh's covenant with David so that a king from the line of David might arise in the future. In this respect, Isaiah's use of arboreal imagery to speak of a new start for the house of David beyond the experience of exile is particularly relevant. It is important to note that kings are often likened to trees in the Hebrew Bible and other ancient Near Eastern literature.[7] So, in Isa 11:1, after the removal (or cutting down) of the king in judgment, a new beginning is promised: "There shall come forth a shoot from the stump of Jesse, and a branch from his roots shall bear fruit." Just as the stump speaks of the judgment of the house of David (cf. Isa 7), so the shoot (חטר) and the branch (נצר) speak of a new beginning that will come with a new Davidic king (cf. Isa 9:6–7). The reference to Jesse, the father of David, also implies a rejection of what the house of David had become and the need for a radically new beginning. However, the new growth will not arise from a completely new dynasty, but come from the judged stump or roots of the Davidic house, affirming Yahweh's faithfulness to his promises to David. This connection to David is made explicit in Isa 9:7 where this future king is said to rule "on the throne of David and over his kingdom."[8]

In the wider context of Isaiah, this new beginning for the house of David will see the renewal of the people and the land. Just as the land would be laid waste (e.g. Isa 5), so too there would be new growth (Isa 4:2): "In that day the branch (צמח) of the LORD shall be beautiful and glorious, and the fruit of the land shall be the pride and honor of the survivors of Israel." Here the term צמח is used of new growth that will shoot up in the land after the desolation of judgment. It is an image of the abundance and prosperity of a future age that will be experienced by a remnant of the people.[9]

---

6. See Isa 9:6–7; 11:1–10; 16:5; Jer 23:3–6; 33:14–22; Ezek 37:21–25; Hos 3:4–5; Amos 9:11–12; Mic 5:2–5.

7. E.g. Judg 9:7–15; 2 Kgs 14:9; Isa 2:6–21; 10:5–34; 14:3–23; Jer 21:11–14; 22:1–22; 23:5; 33:15; Ezek 17; 31; Dan 4:22; Amos 2:9. See K. Neilson, "ʿēṣ," *TDOT* 11:268–77 (274). H. Ringgren, "ʿēṣ," *TDOT* 11:265–67 (267), notes Sumerian royal hymns that liken the king to a tree.

8. See also Isa 16:5; 55:4–5.

9. While some have understood צמח in Isa 4:2 as a reference to the future Davidic king (e.g. Baldwin, "Ṣemaḥ," 93–94; J. A. Motyer, *The Prophecy of Isaiah* [Leicester: IVP, 1993], 65), this seems unlikely. The text does not speak of a future king at this point. See further Rose, *Zemah*, 107; Boda, *Commentary*, 257.

Hence, the arboreal imagery of Isaiah aptly captures three important ideas: first, it expresses the idea of something new springing from what had been cut down; second, it expresses the idea of some measure of continuity between the old and the new; third, it captures the idea of the small or humble beginnings of the new growth which at the same time will grow to produce something magnificent. While Isaiah does not use the term צמח to refer to the future king, Jeremiah certainly reflects Isaiah's use of this arboreal imagery in relation to the house of David, and for Jeremiah the Shoot (צמח) becomes a term for the future Davidic king.[10]

Jeremiah prophesies the coming judgment on the inhabitants of Jerusalem for their rejection of Yahweh. In Jer 22, in a passage that addresses the king of Judah who sits on the throne of David, Jeremiah likens the house of David to Gilead and Lebanon with its choice cedars that will be cut down and cast into the fire (22:6–7).[11] Nevertheless, Jeremiah looks to a time beyond the Babylonian destruction, after the judgment of the shepherds "who destroy and scatter the sheep of my pasture" (23:1), when Yahweh will gather his remnant out of the countries to which they were driven, and "bring them back to their fold" (23:3). At this time he will set up over them shepherds who will care for them (23:4), and raise up the Shoot (23:5–6): "Behold, the days are coming, declares the LORD, when I will raise up for David a righteous Branch (צמח), and he shall reign as king and deal wisely, and shall execute justice and righteousness in the land. In his days Judah will be saved, and Israel will dwell securely. And this is the name by which he will be called: The LORD is our righteousness."

Again, the context of this oracle is significant. In the previous chapter, the house of David, specifically each of the sons of Josiah, is condemned for unrighteousness and injustice. This condemnation culminates in the following curse on Coniah, son of Jehoiakim (son of Josiah): "Thus says the LORD: 'Write this man down as childless, a man who shall not succeed in his days, for none of his offspring shall succeed in sitting on the throne of David and ruling again in Judah'" (Jer 22:30). The sense here is not that Coniah will have no offspring, for in fact seven sons are recorded in 1 Chr 3:17–18. Indeed, Thompson suggests that the eldest

---

10. Note the argument of R. P. Carroll, *Jeremiah: A Commentary* (London: SCM Press, 1986), 446, that Jer 23:5–6 pre-dates Zech 3:8 and 6:12. So too, Tollington, *Tradition*, 171: "It is unlikely that Zechariah chose the same motif independently of Jeremiah and therefore the probability is that he used צמח in the same way."

11. J. A. Thompson, *The Book of Jeremiah* (NICOT; Grand Rapids: Eerdmans, 1980), 474, notes that Gilead and Lebanon were renowned for their forests and that the royal palace was built with timbers from these areas.

may already have been born at the time when this prophecy was first delivered.[12] The curse implies that Coniah will have offspring, but that none of these will sit on the throne of David, and in this sense Coniah is as good as childless. However, Jeremiah is not unaware of the promises to David of an eternal dynasty (cf. 2 Sam 7), and there may even be an echo in the Shoot terminology of David's last words concerning his house (2 Sam. 23:5): "For does not my house stand so with God? For he has made with me an everlasting covenant, ordered in all things and secure. For will he not cause to prosper (יצמיח) all my help and my desire?"[13]

While the house of David is judged and cut down with the removal of the king from the throne, the promise of a Shoot speaks of a future descendant of David who will be restored to the throne and establish justice and righteousness in the land. This promise is repeated later in Jer 33:14–18:

> [14] Behold, the days are coming, declares the LORD, when I will fulfil the promise I made to the house of Israel and the house of Judah. [15] In those days and at that time I will cause a righteous Branch (צמח) to spring up (אצמיח) for David, and he shall execute justice and righteousness in the land. [16] In those days Judah will be saved and Jerusalem will dwell securely. And this is the name by which it will be called: "The LORD is our righteousness."
>
> [17] For thus says the LORD: David shall never lack a man to sit on the throne of the house of Israel, [18] and the Levitical priests shall never lack a man in my presence to offer burnt offerings, to burn grain offerings, and to make sacrifices forever.

The Shoot is fitting imagery to describe a new beginning for the house of David beyond the judgment of the exilic experience. Jeremiah reflects each aspect of Isaiah's imagery: the new beginning; the continuity with the past with the coming of the Shoot seen as a fulfilment of the promises made to David (Jer 23:5; 33:15) and to the houses of Israel and Judah (Jer 33:14); and also the small or humble beginnings from which will grow something much larger and fruit-bearing, producing the fruit of justice and righteousness in the land (cf. Isa 11). Because of each of these connotations, it seems better to translate צמח as "Shoot" rather than "Branch." While there is no simple equivalent in English, "Shoot" captures better both the idea of something new, and the idea of small or humble beginnings, whereas "Branch," suggests something older and more established.

12. Ibid., 485.
13. Noted by Dempster, *Dominion*, 166–67.

Jeremiah also makes an important connection here between the Shoot and the Levitical priests. Just as the Davidic dynasty will continue, so too the Levitical priests will never lack a man, presumably the high priest, to make sacrifices in the temple. This connection between the Shoot and the high priest is significant for Zechariah, and connects the future Davidic king with the temple.

Before turning to Zechariah, it is worth also noting Ezekiel's similar use of arboreal imagery to speak of a new beginning beyond the judgment of exile. In Ezek 17 there is an allegory of the events of the first deportation in 597 B.C.E. In this allegory, the first eagle refers to the king of Babylon, Nebuchadnezzar (17:12). The top of the cedar and the twigs refer to king Jehoiachin and the first exiles (17:12). The seed refers to Zedekiah, whom Nebuchadnezzar planted in Jerusalem.[14]

> [3] Thus says the Lord GOD: A great eagle with great wings and long pinions, rich in plumage of many colors, came to Lebanon and took the top of the cedar. [4] He broke off the topmost of its young twigs and carried it to a land of trade and set it in a city of merchants. [5] Then he took of the seed of the land and planted it in fertile soil. He placed it beside abundant waters. He set it like a willow twig, [6] and it sprouted (ויצמח) and became a low spreading vine, and its branches turned toward him, and its roots remained where it stood. So it became a vine and produced branches and put out boughs. (17:3–6)

In Ezek 17:11–21 the allegory is explained. On account of Zedekiah forming an alliance with Egypt, the vine that represented his house, which had initially sprouted and grown, would wither and eventually perish.[15] Zedekiah would fall under judgment in Babylon along with the pick of his troops (17:20–21). However, Yahweh promises:

> [22] Thus says the Lord GOD: "I myself will take a sprig from the lofty top of the cedar and will set it out. I will break off from the topmost of its young twigs a tender one, and I myself will plant it on a high and lofty mountain. [23] On the mountain height of Israel will I plant it, that it may bear branches and produce fruit and become a noble cedar. And under it will dwell every kind of bird; in the shade of its branches birds of every sort will nest." (17:22–23)

It is clear from the context that arboreal imagery is used to speak of a new beginning for the house of David while at the same time capturing

---

14. See further, Duguid, *Ezekiel*, 33–35, 44–45; C. J. H. Wright, *The Message of Ezekiel* (The Bible Speaks Today; Leicester: IVP, 2001), 170.

15. The word צמח is used twice in Ezek 17:9–10, referring to the new growth of the vine.

the sense of continuity with the past.[16] While the term צמח is not used in relation to the second transplanted cedar top, the imagery of a twig being plucked and replanted speaks of the new start that has some measure of continuity for the house of David with what went before, reflecting Isaiah and Jeremiah.[17] Furthermore, the fragility of the young and tender twig also speaks of the humble origins of this new Davidic king, who will grow to produce something magnificent. In conjunction with the restoration of the house of David, Ezekiel envisions the restoration of the other house of David—the temple (Ezek 40–48).

To summarize, the meaning of the term צמח in Zechariah must be understood against the wider background of what Zechariah calls the "former prophets."[18] Here we find the use of differing terminology, but a common metaphor to depict the hope for the house of David beyond the exile, based on the covenant with David and the earlier expectation of a royal deliverer. The prophets Isaiah, Jeremiah, and Ezekiel each liken the house of David to a tree that is cut down or severed in judgment, and from which new growth will come and grow into something vast. This Shoot is a Davidic king of humble origins, who will bring in the kingdom of Yahweh with all its blessings. Jeremiah uses the term "Shoot" (צמח) to capture these common ideas, and it is this term that is utilized by Zechariah. With this background in mind, its use in Zech 3:8 and 6:12 will now be examined.

4.3. *Signs of the Coming Shoot (Zechariah 3:8–10)*

[8] "Hear now, Joshua the high priest, you and your associates sitting before you, for they are men of a sign: For I will bring my servant the Shoot. [9] For behold, the stone that I have placed before Joshua: upon a single stone with seven eyes, I will engrave its inscription, declares Yahweh of hosts, and I will remove the iniquity of this land in a single day. [10] In that day, declares Yahweh of hosts, each of you shall invite your [his] associate [to come] under [your] vine and under [your] fig tree." (author's translation)

16. Note Duguid, *Ezekiel*, 44–45: "Yet, for Ezekiel, the death of the contemporary Davidides does not mean the end of the road for the Davidic monarchy. A new sprig from that same tree will be planted and will flourish under the blessing of Yahweh's protection… [I]n spite of the failure of the individual Davidic kings and the doom which has been pronounced upon them, there remains a future for the Davidic line."
17. Dempster, *Dominion*, 170–71, supports this.
18. Contra Barker, "Two Figures," 41, who sees no indication that the Shoot is a Davidic title.

The previous chapter examined Zech 3:1–7, a passage that comprises a vision of Joshua cleansed and recommissioned to act as high priest in the reconstructed temple. With this vision explained, the angel of Yahweh declares to Joshua the high priest that his "associates" are a "sign" of the fact that Yahweh will send the Shoot. There are three significant issues in this verse: Who are the "associates"? What does it mean that they are a "sign"? And who is the referent of "my servant the Shoot"?

Joshua's associates have not been mentioned to this point in the vision. We are given three descriptions of them: first, they are "friends" or "associates"[19] of Joshua; second, they "sit before" him, which, along with the first description, suggests that they are Joshua's fellow priests;[20] and third, they are a sign that Yahweh will bring "my servant the Shoot." The fact that they are priests is significant for understanding how they function as a sign, as will be seen.

The word מופת is used in other parts of the Hebrew Bible to mean "portent" or "sign."[21] Rose discusses this and concludes: "Most scholars interpret the function of מופת in 3:8 as providing a guarantee that the oracle about the coming of צמח will be fulfilled."[22] While agreeing with this, the question still remains: How will Joshua's associates serve as a sign that Yahweh will send the Shoot?[23] What is it about the priesthood that serves as a sign? When the prophets Isaiah and Ezekiel are described as signs, it is not their mere existence, but what they do that provides the sign.[24] While the actions of Joshua's associates are not spelled out

19. BDB, 946, gives the meaning "associates" here.
20. McComiskey, "Zechariah," 3:1077, argues: "The conclusion that answers best to the textual data is that Joshua's companions were fellow priests over whom the high priest exercised spiritual authority." See also Mitchell, "Zechariah," 147.
21. E.g. Exod 4:21; 1 Kgs 13:3; 2 Chr 32:24; Isa 8:18; Ezek 12:6; 24:24.
22. Rose, *Zemah*, 45, cites these scholars as M. J. Lagrange, "Notes sur les prophéties messianiques des derniers prophètes," *RB* 15 (1906): 67–83 (70–71); M. Bič, *Das Buch Sacharja* (Berlin: Evangelische Verlagsanstalt, 1962), 50; K. Elliger, *Die Propheten Nahum, Habakuk, Zephanja, Haggai, Sacharja, Maleachi* (6th ed.; ATD; Göttingen: Vandenhoeck & Ruprecht, 1967), 124; Ackroyd, *Exile*, 189–90; Baldwin, *Zechariah*, 116; Amsler, "Zacharie," 83; Mason, *Preaching*, 211; Reventlow, *Sacharja*, 55; Hanhart, *Sacharja 1–8*, 194.
23. While the MT appears to exclude Joshua from the sign, it is likely that "they" includes him and there has been a shift of object by the speaker, or the independent personal pronoun is functioning as a copula and is not to be translated. So Merrill, *Zechariah*, 144.
24. See Isa 20:1–5; Ezek 12:6–7, 11; 24:24, 27. The work of K. Friebel, *Jeremiah's and Ezekiel's Sign-Acts* (JSOTSup 283; Sheffield: Sheffield Academic Press, 1999), and "A Hermeneutical Paradigm for Interpreting Prophetic Sign-Actions," *Didaskalia* (2001): 27–46, is useful for understanding the function of prophetic sign acts.

beyond noting that they were "sitting before" Joshua, it can be inferred that it is their priestly duties that are on view, particularly in view of the fact that these duties have been alluded to in 3:7.

This brings us to the highly significant phrase, "my servant the Shoot." Smith notes that the expression "my servant" is used in many different ways in the Hebrew Bible: to refer to individuals such as Abraham, Isaac, Jacob, Moses, David, even Nebuchadnezzar; to refer to the nation of Israel; and to refer to a future suffering figure.[25] In the prophets, it is used with Davidic overtones, not least because the designation "my servant" is used of David 31 times in the Hebrew Bible,[26] including twice in 2 Sam 7, a chapter which is programmatic for understanding the hope for the house of David in the prophets. C. and E. Meyers note that this use of the term for a Davidide places Zechariah in the tradition of earlier prophets such as Isaiah and Jeremiah.[27] Smith also observes Ezekiel's use of the expression "my servant David" in referring to the king of the new age (Ezek 34:24; 37:24) and suggests that Zechariah is here combining "Isaiah's, Jeremiah's, and Ezekiel's concept of the Branch of the line of David with Deutero-Isaiah's idea of the suffering servant to refer to the coming messiah."[28] This possibility shall be explored later, in Chapter 7.

25. Smith, *Micah–Malachi*, 201.

26. BDB, 714.

27. Meyers and Meyers, *Zechariah 1–8*, 68. Note also in reference to the Servant of Isaiah the comments of H. G. M. Williamson, *Variations on a Theme: King, Messiah and Servant in the Book of Isaiah* (Carlisle: Paternoster, 1998), 133: "'My servant': although this is a widespread title for those in the service of God in the Old Testament, the king (and especially David) is certainly included prominently among them."

28. Smith, *Micah–Malachi*, 201. Many have maintained that there is a lack of any hope for the house of David in Isa 40–55 and that the servant songs contain no reference to the Davidic covenant (it is argued that the reference in Isa 55:3–5 democratizes the promises to David). Regarding the identity of the Servant, Williamson, *Variations*, 113–66, believes that the Servant is to be identified with Israel. R. N. Whybray, *Isaiah 40–66* (NCBC; Grand Rapids: Eerdmans, 1975), 138–39, understands it as Isaiah. These represent the two most common critical views. If, however, we acknowledge the unity of the book of Isaiah (even if only an editorial unity), then the question of the relationship between the passages that speak of a future king and the passages that speak of the Servant must be dealt with. Motyer, *The Prophecy of Isaiah*, 14–16; R. Schultz, "The King in the Book of Isaiah," in Satterthwaite, Hess, and Wenham, eds., *The Lord's Anointed*, 141–65; B. G. Webb, *The Message of Isaiah: On Eagle's Wings* (The Bible Speaks Today; Leicester: IVP, 1996), 233–34, have argued that the future Davidic king and the Servant are two portraits of the one person based on several factors including: (1) the royal elements of the servant songs, especially the Servant's role in bringing forth justice; (2) the endowment of both with the Spirit as a sign of divine choice and empowerment (Isa

At this stage it should be noted that the title "my servant" brings to mind David and the hopes that were held for his house. This is reinforced with the parallel term "Shoot," which, as has been argued, uses the terminology of Jeremiah to refer to the hope of the prophets for a future Davidic king of humble origins who will fulfil the promise to David and restore the fortunes of Israel. The background to this term "Shoot," as has been seen, demonstrates Zechariah's clear hope for the house of David beyond the judgment of exile.[29] The identity of this figure will be discussed at the end of this chapter.

Continuing with the details of the vision, we see that the function of the priesthood in acting as a sign of the coming Shoot is complemented in Zech 3:9 by a stone being set before Joshua. Again, there is a variety of opinion on how this stone is to be understood. The two dominant views are that the stone is part of the new temple, or that it is part of Joshua's high-priestly vestments.[30]

The view that the stone is part of the new temple first arose from the supposition that Zech 3:9 was originally joined to 4:6b–10a, both being oracular material.[31] The basis for this is the common reference to the

11:1–2; 42:1); (3) the confirmation of the Davidic covenant in Isa 55:3–5 so close after the exaltation of the servant; and (4) the link between the Servant and the future king in the reference in Isa 37:35 to "my Servant David." (Williamson, *Variations*, 132–34, also itemises support for identifying the servant as a royal figure. However, as noted above, he believes the servant should be identified in the first place as Israel, to whom the covenant promises to David have been transferred. On the democratization of the Davidic covenant, see Chapter 5, n. 34).

29   Sweeney, *Twelve*, 601, supports this: "the term 'branch' here points to the reestablishment of the Davidic monarchy or at least to the fulfillment of the oracles in Isaiah 11 and Jer 23:5–6; 33:14–26." While from much later, it is interesting to note that the Targum translates the term "Shoot" here and in Zech 6:12 as "the anointed One." See R. P. Gordon, *The Targum of the Minor Prophets* (ed. K. J. Cathcart, M. McNamara and M. Maker; The Aramaic Bible 14; Edinburgh: T. & T. Clark, 1989), 192, 198.

30.   VanderKam, "Joshua," 562–67, succinctly presents the two dominant views. There is another view that the stone represents the future Davidic king (e.g. Briggs, *Messianic Prophecy*, 445; van Groningren, *Messianic*, 881), but there is nothing in the text to suggest this.

31.   As advocated by A. Petitjean, "La Mission de Zorobabel et la Reconstruction du Temple; Zach., III:8–10," *Ephemerides Theologicae Lovanienses* 42 (1966): 40–71. More recently, McComiskey, "Zechariah," 3:1078–79, while rejecting the assumption that the text has changed, has argued that the stone is a temple stone on the basis that: (1) it is "set before" Joshua, a notion that he believes favours a large stone rather than a gem stone; and (2) the wider context deals with the construction of the temple. However, the reclothing the high priest and the allusions to his regalia in Exodus and Leviticus seem to be stronger associations at this point.

"seven eyes" of the stone in 3:9 and the "seven eyes" in 4:10b, and the belief that 4:6b–10a breaks the flow of ch. 4 in its references to Zerubbabel as temple builder. The blessing of 3:10 is also seen to parallel the blessing at the completion of the temple (4:7; cf. 6:12–13).

J. C. VanderKam refutes this view at each point, arguing that there is no evidence that the text of 3:9 was ever joined to 4:6b–10a. The seven eyes of 4:10b do not refer to the eyes of 3:9 but to the seven lamps of 4:2. Furthermore, the reference to the eyes falls outside the oracular material which is almost universally accepted as ending at 4:10a. In addition, the picture of blessing in 3:10 is a different picture to that of the joy of 4:7 and 4:10a, and there is no explicit reference to Zerubbabel or the temple in 3:8–10, which would be expected if it was the stone of the temple.[32]

The second view, that the stone is part of the high priest's vestments, is based in the background information on the high priest's regalia found in Exod 28 (cf. Exod 29; 39; Lev 8; 16). Some scholars identify the engraved plate on Aaron's forehead (cf. Exod 28:38) as the referent of Zechariah's stone.[33] However, as VanderKam notes, "a stone and a metallic plate are rather different phenomena."[34] He makes the observation that the ephod of the high priest has two onyx stones set on the shoulder pieces which are engraved with the names of the sons of Israel, six on each stone (Exod 28:9–11a). Similarly, the breastpiece of the high priest has twelve precious stones, each with a name of the twelve tribes (28:21). He proposes:

> It seems that Zechariah alludes to these two unified pieces of clothing by the stone with seven eyes or facets. The text of Zech 3:9 does not talk of a single stone with seven eyes or facets but of one stone with seven pairs of eyes (the noun is dual — עֵינַיִם) or a total of fourteen, as there were fourteen stones in Aaron's garments... It is not impossible that he names just one stone because for him only the house of Judah remained of the twelve tribes. The symbol of the seven pairs of eyes, then, adds the nuance of completeness, despite the presence of only one tribe in the restored community. That the eyes signify the fourteen stones is evident also from the fact that they are said to be *inscribed* on the stone, as the names of the Israelite tribes were engraved on Aaron's stones.[35]

32. VanderKam, "Joshua," 566–67.

33. VanderKam cites the following scholars as holding this view: Mitchell, "Zechariah," 157–59; L. G. Rignell, *Die Nachtgesichte des Sacharja* (Lund: Gleerup, 1950), 130–34; Ackroyd, *Exile*, 190–91; W. Harrelson, "The Trial of the High Priest Joshua: Zechariah 3," *Eretz-Israel* 16 (1982): 116–24 (120); Petersen, *Zechariah 1–8*, 211–12.

34. VanderKam, "Joshua," 564.

35. Ibid., 568–69 (italics original).

VanderKam's proposal has the immediate advantage of explaining the passage in its context, as the high priest's clothing has been one of the key topics in Zech 3:1–5. While it is impossible to know whether Zechariah had in his mind all the parallels to Exodus that VanderKam suggests, the view that sees this stone as an inscribed gemstone that Joshua wore clearly complements the other features of the vision.

This stone with its inscription, worn by the high priest, is to signify the single day in which Yahweh will remove the iniquity of the land (Zech 3:9).[36] In fact, whereas Joshua and his associates were a sign of Yahweh bringing "my servant the Shoot," it is possible that this stone, set before Joshua, functioned as a reminder to Yahweh of his promise to remove the iniquity of this land in a single day (cf. Exod 28:29).[37] Some scholars note that the reference to the "single day" brings to mind the Day of Atonement (Lev 16).[38] The "single day" is a day that will bring peace and prosperity (Zech 3:10), and the terminology "in that day" (v. 10) suggests an eschatological timeframe. Inviting one's neighbour to come under his vine and under his fig tree is an image drawn from the prosperity experienced by Israel in the days of Solomon.[39]

VanderKam concludes that this coming age will be characterized by two things: the coming of the Davidic heir, and the temple cult once more serving its function of removing guilt and atoning for sin.[40] However, given that Zech 3:8 sets up Joshua and his associates as signs of the coming Shoot, then it is better to understand the removal of the iniquity of the land in a single day as coming about not through the temple cult, but rather via the arrival of the Shoot, which is anticipated in the cult.[41]

36. Interestingly, Merrill, *Zechariah*, 143; Webb, *Zechariah*, 88, and Curtis, *Steep*, 135, suggest that the inscription on the stone is "I will remove the iniquity of that land in a single day"; however, it is impossible to be certain about this from the syntax.

37. Compare also the rainbow sign of Gen 9:13–16, which functions as a reminder to Yahweh.

38. E.g. Curtis, *Steep*, 136; Tiemeyer, *Priestly*, 249. Also Boda, *Commentary*, 258. Yet, Boda argues that this day associated with the Shoot will remove guilt permanently and make the Day of Atonement obsolete.

39. So 1 Kgs 4:25 (MT 5:5); cf. Mic 4:4. See further, Kline, *Glory*, 126; Webb, *Zechariah*, 89 n. 137.

40. VanderKam, "Joshua," 569.

41. Compare Laato, *Josiah*, 244: "Just as the High Priest (and his colleagues) are a sign for the coming of the Messiah, the performance of rituals in the Temple should be seen as symbolizing the coming decisive action of YHWH on behalf of his people."

4.4. *The Significance of Zechariah 3:8–10 for the Hope Held for the House of David*

In the flow of the vision of Zech 3, we have seen Joshua as representative of the people of Yahweh accused and defended, cleansed of his filthiness and iniquity, then clothed and commissioned to serve. As Joshua and his associates conduct the various sacrifices and intercede on behalf of the people, Yahweh declares that they will function as a sign of his promise that he will send his servant, the Shoot (Zech 3:8). A further sign of the coming Shoot is an inscribed stone that is placed before Joshua (3:9). Both signs anticipate the coming of the Shoot, in whose arrival the iniquity of the land will (finally) be removed in a single day, and who will usher in the age of prosperity and abundance.

It is clear that the Shoot is a highly significant figure in Zechariah, and at this point there are four provisional conclusions we can draw. First, it seems that Zechariah, in using the term "Shoot," is drawing on the arboreal imagery of Isaiah, Jeremiah, and Ezekiel to speak of the future king who will revive the fortunes of Israel. The use of the co-ordinate term "my servant" makes this almost certain. Second, it is clear in the final form of the text that Joshua is not the Shoot.[42] In Zech 3:8, Yahweh promises Joshua that he will send the Shoot, and the priesthood, which probably includes Joshua, is a sign that the Shoot will come.[43] Furthermore, Joshua's lack of Davidic lineage also weighs against this identification.

Third, Zech 3:9–10 indicates that the arrival of the Shoot is set for a future day, an eschatological day, a day that will usher in an age of peace and prosperity.[44] A question that is raised at this point is whether the priests are envisaged as serving in the reconstructed temple? A number of scholars argue that the single day of the Shoot is after the temple has been rebuilt and this prevents identifying Zerubbabel as the Shoot. VanderKam argues:

---

42. Contra Redditt, *Zechariah*, 66.

43. McComiskey, "Zechariah," 3:1078, is right when he states: "We cannot identify the Branch with Joshua the high priest or with any of those who sit before him, for they are symbolic figures; to do so would be to identify the symbol with the symbol, not with the reality to which it points. The Branch stands outside this vision and is foreseen by it."

44. Tiemeyer, *Priestly*, 31, notes that the use of the participle מביא ("bringing") indicates that in relation to the other events of Zech 3, the coming of the Shoot is a future event.

if Branch in 3:8 is an epithet for Zerubbabel, the text contains a puzzling feature: the Lord says that he is bringing or will bring (מֵבִיא, a participle) Branch. Zerubbabel, however, had been in Jerusalem for years, according to Ezra 2–5. It does seem peculiar that in the prophet's first reference to Zerubbabel, where he fails to name him, he predicts that he will be brought to a place where he has been for eighteen or nineteen years.[45]

Tiemeyer summarizes the evidence that Zerubbabel had been in Yehud for some time with Joshua:

> There is little reason to doubt that the two leaders arrived together in Judah (Ezra 2:2; Neh 7:7). Further, Ezra 3:2ff. states that both Joshua and Zerubbabel were present in Judah *before* the work on the temple was begun in 520 B.C.E. Therefore, the idea that Zerubbabel's coming is yet to take place at the time of the vision in Zech 3 is difficult to accept.[46]

In addition, Pola argues that since Lev 8 suggests that the investiture of a high priest would have to take place at the temple due to the required cultic cleanness, it may be that Joshua's investiture was enacted after the completion of the temple.[47]

Alternatively, some scholars argue that Zerubbabel, for various reasons, was absent from Yehud at the time of this prophecy and therefore he was the Shoot whom Yahweh would bring back.[48] It is also pointed out that the sacrificial activity of the priests in Zechariah's vision does not necessitate a rebuilt temple since Ezra 3 shows that sacrifices were made at the temple site prior to the foundation of the temple being laid. Haggai 2:14 also gives evidence of sacrificial activity prior to the completion of the temple.

However, whether or not the hypothesis of an absent Zerubbabel is correct, the Shoot in the final form of Zechariah must point to a figure beyond Zerubbabel, for it would have been plain to the final editor(s) and those who incorporated the book of Zechariah into the canon that Zerubbabel, even though he had built the temple, had not brought the forgiveness and prosperity promised in Zech 3:9–10.

Fourth, while the coming of the Shoot is connected with Yahweh ultimately dealing with iniquity, the exact nature of the connection is unclear at this point and requires further clarification. However, the fact that the priesthood serves as a sign of the coming Shoot, and the close connection

---

45. VanderKam, "Joshua," 561.
46. Tiemeyer, "Guilty Priesthood," 1 (emphasis original). Also Curtis, *Steep*, 136.
47. Pola, *Priestertum*, 259. Also Rooke, *Zadok*, 136–37.
48. So Mitchell, "Zechariah," 156; Albertz, "Thwarted," 4; Boda, *Commentary*, 262.

between the coming of the Shoot and the removal of the uncleanness of the land suggests that the Shoot may have a priestly function when he comes.

4.5. *The Crowning of Joshua and the Coming Shoot (Zechariah 6:9–15)*

The oracle of Zech 6:9–15 is a key passage for the present purposes.[49] In it, Zechariah is commanded to crown the high priest, Joshua, and then pronounce to him an oracle concerning the coming Shoot. Again, there are many elements of this passage that pose challenges for the interpreter. How many crowns are there? Why are the two lists of the names of the returned exiles different? Which temple is being referred to? And, who is the Shoot? Further, the significance of this symbolic action is debated: Is it intended to generate additional support so that the temple begun by Zerubbabel might continue to be rebuilt? Or, is it a further sign that looks forward to the coming Shoot beyond the temple's construction?

In order to address these questions, I shall first look at the composition and structure of the passage and then provide an overview, dealing with the significant exegetical issues. This will put us in a good position to assess the majority view that Zerubbabel is the Shoot and see that this view poses a number of major interpretative difficulties. The view of Rose and others that the Shoot is a future king beyond Zerubbabel will then be reviewed. While this view also raises difficulties, a possible way through them will be considered.

4.5.1. *Composition and Structure*

Zechariah 6:9–15 comprises an oracle that immediately follows the visions of 1:7–6:8. As was observed in the literature survey of Chapter 2, under the influence of Wellhausen, critical scholarship has long debated both the literary integrity of this unit and the identity of the Shoot—matters which are not unrelated.[50] On this passage, Wellhausen comments:

---

49. Laato, *Josiah*, 247, considers it the *crux interpretum* of messianic expectations in Zech 1–8.

50. Note Rose, *Zemah*, 151, who says on the composition of Zech 6:9–15, "the reasons for suspicion about MT being a reworking partly arose from a particular interpretation of certain elements of the passage."

Jews from Babylon have brought gold and silver to Jerusalem; of these the prophet must make a crown designated for the 'branch' who is to build Yawhè's house and sit king [*sic*] on the throne, but retain a good understanding with the high priest. Zerubbabel is certainly meant here, and, if the received text names Joshua instead of him (6 11), this is only a correction, made for reasons easy to understand, which breaks the context and destroys the sense and the reference of 'them both' in v. 13.[51]

On this view, this text was originally about Zerubbabel, but when for whatever reason the monarchy failed to be restored in him, Joshua's name was substituted in Zech 6:11. It is easy to see the logic behind this interpretation. We have seen in Zech 4 that Zerubbabel was given the task of building the temple, and twice it is explicitly stated that the Shoot will do this (6:12–13). Hence, it seems natural enough to believe that Zechariah understood Zerubbabel to be the Shoot, initially at least. Given that the text now seems to identify Joshua as the Shoot, it is a logical supposition that the names were switched. The context further supports this in the way that it envisages the crowning of Joshua, something unexpected in relation to the high priest, but perfectly explicable for the Davidic governor.

While not all follow this exact reconstruction, for similar reasons a majority of scholars have challenged the literary integrity of this oracle. Rose groups the scholarly views into three categories:

(a) MT is a combination of two (or more) oracles of separate origin. (b) MT is a reworking by a redactor of an original text which is not impossible to reconstruct; in the original text either (i) there was no command to set a crown on the head of someone, or (ii) there was a command to set a crown on the head of Zerubbabel, or (iii) there was a command to set a crown on the head of Joshua and one on the head of Zerubbabel. (c) MT is not without difficulties, but it is preferable to stick to the text as we have it in MT.[52]

Rose provides a detailed discussion of each view and there is no reason to repeat this here.[53] His conclusions, however, are significant and worth recounting. On proposal (a), that there are two literary layers in the text, Rose concludes that the grounds given by scholars for this proposal fail to carry conviction, and that any apparent problems are "overrated if they are taken as indicating the secondary origin of part of the oracles."[54] On

51. Wellhausen, "Zechariah," 5392.
52. Rose, *Zemah*, 151. Rose comments in a footnote that some scholars find a combination of (a) and (b).
53. Ibid., 151–73. See also the discussion of this passage by Laato, *Josiah*, 247–52.
54. Rose, *Zemah*, 174.

proposal (b), that an original text was reworked by a redactor,[55] Rose contends that the factors which led to this proposal can be explained satisfactorily without resorting to a reconstruction of the text.[56] Moreover, the motives that are often given by scholars for a redactor altering the text lack historical support.[57] Rose concludes that it is best to abandon attempts to reconstruct an original text and accept the MT's integrity: "If the quality of arguments determines the plausibility of a specific proposal to label certain oracles as secondary, then in this case there is good reason to abandon the proposal because the grounds are dubious at best."[58]

Furthermore, this whole approach ultimately fails to address the present form of the text. As Laato comments, it does not ask: "How should the text be interpreted in its present form and why did the text take on this shape?"[59] The real gain of Rose's thesis is that it gives a largely satisfying explanation of the final form of the text.[60] I shall seek to do likewise, and at the same time question one or two aspects of his argument in the hope of developing his theses further.

Turning to structure, the introductory phrase "The word of Yahweh came to…" (Zech 6:9) occurs at key structural points in the book (i.e. 1:1, 7; 7:1; cf. 4:8; 7:8). Here it indicates a new section rather than a continuation of the final vision.[61] However, the content of the oracle depends very much on the visions that precede it, bringing several key

---

55. A further proposal is given by Redditt, *Zechariah*, 40. He believes that the original spoke of crowns for the three returning exiles and for Josiah. Zech 6:11b–13 was added later, and the coronation of Joshua (or Zerubbabel) is secondary.

56. The factors being (Rose, *Zemah*, 174): "the inappropriateness of a royal crown on the head of a high priest, the discrepancy between the recipient of the crown (Joshua, the priest) and the contents of the oracle (a royal figure)."

57. Ibid., 174. See also Cook, *Apocalypticism*, 134: "no textual support exists for the suggestion, often adopted since Wellhausen, that the crowning was originally of Zerubbabel but was changed to Joshua (v. 11)." Further, Tollington, *Tradition*, 166, argues that "the evidence does not support the idea that later scribes deliberately and radically altered texts that they were copying."

58. Rose, *Zemah*, 175. Rose quotes a number of scholars in support, including: Seybold, "Die Königserwartung bei den Propheten Haggai und Sacharja," 76; W. D. Stacey, *Prophetic Drama in the Old Testament* (London: Epworth, 1990), 211; Reventlow, *Sacharja*, 71. J. D. Davis, "The Reclothing and Coronation of Joshua; Zechariah iii and vi," *Princeton Theological Review* 18 (1920): 256–68 (268), reached a similar conclusion over 80 years ago.

59. Laato, *Josiah*, 248. See also the critique by B. Beatty, "Who Wears the Crown(s)? A Rationale for Editing Forwards," *Downside Review* 113 (1995): 1–19.

60. Pola, *Priestertum*, 242–47, 63, also argues that these verses have not undergone any editorial process.

61. Contra Baldwin, *Zechariah*, 85, 130.

themes of the visions together.[62] One of the distinctive elements in this oracle is the repetition of the phrase "he will build the temple of Yahweh" in 6:12–13 (with the addition of the pronoun הוא in v. 13). Rose, following van der Woude, suggests that the best explanation for this repetition is to assume that the word of Yahweh that Zechariah is to announce to Joshua finishes at the end of 6:12, and that 6:13–15 provides the explanation of this symbolic action to Zechariah by the interpreting angel.[63] However, it is evident that by 6:15 it is Zechariah himself who is speaking with no evidence of a change of speaker before that, nor any mention of an angel.[64] It seems best to see the oracle of 6:12–15 as being given directly to Zechariah by Yahweh. While the mediating angel was necessary for the interpretation of the visions, the angel should not be read into this oracle since we have moved beyond the visions.[65]

This still does not explain the repetition of 6:13. Baldwin believes that the repetition was a deliberate device aimed at distinguishing between Joshua and the Shoot, as well as the contemporary temple and the one to come.[66] However, Baldwin does not explain how this works, and it seems that it is the Shoot and the same temple that is being spoken of in each verse.

Tidiman notes the way that this passage pivots around 6:12–13.[67] Given this, the repetition of 6:13a forms the centre of a chiasm, and its repetition emphasizes the future work of the Shoot. There are also some other interesting correspondences in this passage which point to it being quite crafted:

62. Note Ollenburger, "Zechariah," 786: "The oracle depends on the whole visionary sequence. Its content depends on what has been accomplished in the visions, particularly in the concluding eighth vision."

63. Van der Woude, "Serubbabel," 145; Rose, *Zemah*, 161.

64. The phrase "You will know that Yahweh of hosts has sent me to you" is found on three other occasions (Zech 2:9, 11; 4:9), and each is best understood as a verification of Zechariah's prophecy to the community, rather than a verification of the angel's words to Zechariah. This same phrase at the end of 6:15 is best understood in the same way. Furthermore, the fact that "you" (6:15) is masculine plural also supports the view that it is intended as authentication of Zechariah's word to the community, rather than the angel's word to Zechariah. *Contra* Sweeney, *Twelve*, 634.

65. So Meyers and Meyers, *Zechariah 1–8*, 338: "This oracle consists of the direct words of Yahweh to the prophet without the intervening comments and queries of the angelic figure who played an important mediating role in the Seven Visions."

66. Baldwin, *Zechariah*, 135–36.

67. Tidiman, *Zacharie*, 150.

A   The Word of Yahweh (v. 9)
   B   Exiles come from Babylon (v. 10a, c)
      C   Exiles named (v. 10b)
         D   A crown to be made (v. 11a)
            E   Joshua the high priest (v. 11b)
               F   The Shoot introduced (v. 12a)
                  G   Build the Temple of Yahweh (v. 12b)
                  G'   Build the Temple of Yahweh (v. 13a)
               F'   Bear majesty, sit and rule (v. 13b)
            E'   A priest (v. 13c)
         D'   Crown in the temple (v. 14a)
      C'   Exiles named (v. 14b)
   B'   Far off ones shall come (v. 15a)
A'   The voice of Yahweh (v. 15b)

The following basic structure will be followed in my treatment of this passage:

     6:9–11   A symbolic crowning
     6:12–13   An oracle concerning the Shoot
     6:14–15   A memorial established

4.5.2. *A Symbolic Crowning (Zechariah 6:9–11)*

> [9] The word of Yahweh came to me saying, [10] "Take from the exiles, from Heldai, Tobijah and Jedaiah who have come from Babylon, and you go, on that [same] day, go to the house of Josiah, son of Zephaniah. [11] Take silver and gold and make a crown and set it upon the head of Joshua son of Jehozadak the high priest." (author's translation)

Zechariah is commanded to take silver and gold from three named exiles returning from Babylon (Zech 6:10).[68] Presumably, the precious metals

---

68.   In terms of their names, it is difficult to know why two of the names have been changed between Zech 6:10 and 6:14 (Heldai to Helem and Josiah to Hen). The usual explanation is that these names reflect different textual traditions (e.g. Laato, *Star*, 205, "The differences between these two lists of names may indicate that the names in v 14 belong to a later stratum in the text"). Others suggest a scribal error (e.g. D. Baron, *The Visions & Prophecies of Zechariah: An Exposition* [London: Morgan & Scott, 1918], 203). A. Demsky, "The Temple Steward Josiah ben Zephaniah," *IEJ* 31 (1981): 100–102, suggests that they might be terms for official positions in the temple or provincial court, and that between taking the offerings (Zech 6:10–11) and placing the crowns in the temple (6:14), these two men had taken new positions. Similarly, Thomas, "Zechariah," 1080, notes that all the names apart from Josiah are treated as appellatives in the LXX and translated this way. In this case, there may have been more than three or four in this group, and different names from the group are referred to in the two lists. However, this seems unlikely as the appellations of these names do not reflect temple positions. Meyers and

were intended as an offering.[69] The gold and silver is to be taken to the house of Josiah, where he will make either a "crown" or "crowns" (עטרות).[70] A modified form of this same word is also found in 6:14 (והעטרת). The significance of this reference has been widely discussed by scholars, and Rose summarizes the three main positions: "(a) In both cases the noun is singular, and only one crown is intended. (b) The noun is plural in both v. 11 and v. 14. (c) in v. 11 עטרות is plural and refers to two crowns, one of which is commented upon in v. 11, the other of which appears in v. 14 where עטרת is to be taken as singular."[71]

Rose believes that the noun עטרות is feminine singular.[72] The two main lines of evidence that he uses for support are the singular form of the verb in Zech 6:14 (תהיה) and the fact that Zechariah's usual practice is to number items (e.g. 1:18, 20; 3:9; 4:2, 14; 5:9; 6:1), something that

Meyers, *Zechariah 1–8*, 340, suggest that Heldai was a name with two forms, the Babylonian form being used first, and then the other being reverted to when he returned to Judah. However, it seems strange to use these two different names in such close proximity. More likely is that Helem in 6:14 functions like a nickname, and Hen refers to the grace of the son of Zephaniah (Petersen, *Zechariah 1–8*, 278, makes the suggestion that they are both nicknames; Baron, *Zechariah*, 203, suggests that rather than referring to the son of Zephaniah by his proper name in 6:14, the name "Hen" reflects the grace or kindness of the son of Zephaniah in this symbolic act; see also the useful treatment by Clark and Hatton, *Handbook*, 176–77). Whatever the explanation, it is clear that it is the same group of individuals that are being referred to in each instance, and that the differences in the names between the two verses does not necessitate seeing different textual layers. Further, if it was the redaction of two texts, it is difficult to explain why a redactor would not have simply brought the two lists into line.

69. "Take" (Zech 6:10) has no object. Ollenburger, "Zechariah," 787, notes that in the priestly legislation, לקח can refer to the taking of an offering. The repetition of the command in 6:11, this time with the stated objects, namely silver and gold, makes it clear that this is the sense in which "take" is to be understood in 6:10. Petersen, *Zechariah 1–8*, 274, helpfully suggests that the lack of object in 6:10 places the primary emphasis on those from whom the offering is to be taken.

70. Pola, *Priestertum*, 263, suggests that Josiah son of Zephaniah is possibly a grandchild of the priest Zephaniah, son of Maaseiah, who was the representative of the high priest (Jer 21:1; 37:3; cf. Jer 29:25; 2 Kgs 25:18). In this case, the place of the crowning of the grandchild of the last pre-exilic high priest (Joshua) would be the house of the grandchild of the last representative of the high priest (Josiah).

71. Rose, *Zemah*, 47.

72. Ibid., 84–86, dedicates an excursus to discussing this issue. However, note the criticism of Rose by Renz, "Review," 136: "he reads ʿăṭārôt as an archaic singular (but without providing a reason why an archaic form should have been used here)." See further Tollington, *Tradition*, 165 n. 2. Pola, *Priestertum*, 224 n. 8, takes it as an abstract plural which does not necessarily imply a factual plurality.

would be expected here if there were more than one crown. Most scholars who argue for (b) argue that the plurals reflect an earlier form of the text and agree that reading עטרות as a plural does not make sense of the text as it stands.[73] Many scholars believe that the presence of the singular verb in Zech 6:14 makes it certain that only one crown is on view in the entire passage. The fact that in Job 31:36 the identical plural form is used to refer to only one crown further supports this view.[74] The most plausible reason for the plural form is the suggestion that the crown is two-tiered, or composite, with gold and silver rings forming the one crown.[75] I will argue that a single crown makes best sense in the context.

Having made the crown, Zechariah is told first to set it upon the head of Joshua son of Jehozadak the high priest (Zech 6:11), and then to pronounce an oracle (6:12–13). Many interpretations hinge on the significance of this crowning. If the placing of the crown on Joshua's head is to be understood as a coronation, then it would support those who contend that we have here an elevation of the status of the high priest, with Joshua being given the prerogatives of the pre-exilic monarch (the same interpretation is offered in relation to ch. 3). Similarly, the proposal that Joshua's name has been substituted for Zerubbabel's name rests largely on this action being understood as a coronation and the difficulties inherent in the high priest being crowned as king (i.e. the high priest would not be crowned, so it must have originally referred to Zerubbabel).

Rose first looks for the explanation of the crowning of the high priest in the semantics of עטרה. Exploring the usage of this term in the Hebrew Bible, Rose questions the interpretation that identifies this crown in 6:11, 14 with a crown used in the coronation of kings,[76] and so questions,

---

73. Most would also agree with Floyd, *Minor Prophets*, 403, that "it is not necessary to resolve this text-critical problem in order to grasp the significance of the command that is enjoined on the prophet and hence the overall significance of the action."

74. So Clark and Hatton, *Handbook*, 172.

75. So Baron, *Zechariah*, 190; Unger, *Zechariah*, 112; Baldwin, *Zechariah*, 133; Smith, *Micah–Malachi*, 218; Heater, *Zechariah*, 54; McComiskey, "Zechariah," 3:1112–13; Kline, *Glory*, 220; Webb, *Zechariah*, 107. Kline and Baldwin also suggest that it may be the superlative plural of excellence (cf. Elohim).

76. Rose, *Zemah*, 48–59, clearly shows that not every use of the word עטרה is with reference to a "royal crown" (e.g. the use in Prov 4:9; 12:4; 14:24; 16:31; 17:6). Rose is also concerned to show that "coronation crowns" are different from "royal crowns," and to do this he includes an excursus on the crown of Ps 21:4 on pp. 86–88. Tollington, *Tradition*, 167, has a useful discussion here, and rightly concludes: "it may be unwise to assume that either Hebrew word for crown had a distinctive meaning at the time of Zechariah."

along with Petersen, "the belief that what we are dealing with in 6:9–15 is a coronation."[77] This has obvious implications for those who argue that the crowning of Joshua here indicates the elevation of the high priest's political status.

However, at this point in his argument, Rose draws too much from the semantic evidence, and it must be asked whether the distinction between a king's crown and a coronation crown is somewhat anachronistic. Semantics alone cannot prove that this is not a coronation, particularly when עטרה is associated on a number of occasions with kings.[78] However, Rose's discussion of the crowning moves in a more convincing direction when he turns to examine this action in the context of the oracle (6:12–13), and to compare this crowning of Joshua with the other symbolic actions of ch. 3. This, he argues, "opens the possibility of interpreting the action not as a coronation but as a crowning for a different purpose...as a sign providing the guarantee for the fulfilment of the promise concerning the coming rule of the figure called Zemah."[79] Before evaluating Rose's proposal, the oracle will be examined.

4.5.3. *An Oracle Concerning the Shoot (Zechariah 6:12–13)*

[12] "And you say to him, 'Thus says Yahweh of hosts, behold a man, Shoot is his name, and from beneath him he will shoot up and he will build the temple of Yahweh. [13] He will build the temple of Yahweh, and he will bear majesty, and he will sit and rule upon his throne, and he will be a priest [a priest will be] upon his throne, and a counsel of peace will be between the two.'" (author's translation)

Yahweh here gives the prophet Zechariah an oracle to pronounce to Joshua that accompanies and helps to explain the action of crowning him. Zechariah is to speak of a man whose name is Shoot. Rose gives three reasons why "a man" refers not to Joshua, but to a third party.[80] First, he argues that one would expect the addition of the article and the second person if Joshua were to be identified (i.e. "You are the man"). Second, the narrative construction איש + a personal name + שמו only makes sense if האיש is taken to refer to a third party.[81] Third, when

---

77. Rose, *Zemah*, 57; cf. Petersen, *Zechariah 1–8*, 275. Contra Davis, "Reclothing," 257; Baldwin, *Zechariah*, 137; Merrill, *Zechariah*, 197.

78. E.g. Jer 13:18; cf. Song 3:11.

79. Rose, *Zemah*, 59.

80. Ibid., 125–26. See also Pola, *Priestertum*, 245–46.

81. Rose, *Zemah*, 126, notes that if it was a name change, or the giving of a new name, that it would be usual to mention both names (e.g. Gen 17:5, 15; 32:29; Dan 1:7). Cf. McComiskey, "Zechariah," 3:1113: "Zechariah's reference here to 'a man'

this construction is used and the name is a noun or adjective, or is not a real personal name, the attention is focused on a particular characteristic of the person that finds expression in the name.[82] Hence, rather than being the Shoot, for the purposes of this symbolic action, Joshua represents the Shoot.

There are seven descriptions of the Shoot in the oracle. First, as we have just seen, the Shoot is a man. This suggests that the Shoot of Jeremiah was a known and hoped for figure in Zechariah's day, and that the Shoot is to be interpreted against this background.

Second, there is a play on the Shoot's name in the description ומתחתיו יצמח. The same verbal form יצמח occurs in Gen 2:5 and Job 5:6 to refer to growth from the ground.[83] The difficulty in this description is the expression ומתחתיו (lit. "from beneath him"). Who will the Shoot shoot up from beneath? It is generally taken to refer to the Shoot himself; the ESV translation, for instance, reads: "he will branch out from his place." However, it is not exactly clear what this means. It seems significant that the related expression תחתיו occurs 97 times in the Hebrew Bible, and in well over 80 of these instances it refers to a king's son taking his father's place as king (e.g. 2 Sam 10:1; 2 Chr 1:8). It may be that the Shoot will replace Joshua in some sense as he takes the crown that is now on Joshua's head. More likely, given the background of the Shoot in Jeremiah where the Shoot will "shoot up" (אצמיח) for David (Jer 33:15), is the suggestion that "from beneath him he will shoot up" is a way of indicating that the Shoot will come from the line of David.[84] In the context of this symbolic action, the sense may be that the Shoot will be a legitimate descendant of David, unlike Joshua, who simply represents the Shoot.[85]

---

leads us to expect him to be one who stands apart from the activity narrated in this text. This makes it unlikely that it refers to Joshua, who by virtue of his symbolic role is already a part of the events this text describes."

82. Rose, *Zemah*, 127, cites two places where this refers to a future figure: 1 Chr 22:9–10 and 1 Kgs 13:2.

83. The other two occurrences are in 2 Sam 10:5 and 19:5 where it refers to the growth of a beard.

84. Meyers and Meyers, *Zechariah 1–8*, 356, 71, also see the parallel with Jeremiah, arguing that this expression "represents a kind of commentary on Jer 33:17," reflecting the fact that David will never lack a successor to sit on his throne. Pola, *Priestertum*, 252, believes this phrase is connected to Ps 132:17 and points to a conception of kingship that is oriented towards David. This is certainly true, but it seems that Jeremiah is in the immediate background.

85. So Mackay, *Zechariah*, 138.

The third description says that the Shoot "will build the temple of Yahweh," a task that is repeated in Zech 6:13a.[86] This feature, in the light of 4:6–10 where Zerubbabel is said to build Yahweh's house, has led many to conclude that the Shoot is to be identified with Zerubbabel. However, this raises a number of major interpretational difficulties, as will be seen. An alternative identification will be offered shortly.

The fourth description of the Shoot is that "he will bear majesty." While הוד can simply mean "glory" or "honour" (e.g. Ps 8:2; Zech 10:3), when it is used in connection with a king, including Yahweh, it is best translated "majesty."[87] In Jer 22:18 it refers to the majesty of king Jehoiakim, and since this passage is in the background of Zech 6:12–13, with its reference to the Shoot, this meaning seems certain here.

Several scholars propose that in Zech 6:13, Zechariah is speaking to Zerubbabel and Joshua in turn.[88] So, "[Zerubbabel] will build the temple of Yahweh, and [Joshua] will bear majesty, and [Zerubbabel] will sit and rule upon his throne, and [Joshua] will be a priest upon his throne, and the counsel of peace shall be between them both." This phrase would then be descriptive of Joshua as high priest, rather than the Shoot. However, it seems very strained to argue that such a conversation was occurring between Zechariah, Joshua, and Zerubbabel. If such a conversation took place, one would expect the speakers to be more explicitly identified. The most natural way of taking the pronouns in this verse is to see all of them as referring back to and being descriptive of the Shoot.

Fifth, it is stated "he will sit and rule upon his throne." While Rose questions whether the verb משל is appropriate for describing the rule of a king (as opposed to מלך), C. and E. Meyers note that it is used of David, Solomon, and Hezekiah, monarchs whose kingdoms extended beyond the borders of Judah, and that Yahweh's rule is similarly denoted by משל.[89] Regarding the phrase "sit…upon his throne," Rose has no doubts that this is the usual description of a king in office (e.g. 1 Kgs 1:46; 16:11), noting that in the context it is "abundantly clear that צמח is indeed a royal figure."[90] Boda observes that the only other place in the Hebrew Bible where the combination "sit…rule…throne" appears is

---

86. See the comments on this repetition in §4.5.1, above.

87. E.g. 1 Chr 29:25; Pss 21:5 (MT 21:6); 45:3 (MT 45:4); 96:6; 104:1; 111:3; Jer 22:18. Note Petitjean, *Oracles*, 294–96 (cited by Rose, *Zemah*, 129), who criticizes those who minimize the royal connotations here.

88. E.g. Ackroyd, "Zechariah," 649; Jones, *Commentary*, 92.

89. E.g. Isa 40:10; Pss 22:29; 59:14; 1 Chr 29:12. Meyers and Meyers, *Zechariah 1–8*, 360.

90. Rose, *Zemah*, 130.

Jer 22:30, the passage that denies these things to Jehoiachin just before the promise of the Shoot.[91] This clearly connects this description with kingly rule.

It is disputed whether the sixth description should be translated "he will be a priest upon his throne" or "a priest will be upon his throne." Is this a further description of the Shoot who sits on the throne that was mentioned in the previous phrase, or is it another figure, generally understood as Joshua, sitting on a second throne? A majority of scholars holds the second view on the basis that Zech 6:13 refers to two people and that Zechariah is developing the thought of Jer 33:17–22 which promises a Levitical priest along with the Shoot.[92]

However, a significant minority of scholars believes that the Hebrew syntax points to it being a further description of the Shoot, with the initial *waw* consecutive continuing the subject from the previous clauses.[93] Rose notes the lack of specificity with reference to the description of the priest: "The absence of the article should make us suspicious of a simple identification of the figure called כהן with Joshua, the high priest."[94] In addition, V. M. Jauhiainen notes "the fact that vv. 12–13 first mention Zemah and then go on to tell what he will do (…a total of five third masculine singular imperfective verbs whose subject is Zemah) would lead one to think that the immediately following verb in the same form (והיה) also has Zemah as its subject."[95] As noted above, a decision about the interpretation of this description is closely connected to our understanding of the next one.

Seventh, and finally, the oracle states: "a counsel of peace will be between the two." These two figures are generally understood as the Shoot and the priest of the previous phrase. However, if the priest is understood to be the Shoot, rather than introducing another individual, then who is the second member of this duo? A significant number of scholars interprets the phrase to mean that the two roles of priest and king will merge in the person of the Shoot.[96] Often, on this interpretation,

91. Boda, *Commentary*, 340 n. 25.

92. Note Meyers and Meyers, *Zechariah 1–8*, 362: "The text is explicit in stating that peaceful harmony will exist between *two* individuals."

93. See further Davis, "Reclothing," 260; Baldwin, "Ṣemaḥ," 96; Barker, "Two Figures," 44; McComiskey, "Zechariah," 3:1116; Block, "Servant," 36. Cf. Kline, *Glory*, 223, who says, "The only warranted translation of *wĕhāyâ kōhēn* in v. 13d is: 'and he shall be a priest'."

94. Rose, *Zemah*, 60.

95. Jauhiainen, "Turban," 509.

96. So, Keil, "Zechariah," 300; Moore, *Zechariah*, 98; Unger, *Zechariah*, 114; Hengstenberg, *Christology*, 295; Baldwin, *Zechariah*, 137; Calvin, "Zechariah,"

"a counsel of peace" is understood as the harmony of these two roles as they are established in the one person. While popular, this interpretation seems to strain the natural meaning of "the two," as it more naturally refers to individuals rather than roles. Furthermore, the "counsel of peace" better describes the result of this union, more than the nature of it.[97] That is, the counsel between these two individuals will bring peace, or well-being, to the community.[98]

Ancient scholars and several modern ones offer another interpretation to overcome these difficulties.[99] They suggest that the second figure is Yahweh himself. While it may be argued that Yahweh as a subject is too far away from the reference to "the two," if Yahweh is also the subject of "his throne," then this brings Yahweh as a subject into a position in the sentence that more readily identifies him as the second figure.[100] In this case, what is being said is that the coming of the Shoot to rule from Yahweh's throne will issue in peace for the community as Yahweh and the Shoot rule together. There are similarities in this presentation with Pss 2 and 110. In Ps 2, Yahweh installs his king "on Zion, my holy hill" (Ps 2:6). The place from which the anointed king rules is Yahweh's. In addition, the joint reign of Yahweh and his anointed king results in blessing for those who take refuge in him (Ps 2:12). Similarly, in Ps 110, the joint reign of Yahweh and his king results in blessing for Yahweh's people with the king's enemies overthrown.[101] Significantly for the present purposes, the king of Ps 110 is also identified as a priest (Ps 110:4): "The LORD has sworn and will not change his mind, 'You are a priest forever after the order of Melchizedek'." The Psalms therefore provide support for this interpretation, which understands the Shoot as Yahweh's

160; Heater, *Zechariah*, 55; Bentley, *Building*, 153; Kaiser, *Micah–Malachi*, 358; Tidiman, *Zacharie*, 150; McComiskey, "Zechariah," 3:1116; Mackay, *Zechariah*, 140; Webb, *Zechariah*, 109.

97. Many scholars compare this with the phrase "the chastisement that made us whole" in Isa 53:5, which is a genitive of effect. See, for example, the discussion in Rose, *Zemah*, 65.

98. As Rose (ibid., 65 n. 66) rightly comments, this phrase "cannot be taken as evidence for a rivalry between Zerubbabel and Joshua or king and priest."

99. So Pusey, *Zechariah*, 144–45; Baron, *Zechariah*, 201–2; Higginson, "Zechariah," 793; Kline, *Glory*, 223–24; Jauhiainen, "Turban," 509. The ancient scholars cited by Hengstenberg, *Christology*, 1000, are Jerome, Cocceius, Vitringa, and Reuss.

100. Yahweh is therefore identified three times: twice as the owner of the temple, and once as the owner of the throne that the Shoot shall sit on.

101. While later than Zechariah, 1 Chr 29:23 and 2 Chr 9:8 also speak of the king being seated on the throne of Yahweh.

agent who rules on earth to bring peace to the community. The implicit contrast is with the kings of the past who have ruled without regard for Yahweh and brought destruction on the community.[102] If "the two" are Yahweh and the king, then it allows for the possibility of the previous phrase being translated "he will be a priest on his throne."

These last two descriptions are clearly significant in determining the nature of the Shoot. However, their interpretation is difficult. Thankfully, their meaning does not unduly impact the question of the identity of the Shoot in Zechariah, since there is enough given in the other five descriptions (and Zech 3) to provide guidance. The notion of the Shoot being a priest will be discussed again (in section 7 of this chapter) in the light of some further themes of the Hebrew Bible. It will also be discussed (in section 3 of Chapter 7) with the broader context of the Davidic hope of the book of Zechariah in view.

4.5.4. *A Memorial Established (Zechariah 6:14–15)*

> [14] "And the crown will be a memorial in the temple of Yahweh to Helem, Tobijah, Jedaiah, and to the grace of the son of Zephaniah. [15] And the ones who are far off shall come and build in the temple of Yahweh. And you will know that Yahweh of hosts has sent me to you. And it will come to pass if you diligently obey the voice of Yahweh your God." (author's translation)

The key to the ongoing significance of the crowning of Joshua is found in these verses. After being placed on the head of Joshua, the crown is to be placed in the temple as a memorial. It is not uncommon for an object to be designated the role of memorializing a person, object, or event.[103] We have already seen this in Zech 3, where both the priesthood and the inscribed stone placed before Joshua function as signs of the coming Shoot, who in his coming would remove the iniquity of the land in a single day and bring in the day of peace and prosperity. It is significant that both of these reminders are concerned with the coming Shoot and his rule. It is difficult to know whether this memorial crown is *for* the exiles, or *of* them, and scholars are divided.[104] The decision largely depends on the identity of the Shoot.[105]

---

102.   Note Jauhiainen, "Turban," 509–10: "The עצת שלום is between Yahweh and Zemah and is thus set in stark contrast to the relationship between Yahweh and the wicked king, who brought about the exile."

103.   E.g. Exod 13:9; 28:12, 29; Num 10:10; 31:54.

104.   The prefix ל on the names could be understood in both senses (e.g. Exod 12:14; cf. 28:12). Those who argue that the crown or crowns were memorials *of* these exiles include Petersen, *Zechariah 1–8*, 275; Floyd, *Minor Prophets*, 405.

The oracle continues with the promise that "the ones who are far off shall come and build in the temple of Yahweh." There is debate over the identity of these people. The phrase "the ones who are far off" clearly refers to the Israelite exiles in Ezra 6:12, Est 9:20, and Dan 9:7. However, Zechariah also envisages the nations sharing in the blessings of Israel, as do the "former prophets."[106] Isaiah envisages the nations inquiring of the root of Jesse (Isa 11:10), and also of the nations coming to the temple (Isa 56:4–7) and bringing their offerings (Isa 60:6–7). Zechariah's contemporary, Haggai, also speaks of the nations contributing their treasures to the temple (Hag 2:6–9). It is difficult to make a decision between Jewish exiles and the nations, and both groups may indeed be covered by the phrase. It may be significant that these ones who are far off are not said actually to build the temple, but to build *in* the temple (בהיכל).[107] This suggests that the temple structure is envisaged as having been completed, and these people shall contribute to the furnishing of the temple, as pictured in Isaiah and Haggai above.

As in Zech 4:9, the completion and furnishing of the temple is linked to the authenticity of the prophet Zechariah's ministry (cf. 1:16; 2:9, 11). However, a conditional statement is added: "And it will come to pass if you diligently obey the voice of Yahweh your God." This is sometimes understood as a later addition to explain why Zechariah's expectations for Zerubbabel to be installed as king were unfulfilled, namely, because the people did not obey the voice of Yahweh.[108] However, this conditionality may simply be understood as another expression of Deuteronomic theology (cf. 1:3, 16–17; 3:2).[109] The completion of the temple and the coming of the Shoot are conditional on obedience. However, there is also an unconditionality inherent in the promises of Yahweh, an unconditionality that Zechariah staked his reputation on, as seen in way that the completion of the temple would authenticate his ministry. As noted before, this blend of conditionality and unconditionality has an important

---

Those who argue that it was a memorial *for* them include Keil, "Zechariah," 300; Ollenburger, "Zechariah," 788.

105.   If the crown is understood as a memorial for the exiles, then it may suppose that Zechariah expected the arrival of the Shoot within their lifetime. Scholars do not always recognize this.

106.   E.g. Isa 2:1–3; 49:6; Zech 2:11 (MT 2:15); 8:20–23; 9:10. Cf. Gen 12:3; 22:17–18.

107.   ב is being used spatially, to indicate where the building is taking place, not what is being built (cf. v. 14).

108.   So, e.g., Laato, *Star*, 206.

109.   Ackroyd, "Zechariah," 650, notes this as a possible allusion to Deut 28:1.

rhetorical function.[110] The effect is to challenge the community to trust the promise of Yahweh that they have heard, and diligently to obey his voice.

4.6. *The Identity of the Shoot*

Having closely examined the text of Zech 3 and 6, the various options for the Shoot's identity can now be assessed. While exegeting these chapters, the impossibility of Joshua being identified as the Shoot has already become evident. The syntax, Joshua's lack of Davidic ancestry, and the clear distinction between Joshua and the Shoot in ch. 3 prohibits this. Alternatively, a majority of scholars holds the view that Zerubbabel is the Shoot.[111] Boda is a recent proponent of this view. He takes the absence of any reference to Zerubbabel as an indication that Zerubbabel was not in fact present in Jerusalem.[112] Instead, the crowning of Joshua is a sign that Zerubbabel will soon arrive and confirm the prophetic word, and rebuild the temple.[113] Boda states the chief grounds for identifying Zerubbabel with the Shoot: "Twice it is claimed that this *ṣemaḥ* will 'build the temple of the Lord' (6:12–13), an activity linked to Zerubbabel in the oracle in 4:6b–10a as well as the tradition of the books of Haggai and Ezra."[114]

Further support for this identification is found in Zerubbabel's Davidic ancestry, and the background of Jeremiah where the coming of the Shoot is the answer to the disaster that was to fall on the Davidic line as announced in Jer 22. Boda understands Zechariah to be here indicating that Zerubbabel is the one promised by Jeremiah who will rebuild [*sic?*] the land and restore the house of David.[115] Given this, Boda goes on to identify the two figures of Zech 6:13 as most likely being Joshua and Zerubbabel, the latter of which has not yet returned from Babylon.[116]

110.   See further Millar, *Deuteronomy*, 55–62.
111.   E.g. Mitchell, "Zechariah," 104; Rignell, *Nachgesichte*, 218–42; Merrill, *Zechariah*, 197; Conrad, *Zechariah*, 126–27; Floyd, *Minor Prophets*, 405–6.
112.   Boda, *Commentary*, 336.
113.   Ibid., 335. Boda believes that two crowns were made to symbolize the endurance of the royal and priestly lines. Joshua is only crowned with one of the crowns.
114.   Ibid., 338. Compare with Floyd, *Minor Prophets*, 405: "In view of the fact that Zerubbabel has previously been identified as the builder of the temple (4:9), he must be the one like a 'branch,' whose role is defined by the prophet's dramatic act."
115.   Boda, *Commentary*, 340–41. Boda presumably means restoring the land and rebuilding the Davidic house.
116.   Ibid., 341.

Hence, Boda understands this oracle as functioning to assure the priestly house that they will have a key role in the Davidic court, and also to remind them that the royal line will have pre-eminent authority and responsibility. The two crowns (on Boda's reading) that are given to the exiles will function as symbolic reminders of this prophetic action, and they are to keep the crowns in safekeeping because, Boda believes, the temple has not yet been constructed.

While there are variations on this interpretation, it represents a recent attempt to explain the final form of the text with Zerubbabel as the Shoot. However, there are a number of major interpretative difficulties with it. First, there is absolutely no evidence that Zerubbabel ever bore majesty, or sat and ruled on Yahweh's throne—two designations of the Shoot. Furthermore, if the phrase "he will be a priest on his throne" is a further description of the Shoot, this makes it even less likely to refer to Zerubbabel. If Zechariah is identifying Zerubbabel as the Shoot, then the failure of his prophecy at this point must raise serious questions about his authenticity, especially in the light of his comment that with these things happening, "you will know that Yahweh of hosts has sent me to you." Boda seems to suggest that Zechariah envisaged that, as the Shoot, Zerubbabel would only restore the Davidic line. However, the descriptions of the Shoot go far beyond this, as has been demonstrated.[117] If Zechariah understood Zerubbabel to be the Shoot, his prophecy here clearly failed. Given the way that false prophecy is criticized elsewhere in the book of Zechariah (e.g. 10:2; 13:2–6), why then did Zechariah's prophecy continue to be treated as authoritative within the community? This point has not been given due consideration by those who consider Zerubbabel to be the Shoot.

A second problem, which is obscured by Boda, is the fact that the crown is said to be a memorial *in* the temple of Yahweh.[118] Presumably the crown is for the coming Shoot, since the crown is a symbol of his kingship. If the crown is being kept for the coming Shoot who will build the temple, how is it that the crown can be placed in this same temple until the Shoot comes? If Zerubbabel is the Shoot, the temple clearly will not be built until he arrives.[119]

---

117. Tollington, *Tradition*, 173–75, also downplays the royal connotations of these descriptions.

118. Boda, *Commentary*, 342, says: "The four men are to keep the crowns in safekeeping because the temple has not yet been constructed." However, the text says that the crown will be "in the temple of Yahweh."

119. Boda avoids this difficulty by arguing that the crown does not represent the coming Shoot, but the ongoing relationship between the priesthood and the royal line. My exegesis does not sustain this interpretation.

Third, if we consider the identity of the Shoot in the light of the rest of the book of Zechariah, in Zech 3 we saw the coming of the Shoot would usher in the day of peace and prosperity. This day never arrived, even though the temple was completed by the time the book reached its final form. Similarly, in 9:8 Yahweh says: "Then I will encamp at my house as a guard, so that none shall march to and fro; no oppressor shall again march over them, for now I see with my own eyes." Significantly, ch. 9 envisages the future king coming to Jerusalem *after* the construction of the temple (9:9), and bringing the age of peace and prosperity. If Zerubbabel is the Shoot who will build the temple, how can these other passages that speak of him arriving after the construction of the temple and ushering in a day of peace and prosperity be accounted for?

All these factors make the identification of the Shoot as Zerubbabel in the final form of the book incongruous. Whether Zechariah ever made this identification in an earlier form of the text is purely speculative.[120] While a case can be made that he did, it is clear that it cannot sit as a legitimate reading of the text in its final form.

An alternative explanation is that the Shoot is an eschatological figure, beyond Zerubbabel, who will come and reign as king and so fulfil the hopes of Jeremiah and the prophets. In 3:8–10, we saw that the coming of the Shoot was set for a future day, an eschatological day. In 6:9–15, the use of the same Shoot terminology as Jeremiah and ch. 3 also suggests that the final form of Zechariah looks beyond Zerubbabel for the fulfilment of the prophecy concerning the Shoot.[121] Rose and Pola have recently put forward this view.[122]

Pola believes that the act of crowning Joshua and then depositing the crown in the temple is an act that honours the Zion-oriented contributions of the exiles, but also is meant to remind Yahweh of the so

---

120.   Suggestions of layers in the text that come from before and after the temple reconstruction, such as given by Laato, *Star*, 204–5, ultimately fail to explain the meaning of the final form of the text.

121.   The expression "days are coming" in Jer 33:14 looks to the eschatological future.

122.   For the same identification, see also Baldwin, "Ṣemaḥ," 93–97, and *Zechariah*, 136–37; Cook, *Apocalypticism*, 134–35; R. Nurmela, *Prophets in Dialogue: Inner-Biblical Allusions in Zechariah 1–8 and 9–14* (Åbo: Åbo Akademi University Press, 1996), 65; Webb, *Zechariah*, 107–11; Curtis, *Steep*, 146. Note Childs, *Introduction*, 478: "Wellhausen's argument that originally Zerubbabel was the recipient of the crowning has been followed by many modern commentators…but even if this were the case, this level of the tradition has been completely eliminated (cf. the LXX). Joshua's crowning now functions symbolically to foreshadow the coming of the future messianic figure of the 'Branch'."

far unfulfilled prophecy of Jeremiah and his school. The crown is no ephemeral requisite, but a memorial for Yahweh to bring about the Shoot: "With the depositing of the crown in the temple, and also within the frame of the priesthood and the high priest, the expected ruler to come is symbolically (מוֹפֵת, 3:8) and in a hidden way present in the temple."[123] Later Pola says, "While in Zechariah 3:8 the צֶמַח is already secretly present in the association of priests, the crown deposited in the temple in Zechariah 6:12ff. additionally stands for the hidden yet actual experiential presence of the צֶמַח in the temple."[124] Hence, Pola understands the crown in the temple as representing the presence of the future king hidden in the temple, and within the company of the priests. Elsewhere he says, somewhat enigmatically: "The 'servant shoot' is already present in the temple and its priesthood in a mystical sense."[125] However, while Pola rightly sees the Shoot as a future figure, he has over-realized Zechariah's expectations for the Shoot. The crown does not represent the Shoot "already present in the temple and in its priesthood in a mystical sense," but it was deposited in preparation for the coming of the future king to the temple (cf. Mal 3:1). The priesthood certainly anticipated the coming of the future king as they performed the cultic rituals, but the expectation was for something greater when the Shoot arrived. The Shoot is future and anticipated, not present and hidden.

An apparent difficulty in identifying the Shoot as a future figure is the repeated statement in Zech 6:12–13 that he will build the temple of Yahweh. This difficulty is felt more acutely if one is convinced that Zechariah identified Zerubbabel as the Shoot at some point. For the first readers of the final form of the book, for whom it was evident that Zerubbabel was not the Shoot, they would clearly have needed to have understood this temple to be a different construction to Zerubbabel's temple— but what exactly? Rose offers a couple of alternatives. First, noting that the Hebrew בנה covers a range of nuances including "rebuild," "continue building," "finish building," or "add to present construction," Rose suggests that the temple which the Shoot will build could be an addition to the same building that Zerubbabel had finished, or a new structure in addition to the existing one.[126] A second suggestion is that it could refer to an eschatological temple.[127] Davis offers a third view:[128] since בית

---

123. Pola, *Priestertum*, 255 (author's translation).
124. Ibid., 261 (author's translation).
125. Pola, "Form," 165.
126. Rose, *Zemah*, 138. Compare van der Woude, "Serubbabel," 151; Cook, *Apocalypticism*, 136 n. 48.
127. Rose, *Zemah*, 138. Rose is rather unclear at this point, and does not develop this suggestion in any detail. Curtis, *Steep*, 146, believes "it is not the Zerubbabel

is used on a number of occasions to refer to the community of Yahweh's people (e.g. Num 12:7; Jer 32:7; Hos 8:1), he suggests that here היכל יהוה is being used for the first time to convey the same metaphor, namely, the community of Yahweh's people.[129]

Before considering these alternatives, it is worth noting that Zech 6:12–13 is not a quotation of ch. 4. The closest statement to Zerubbabel building the temple is 4:9: "The hands of Zerubbabel have laid the foundation of this house (הבית), and his hands will finish it." The statement in ch. 6 is quite different, and uses different terminology for the temple: "[The Shoot] will build the temple (את־היכל) of Yahweh."[130] While the vocabulary is different, too much must not be made of this.[131] My exegesis suggests that the temple in 6:14–15 is the contemporary temple, and the same vocabulary is used in 6:12–13. Furthermore, in 8:9, היכל is used in parallel with בית to refer to the contemporary temple.

The proposal of Davis and others that the temple that the Shoot will build is the community of the people of Yahweh is an attractive possibility. There are places where a close connection between Yahweh's house and the community is evident (e.g. 9:8). However, there is no other instance in Zechariah where they are used synonymously. Therefore, it seems unlikely from the wider and immediate contexts that the temple that the Shoot will build has become a metaphor for the community of Yahweh's people.

It is more likely that just as those whom Zechariah calls the "former prophets" speak of an eschatological temple (e.g. Isa 2:2–4; Jer 3:16–18; Ezek 40–42; Mic 4:1–5; Hag 2:7–9), so too Zechariah here speaks of the Shoot building a temple of this character, in contrast to the temple of

---

temple, or if so, it is a substantial enlargement or renovation of that temple, which is likely under the influence of the temple vision in Ezek 40–48," and later (p. 147) refers to it as "the eschatological temple." Note Meyers and Meyers, *Zechariah 1–8*, 356: "The building of this temple is a future and probably eschatological event." Also, Baldwin, "Ṣemaḥ," 96: "We conclude that the prophet had in mind a future temple; the very repetition suggests that he is not thinking of the temple completed in 516."

128.   Davis, "Reclothing," 257 n. 2.

129.   This is also suggested by Hengstenberg, *Christology*, 294; Bentley, *Building*, 152; Marinkovic, "Zechariah 1–8," 101; Mackay, *Zechariah*, 138.

130.   Of the five instances of היכל in Zechariah, four occur in 6:12–15. The other is 8:9.

131.   Rose, *Zemah*, 138, following van der Woude, "Serubbabel," 151, suggests that the reference to a different temple may account for the different vocabulary used here to refer to the temple building: היכל יהוה rather than בית (cf. 1:16; 3:7; 4:9). See the criticism of van der Woude by Laato, *Josiah*, 249.

Zerubbabel.[132] Zechariah 14 envisages a future temple in Jerusalem that is of a different character to the temple of Zerubbabel. It is a temple that survives the eschatological battle. No longer will the holiness of Yahweh be confined to it, but Yahweh's holiness will spill out into Jerusalem and the whole region of Judah (14:21). It is a temple that results from the death of the coming eschatological king, as will be seen (12:10; 13:7).

Since there is this wider hope for an eschatological temple expressed by those whom Zechariah calls "former prophets," and elsewhere in Zechariah, it is only natural that the building of this eschatological temple is attached to the hope for a future Davidic king, since temple-building is the task of a Davidide, as has been noted.

In conclusion, the final form of the text looks beyond Zerubbabel to the eschatological king promised by the "former prophets." I concur with Rose:

> The view which considers Zemah to refer to an unidentified future figure can deal with the details of the portrait of Zemah in a much more satisfactory way… [T]he prophet Zechariah pointed the people of Jerusalem to look to the future, when better things would come, including a ruler who would truly build the temple. The choice of the name Zemah implied that Zerubbabel was not that ruler.[133]

This oracle functions to shift the readers' focus away from the present historical reality to a future day.[134] The structure of the passage, which

---

132.   Note also McComiskey, "Zechariah," 3:1114: "The time of the appearance of the Branch is indefinite and does not seem to be part of the community's immediate expectation. This fact, coupled with the urgency to complete the temple that permeates this book, places the *hêkal* (temple) that the Branch builds outside the purview of the community." Others who suggest it is an eschatological temple include Kaiser, *Micah–Malachi*, 358, and G. K. Beale, *The Temple and the Church's Mission: A Biblical Theology of the Dwelling Place of God* (NSBT 17; Leicester: Apollos, 2004), 113, who argues that the prophets speak of "a greater temple with a greater glory than a mere physical one, not only expanding to encompass all of Jerusalem…but the entire earth."

133.   Rose, *Zemah*, 140–41. The same conclusion is reached by Cook, *Apocalypticism*, 135: "Rather than elevating a contemporary figure, either Zerubbabel or Joshua, the text looks forward to the coming of a future Davidide, the Branch." Also Tollington, *Tradition*, 172: "[Zechariah] appears to have no specific individual in mind but uses the [צמח] motif as a typological identification for the ruler in the new age that Yahweh will inaugurate."

134.   It is clear from other writings that there was a measure of dissatisfaction with Zerubbabel's Temple. For example, Ezra 3:12–13 recounts the mourning of the older men who could remember Solomon's temple upon seeing the foundation of Zerubbabel's temple. Daniel speaks of the desecration and destruction of

highlights the eschatological temple that the Shoot will build, supports this. Furthermore, the symbolic action of crowning the high priest looks forward to the king who will take up the crown. Before the Shoot comes, the crown in the temple acts as a memorial of the exiles and the hope that they had for his coming.[135]

4.7. *The Shoot and Forgiveness*

There is one further theme that throws light on the nature of the Shoot. O'Kennedy has recently demonstrated that forgiveness was an important theological issue for the post-exilic community in Jerusalem.[136] Since the prophets clearly connected the exile with the sin of the community, and in particular with the house of David, the cleansing from sin for the returned exiles would be connected with the restoration of both the houses of David—temple and king. Laato also notes this connection, arguing that since the collapse of the Davidic dynasty and the exile were directly regarded as Yahweh's punishment on sin, it was natural to connect the restoration of the Davidic dynasty with forgiveness.[137]

In this respect, one of the features associated with the coming of the Shoot that was noted in Zech 3:8 was the removal of the iniquity of the land in a single day. The cleansing of Joshua as high priest foreshadowed another greater cleansing that would accompany the coming Shoot. Furthermore, until the Shoot came, the priesthood would function as a sign of his coming as they carried out their priestly duties. Hence, ch. 3 hints that the Shoot might have some sort of priestly function in removing sins when he comes. The close connection between the priesthood and the Shoot in 6:13 has also been noted.

The connection of the future king and the priesthood is not unique to Zechariah. As has been noted, Ps 110 connects the future Davidic king

---

Zerubbabel's temple in Dan 8:11–14; 11:31; 12:11. For apocryphal works that deal with this theme, see R. T. Beckwith, "The Temple Restored," in *Heaven on Earth: The Temple in Biblical Theology* (ed. T. D. Alexander and S. Gathercole; Carlisle: Paternoster, 2004), 71–79 (75–79).

135.   Pola, *Priestertum*, 255, believes that the memorial was set up for Yahweh to remind him of his yet unfulfilled promise regarding the Shoot (cf. Ackroyd, *Exile*, 200).

136.   O'Kennedy, "Forgiveness," 410–22.

137.   Laato, *Star*, 239: "Zech 3:8–10 emphasizes that the sins would be removed from Israel when the promised Branch, the Messiah, comes. Until this time, the High Priest and his colleagues were signs in Israel. The atonement rituals performed at the Temple presaged the eschaton when sins would be finally removed."

with the priesthood of Melchizedek, not the tribe of Levi.[138] In this way, the future king from the line of David can be both king and priest. Psalm 132:17–18 also makes some interesting priestly associations with the future Davidic king: "There I will make a horn to sprout (אצמיח) for David; I have prepared a lamp for my anointed. His enemies I will clothe with shame, but on him, his crown will shine." Here the future king is a sprouting horn, which uses the verbal form of "Shoot." The crown that is on the anointed one is the same word that is used of the priest's mitre (e.g. Exod 29:6). Similarly the verb "will shine" (ציץ) is literally "will blossom" and the same verb is used of Aaron's staff in Num 17:8 (MT 17:23).[139] Jeremiah 30:21 also envisages a priestly dimension to the future Davidic ruler: "Their prince shall be one of themselves; their ruler shall come out from their midst; I will make him draw near, and he shall approach me, for who would dare of himself to approach me? declares the LORD."

Hence, the thought in Zech 3 and 6 that gives the coming Davidic ruler a priestly function is not unique. The basis for it is probably to be found in the life of David himself, who on several occasions acted as a priest. As Merrill notes:

> The strongest suggestion of Davidic royal priesthood occurs in 2 Samuel 6 (cf. 1 Chron. 15), which recounts the procession of the ark into Jerusalem from Kiriath-jearim, where it had been housed for a century or more. The entire enterprise was at the initiative of David and though the regular Aaronic order of priests and Levites was involved, David himself was in charge, leading the entourage and, clothed in priestly attire, offering sacrifices and issuing priestly benedictions.[140]

Similarly, David's son Solomon also offered sacrifices (1 Kgs 3:3–4, 15), prayed for (1 Kgs 8:22–26), and blessed the people (1 Kgs 8:14, 55–61). David's sons are also called "priests" (כהנים) in the list of his officials in 2 Sam 8:18. While Uzziah is often cited as an example of a king who is punished for taking over the priestly prerogatives, Merrill contends that Uzziah is not condemned for having assumed a priestly role in general,

---

138. Block, "Servant," 43, correctly notes that this passage attaches priestly prerogatives to the monarchy, rather than royal prerogatives to the priesthood and looks to the future in terms of the kind of kingship that existed in Jerusalem at the time of Abraham, the father of Israel.

139. It is also possible that Ps 118:26–27 envisages the entry of the king into the temple, who then performs a priestly ritual.

140. E. H. Merrill, "Royal Priesthood: An Old Testament Messianic Motif," *BibSac* 150 (1993): 50–61 (60).

but for the specific indiscretion of burning incense (cf. 2 Chr 26:18), specifically limited to the descendants of Aaron in Num 16:40.[141]

There is also a wider biblical tradition that may have contributed to the future Davidic king being understood as a priest. Several scholars have noted the sanctuary associations of Eden that establish Adam as the original priest-king. Dumbrell, for instance, notes how Ezek 28:13–14 conceives of Eden as a mountain sanctuary with the king of Tyre adorned with stones like those on the high priest's breastplate (cf. Exod 28:17–20).[142] Later, in Ezek 47:1–12, the temple is described in Edenic terms.[143] Dumbrell concludes: "By implication, the original inhabitant of the garden, Adam, is a decidedly priestly/kingly character. If Gen 1 emphasizes humankind's kingship, Gen 2 presents Adam as God's priest."[144]

This priestly kingship is later devolved upon the nation of Israel at Sinai. They are to be "a kingdom of priests and a holy nation" (Exod 19:6). As Alexander notes, the expression "a kingdom of priests" can also be translated "priestly kings."[145] Israel is saved (pictured as an act of creation in the song of Moses in Exod 15), to function as a new Adam. Like Adam, Israel is created to serve Yahweh in his sanctuary, this time the land of Canaan.[146] Yet also like Adam, the people of Israel sinned and were cast out of the sanctuary in the exile.

The way in which the Davidic kings acted as priests has already been noted, and this lends support to the translation of Zech 6:13 as "he will

---

141.　Merrill, "Royal Priesthood," 60–61: "The infraction was not that of a king functioning cultically, but of a king undertaking a cultic ministry limited to another order of priests."

142.　W. J. Dumbrell, *The Search for Order* (Grand Rapids: Baker, 1994), 25. G. K. Beale, "The Final Vision of the Apocalypse and Its Implications for a Biblical Theology of the Temple," in Alexander and Gathercole, eds., *Heaven on Earth*, 191–209 (197–99), observes ten features that hint that the Garden of Eden was the archetypal temple.

143.　Note also how Ps 78:69 compares the building of the sanctuary with the creation of the earth.

144.　Dumbrell, *Search*, 25. Note also Beale, *Temple*, 81: "Genesis 1–2 not only portrays Adam as a kingly gardener and watchman but does so in language that rings with the notion of worshipful obedience [ʿābad, šāmar]. Consequently…Adam is being portrayed as a priest in this task."

145.　T. D. Alexander, *From Paradise to the Promised Land: An Introduction to the Pentateuch* (2d ed.; Carlisle: Paternoster, 2002), 177.

146.　The land of Canaan is described in Edenic terms in Gen 13:10; Isa 51:3; Ezek 36:35; 47:12; Joel 2:3. Interesting also, in the light of the menorah vision of Zech 4, is the way that Edenic imagery permeated the tabernacle, particularly with the tree-like menorah. See further, Longman, *Immanuel*, 55–57.

be a priest on his throne."[147] It may be that the designation of the Shoot as a priest in 6:13 draws on this tradition of the priest-king, yet this wider tradition has been largely neglected in the study of Zechariah. Indeed, at this point in Zechariah it is unclear exactly how Zechariah envisaged the Shoot functioning as a priest to remove the iniquity of the land in a day. However, we shall see in chs. 9–14 that the future Davidic king has a key role in providing cleansing from sin. In light of the book as a whole, the case for understanding the future king as having a priestly function is strengthened.[148]

While we have seen that the crown is to be kept in the temple as a memorial, the purpose of placing the crown on the head of Joshua the high priest has not yet really been established. The background of cleansing and forgiveness for the sins that led to the exile may explain the significance of this. Psalm 89 speaks of the rejection of the king at the exile as a defiling of the crown: "But now you have cast off and rejected; you are full of wrath against your anointed. You have renounced the covenant with your servant; you have defiled his crown (נזרו) in the dust. You have breached all his walls; you have laid his strongholds in ruins" (Ps 89:38–40 [MT 89:39–41]).

As the high priest, Joshua was in a position to cleanse and sanctify objects that had become defiled. In the account of the consecration of Aaron and his sons in Exodus, a holy crown (נזר) is said to be put on Aaron's head: "And you shall set the turban on his head and put the holy crown on the turban" (Exod 29:6). While it is difficult to be certain, against the background of the purification rituals of the Torah, it may be that the crown that is made by Zechariah from the offerings of the returned exiles is placed on the head of the high priest in order to sanctify it. Having been sanctified, the crown that had symbolically been defiled by the exile is ready to be taken up again by the future righteous king when he comes. In the mean time, it is kept in the temple for safe-keeping as well as functioning as a memorial to the exiles. There may also be the thought that when the Shoot takes up the crown, he will not defile the crown as previous kings from the house of David had done. He will be holy enough to wear the crown without defiling it. While these

---

147. See further C. E. Armerding, "Were David's Sons Really Priests?," in *Current Issues in Biblical and Patristic Interpretation* (ed. G. F. Hawthorne; Grand Rapids: Zondervan, 1975), 75–86; H.-J. Kraus, *Theology of the Psalms* (Minneapolis: Augsburg, 1986), 111; Rooke, "Kingship," 187–98.

148. M. G. Kline, "The Structure of the Book of Zechariah," *JETS* 34 (1991): 179–93, argues from the structure of Zechariah that the theme of the "priest-king" is dominant. I agree with this, but disagree with elements of his structure.

ideas are not explicit in the text, they are natural connections given the background that closely associates the priesthood with cleansing in the temple. What is clear is that the symbolic action of crowning of the high priest anticipates the Davidic king who will come and build the eschatological temple.

4.8. *The Shoot and the Hope for the House of David*

Zechariah uses the term "Shoot" against the background of the earlier prophets Jeremiah, Isaiah, and Ezekiel. While Jeremiah is the only prophet to use the term to refer the future Davidic king outside Zechariah, the imagery is certainly used by Isaiah and Ezekiel to capture the idea of a future figure from the house of David who will restore the fortunes of Yahweh's people. This arboreal imagery captures the ideas of a new and humble beginning for the house of David, after its judgment, that has continuity with the past, and will grow into something magnificent.

While Rose believes that צמח is a future figure, his understanding of the meaning of this word as "vegetation, greenery, growth" leads him to contend that Zechariah used this term in contradistinction to Isaiah's arboreal imagery (Isa 11:1, 10).[149] Rose argues that Zechariah used the term to indicate that any hopes held for a future ruler are not to be sought in a "simple historical development," but through the direct intervention of God. Rose is quite elusive as to what he means by "simple historical development," but seems to be saying at least that the term צמח means that a future king will not come from the restored monarchy, but from God alone.[150] In a later article he is clearer: "To sum up: the point of the צמח imagery…is to indicate that not a simple historical continuity in the form of physical descent, but a special intervention by God will be the way in which future kingship will be guaranteed, a kingship with respect to which the role of 'David' will be more one of receiving than contributing to."[151]

Rose notes in support of his thesis the absence of any reference to David in Zech 6:9–15.[152] In other words, Rose argues that while Isaiah uses arboreal imagery to express the idea that there was still hope for the

149.   Rose, *Zemah*, 106.
150.   Ibid., 119–20.
151.   Rose, "Messianic," 179.
152.   Rose, *Zemah*, 130: "What is perhaps somewhat striking is the absence of anything that in one way or another may be associated with David or his house (for example why not 'the throne *of David*'?)"

restoration of the monarchy and for an active role for the Davidic dynasty in that restoration, he holds that Zechariah uses the term צמח to say that any hopes held for a future ruler will only come through the intervention of God, with no room for the input of the house of David. He thereby removes any idea of Davidic continuity from these passages.[153]

However, Rose has relied too much on the semantics of the word צמח and has not paid close enough attention to the context of both Zechariah and the earlier prophets at this point.[154] As was seen in the above treatment of Isaiah, Isaiah does not see an "active role" for the Davidic dynasty in its restoration if what is meant by an "active role" is a restoration of the glory of the monarchy from which the future king will come. The Davidic dynasty will fall under the judgment of Yahweh. However, the line of David is still important because of the promises made to David in 2 Sam 7. Isaiah envisages the future king being given by Yahweh not from a completely new dynasty, but from the judged stump or roots of the Davidic house. Indeed, one of the key aspects of the arboreal imagery is that it conveys a measure of continuity from past failure to future glory.

Rose is right to see that the צמח imagery "suggests that only a divine intervention can safeguard the future of the Davidic dynasty."[155] However, he makes a false dichotomy when he sets the input of the house of David against the action of Yahweh. The action of Yahweh in sending the Shoot does not necessarily bypass any contribution by the house of David. Rose's dichotomy means that the significant role that the house of David did play in the post-exilic period in rebuilding the temple, providing leadership, and supplying the line of seed from which the Shoot would come is effectively ignored. Furthermore, while it is true that there is no explicit reference to David in Zech 1–6, the descriptions of the Shoot in Zech 6 make it clear that Yahweh's covenant with David in 2 Sam 7:5–16 is on view, particularly the prerogative of constructing the temple and his right to the throne. The allusion to Jeremiah, where the Shoot will "spring forth" (Zech 6:12; cf. Jer 33:15), also supports the Davidic associations, as in Jeremiah it is explicit that the Shoot will spring forth for David (cf. Jer 12:5).[156] It was noted that the expression

153. Renz, "Review," 136, also makes this assessment of Rose.

154. Furthermore, the semantics of צמח, particularly in Ezek 17:9–10 and Hos 8:7, clearly do not favour Rose's case. Rose acknowledges this in his discussion (pp. 97–99), but still builds his argument regardless.

155. Rose, *Zemah*, 120.

156. I concur with Tollington, *Tradition*, 171: "It is unlikely that Zechariah chose the same motif independently of Jeremiah and therefore the probability is that he used צמח in the same way."

"from beneath him" in Zech 6:12 most likely expresses continuity with the house of David. Furthermore, Ps 132 connects the Shoot with the promises to David, which also gives the house of David, as descendants of David, a significant place:

> [11] The LORD swore to David a sure oath from which he will not turn back: "One of the sons of your body I will set on your throne. [12] If your sons keep my covenant and my testimonies that I shall teach them, their sons also forever shall sit on your throne"... [17] There I will make a horn to sprout (אצמיח) for David; I have prepared a lamp for my anointed. [18] His enemies I will clothe with shame, but on him, his crown will shine." (Ps 132:11–12, 17–18)

It is also worth noting that Rose bases his thesis only on Zech 1–6 and does not deal with chs. 7–14. What will be seen in this later part of the book is that Zechariah clearly envisages an ongoing place for the house of David. We must wait to see how this develops, but there are no indications to this point that the Shoot imagery is operating in a different way to Isaiah or Jeremiah. While there is a discontinuity in terms of judgment, continuity with the house of David is fundamental to the way that the Shoot image functions. It is this continuity that is essential to the promise in 2 Sam 7. The Shoot implies new growth, but a new beginning that is continuous with the past. Indeed, Zechariah drew on the terminology of Isaiah, Jeremiah, and Ezekiel to keep the hope for the house of David alive.

I must at this point also comment on the recent trend, as seen in Rose's monograph, not to translate צמח into English, but transliterate it to a proper name Zemah (or *ṣemaḥ*).[157] While agreeing that "Branch" is not the best translation of this term, simply to use the transliteration fails to convey any of the connotations that go with the imagery. "Shoot" is not only a legitimate translation, but also best captures in English the ideas, particularly of continuity, that lie behind Zechariah's use of the term צמח.

Let me summarize Zechariah's hope for the Shoot. In the vision of Zech 3, Joshua the high priest is cleansed and commissioned to serve in the new temple along with his fellow priests. The reinstitution of the priesthood functions as a sign of the coming Shoot and so too does an inscribed stone that is placed before Joshua. Zechariah 3 promises that, with the coming of the Shoot, the iniquity of the land will be removed in a single day and that the day of prosperity and abundance will arrive.

---

157. So Rose, *Zemah*, passim; Boda, *Commentary*, passim. This is also done by Keil, "Zechariah," 259–62, 300, who uses "*Tsemach*."

While many scholars challenge the literary integrity of the oracle of Zech 6 and offer interpretations that ultimately fail to address the final form of the text, it is possible to make sense of the text as it stands if the Shoot is understood to be the future Davidic king of prophetic expectation. Zechariah is told to take silver and gold from named returned exiles and make a composite crown and place it on the head of Joshua. Accompanying the crowning, Zechariah is to pronounce an oracle to Joshua that concerns the coming Shoot. The pronouncement makes it clear that the crowning of Joshua anticipates the crowning of the Shoot. The Shoot is a man who is a legitimate descendant of David who will build the temple of Yahweh. Furthermore, he will bear majesty as he sits and rules on Yahweh's throne as king. While Jer 33:14–22 suggests that the throne of the Shoot will be supported by a priest, we have also seen that a good case can be made for seeing the Shoot here as being identified as a priest with the joint rule of Yahweh and the Shoot ushering in wellbeing for the community of Yahweh's people. After announcing this promise, the crown was to be placed in the temple as a memorial to the exiles and their act performed in hope of the Shoot.

In this way, the crowning of Joshua and the accompanying oracle, coming immediately after Zechariah's night visions, shifts the readers' focus from the present historical reality to a future day, just as several of the visions have done. This oracle, like Zech 3, looks beyond the present circumstances to the day of the Shoot. Just as the vision in Zech 3 established the priesthood and the inscribed stone placed before Joshua as signs of the coming Shoot, so the actions of Zech 6 further raise the hope for the coming Shoot. This future was held out to Zechariah's readers as an encouragement to obey the voice of Yahweh their God until the Shoot should come.

Against the background of the sin that led to the exile and the forgiveness that would ultimately come with the Shoot, the act of placing the crown on the head of the high priest could also function to sanctify the crown in preparation for the coming of the Shoot. The placement of the crown in the temple as a memorial pushes the coming of the Shoot into the more distant future, to a time when the events surrounding the building of the temple under Zerubbabel and Zechariah's prophecies may have been forgotten. It seems very unlikely that the crowning was in any sense a coronation designed to give an enhanced position for the high priest. The crowning of the high priest was part of the symbolism of this action. The crown, which was a symbol of kingship, being placed on the head of the high priest, may point to the rule of the Shoot as both priest and king. The priest-king tradition that is found in other places in the

Hebrew Bible (e.g. Adam, Melchizedek, Israel, David, Solomon) is a neglected theme in the interpretation of this passage. It highlights the close association between the king and the temple and explains how the reconstruction of the temple under Zerubbabel would naturally raise the hope for a king to come.[158] In addition, if the Shoot is being described as a priest, it hints at how Yahweh will remove the sin of the land in a single day with his coming (Zech 3:9).

Given this, what can be concluded at this point about Zechariah's hope for the house of David? It has been demonstrated that neither Zech 3 nor 6 can sustain the view that Joshua was the Shoot. Furthermore, Joshua's lack of Davidic ancestry weighs against this identification, an important requirement given the background of Jeremiah, Isaiah, and Ezekiel. Neither was Zerubbabel envisaged as the one to take the throne. While Zerubbabel was of Davidic descent, and a temple builder, Zerubbabel never came close to the descriptions of the oracle in 6:12–13. Neither did he usher in the age of peace and prosperity pictured in 3:10. Moreover, Zerubbabel could not have been the Shoot, for the temple that he built had a key role to play in containing the crown for a time before the Shoot should come. The final form of Zechariah identifies the Shoot as a future ruler beyond Zerubbabel and beyond Zechariah's day.[159] Drawing on the imagery of the "former prophets," Zechariah used the term "Shoot" (צמח) to keep the Davidic hope alive and to push it into the future.

---

158. Note how as a priest-king Adam served in the sanctuary of Eden and Israel served in the sanctuary of Canaan (Exod 15:17; Ps 78:54; cf. Isa 51:3; Ezek 36:35).

159. I concur with Rose, *Zemah*, 141, that "the צמח oracles [in Zech 3 and 6] are not royalist, that is, they do not announce, encourage or instigate a restoration of the monarchy in the person of Zerubbabel."

Chapter 5

THE COMING KING

5.1. *Introduction*

Reading Zech 9–14, it quickly becomes evident that we are dealing with a different style of literature to the visions of chs. 1–6, and the narrative of chs. 7–8. For this and other reasons that were dealt with in the Introduction, the consensus of scholarly opinion has been that these chapters arose separately. Either as a reason for this opinion, or as a consequence thereof, many see a sea change in the hope expressed for the house of David between these different parts of the book of Zechariah. It is thought that the hope held for the Shoot in chs. 1–8 has been somewhat modified in chs. 9–14, generally because of the supposed failure of this earlier hope to eventuate under Zerubbabel. Some argue that the hope for the house of David has been modified in a "democratizing" direction, or that this section of Zechariah envisages the demise of the house of David with the direct rule of Yahweh himself replacing it. These views need to be closely assessed, especially if, as we have seen, the Davidic hope in Zech 1–8 is not tied to Zerubbabel.

5.2. *The King of Zechariah 9*

Rather than transforming the hope of Zech 1–8, it is my contention that Zech 9–14 restates and develops the hope that has already been seen. This begins with the hope for a coming Davidic king expressed implicitly and explicitly in Zech 9.

5.2.1. *Structure of Zechariah 9*

The extent of the unit beginning with Zech 9:1 is debated, but most scholars regard 10:1 as the start of a new unit, marked by the imperative "ask." This leads into the development of the theme of leadership in chs. 10–11. Zechariah 9:1–17 can be structured thematically as follows:

vv. 1–8   The restored land
vv. 9–10   The restored king
vv. 11–17   The restored people

The structural markers supporting the above division of Zech 9:1–17 include: the weak paragraph marker at the end of 9:8 in the MT; the sharp imperatives that begin 9:9; and the use of נם־את in 9:11, which shifts the topic from the king to what the coming of the king will mean for his people.

There are also structural links between these sections. So, while there is clearly a change in subject at Zech 9:9 with the imperatives to "rejoice" and "shout," there is also continuity from 9:8 as Yahweh continues to speak in the first person. While 9:11–17 deals with the theme of Yahweh's people, 9:11–13 continues to have Yahweh speaking in the first person. This then changes to the third person in 9:14–17 with four references to what Yahweh will do for his people. Similarly, while the נם־את of 9:11 functions as a transition, it also presupposes what has gone before.[1] Therefore, while ch. 9 can be divided thematically, it also functions as a coherent unit.

5.2.2. *The Restored Land (Zechariah 9:1–8)*

[1] An oracle. The word of Yahweh is against the land of Hadrach, and Damascus is its resting place, so to Yahweh is the eye of man and all the tribes of Israel. [2] And Hamath also, which borders on it. Tyre and Sidon, for it is very wise. [3] Tyre has built a fortification for herself and has heaped up silver as dust and gold as mud of the streets.

[4] Behold! The Lord will dispossess her and strike down her army in the sea, and she will be consumed by fire. [5] Ashkelon will see it and be afraid, and Gaza will tremble greatly; and Ekron, for her hope has been put to shame. A king from Gaza will perish, and Ashkelon will not be inhabited. [6] A bastard will dwell in Ashdod and I will cut down the pride of the Philistines. [7] I will remove its blood from its mouth, and its abominations from between its teeth; and, moreover, it will remain for our God. And it will be like a clan in Judah, and Ekron like a Jebusite.

[8] I will encamp at my house as a guard against the one passing through and returning, and an oppressor will not pass through them again. For now I have seen with my eyes. (author's translation)

Zechariah 9 begins with משא, generally translated "an oracle." Attempts to define this word etymologically tend to go in one of two directions: either it is understood as something weighty or burdensome, and hence

---

1. See further, Butterworth, *Structure*, 73, and Webb, *Zechariah*, 131.

משׂא is descriptive of a prophecy of doom;[2] or, it is understood along the lines of "lifting up" one's voice, hence it is a "pronouncement" or "proclamation."[3] Floyd, building on the work of Weis, argues that "prophetic books of the משׂא sort seem to be concerned with reinterpreting prophecies that have over time become problematic in some way."[4] However, as was argued earlier, in the treatment of chs. 1–8, there are no grounds for the presupposition that earlier prophecies had become problematic.[5] While chs. 9–14 deal with earlier prophetic material, so too do chs. 1–8, so this cannot be the distinctive feature of a משׂא. In a recent study, Boda concludes that it is a structural device that, rather than curtailing or transforming prophecy, introduces "the word of Yahweh" that renews prophecy along the lines of earlier prophecy.[6]

The oracle begins with judgment on several foreign cities. While most scholars look for contemporary historical events being reflected here so as to date the oracle, the lack of consensus demonstrates that this is probably not the best approach to interpreting the text. These cities are not chosen because of any contemporary threat that they posed. Rather, it seems that they have been listed because they were the traditional enemies of Israel and because their geography was significant in circumscribing the ideal land of Israel.[7] In support of this is the fact that none of these cities really posed a threat to Israel during the Persian period, or for that matter during the Babylonian or Assyrian periods, while prior to that

---

2. E.g. P. A. H. de Boer, "An Inquiry into the Meaning of the Term משׂא," in *Oudtestamentische Studiën* (ed. P. A. H. de Boer; Leiden: Brill, 1948), 197–214. R. B. Y. Scott, "The Meaning of *Maśśā᾿* as an Oracle Title," *JBL* 67 (1948): v–vi, suggests that it derived from the lifting up of the hand as "a solemn oath or prophetic curse."

3. See further M. H. Floyd, "The משׂא (*MAŚŚĀ᾿*) as a Type of Prophetic Book," *JBL* 121 (2002): 401–22.

4. Ibid., 422. Cf. R. D. Weis, "Oracle," *ABD* 5:28–29 (29): "Here a *maśśā᾿* is the prophet's response to a generalized complaint that God's intention expressed in the prior communication has not shown itself in human affairs as expected."

5. This view owes more to the presuppositions of Wellhausen than the text (see Chapter 1, §1.3).

6. M. J. Boda, "Freeing the Burden of Prophecy: *Maśśā᾿* and the Legitimacy of Prophecy in Zech 9–14," *Biblica* 87 (2006): 338–57 (356).

7. There is a geographical movement from north to south, beginning with Syria and moving to Phoenicia, Philistia, and finally to Judah. Cf. Hanson, *Apocalyptic*, 317: "The borders of that area are not arbitrarily set, but outline what ancient Israelite tradition held to be the ideal kingdom of the Jews." See also T. R. Hobbs, "The Language of Warfare in Zechariah 9–14," in *After the Exile: Essays in Honour of Rex Mason* (ed. J. Barton and D. J. Reimer; Macon: Mercer University Press, 1996), 103–28 (121).

time they had. The other significant fact concerning these cities is that under the reign of David, many of them were brought under his rule, or were favourable towards his empire. The evidence for this will now be surveyed.

In Syria, the capital Damascus and Hamath are mentioned (Zech 9:1–2a).[8] From the time of the Israelite settlement, Damascus was a threat to Israel. Significantly, under David it was subdued and incorporated into his empire (2 Sam 8:5–6), but then was lost under Solomon when Rezon captured it and proclaimed himself king (1 Kgs 11:24–25).[9] It continued to pose a threat to the northern borders of Israel throughout the monarchy until the first half of the eighth century, when Jeroboam II seems to have established it as a vassal of Israel (2 Kgs 14:25, 28). Damascus was defeated by the Assyrian king, Sargon II, in 720 B.C.E., and it then came under Babylonian control in 604 B.C.E.[10]

Hamath is never said to be hostile to Israel during the settlement. Instead, they gave gifts to David (2 Sam 8:9). Solomon later controlled it (2 Chr 8:4). The city must have again passed out of Israelite control because Jeroboam II is said to have restored Damascus and Hamath to Judah in 2 Kgs 14:28. Both cities eventually threw off this control and Hamath reached its greatest power at the beginning of the eighth century. However, by 720 B.C.E., the Assyrians had ravaged Hamath, and what remained was incorporated into their empire.[11]

In Phoenicia (Zech 9:2b–4), Tyre and Sidon are paired, though only the description of Tyre is elaborated upon. Tyre was never hostile towards Israel; in fact, the king of Tyre built houses for David (2 Sam 5:11; cf. 1 Chr 14:1) and Solomon (1 Kgs 9:11; cf. 2 Chr 2:3). As a trade port, it was quite a wealthy city, and it is probably this that gave it a reputation of pride in its own skill and ability (Zech 9:3–4). On account of this, Yahweh will bring her down: "The Lord will dispossess her and strike down her army in the sea, and she will be consumed by fire." However, this had largely occurred by the Persian period. After the Babylonian conquest of Jerusalem in 586 B.C.E., Nebuchadnezzar besieged Tyre for 13 years (ca. 585–573/2 B.C.E.), a siege that ended in a treaty with the royal Tyrian house residing in Babylon. But Tyre as a

---

8. The "land of Hadrach" in Zech 9:1 is not mentioned elsewhere in the Hebrew Bible. It appears to be a district (so Meyers and Meyers, *Zechariah 9–14*, 91–92; Petersen, *Zechariah 9–14*, 43).

9. Keil, "Zechariah," 324–25, neglects this fact when he argues on the basis of Num 34:1–12 that Damascus was never within the ideal boundary of Israel.

10. W. T. Pitard, "Damascus: Pre-Hellenistic History," *ABD* 2:5–7.

11. M.-L. Buhl, "Hamath," *ABD* 3:33–36.

power had been totally exhausted. We do not know as much about Sidon. While Nebuchadnezzar conquered it, during the Persian period it seems to have been an important administrative centre for the Persian Empire.[12]

Moving to the region of Philistia (Zech 9:5–7), it must be noted that the Philistines dominated the Palestinian seacoast in the twelfth and eleventh centuries, with their centre of power being a Pentapolis comprising Gaza, Ashkelon, Ashdod, Ekron, and Gath (cf. Josh 13:2–3). Four of these five cities are mentioned here. While the Philistines were initially vassals of Egypt, it seems that they gained their independence as Egypt declined in power. They had a reputation for being a strong military force, with iron weapons, chariots, and formidable fighters.[13] While they are cited as defining the borders of the territory of Judah (e.g. Josh 15:11, 46–45), they also threatened the Israelites from the time of the Judges until, significantly, David subdued them in the tenth century (2 Sam 5:17–25; 21:15–22). This defeat seems to have ended the Pentapolis, with each city operating independently after this time.[14] Many of these cities were subdued or destroyed in the Assyrian and Babylonian periods, and by the Persian period were certainly a spent force.[15]

Given the history of these cities, this oracle seems to envisage a restoration of the boundaries of the land as it was under King David. That the author had in mind the link with David is strengthened by three things: the mention of the Jebusites (Zech 9:7); Yahweh's statement, "I will encamp at my house" (9:8); and the reference to "all the tribes of Israel" (9:1). Each of these will now be dealt with.

The Jebusites were the inhabitants of Jerusalem before it was captured by David (2 Sam 5:6–9; 1 Chr 11:4–9). Although the city was taken, there is evidence that not all the Jebusites were annihilated. According to 2 Sam 24:18–24, David is said to have bought the threshing floor of Araunah the Jebusite.[16] This is supported by the reference in Zech 9:7 to Ekron being like a Jebusite in the context of the Philistines being a remnant ("it will remain for our God"). Hanson helpfully suggests that this is saying: "Israel's traditional enemies and rivals alike would be

---

12. P. C. Schmitz, "Sidon (Place)," *ABD* 6:17–18.
13. J. Bright, *A History of Israel* (3d ed.; London: SCM Press, 1981), 176, 185.
14. H. J. Katzenstein, "Philistines," *ABD* 2:326–28.
15. For details, see following articles: M. Dothan, "Ashdod," *ABD* 1:477–82; T. Dothan and S. Gitin, "Ekron," *ABD* 4:415–22; D. L. Esse, "Ashkelon," *ABD* 1:487–90; Katzenstein, "Philistines," 326–28; H. J. Katzenstein, "Gaza: Prehellenistic," *ABD* 5:912–15.
16. S. A. Reed, "Jebus," *ABD* 3:652–53 (53). Reed overlooks this reference to Zechariah in his article.

absorbed into a kingdom surpassing even that of David."[17] The idea of this kingdom encompassing the nations is not new; it was a feature of the coming of Yahweh to dwell in the midst of his people in Zech 2:11 (MT 2:15). Furthermore, the expression "encamp at my house" (9:8) also has strong tabernacle associations due to the use of the verb הנה. While בית is frequently used of the temple, it also refers to the tabernacle on six occasions.[18] Hence, there is the possibility that this picture of the future, where Yahweh will "camp" at his house, may also provide a subtle allusion to the reign of David, as it was only ever during this period that God's house was in a tent in Jerusalem.[19] Finally, the way that the oracle begins with a reference to "all the tribes of Israel" (9:1) seems to envisage the united kingdom at the time of David (and Solomon), something that is also reflected in the relationship between Judah and Ephraim in 9:10–13.[20]

This section finishes with Yahweh saying "I have seen with his own eyes." This could be understood as a further reference to Yahweh keeping watch over, or guarding, his people from his house.[21] Alternatively, it could function in a similar fashion to the phrase וירא אלהים את־בני ישראל in Exod 2:25 where the "seeing" of God invokes his memory of the covenant that he had made with his people (cf. Zech 9:11) and raising up Moses as a saviour (cf. Zech 9:9). This would provide a direct link with the next section, where the king comes bearing salvation.

While there have been numerous attempts to give this oracle either a pre-exilic date to reflect the time when these nations were a force to be reckoned with, or a date in the fourth to third centuries B.C.E. to reflect the campaign of Alexander the Great, none of these historical situations corresponds exactly with the text.[22] Furthermore, none of these readings adequately explains the present form of the text and particularly why it

17. Hanson, *Apocalyptic*, 319–20.

18. Judg 18:31; 19:18; 1 Sam 1:7, 24; 2 Sam 12:20; 1 Chr 9:23. See especially 2 Sam 12:20 with reference to David.

19. There is a reference to Yahweh encamping against Jerusalem in Isa 29:3, but this is with a view to besieging Jerusalem with the forces of Babylon, not to protecting Jerusalem from his house. It was the common practice of besieging armies to camp in tents.

20. Boda, *Commentary*, 420, helpfully traces this background to the references to Ephraim and Judah in Zech 9:9–13 and concludes: "Both north and south will return together to Zion to form a united kingdom under a Davidic monarch."

21. Petersen, *Zechariah 9–14*, 53; Webb, *Zechariah*, 130.

22. Cf. Meyers and Meyers, *Zechariah 9–14*, 92: "the particular sites and districts mentioned in Zech 9 do not reflect the geopolitics of the late sixth or fifth century." Similarly, Coggins, *Zechariah*, 65.

has been juxtaposed with an oracle that speaks of a king coming to deliver his people (Zech 9:9–10). Rather than looking to the contemporary historical situation, these cities were chosen for what they represented, namely, the extent of the kingdom at the time of David.[23] The message of the oracle is therefore that Yahweh is coming to re-establish the kingdom promised to David.[24] In doing so, the nations shall be judged and also incorporated into the people of God, as had been the case for the Jebusites in David's day. The coming of Yahweh to his house will mean the protection of his people, and the fulfilment of his promises.

5.2.3. *The Restored King (Zechariah 9:9–10)*

[9] Rejoice greatly, daughter of Zion! Shout, daughter of Jerusalem! Behold, your king will come to you. He is righteous and saved, humble and riding upon a donkey, upon a colt, the foal of a donkey. [10] I will cut off the chariot from Ephraim and the horse from Jerusalem, and the battle bow will be cut off, and he will speak peace to the nations. His rule will be from sea to sea, and from the river to the ends of the earth. (author's translation)

With the reclamation of the land, and the encamping of Yahweh at his house, the prophecy envisages the coming of the king to Jerusalem and exhorts the inhabitants of the city to "rejoice greatly" and "shout." This is a moment of great exuberance; Jerusalem's king is coming. The king is described as "your" king, that is, Jerusalem's king. The addition of the pronominal possessive pronoun suggests that this was not just any king, but the king that the inhabitants of Jerusalem were expecting, presumably on account of the Davidic dynasty tradition.[25]

The call for "daughter Zion" to "rejoice greatly" and "shout" recalls Zech 2:10 (MT 2:14), where the daughter of Zion is exhorted to sing and

---

23. Note Klausner, *Messianic*, 203: "Zechariah prophesies of a kingdom as extensive as was the kingdom of David in his time: it will reach from the Mediterranean to the Red Sea and from the River Euphrates to the limits of the land of Canaan."

24. Cf. Redditt, *Zechariah*, 102: "Zechariah 9–14 opened with a chapter of diverse literary genres depicting God's recapturing the old Davidic empire (9:1–8)." Also, Curtis, *Steep*, 169: "Yahweh reasserts Davidic empire for the postexilic context."

25. Cf. C. L. Feinberg, "Exegetical Studies in Zechariah," *BibSac* 100 (1943): 513–23 (518); F. d. T. Laubscher, "The King's Humbleness in Zechariah 9:9. A Paradox?," *JNSL* 18 (1992): 125–34 (130): "With the appeal to Zion in verse 9, the king, described idealistically here as צַדִּיק, is linked to the traditional Davidic dynasty."

rejoice because Yahweh is coming to dwell in her midst.[26] Mason notes several points in common between these passages: first, both fall in the context of judgment against the nations (2:8–9; cf. 9:1–8); second, the promise that Yahweh will come and dwell in the midst of his people in Zion implies the centrality of the temple in the new age, something that is seen throughout chs. 1–8 and here in 9:8; third, the notion that nations shall join themselves to Yahweh's people (2:11) is also found in 9:7.[27]

Another phrase similar to that of Zech 9:9 is found in Zeph 3:14: "Sing aloud, O daughter of Zion; shout, O Israel! Rejoice and exult with all your heart, O daughter of Jerusalem!" Again, Mason notes the parallel ideas in the surrounding contexts: both refer to Zion and Israel (cf. Ephraim and Jerusalem in Zech 9:10); both have Yahweh turning away their enemies, and dwelling in their midst as king; in both instances this results in salvation, restoration, and blessing; further, the contexts also speak of judgment against the nations (Zeph 3:1–8), as well as their inclusion in the people of God (Zeph 3:9).[28]

These parallels have led some scholars to believe that the king is Yahweh himself.[29] However, the description of the coming king as riding on a donkey clearly speaks against this identification.[30] So too, the description of the king as "saved."[31] Leske argues that the "king" represents God's faithful people, who will embody Yahweh's gracious rule to the nations through their covenant life.[32] This is based on reading Isa 55:1–5 as a democratization of the Davidic covenant, and arguing that this is what lies behind Zech 9:9. Petersen similarly concludes:

---

26. Meyers and Meyers, *Zechariah 9–14*, 121, argue that the idiom "daughter" refers to the place itself, personified as a daughter: "Just as unmarried daughters cannot act independently of their parents, so Yahweh's people must rely on God and on the king who is coming for their future to be arranged."

27. Mason, "Earlier," 30.

28. Ibid., 31–32.

29. So Hanson, *Apocalyptic*, 292–324.

30. The first-person references in Zech 9:7–8, which clearly refer to Yahweh, may indicate that Yahweh is also speaking in Zech 9:9, which would also make identifying him as the king difficult. However, the final phrase in Zech 9:8, "for now I see with my own eyes," may be attributed to the prophet, in which case it is less clear who is speaking in Zech 9:9.

31. Jones, *Commentary*, 130, rightly observes: "That he is described as 'saved' shows that it is the Davidic king, not Yahweh, who is in mind. The whole context confirms this."

32. Leske, "Context," 663–78. Cf. Mason, "Earlier," 62, who concluded "that traditional 'messianic' hopes have been modified in a 'democratizing' direction."

This is no standard royal or messianic expectation, namely, the return of a real or ideal Davidide. This expectation has little in common with the hope for a prince (Ezekiel 40–48), a crowned Zerubbabel (Hag. 2:23); a Davidide à la the oracles of Zechariah (Zech. 4:6–10). Instead, the poet focuses on collectivities, addressed through the technique of personification.[33]

However, there are several difficulties with this interpretation of Isa 55, and so the grounds for interpreting the king of Zech 9:9 as a corporate figure are wanting.[34] C. and E. Meyers reflect the majority consensus: "The term *melek* ('king') itself is a loaded one in the present context,

---

33. Petersen, *Zechariah 9–14*, 59. Mason, "Earlier," 42–45, also favours this interpretation, arguing that the messianic role was being interpreted in the light of the suffering servant of Isa 40–55 and taken further to refer to the prophetic office.

34. It is difficult to know who is being addressed as "you" in Isa 55:3–5. In Isa 55:3 it is plural and this forms the basis for the suggestion that there is a democratization of the Davidic covenant. That is, the promises that were once made to David are now promised to Israel (e.g. C. Westermann, *Isaiah 40–66: A Commentary* (trans. D. M. G. Stalker; OTL; London: SCM Press, 1969), 284–85; Williamson, *Variations*, 117–19). The parallel between vv. 4 and 5 seems to bear this out: as David was once a commander and leader of nations, the new community will now rule from Zion over the world, and witness that Yahweh rules over the nations. While the "you" in Isa 55:5 is singular, this may be taken as referring to the community as a whole, that is, to Israel as a restored community. The result of this interpretation is that it effectively removes a future Davidic king from Isa 40–55. Scholars argue that just as "my anointed" is transferred to Cyrus, so the Davidic covenant is taken from David and given to the restored community. Motyer, *The Prophecy of Isaiah*, 454, argues: "In context, however, the interpretation is unlikely, indeed impossible." He contends that the covenant (Isa 55:3c) must be a pledge of the blessings that are promised to individuals, and that the singular verbs in Isa 55:4–5 are addressing a single person. He translates Isa 55:3: "I will bring you [plural] into covenanted blessings, namely the promises to David of world rule and an enduring throne." C. R. Seitz, *Word Without End: The Old Testament as Abiding Theological Witness* (Grand Rapids: Eerdmans, 1998), 150–67, also argues against a democratization of the Davidic covenant in Isa 55:3 on the basis of comparing the book of Isaiah in its entirety with the Psalter in its entirety. He argues (p. 160): "the sharp lament perspective at the close of Psalm 89 is not anticipating the sort of transformation of these original promises that Westermann claims Deutero-Isaiah is proposing." Hence, the covenant that is established in Isa 55:3 by the work of the Servant is best understood as steadfast love shown *to* David (i.e. it means that the promises to David have been kept). The "everlasting covenant" is not a transferral of Davidic covenant to the nation, but as an extension of it. That is, the "everlasting covenant" comes as the Davidic covenant is fulfilled (by the Servant). See further P. R. Williamson, *Sealed with an Oath: Covenant in God's Unfolding Purpose* (NSBT 23; Nottingham: Apollos, 2007), 161–62. The conclusions drawn in the present study from the book of Zechariah will support this.

which is unmistakably eschatological and which foreshadows the emer-
gence of messianic language in intertestamental literature and the New
Testament."[35]

Several scholars are happy to leave the ambiguity between Yahweh
and the king, and see in Zech 9:9 both a distinction and a merging of the
two.[36] Others argue that the activity of the king becomes passive, with
Yahweh becoming the active party.[37] Still other scholars argue on the
basis of the parallels with Zech 2:10 (MT 2:14) and 3:14 that what is
being said is that the arrival of the king deserves the same reception as
that of Yahweh.[38] For the present, it can be noted that this king has a
central role in the coming of Yahweh's kingdom, but this relationship
between the king and Yahweh is something that will be developed in the
subsequent chapters of Zechariah.

There are four further descriptions of the king, grouped in pairs, the
first pair being צדיק ונושע הוא. Some scholars understand צדיק in a
military sense, translating it "triumphant,"[39] and see here a king returning
victorious from battle. Other scholars translate it as "legitimate," usually
against the proposed background of Zerubbabel's failure to take the
throne.[40] While it is true that there is a battle victory in the background
(9:1–8) and the context speaks of a rule of peace that the king will bring,
and furthermore, speaks of this king certainly being legitimate, it seems
best to translate צדיק in its usual sense of "just" or "righteous" and see in
it a reference to the character of the king and hence the nature of his rule.
Yahweh is often described as צדיק where this refers to his just rule or
just judgments.[41] Since the king is Yahweh's representative on earth,

35. Meyers and Meyers, *Zechariah 9–14*, 123.

36. Stuhlmueller, *Rebuilding*, 121–25; Merrill, *Zechariah*, 252.

37. So for instance Duguid, "Messianic," 267, who argues that there is a sharp
contrast between Ps 72 and Zech 9. Whereas in Ps 72 it is the Davidic king who is
active in bringing blessing, Duguid argues: "In contrast, in Zechariah 9 it is the Lord
alone who is the active party, bringing about the state of world domination single-
handedly." In a similar vein, Sweeney, *Twelve*, 664, argues that Zechariah envisions
Judah's monarch along much the same lines as the final form of the book of Isaiah as
first a Davidic monarch, then a Persian monarch, and ultimately Yahweh. However,
there is nothing to suggest that the king was not actively involved in the campaign of
Zech 9:1–8 as Yahweh's agent. Both Ps 72 and Zech 9 envisage the Davidic king as
having a central role as agents of Yahweh's blessing, though it is true that it is not as
explicit in Zech 9 as it is in Ps 72.

38. Petersen, "Zechariah, Book of (Zechariah 9–14)," 57–58; Ham, *King*, 25.

39. Hanson, *Apocalyptic*, 294. Cf. the translation given in the RSV.

40. E.g. Ollenburger, "Zechariah," 807.

41. E.g. Deut 32:4; 2 Chr 12:6; Ps 7:11; Lam 1:18; Dan 9:14; Zeph 3:9.

righteousness was to be a mark of his rule, and hence a characteristic of the future Davidide's rule.[42] Significantly, righteousness is a characteristic of the Shoot in Jer 23:5.

Second, this king is "saved" (ונושע). The Niphal participle here has been variously understood. Most take it as a passive, so that with Yahweh's victory over his enemies, the king has been "saved," and is thereby enabled to assume power.[43] If a close connection is seen between Yahweh and the king, so that the victory of Yahweh is the victory of the king, then it is translated as "victorious."[44] Others take it as a reflexive with an active sense of "bearing salvation."[45]

There are only two other occurrences of this form of the verb in the Hebrew Bible, and in both contexts they have a passive sense (Deut 33:29; Ps 33:16). Particularly interesting is Ps 33:16–17: "The king is not saved (נושע) by his great army; a warrior is not delivered by his great strength. The war horse is a false hope for salvation, and by its great might it cannot rescue."[46] Given this usage, it seems best to understand Zech 9:9 as a description of the coming king having been saved, not by his own might, but by Yahweh's. Yet in the context of Yahweh's victory in Zech 9:1–8, it also seems appropriate to understand the king's salvation in the sense of a victory that he brings to share with others. The salvation of the king means the salvation of his people, and in this sense the king "has salvation" or "brings salvation" and so the difference between the passive and the reflexive is not that great when it comes to the final meaning.[47]

The third description, עני, most often occurs in the Hebrew Bible with the sense of "affliction" (e.g. Ps 22:24) and this has led some scholars to read it against the background of the suffering servant in Isaiah.[48] While

---

42. E.g. 1 Sam 24:17; 2 Sam 23:3–5; Ps 72:1–7; cf. Isa 9:7; 11:4–5; 32:1.

43. Meyers and Meyers, *Zechariah 9–14*, 127.

44. Mitchell, "Zechariah," 273; Lamarche, *Zacharie IX–XIV*, 131; Baldwin, *Zechariah*, 165; Stuhlmueller, *Rebuilding*, 124; McComiskey, "Zechariah," 3:1166.

45. Unger, *Zechariah*, 162–63. The strongest argument for taking נושע in this way is that the ancient versions (e.g. the LXX, the Targum, the Syriac Peshitta and Latin Vulgate) all render it in an active sense.

46. Mason, "Earlier," 36, wonders whether this psalm was in the writer's mind, given the reference to the war horse in the next verse.

47. Note Meyer, "Messianic Metaphors," 27: "an examination of these passages suggests that the distinction between reflexive and passive is probably not as significant as might at first appear." Also T. Collins, "The Literary Contexts of Zechariah 9:9," in Tuckett, ed., *The Book of Zechariah and Its Influence*, 29–40 (38).

48. This term is applied to the servant in Isa 53:4, 7. The servant is also called "righteous" in Isa 53:11.

the servant figure of Isaiah may be in the broader background, a question that I shall return to later, here the combination with the second description suggests that עָנִי be understood in the sense of "humble," as it is in several other passages.[49] Rather than a war horse (Zech 9:10; cf. Ps 33:17), the king comes "riding upon a donkey, upon a colt, the foal of a donkey." Laato is very helpful in providing the background for this image of a king riding on a donkey.[50] While there are a few favourable references to the king riding in a chariot (Jer 17:25; 22:4), 2 Sam 15:1 and 1 Kgs 1:1–5 portray this motif in a negative light.[51] Furthermore, Laato argues that texts such as 1 Kgs 1 explicitly contrast two ideologies of kingship: "one which is based on the king's own might and despotism and is symbolized by horses, chariots and an army, and the other which is based on the ancient notion of charismatic leadership which is closely connected with the archaic tribal society and Yhwh war, and which is symbolized by the king riding on an ass."[52]

This is the background against which the image of the king coming, riding on a donkey should be understood. It is a king who has his confidence in Yahweh and not in military might. This background is made even more certain in Zech 9:10 when we are told that with his coming, Yahweh will "cut off the chariot from Ephraim and the horse from Jerusalem, and the battle bow will be cut off" (cf. Zech 10:3b–5; Hos 1:7).

While less certain, there may also be an allusion to Gen 49:11 where the future rule of Judah is linked to him tethering his donkey to a vine after washing his garments in the blood of grapes (cf. Zech 9:15).[53] The wider concern for Ephraim (Zech 9:10, 13), and possible allusion to Joseph (9:11) strengthen the case for an allusion here, and hence bring to mind the wider Davidic dynasty tradition.

Two further descriptions of the king are given. First, the king proclaims peace to the nations. This peace (שָׁלוֹם) is not just the absence of war. The peace that is on view here is the peace of salvation, the peace of

---

49. I.e. 2 Sam 22:28; Ps 18:28; Isa 66:2; Zeph 3:12.

50. Laato, *Star*, 209–10.

51. Black, "Messiah," 68–69, also notes echoes with the reign of David. When the kingdom was divided after Absalom's revolt, David and his household were given some donkeys to ride on by Mephibosheth's servant (2 Sam 16:1–4). At the same time, Absalom acquired a chariot and horses, and fifty men to run before him (2 Sam 15:1). It is David who eventually puts down the revolt in a battle against Israel in which Absalom is killed, and David reunites Israel and restores peace.

52. Laato, *Star*, 209. Other passages include Deut 17:14–20; 2 Sam 24; Pss 20:7–9; 33:16–17.

53. See further Duguid, "Messianic," 267–68; Sweeney, *Twelve*, 663; Boda, *Commentary*, 417; Ham, *King*, 29.

Yahweh's kingdom being re-established with all its covenant blessings (as is seen as the oracle continues).[54] The kingdom that had been divided is now unified, as it had been under David (cf. 2 Sam 2:10–11; 5:1–5). This king is the counter to the strength, wealth, and might of the nations depicted in Zech 9:1–8.

Second, this king will rule "from sea to sea, and from the river to the ends of the earth." This phrase is also found in Ps 72:8 as part of a prayer for the king's son.[55] In the final form of the Psalter, and against the background of 2 Sam 7, it can be understood as a poetic way of describing the universal extent of this future Davidic king's dominion.[56] Rather than focusing on the actual geography of his kingdom (as in Zech 9:1–8), here it expresses the fact that he will reign over all the earth, encompassing all the nations. That the future king will rule over the nations is a common feature in the presentation of the Psalms and Isaiah.[57]

Before moving on from these verses, there are two further views that we must consider. Laato is one of a number of scholars who understand chs. 9–14 as representing a modification of the messianic hopes expressed in chs. 1–8. He states:

> This difference [between Zech 9:9–10 and Zech 2:14–15] can be best explained against the background of disappointed messianic hopes connected with Zerubbabel. Our examination of Zech 3:8–10 and 6:9–15 revealed that the messianic hopes which were originally connected with Zerubbabel were later modified to refer to the future. Thus it is plausible to assume that these reasonably concrete messianic hopes were reinterpreted to refer to a final act of salvation from Yhwh. In light of this development, the connection between Zech 2:14–15 and 9:9–10 becomes understandable. The last mentioned passage must be read as an eschatological interpretation of the first mentioned. Yhwh will bring his Messiah to Jerusalem in order to bring about the final restoration promised in Zechariah 1–8.[58]

54. See further Meyers and Meyers, *Zechariah 9–14*, 135; Webb, *Zechariah*, 132. Note the parallel with many of the ideas of Isa 52:7–10.

55. There is a similar expression in Ps 89:25 (MT 89:26).

56. See further, M. Sæbø, *On the Way to Canon: Creative Tradition History in the Old Testament* (JSOTSup 191; Sheffield: Sheffield Academic Press, 1998), 122–30; Dempster, *Dominion*, 195–96. Cf. Meyers and Meyers, *Zechariah 9–14*, 137, who conclude: "In sum, the 'sea to sea' combination, intensified by the imagery of the next line ('river to the ends of the earth'), constitutes language that conveys the universality of the king's domain. The directional imagery functions as a kind of merism: all points and thus everything in between."

57. E.g. Pss 2:7–8; 89:26–28 (MT); 110:1–2; Isa 9:1–6; 11:10; 42:2–4; 49:6–7; 52:15; 55:3–5; cf. Gen 49:10–12.

58. Laato, *Star*, 210–11.

The logic entailed in this view, however, seems to be wanting. Laato states that given the failure of Zerubbabel to take the throne, "these concrete messianic hopes [presumably about Zerubbabel] were reinterpreted to refer to a final act of salvation from Yhwh." However, given this logic, surely one would expect Zech 9:9–10 to talk about the coming of Yahweh, and 2:14–15 to talk about the coming of the king, but in fact the reverse is the case. Moreover, it has been demonstrated that 3:8–10 and 6:9–15 speak of the coming of a Davidic king, namely, the Shoot, who is not to be identified with Zerubbabel. It is this same king that 9:9 speaks of. Hence Laato's grounds for arguing that ch. 9 reflects a later modification of the hope for a future king in chs. 1–8 are dissolved.

Floyd has recently argued that the description of the king in 9:9–10 is ambiguous: "Such language might apply to one of David's successors in pre-exilic times, to one of the emperors that imposed their rule over Judah in postexilic times (cf. the application of the term 'messiah' to Cyrus in Isa 44:28–45:3), or to a late postexilic pretender to the restored Davidic throne (e.g. *Pss. Sol.* 17)."[59] However, reading the book of Zechariah in its final form, something that Floyd himself is keen to do, this king can only be the promised Shoot (cf. Zech 3:8; 6:12).[60] Zechariah 1–8 must inform the understanding of this king in the final form of the book.[61]

These verses do not democratize the Davidic covenant, or reduce the significance of the house of David with respect to the coming of Yahweh. They speak of the key role of the king in Yahweh's eschatological purposes for his people. This is not just any king; this is the Davidic king of prophetic expectation, the king who will be the agent of Yahweh. The descriptions of the king (righteous and saved, humble and riding on a donkey), demonstrate that there is continuity with the earlier Davidic dynasty tradition and Zech 1–8. The positioning of these verses at the centre of this unit highlights the key role that the king will have in the future of Yahweh's purposes. C. and E. Meyers rightly capture the importance of this figure in Zech 9. "The restored royal figure is the lynchpin of the restored land and people."[62]

---

59. Floyd, *Minor Prophets*, 467.
60. This case is well put by Webb, *Zechariah*, 131. For Floyd's concerns to deal with the book of Zechariah as a whole, see Floyd, "Changing Views," 257–63.
61. O'Brien, *Zechariah*, 239, also argues that "Zech 9:9–10 may be intentionally ambiguous, blurring the distinction between Yahweh and Yahweh's agents." However, O'Brien downplays the significance of the "Shoot" prophecies in Zech 3 and 6 (she does not mention Zech 3), and overplays the possibility that Yahweh is "described in the anthropomorphic language of riding an animal" to justify the supposed "ambiguity."
62. Meyers and Meyers, *Zechariah 9–14*, 169.

5.2.4. *The Restored People (Zechariah 9:11–17)*

[11] You also, because of the blood of your covenant, I will set free your prisoners from the pit—there is no water in it. [12] Return to a stronghold, prisoners of hope. Moreover, today I declare that I will restore to you double. [13] For I will bend Judah to myself as a bow; I will fill it with Ephraim, and I will incite your sons, Zion, against your sons, Greece. And I will make you as a warrior's sword.

[14] And Yahweh will appear over them, and his arrow will go forth as lightning, and the Lord Yahweh will sound the trumpet and go forth in storms of the south. [15] Yahweh of hosts will defend them, and they will devour and will subdue the sling stones and they will drink and will roar as with wine, and they will be full like the bowl, like corners of an altar.

[16] Yahweh their God will save them on that day as a flock of his people, so that they will be jewels of a crown shining upon his land. [17] For how good is it and how beautiful is it! Grain will make young men flourish and new wine young women. (author's translation)

With the return of the king to Zion, the oracle shifts to address the people, spelling out the benefits of the king's rule.[63] This unit begins with Yahweh continuing to speak in the first person, as had been the case from Zech 9:7. In 9:14 there is a shift to the third person with four references to what Yahweh will do for his people (cf. 9:1, 4).

The oracle begins by proclaiming that the prisoners shall be set free, whereupon they are to return to their stronghold, where they shall be restored double (9:11–12). Some scholars suggest an allusion to the Joseph story in the description of the "waterless pit" (cf. Gen 37:24), believing that Israel's present situation parallels the low point in Joseph's life, with the hope of better things to come.[64] Similarly, it is suggested that there is an allusion to Jeremiah's experience in Jer 38:6 (cf. Pss 40:3; 69:15). Even if these allusions are not present, the waterless pit is clearly a metaphor for Israel's exile.[65]

A clearer allusion, given the many other references to the Exodus in this section, is seen in the phrase "I will set free," which corresponds to the many instances where Moses calls upon Pharaoh to let the Israelites go (e.g. Exod 5:1).[66] Upon their release, these prisoners are to return to

---

63. As noted already, this chapter moves from the restored land (Zech 9:1–8), to a restored people (Zech 9:11–17) via the restoring king (Zech 9:9–10). The feminine singular "you" indicates that the daughter of Zion is again being addressed.

64. E.g. Stuhlmueller, *Rebuilding*, 126; Meyers and Meyers, *Zechariah 9–14*, 142; Petersen, *Zechariah 9–14*, 60; Mason, "Earlier," 49; Boda, *Commentary*, 420.

65. So Clark and Hatton, *Handbook*, 248: "Here the waterless pit is used as a symbol for the exile of the Jews from the Promised Land."

66. Meyers and Meyers, *Zechariah 9–14*, 140.

their stronghold, best understood as Jerusalem in the present context. The double restoration conveys the idea of recompense, perhaps for those who were suffering for the sins of earlier generations.[67]

The grounds of this restoration by Yahweh is "the blood of your covenant." This phrase is found in only one other place in the Hebrew Bible, in Exod 24:8, where it refers to the Mosaic covenant. Just as Israel had been released from captivity in Egypt, so they shall be set free again on account of the covenant that Yahweh had made with his people at Sinai, the blood being the element of covenant ratification whereby the people committed themselves to obey Yahweh, and Yahweh bound himself to keep his words.

The means of the restoration is Yahweh himself, who will use his people as his weapons against their enemies (Zech 9:13).[68] Concerning the reference to Greece that many have used to give a late date to this part of Zechariah, Boda notes that in the early Persian period, the Persians sought to incorporate Greece into their empire, but with limited success.[69] He also notes the reference to the "sons of Javan" in the table of nations in Gen 10:4, and helpfully suggests: "The allusion to the 'sons of Javan' here links together the historical tensions of the early Persian period with traditional enemy language in the Old Testament."[70]

The exodus theme continues, with Yahweh pictured as a warrior, driving out his enemies and saving his people (cf. Exod 15:1–21).[71] The reference to the "storms of the south" has puzzled many scholars, since it

67. Ibid., 144–45. Mason, "Earlier," 47, suggests that this recalls the promise of Isa 61:7 (cf. Jer 16:18) where an earlier "double" judgment (Isa 40:2) is reversed by a double restoration (cf. Job 42:10). However, the double judgment of Isa 40:2 may not mean that the Israelites received twice what they deserved, but that the judgment exactly met the sin. Clark and Hatton, *Handbook*, 249, suggest that it is a doubling of Jerusalem's population that is promised. This is possible, but not certain.

68. Calvin, "Zechariah," 265–66, comments on the description of Judah as a bow and Ephraim as its arrow that it was a reminder to the Jews of Yahweh's own power, "that they might not regard their own strength, but acknowledge that they were made strong from above, and that strength to overcome their enemies would be given them."

69. Boda, *Commentary*, 421. See further Webb, *Zechariah*, 45, who says: "Greece loomed large in everyone's mind in the early Persian period. It is no wonder, then, that Zechariah should have seen it as a potentially hostile power on the western horizon." Greece is also mentioned in Isa 66:19 and Ezek 27:13. It is recorded as a hostile power during the Babylonian period in Dan 8:21; 10:20; and 11:2.

70. Boda, *Commentary*, 421.

71. For the background of the divine warrior theme, see Hanson, *Apocalyptic*, 292–324.

is believed that any threat for Yahweh's people at this time would come from the north. However, if this is simply applying exodus themes to the future salvation that Yahweh will work, then rather than being a reference to a contemporary situation, it is a further allusion to the past and it also throws further light on Zech 9:9–10.[72] Horbury argues that many of the prophetic texts that speak of a coming saviour (e.g. Isa 19:20; 59:10; 62:11; Obad 21) have in their background a corporate recollection of the exodus (e.g. Isa 63:11–14).[73] Emphasis is placed on Yahweh's deliverance by means of a shepherd of his flock (cf. Moses, or Moses and Aaron), and the king plays this role here.

The return to the land will see a restoration of the people of Yahweh to paradise. There is some debate as to whether Zech 9:15 envisages the people of Yahweh obliterating their enemies in war, or whether it should be understood as part of the prosperity that Yahweh's saved people shall enjoy. If the former, then ואכלו and ושתו are understood as "they shall devour" their enemies, and "they shall drink" their blood, respectively.[74] If the latter, then these descriptions are understood as "they shall eat" and "they shall drink" at some form of victory banquet.[75] The difficulty lies in the fact that there is no object supplied for either of these verbs, and while the context of Zech 9:14 favours the war interpretation, 9:16–17 favours the feasting. The description that they "will subdue the sling stones" may tip the balance in favour of the war interpretation. However, Jones makes the observation that sling stones were only really ever used at the time of David, and that this is purposefully anachronistic. He argues that the sense here is that the weapons that David used against the Philistines "will stay where they belong and not be collected together to be used as missiles."[76] If this is the case, we have a further allusion to the time of David, this time to the peace and prosperity that he brought to

---

72. Webb, *Zechariah*, 134 n. 81, notes that this expression is "especially reminiscent of God's revelation of himself to Israel at Mount Sinai (to the south of the land of Canaan) at the time of the exodus (Exod. 19:16)." Calvin, "Zechariah," 268–69, also argues that it is a reference to God making himself known at Mount Sinai.

73. Horbury, *Messianism*, 43–44.

74. E.g. Mitchell, "Zechariah," 280; Keil, "Zechariah," 342; Petersen, *Zechariah 9–14*, 65; Sweeney, *Twelve*, 667.

75. E.g. Baldwin, *Zechariah*, 169–70; Calvin, "Zechariah," 269–70. McComiskey, "Zechariah," 3:1172, understands this as a combination of the two: "Thus satisfied by Yahweh's provision, the people of God wage war victoriously, covered by the blood of their conquered foes." Redditt, *Zechariah*, 117, also sees it as a combination, but the other way around, with the eating referring to victory, and the drinking referring to plenty!

76. Jones, "Fresh," 249.

Israel. Jones's interpretation, however, seems to be built on a slender thread, and overlooks the stones for slinging used much later by Uzziah (2 Chr 26:14–15) and the fact that the description of treading down sling stones most naturally favours a war context. On balance, given the reference to Yahweh using his people as weapons (Zech 9:13), Zech 9:15 seems to further this war image.

Zechariah 9:16–17 provides a summary of what has been seen in this chapter, and its outcome. "That day" is the day of salvation, the day of victory, the day of conquest that ushers in prosperity and abundance (cf. 3:9b–10). This phrase sets this chapter in an eschatological context and clarifies for us that the king of 9:9 is the future Davidic king (i.e. the same king envisaged in chs. 1–8). There are three other significant features here. First, the description of Yahweh as "their God" calls to mind the covenant that Yahweh had made with his people and looks to the past. Second, Yahweh's people are described as "a flock." This description will become all-important in the coming chapters as it prepares for shepherd imagery. Here it points to Yahweh as the Shepherd who saves his people with his king. The third significant feature is the mention of the land (9:16) that brings forth grain and new wine (9:17). This is where the logic of the exodus theme finds its fulfilment. Just as Yahweh had saved his people from the oppressive nations and brought them into the Promised Land, establishing them under David, so he will again save and establish them in the land under the heir of David's throne.

5.3. *The Coming King and the Hope for the House of David*

On the hope for the house of David expressed in the book of Zechariah, C. and E. Meyers comment:

> The future Davidide is relegated to the eschatological future both here [in Zech 9] and in First Zechariah; yet the present reality recedes here in a way that it does not in First Zechariah. Still, this prophecy accords well with the earlier ones in First Zechariah; and the fact that they mesh so well may be evidence of redactional or editorial skill, or of the author's intentional utilization of themes and language of his immediate predecessor.[77]

What C. and E. Meyers mean when they say that "the present reality recedes here in a way that it does not in First Zechariah" is unclear. Presumably they mean that the contemporary figures like Joshua and Zerubbabel are not referred to. The present reality of Zion (Jerusalem) is

---

77. Meyers and Meyers, *Zechariah 9–14*, 126. In their "Fortunes," 211, Meyers and Meyers make the comment that "the ideological similarity of 9:9–10 to 3:8, 4:6b–10a, and 6:12 is striking."

no less in focus, and the hope for a future king, in some ways, becomes sharper. Elsewhere they argue: "It is even possible that the editor or redactor of ch. 9 or even the compiler of the book of Zechariah has inserted these verses [Zech 9:9–10] into the divine warrior hymn in an attempt to make it more compatible with the earlier materials of Zechariah."[78]

This of course raises the question whether "the fact that they mesh so well" may also be evidence of authorial unity between the two parts of the book, the differences being accounted for simply by the different occasion and genre. In any case, C. and E. Meyers note that the Davidic hope expressed in Zech 9 is broadly continuous with what has gone before.

In conclusion, the grounds are wanting for seeing a diminished Davidic interest or a democratization of the Davidic covenant in Zech 9. There is no evidence that the Davidic hope has been modified or made ambiguous. The hope that is expressed in this chapter for the house of David is no different to that of Zech 1–8, nor to those whom Zechariah calls "former prophets" (cf. 1:4; 7:6). Drawing on the Davidic dynasty tradition, Isaiah spoke of the coming king who would rule with justice and righteousness (Isa 9:6–7; 11:1–10; cf. 16:5). Similarly, Jeremiah promised a righteous Shoot of David who would reign as king (Jer 23:3–6; 33:14–22). Ezekiel promised a Davidic king who would rule over a cleansed and united people (Ezek 37:21–25). Hosea looked forward to the children of Israel seeking David their king (Hos 3:5). Micah spoke of kingship returning to Jerusalem with one from the clan of Judah who would reunite the people of Israel and bring peace (Mic 4:8–5:5 [MT 4:8–5:6]). Amos promised the restoration of David's fallen booth with a return to the land, accompanied by abundant wine (Amos 9:11–15). Zechariah stands in the same tradition and holds out the same hope.[79]

In Zech 1–8 we saw the expectation of the coming Shoot: a Davidic figure in whose coming the iniquity of the land would be removed in a single day, by whom the eschatological temple would be built, and through whom the day of peace and prosperity would be ushered in for Yahweh's people and the nations (cf. Zech 6:15; Isa 11:10). In Zech 9, this hope continues to be held out with the coming of Zion's king at a time after the temple had been built (Zech 9:8). With his coming, Yahweh will re-establish his kingdom, both judging the nations and

---

78. Meyers, "Messianism," 135.

79. If there is also an allusion to the servant figure of Isaiah with the king's humility, righteousness, and the peace that he brings and speaks to the nations (I deal with this in Chapter 7, §7.3), then these links are strengthened still.

incorporating them into his people. Indeed, the future Davidic king is the lynchpin of a restored land and people. Zechariah draws on the past, especially the promise to David of a future king, as the basis for future hope. If there is anything new here in relation to the presentation of the coming of the king in the book of Zechariah, it is simply the use of exodus imagery to describe the true end of Israel's exile (9:11–12) with the victory of Yahweh's people (9:13–15), resulting in the abundant blessings of the new age (9:16–17; cf. 3:10).[80]

---

80.   This theme is not new in itself. Note Horbury, *Messianism*, 31: "At the heart of the Pentateuch, then, is a figure [Moses] which could be and was interpreted as that of a royal deliverer."

Chapter 6

THE SHEPHERD

6.1. *Introduction*

Shepherd imagery features prominently in Zech 9–14. In 10:1–11:3, the people's afflictions are attributed to their lack of a shepherd (10:2). At the same time, Yahweh promises to punish and remove shepherds who oppress his people by their rule (10:3; 11:1–3). In 11:4–17, Zechariah is told to act out the role of two different shepherds: the first rejects the flock after removing three unmerciful shepherds (11:4–14); and the second devours the flock (11:15–17). In 13:7–9, judgment is announced against Yahweh's shepherd, a judgment that brings about a scattering and refinement of the flock.

   In order to understand these passages and the hope for the house of David that they exhibit, it is necessary to identify the shepherds in each instance and to establish the way that the passages relate to each other. The issues of interpretation are complex, particularly those surrounding the two sign-actions of ch. 11, a chapter upon which many of the interpretations of the Davidic hope in the book hinge. This chapter will first summarize the background to the shepherd imagery in the Hebrew Bible. Against this background, the following sections in which the Shepherd imagery occurs will be closely examined: 10:1–11:3; 11:4–17; and 13:7–9. In doing this, the question that this chapter will seek to answer is: To what extent do these chapters raise the expectation that the answer to troubles of the post-exilic community lay in a coming shepherd, the future Davidic king?

6.2. *Background to the Shepherd Imagery of Zechariah*

Shepherding was a central part of Israel's economy, and on account of this, it was a well-understood metaphor for leadership.[1] Yahweh is said

---

   1. For further details, see L. Ryken, J. C.Wilhoit, and T. Longman III, "Sheep, Shepherd," in *Dictionary of Biblical Imagery* (Downers Grove: IVP, 1998), 782–85.

to be shepherd of his people, who are his flock.[2] When this metaphor is explained, it is in terms of Yahweh guiding (e.g. Pss 77:20; 80:1), protecting (Ps 78:52; Isa 40:11), saving (Ezek 34:22), gathering (Isa 40:11; Jer 31:10), and nourishing (Jer 50:19; Mic 2:12–13) his people.[3]

Shepherd imagery is also applied to human leaders such as Moses and the Persian king Cyrus as they act as agents of Yahweh.[4] The importance of this theme for the Davidic dynasty tradition is seen in the reference to King David as the human shepherd par excellence: "[Yahweh] chose David his servant and took him from the sheepfolds; from following the nursing ewes he brought him to shepherd Jacob his people, Israel his inheritance. With upright heart he shepherded them and guided them with his skillful hand" (Ps 78:70–72). While David is said to shepherd Israel (cf. 2 Sam 5:2), scholars note that there seems to be some reticence to use the term "shepherd" for Israel's kings; this may be to avoid the way it was used in other ancient Near Eastern contexts.[5] However, there is no reluctance in using this title in denouncing unworthy leaders of Israel or the nations. Ezekiel and Jeremiah both refer to the unworthy leaders of Judah and Israel as shepherds.[6] Other prophets also hold corrupt shepherds responsible for the scattering of the flock and the experience of the exile.[7] These shepherds were past and present kings of Judah and Israel.[8]

The failure of the monarchy and its culpability for the experience of exile is a theme of the latter chapters of Hosea. Hosea 13:4–11 goes as far as saying that kingship became part of Yahweh's judgment on his people. W. Eichrodt summarizes the situation well:

---

2. E.g. Gen 49:24; Pss 23:1; 79:13; 95:7; 100:3; Isa 40:11; Jer 13:17; Ezek 34:31; Mic 7:14; Zech 9:16; 10:4.

3. Ryken, Wilhoit and Longman, "Sheep, Shepherd," 784.

4. E.g. Isa 63:11 and Isa 44:28, respectively.

5. L. Jonker, "rʿh," *NIDOTTE* 3:1138–43 (1141); G. Wallis, "rāʿâ, rōʿeh," *TDOT* 13:544–53 (550), state that the term "shepherd" was used of foreign gods or deified kings in other ancient Near Eastern contexts, and the reluctance to use the term for Israel's kings was to avoid these associations. E. Beyreuther, "Shepherd," *NIDNTT* 3:564–69 (565), believes that the reason the title is not given to a king of Israel is on account of the association of the title with Yahweh.

6. E.g. Jer 2:8; 10:21; 12:10; 22:22; 23:1–2; Ezek 34:1–10. Cf. Isa 56:11.

7. Note "so they were scattered" in Ezek 34:5, which attributes the exile to false leadership. While its interpretation is disputed, Sweeney, *Twelve*, 365–66, argues that Mic 2:12–13 pictures the Israelite king leading his people into captivity.

8. Wright, *Ezekiel*, 274–75, comments on Ezek 34:1–10: "Ezekiel chooses a metaphor for kingship that was well known throughout the ancient Near East, from Babylon to Egypt—the shepherd of the flock. He then launches into an attack on *the shepherds of Israel*—meaning the historical kings of the period up to the exile."

whenever the monarchy was confronted by any problem it would always
fail to rise to the occasion, and grasp at false expedients. It attempted to
cope with the crisis of the moment by playing the game of alliances with
the great heathen powers, and by deceitful political manoeuvres ([Hos]
10:4; 8:9; 5:13 f.). The bitterest criticism of this state of affairs is to be
found in 10:3 f. To the nation's despairing cry, "We have no king!," the
prophet retorts: "What use is a king to us? To help us to speak swelling
words, and swear false oaths, to conclude alliances, and to break the
law"… [T]he kings entangle both themselves and the people in the sin of
brutal and self-seeking power politics, knowing no maxim but that of
worldly self-aggrandizement by any and every means, and so coming
rapidly to disaster.[9]

The kings of Israel and Judah are indicted for their failure to shepherd
Yahweh's people. However, the judgment of these false shepherds is not
Yahweh's final word. The removal of false shepherds clears the way
for the coming of a true shepherd: "I will rescue my flock; they shall no
longer be a prey. And I will judge between sheep and sheep. And I will
set up over them one shepherd, my servant David, and he shall feed them:
he shall feed them and be their shepherd. And I, the LORD, will be their
God, and my servant David shall be prince among them. I am the LORD;
I have spoken" (Ezek 34:22–24; cf. 37:24–25).

In Ezekiel, this future Davidic prince will reunite Judah and Ephraim,
just as David had done, so that they shall be one nation. Ezekiel dramatically enacts this with the joining of two sticks (Ezek 37:15–23). Jeremiah
also links the future shepherd leadership of Yahweh's people beyond the
exile with the Davidic dynasty tradition. He speaks of the coming Shoot:

> [1] "Woe to the shepherds who destroy and scatter the sheep of my pasture!"
> declares the LORD… [3] Then I will gather the remnant of my flock out of all
> the countries where I have driven them, and I will bring them back to their
> fold, and they shall be fruitful and multiply. [4] I will set shepherds over
> them who will care for them, and they shall fear no more, nor be dis-
> mayed, neither shall any be missing, declares the LORD.
> [5] "Behold, the days are coming, declares the LORD, when I will raise up
> for David a righteous Branch, and he shall reign as king and deal wisely,
> and shall execute justice and righteousness in the land. [6] In his days Judah
> will be saved, and Israel will dwell securely. And this is the name by
> which he will be called: "The LORD is our righteousness." (Jer 23:1, 3–6)

In summary, this background shows that the prophets commonly use the
shepherd metaphor in relation to the leadership of Yahweh's people.
While Yahweh is the ultimate shepherd of his flock, human agents,

9. W. Eichrodt, *Theology of the Old Testament*, vol. 1 (trans. J. Baker; London:
SCM Press, 1961), 450.

particularly the kings of Israel and Judah, are also said to shepherd Yahweh's flock for good or ill. The pre-exilic and exilic prophets place the responsibility for the disaster of exile firmly on the shoulders of corrupt and unworthy shepherds. However, they also draw on the Davidic dynasty tradition, and the notion of David as human shepherd par excellence, to speak of a future Davidic shepherd who will restore Yahweh's people. This shepherd is alternatively called "servant," "prince," "Shoot," and "king" (e.g. Ezek 34:33–35; 37:24–25; Jer 23:5). While many scholars see Zechariah transforming and reinterpreting the way that earlier prophets, particularly Ezekiel, use the shepherd metaphor, it will be demonstrated that Zechariah continues to express exactly the same hope for a future Davidic king who will reunite and shepherd Yahweh's people.

6.3. *Shepherd Leadership in Zechariah 10:1–11:3*

The main theme of chs. 10–11 is leadership and its consequences for the people of Yahweh. First, 10:1–11:3 shall be examined, exploring the way that the shepherd imagery is used and focus on the nature of the new leadership that Yahweh will establish, particularly the metaphors that are used in 10:4. As shall be seen, scholars are divided on the significance of this verse for any hope being expressed for the house of David. Are these different metaphors for the future Davidic king? Or, are they simply speaking of leadership coming from the people, with no king necessarily on view? I shall closely examine this text in its context and then carefully weigh up the scholarly arguments.

6.3.1. *Content and Structure*
Zechariah 10 begins by calling on Yahweh's people to ask him for rain rather than the false prophets. Indeed, the people's dependence on false prophecy was the reason for their affliction and lack of a shepherd (10:1–2). Yahweh promises to punish those who are shepherds and raise up a new leadership (10:3–4) who will save his people from their affliction (10:5). He also promises to gather those from both south and north who remain scattered among the nations (10:6–11), and have them walk in his ways (10:12). This is a huge work, pictured once again as a new exodus (cf. 9:11–17).

Zechariah 11:1–3 functions as a transition. The geography and the mention of shepherds connects it with ch. 10, but the three sharp imperatives mark it as a separate unit. This section reveals that Yahweh's intention to raise up a new leadership and to reunite his people will have devastating consequences for those who are currently shepherds. It also prepares for the further use of the shepherd theme in the two sign-act reports of 11:4–17.

Zechariah 10:1–11:3 will be treated as a unit.[10] It can be structured thematically:[11]

> *Zech 10:1–11:3: The results of good and bad leadership*
> 10:1–2   Affliction for lack of a shepherd
> 10:3–12   The establishment and result of new leadership
> 11:1–3   Shepherds judged

6.3.2. Shepherds under Judgment (Zechariah 10:1–2, 3; 11:1–3)

Zechariah 10 and 11 both begin with announcements of punishment and destruction coming on shepherds. Zechariah 10:1–2 attributes the people's wandering and affliction to the lack of a shepherd. Then, in what seems at first to be a paradox, Yahweh's anger against the people's shepherds is announced in 10:3:

> [1] Ask for rain from Yahweh in the season of the latter rain—Yahweh who makes the thunderbolts. And he gives rain showers to them; to each grain in the field. [2] For the teraphim have spoken iniquity and the diviners have seen a lie—they speak false dreams; they give vain comfort. Therefore they have set out just like sheep. They are afflicted for there is no shepherd.
> [3] My anger has flared against the shepherds and I will punish the leaders, for Yahweh of hosts will attend to his flock, the house of Judah, and will establish them as his majestic horse in the battle. (author's translation)

The shift from saying "there is no shepherd" (10:2) to announcing that Yahweh's "anger has flared against the shepherds" (10:3) has caused some to doubt the literary integrity of 10:1–2.[12] This judgment must not

---

10. Butterworth, *Structure*, 190: "It appears that Zech. 10:1–11:3 has its own integrity."

11. These thematic divisions are supported by the strong paragraph marker (פ) at the end of Zech 10:2 and the weak markers (ס) at the end of Zech 10:12 and 11:3.

12. See, for instance, J. Tromp, "Bad Divination in Zechariah 10:1–2," in Tuckett, ed., *The Book of Zechariah and Its Influence*, 41–52 (49), who concludes: "Zechariah 10:1–2 is best explained if it is *not* read within the context of chapters 9 and 10:3–12" (emphasis original). Tromp makes some important observations of the text, but his methodology is unsatisfying. He believes that the final editor never sought coherence (p. 50): "It can no longer be taken for granted that the editor responsible for the present arrangement believed them to cohere in any other way, or even whether he ascribed them to Zechariah." I believe there are no grounds for this assumption and that a coherent reading can be demonstrated. Moreover, an interpretation that ignores the wider context is impoverished for doing so, as the wider context throws additional light on the meaning of the component parts.

be made too quickly. A closer look at the text and its background indicates that it is most likely two different groups of shepherds that are on view, and that the final form of the text is coherent.

Zechariah 10:1–2 is generally taken to refer to the contemporary situation. It is argued that the Israelites in the post-exilic age were falling into the same trap as their ancestors in turning to teraphim and diviners.[13] However, an alternative interpretation arises by taking into account the background of the idea that Yahweh's people lacked a shepherd.

The idea of Yahweh's people being afflicted for lack of a shepherd is first found in Num 27:17. With Moses' impending death, he cries out to Yahweh to appoint someone to take his place as leader over Yahweh's people so that they may not be "as sheep that have no shepherd." Yahweh responds by appointing Joshua (Num 27:18). This idea is again expressed at the end of 1 Kings, where the prophet Micaiah prophesies the death of king Ahab with the result that Israel will be scattered "as sheep that have no shepherd" (1 Kgs 22:17). Significantly, the sin that led to this judgment was Ahab's willingness to listen to the false prophets (1 Kgs 22:1–16). Of the exilic prophets, Ezekiel links the exile experience with the lack of a shepherd: "So they were scattered, because there was no shepherd, and they became food for all the wild beasts" (Ezek 34:5). Jeremiah 50:6–7 also explains the affliction of the people on account of shepherds who had led them astray. Indeed, one of the sins highlighted by the pre-exilic and exilic prophets as contributing to the disaster of the exilic experience was false prophecy.[14]

Against this setting, 10:1–2 is not necessarily an indication that the post-exilic community was involved in these practices,[15] even if they posed a real threat.[16] In the context of the promised harvest which will ensue on the day when Yahweh's king comes to save his people (cf. 9:17), this is a warning to learn from the past and to look to Yahweh for the rain for their harvests in anticipation of this greater harvest day that Yahweh will bring (cf. 14:17). They are to do this rather than to look to the false prophets who were responsible for their present affliction and who only gave foolish and empty counsel.

13. E.g. Stuhlmueller, *Rebuilding*, 128; McComiskey, "Zechariah," 3:1176; Boda, *Commentary*, 436–40.

14. Cf. Isa 3:2–3; 41:21–29; Jer 14:13–22; 29:8–9; 27:9–10; Ezek 13:8–9; Mic 3:7, 11.

15. For the background of these practices and for evidence that the teraphim were used in ancestor worship, see Meyers and Meyers, *Zechariah 9–14*, 184–92.

16. The judgment of false prophets announced in Zech 13:2–6 is an indication that their presence and threat is real for the post-exilic community. See also the evidence amassed by Webb, *Zechariah*, 135–37.

Therefore, Zech 10:1–2 draws on the past as much as it refers to the present situation.[17] The background to these verses indicates that the people's present lack of a shepherd was Yahweh's judgment on the failure of the kings of Israel and Judah. Given the significance of the shepherd metaphor and the reference to Yahweh's people being afflicted for lack of a shepherd, it is clear that the shepherd which the people lacked in 10:2 was a king of their own: "Therefore [the people] have set out just like sheep. They are afflicted for there is no shepherd." The implication of this verse is that the coming shepherd-king will solve the problem of the flock's present affliction (cf. 9:16). Indeed, Zech 1–8 has created the expectation for a coming king and 9:9 has just reasserted this expectation. When the Davidic king comes the people shall be afflicted no more. It is against this background that we are to understand the new leadership that Yahweh will provide for his people (10:4).

The shepherds of 10:3 are often understood to be the same shepherds (or lack thereof) as those in 10:2. However, a closer look at 10:3 suggests that they are not.[18] Yahweh's anger is not only against the shepherds; the text also says that his punishment will fall on the leaders, or literally, the "he-goats" (העתודים). This term is used on several occasions to refer to the leaders of foreign nations, in particular, their kings. It is never used of Israel's kings. For instance: "Sheol beneath is stirred up to meet you when you come; it rouses the shades to greet you, all who were leaders (עתוד) of the earth; it raises from their thrones all who were kings of the nations" (Isa 14:9), and "You shall eat the flesh of the mighty, and drink the blood of the princes of the earth—of rams, of lambs, and of he-goats (עתודים), of bulls, all of them fat beasts of Bashan" (Ezek 39:18).

In terms of the syntax of 10:3, either the term "he-goats" functions in parallel to the "shepherds" to further describe the same group, or the "he-goats" may be a different group of leaders. Yahweh's judgment of shepherds is also depicted in 11:1–3, and this aids identification:

[1] Open your doors, Lebanon, so that fire may consume your cedars. [2] Wail, cypress, for a cedar has fallen, whose glory has been ruined. Wail, oaks of Bashan, for the dense forest has been felled. [3] A sound of the shepherds wailing, for their glory has been ruined. A sound of lions roaring, for the thicket of the Jordan has been ruined. (author's translation)

17. Mason, "Earlier," 64, is right to infer that "we should see here a conscious re-application of traditional prophetic teaching." Mason highlights the connections that this passage has with Jer 14 (pp. 64–66). Cf. Larkin, *Eschatology*, 87–90; Mackay, *Zechariah*, 196–98.

18. The strong paragraph marker (פ) at the end of Zech 10:2 indicates a division before Zech 10:3 and suggests the introduction of a new idea.

This passage functions as a transition between ch. 10 and the two shepherd sign-actions of 11:4–17. It speaks of the judgment that is coming on the cedars of Lebanon and the oaks of Bashan. Lebanon had a reputation for its cedars and cypress, which, as 1 Kings records, were even used in the construction of the Jerusalem temple and Solomon's palace (1 Kgs 5:6; 7:2). Bashan was known for its mighty oaks (e.g. Isa 2:13; Ezek 27:6). While Lebanon and Bashan had been in Israelite hands for a time, Israel is not mentioned as being in Lebanon after Solomon, and the Israelites were removed from Bashan by Tiglath-pileser III of Assyria in the eighth century B.C.E.[19] For the pre-exilic and exilic prophets, Lebanon and Bashan epitomized all that was proud (e.g. Isa 2:13). Bashan was an idolatrous place (Amos 4:1). Both were the objects of Yahweh's wrath.[20]

Many scholars note the way that prophetic literature frequently appropriates arboreal imagery to speak of the majesty and power of rulers that often precedes their fall.[21] Like a "shepherd," the image of a tree or a plant is frequently used in relation to kingship, as has already been noted with the related term "Shoot."[22] Zechariah 11:1–2 speaks of the destruction that is coming on these proud nations, particularly their kings. It is closely connected with Zech 10:1–12, where Yahweh promises to bring the exiles home, back from such far-off countries as Egypt and Assyria (10:9–10a). In a new exodus, they will return to the land of Gilead and Lebanon (10:10b–11). The geography here is not arbitrary. Gilead refers to the region of Transjordanian land that was occupied by the tribes of Reuben, Gad, and the half-tribe of Manasseh, including Bashan in the north.[23] It was the territory through which Israel first approached the Promised Land under Moses (Deut 1:4; 3:1–11), and here naturally describes the route of the exiles returning from Egypt (Zech 10:10). Lebanon is also used to define the northernmost extent of the Promised Land (e.g. Deut 11:24; Josh 1:4). While separate from Israel for most of Israel's history, 1 Kgs 9:19 claims that Lebanon was part of Solomon's dominion. In a similar way to Gilead, Lebanon was the region through which those from Assyria would return (Zech 10:10). The Jordan (Zech 11:3) was also very significant in the entry of the Israelites into the Promised Land under Joshua (Josh 1–4).

19. J. C. Slayton, "Bashan," *ABD* 1:623–24 (624).

20. Hanson, *Apocalyptic*, 336 n. 33.

21. E.g. Smith, *Micah–Malachi*, 267; Merrill, *Zechariah*, 285–86; Sweeney, *Twelve*, 676.

22. See Chapter 4, §4.2.

23. E.g. Deut 23:6; 34:1; Judg 10–12; 20:1; 1 Kgs 4:13; 2 Kgs 15:29. See K. A. Kitchen, "Gilead," in *New Bible Dictionary* (ed. J. D. Douglas et al.; 2d ed.; Leicester: IVP, 1982), 421.

Hence, in preparation for the return of his people, Yahweh will clear the way by felling as trees and destroying with fire those who held sway in the land. In many ways, Zech 11:1–3 is a return to the theme of 9:1–8, which pictured Yahweh coming to re-establish the kingdom promised to David. Just as 9:1–8 chose cities that represented the extent of the land during David's reign, here Gilead, Lebanon, and the Jordan represent the borders of the land through which the returning exiles shall pass.[24]

The destruction of the nations and their leadership (Zech 11:1–2) results in the wailing of shepherds (11:3a). There is also a parallel phrase that speaks of the roaring of lions (11:3b), and a reason given for the animals' behaviour: "the thicket of the Jordan has been ruined" (11:3c). Are the lions the same group as the shepherds?

Sweeney suggests that the shepherds are the leaders of the nations whose glory shall be ruined, and that the image of the roaring lions brings to mind associations from other parts of the Hebrew Bible, namely, the lion of the tribe of Judah and hence the house of David.[25] He states:

> The use of this imagery suggests that the "trees" of the leaders who are to be destroyed are Jerusalem's or Judah's oppressors and that the "lion" who will be left to roar over their demise is Judah or the house of David. Certainly, such a scenario fits well with Zechariah 12–14, which describe YHWH's actions against the nations who threaten Judah and the continuing role of the house of David.[26]

At one level, this is an attractive interpretation, for it links this verse back to the future leadership that Yahweh will raise up in Zech 10:4 to replace the shepherds of 10:3. However, this interpretation largely depends on the lion image being equated with Judah on the basis of Gen 49; the problem is that it is not at all clear that this link is intended.[27] Furthermore, there is no indication that the roaring of the lions is celebrating the demise of the shepherds; in fact, the roaring of the lions is explicitly the result (כִּי) of their loss of habitat. Therefore, it seems unlikely that the lions are the new leadership that Yahweh will raise up (Zech 10:4) and hence this verse is not expressing the hope for the house of David that Sweeney suggests. It is more likely, as a number of scholars argue, that the juxtaposition of the two figures invites the identification of the shepherds who wail with the lions who roar. Floyd states: "This identification

---

24. For details on "the Jordan," though a different interpretation of its significance, see Meyers and Meyers, *Zechariah 9–14*, 248. Also H. O. Thompson, "Jordan River," *ABD* 3:953–58.
25. E.g. Gen 49:9; 1 Sam 17:34–36; Amos 1:2. See Sweeney, *Twelve*, 676.
26. Ibid., 677.
27. This shall also be seen shortly in relation to Zech 10:4.

suggests that the shepherds have been more like predators than protectors, and that they are more upset by their own loss of a resource to exploit than by any damage done to the flock's own well-being."[28]

Scholars are undecided regarding whom this group of shepherds/lions represent. Some argue that they are the leaders of the nations who oppressed Israel,[29] others that they are Israel's own worthless leaders.[30] However, the immediate context suggests that they are the leaders of foreign nations, namely, the cedars of Lebanon and oaks of Bashan.[31] Support for this comes from a very useful article that surveys the use of the "Shepherd-Ruler Metaphor" in the Hebrew Bible.[32] J. G. S. S. Thomson identifies several passages that speak of the leaders of foreign nations as shepherds.[33] In particular, Jer 12 speaks of the desolation of the exile that is the direct result of Yahweh abandoning his heritage, Israel. The shepherds who have brought about this desolation (12:10) are identified as being of the nations (cf. 12:14–17).[34] Significantly, these shepherds are also likened to wild beasts that devour Yahweh's people (12:9). To this we may add Jer 50:17, where the king of Assyria and the king of Babylon are both called lions. These passages give further grounds for understanding Zech 11:3 as simply switching metaphors to speak of the same group—foreign kings who have ruled over and afflicted Yahweh's people.[35] The "shepherds" who are under Yahweh's judgment in 11:3 are therefore the foreign kings who have oppressed Yahweh's people.

Given the way that "he-goats" refers exclusively to foreign kings elsewhere in the Hebrew Bible, and given that the "shepherds" of Zech 11:3 are clearly foreign kings, it seems best to understand these two terms in 10:3 as operating in parallel to refer to the same group, namely, foreign kings who have ruled and oppressed Yahweh's people. This is the group with whom Yahweh is angry and is about to punish, for he

28. Floyd, *Minor Prophets*, 482. Cf. Merrill, *Zechariah*, 286.

29. So Mitchell, "Zechariah," 298; Jones, "Fresh," 251; Baldwin, *Zechariah*, 178; Conrad, *Zechariah*, 171–72.

30. So Baron, *Zechariah*, 344; Hanson, *Apocalyptic*, 335; Smith, *Micah–Malachi*, 267; Stuhlmueller, *Rebuilding*, 132; McComiskey, "Zechariah," 3:1188.

31. The description in Zech 11:2: "whose glory is ruined" matches Zech 11:3: "their glory is ruined."

32. J. G. S. S. Thomson, "The Shepherd-Ruler Concept in the Old Testament and Its Application in the New Testament," *SJT* 8 (1955): 406–18 (410–11).

33. Isa 44:28; Jer 6:3; 12:10; Mic 5:5–6; Nah 3:18.

34. See Thompson, *Jeremiah*, 358.

35. See also Larkin, *Eschatology*, 103, who argues that as well as Jeremiah, the Targum tradition that the shepherds are leaders of foreign nations should be taken into account in the interpretation of Zech 11:3.

cares for the house of Judah. This explains the transition between 10:2 and 10:3: Yahweh's people had no shepherd (of their own) (10:2) and Yahweh's anger burned against the shepherds (from the nations) (10:3). It was the kings of the nations who ruled over Yahweh's people in the post-exilic period when they had no king of their own. Yahweh here promises to act against this group by raising up an alternative leadership for his people. By implication, this group would include their own shepherd.[36]

6.3.3. *A Shepherd for Joseph and Judah (Psalm 78)*

Psalm 78 provides an important perspective on the relationship between the house of Judah and the house of Joseph that features in Zech 10. It is a psalm that rehearses the history of Israel and highlights their repeated rebellion. It climaxes in Yahweh's rejection of his people on account of their high places and idolatry (Ps 78:58; cf. Zech 10:1). As well as delivering his people to captivity (Ps 78:61), the psalm speaks of Yahweh spurning the northern tribes: rejecting the tent of Joseph and not choosing the tribe of Ephraim (78:67); and forsaking his dwelling at Shiloh (78:60). However, the psalm ends on a note of hope as it recounts Yahweh choosing the tribe of Judah, building his sanctuary in Zion (78:68–69), and choosing David his servant to shepherd his people (78:70–72). The message of the psalm is that Yahweh's rejection of his people is not total. Instead, the future is to be found in his choice of Zion, Judah, and his shepherd, David.[37]

In Zechariah's day, the question that the people would have asked was: If Yahweh could reject the line of Ephraim, might he not also have done the same to Judah? Indeed, Jer 26:4b–6 prophesies of Judah: "If you will not listen to me, to walk in my law that I have set before you, and to listen to the words of my servants the prophets whom I sent to you urgently, though you have not listened, then I will make this house like

---

36. Hanson, *Apocalyptic*, 336, mistakenly argues that because it is the Jordan that is destroyed rather than some "some foreign capital," that it must refer to Israel's leaders. Hanson fails to take into account that Israel was presently being ruled by foreigners in the land (cf. Zech 1:1, 7; 7:7).

37. Alexander, *Paradise*, 106, 26, shows the way in which these themes are also seen in Genesis to 2 Kings. At the end of Genesis it appears that Joseph has the status of "first-born." However, Gen 38 interrupts the Joseph story with the account of Judah's seed. Alexander suggests that the account of the birth of Judah's twins, where Perez "breaks out" in front of the "first-born" Zerah, is significant in the light of the larger story. While Israel's leadership initially comes from Ephraim (e.g. Joshua and Saul), the "first-born" line of Ephraim is eventually rejected in the time of Samuel and replaced by David from the tribe of Judah (cf. Ps 78).

Shiloh, and I will make this city a curse for all the nations of the earth."
Against this background, the restoration of the temple in Jerusalem under
Zerubbabel in Zechariah's day is highly significant. It would rightly be
seen as a reaffirmation of Yahweh's commitment to Jerusalem and the
house of David. Jerusalem is not like Shiloh. It has not been rejected
forever. Indeed, in Ps 78, the coming of a Davidic king will not only see
the house of Judah being saved, but will also see the salvation of the
house of Joseph. Psalm 78 envisages the coming of a Davidic king who
will shepherd "Jacob" and "Israel" (v. 71). These names point to restoration and reunion of the nation as a whole under a Davidic king. The
references to the house of Judah and the house of Joseph/Ephraim in
Zech 10–11 must be understood against this background.

6.3.4. *An Alternative Leadership (Zechariah 10:4–5)*

After first announcing judgment on foreign leaders (Zech 10:3a), Yahweh
turns to affirm his commitment to his people, both the house of Judah
(10:3b–6a) and the house of Joseph/Ephraim (10:6b–7). What is envisaged is a restoration and reunification of the nation as a whole. Drawing
again on the imagery of warfare, Yahweh announces that he will
strengthen Judah so that they shall become like a majestic horse in battle
(Zech 10:3), and Ephraim will become like a mighty warrior (10:7). Key
to this strength and victory in battle is an alternative leadership that
Yahweh will provide for his people (10:4–5):

> [3] My anger has flared against the shepherds and I will punish the leaders,
> for Yahweh of hosts will attend to his flock, the house of Judah, and will
> establish them as his majestic horse in the battle.[4] From him a keystone,
> from him a peg, from him a battle bow, from him shall go forth every ruler
> together. [5] And they shall be as mighty men, trampling down in the mud of
> the streets in the battle, and they will fight, for Yahweh is with them, and
> they will put to shame the riders of horses. (author's translation)

Zechariah 10:4 piles up a number of leadership metaphors that four times
are said to come "from him" (ממנו). It is uncertain whether the antecedent
of this is the house of Judah or Yahweh himself. The wider theology of
the Hebrew Bible suggests the former, as it was from Judah that the
nation's leadership would arise (cf. Gen 49:10).[38] On the other hand, the

---

38. Keil, "Zechariah," 347, argues that the expression ממנו יצא at the end of
Zech 10:4 mitigates against it being Yahweh, as he believes it is "unheard-of and
unscriptural" that any leader will go forth or come forth out of Yahweh. However,
McComiskey, "Zechariah," 3:1180, contends that they must come from Yahweh,
because Yahweh is the one who cuts off the war bow (Zech 9:10) and sovereignly
supplies his people's needs (9:8, 11–16; 10:3, 6, 8–10). McComiskey understands

syntax and the context, which stress Yahweh's activity, favour Yahweh as the antecedent of ממנו.[39]

Dealing in a preliminary way with the metaphors, the "keystone" (פנה, literally "corner") often refers to the corner of a structure.[40] When it denotes a part of a building, it can refer to either a capstone that completes the building (e.g. Ps 118:22), or to the cornerstone of the foundation (e.g. Isa 28:16).[41] In both cases it designates a crucial stone in the structure from which the building finds its stability (hence it is translated "keystone" here). It is used as a metaphor for leadership in Judg 20:2; 1 Sam 14:38; and Isa 19:13.[42] Similarly, in Zech 10:4 it refers to a leader, who, given the way the metaphor works, should be understood as a key figure for strengthening the house of Judah and saving the house of Joseph (cf. Zech 10:6). Given the importance of the keystone for a house, the metaphor may also function at another level with an association between the keystone and the support that it will provide for the "house" of Judah and the "house" of Joseph.

The "peg" (יתד) most commonly refers to one of the pegs that secured the tabernacle (e.g. Exod 27:10; Num 3:37), but can also refer to a peg for hanging items from (e.g. Ezek 15:3).[43] A peg provides support for the object that it holds, and as a metaphor conveys a very similar meaning to the keystone. It is used as a metaphor for leadership in Isa 22:22–25. Here in Zech 10:4, the peg is a leader who strengthens the house of

---

ממנו in terms of agency. We note that ממנו can convey the sense of "out of" (e.g. Gen 26:16; 48:19; Jer 42:11), as well as agency (e.g. Nah 1:5, 6), so McComiskey's distinction is not decisive.

39. In terms of syntax, the plural reference to the house of Judah (אותם) in Zech 10:3 indicates that this may not be the antecedent. These two observations concerning syntax and context are made by Duguid, "Messianic," 271. Cf. Mason, "Relation," 236–37, who says: "The context, however, appears to place emphasis on the victory which Yahweh enables the community to achieve and this may tilt the balance towards the thought that emphasis is not on the leadership as such, but on Yahweh as the source of leadership and military prowess."

40. G. H. Matties and J. Walton, *"pinnâ," NIDOTTE* 3:640, cite the following uses: the corner of the altar (Exod 27:2); the ledge of the altar (Ezek 43:20); houses (Job 1:19); gates (Jer 31:40); city walls (Neh 3:24); corner towers (Zeph 1:16; 3:6); the city itself (2 Chr 28:24); one of Jerusalem's gates (2 Kgs 14:13; 2 Chr 26:9; Jer 31:38; Zech 14:10); and the corner of the street (Prov 7:8, 12).

41. M. Oeming, *"pinnâ," TDOT* 11:586–89 (587), cites references where it is a capstone (e.g. 2 Chr 26:15; Prov 21:9; 25:24; Zeph 1:16; 3:6) and where it is a cornerstone (e.g. Job 38:6).

42. BDB, 819, gives the meaning in these instances as "chief, ruler."

43. It can also refer to a digging implement (Deut 23:13) or a weaving pin (Judg 16:4). See BDB, 450. Also A. Tomasino, *"yātēd," NIDOTTE* 2:568–70.

Judah and saves the house of Joseph (cf. Zech 10:6). K. A. Kitchen notes that "tent" in ordinary speech came to be used of any kind of dwelling,[44] and so again there may be another level of association between the "peg" and the "house" of Judah and the "house" of Joseph (elsewhere called the "tent of Judah" in Zech 12:7, and the "tent of Joseph" in Ps 78:67).

The "battle bow" (קשת מלחמה) is not used as a metaphor for leadership anywhere else in the Hebrew Bible. However, it can readily be related to the ideas in the previous two metaphors. A strong bow leads to victory in battle, a weak or broken bow to defeat.[45] In Zech 9:13, Judah has been described as Yahweh's bow, the associations being ones of warfare and conquest.[46] In Gen 49:22–26, the bow of Joseph is said to be unmoved against the attacks of his enemies. It is clear that, as a metaphor for leadership, the bow pertains to a leader's military strength. This image ties in with the warfare that will secure the salvation of the house of Judah and the house of Joseph from their enemies (cf. Zech 10:5, 7).

The final description, "every ruler" (כל־נוגש), is best understood as a description of the previous metaphors collectively, with the sense of the verb יצא being understood for each of them. Surprising perhaps is the fact that "ruler" (נוגש) is otherwise used in a negative sense in the Hebrew Bible, describing an oppressor or tyrant.[47] Mason plausibly suggests that what is on view here is a reversal of roles, with those who had persecuted Israel now being oppressed.[48] This is certainly consistent with the description of their exploits in Zech 10:5.

What is the significance of these metaphors? Some scholars argue that they are all images of the future Davidic king. For instance, Cook states: "Within this chapter it is likely that Zech 10:4 contains a triple messianic designation. According to this verse, 'the cornerstone,' the 'tent peg,' and the 'bow of battle' will come from Judah. The Targum's messianic interpretation of these designations is probably on target."[49]

---

44. K. A. Kitchen, "Tent," in Douglas et al., eds., *New Bible Dictionary*, 1175.

45. See further, T. Kronholm, "*qešeṯ, qaššāṯ*," *TDOT* 13:201–8.

46. Mason, "Earlier," 82, cites Egyptian literature, where the enemies of Egypt are described as "bows."

47. E.g. Exod 3:7; Job 3:18; Dan 11:20; Zech 9:8.

48. Ibid., 83: "That which their traditional persecutors have been to them throughout their history, they will in turn become to them."

49. Cook, *Apocalypticism*, 137. Cf. C. L. Feinberg, "Exegetical Studies in Zechariah," *BibSac* 101 (1944): 434–45 (435); Rudolph, *Sacharja*, 196; Smith, *Micah–Malachi*, 265; Tidiman, *Zacharie*, 218. Wellhausen, "Zechariah," 4:5393, also understood this verse as a messianic prophecy analogous to that in Zech 9:9. Cf. J. Wellhausen, *Die Kleinen Propheten* (Berlin: de Gruyter, 1963), 192.

Merrill contends that all four elements contain "a strong mixture of messianic language," particularly the "battle bow," which, because of its associations with Judah in Zech 9:13, is consistent with the messianic theology of Gen 49:10, and "every ruler" coming from Judah, which is "a major OT theme."[50] Duguid believes that while the keystone and peg are not exclusively royal, they have strong royal associations.[51] Arguing that royalty from David's line is on view in this verse, Ollenburger believes that the metaphors are similar to the use of the Shoot in Zech 3:8 and 6:12.[52] C. and E. Meyers also understand these metaphors as being descriptive of the future Davidic king, particularly the keystone and peg.[53] They also suggest that Ezra 9:8–9 provides a retrospective view on Zech 10:4 in "reaffirming in eschatological language Israel's age-old preoccupation with Davidic rule."[54]

On the other hand, several scholars argue that these are simply metaphors for leadership, with no hope for a future Davidic king being expressed. So for instance, Redditt states that they are "three titles for the commanders who would emerge from Judah to lead her."[55] These shall be warriors, led by Yahweh in holy war. Similarly, Petersen argues that they are images of the military resources that Judah will provide; symbols of human strength, warriors.[56] Sweeney sees these metaphors covering both leadership and warlike action, and believes that they make no reference to any eschatological ruler.[57] Leske is adamant that the context demands that these be understood as titles that emphasize leadership coming from the people, rather than as references to a future Davidic king.[58]

There are other scholars who offer a different perspective on this verse. Mitchell agrees that the "keystone" and the "peg," and possibly also the

50. Merrill, *Zechariah*, 272–73.
51. Duguid, "Messianic," 271–72.
52. Ollenburger, "Zechariah," 814. Ollenburger also observes that in Zechariah the confounding of the cavalry comes after, rather than precedes, the presence of a cornerstone and tent peg.
53. Meyers and Meyers, *Zechariah 9–14*, 200. See also Meyers and Meyers, "Fortunes," 212–15.
54. Duguid, "Messianic," 271–72, follows C. and E. Meyers in seeing strong royal associations in the cornerstone and tent peg imagery, even of a new David. At the same time, he understands the battle bow as an image of military power and "every overseer" as a second class of leadership.
55. Redditt, *Zechariah*, 120.
56. Petersen, *Zechariah 9–14*, 74.
57. Sweeney, *Twelve*, 671–72. Cf. van Groningren, *Messianic Revelation*, who makes no reference to Zech 10:4 in his treatment of the messianic hope in the Old Testament.
58. Leske, "Context," 674 n. 30.

"bow," are all references to the king who will bear the responsibilities of government (cf. Isa 19:13; 22:23), and he backs this up by saying, "It is the Messiah, according to the Targum, who is meant."[59] However, he also believes that this verse is a scribal gloss that "has no particular fitness in this connection."[60] Mason argues from the connections with Ps 118 that Zech 10:4 has messianic connotations.[61] This is supported, Mason contends, by later Judaism, which identifies the stone in Ps 118:22 with the Messiah (Rashi on Mic 5:1), just as the Targum on Zech 10:4 identifies the corner with the Messiah. However, Mason believes:

> It is much more understandable that a later hand, seeing the Messianic connotation possible in these descriptions of leadership, should, in the light of Gen. 49:10, and the general Davidic and Messianic hopes attached to Judah (cf. Mic. 5:2; Isa. 11:1, etc.) introduce the name of Judah as the only possible source of such leadership. Yet a feature of these chapters is the close unity of North and South (cf. Zech. 9:10; 10:6). If this is so, then the gloss represents an early re-interpretation of this original verse along Davidic lines as we have in Micah.[62]

Earlier, Mason states that Zech 10:4 "seems to be more the promise of a general provision of adequate leadership to replace the unworthy ones than to a Messianic figure specifically of the Davidic line."[63]

The variety of opinions shows the tentative nature of a conclusion about allusions to a future Davidic king in these metaphors. Indeed, decisions concerning the nature of the Davidic hope elsewhere in the book of Zechariah largely determine whether or not these metaphors are seen by scholars to convey a hope for a future Davidic king. Nevertheless, there are several other exegetical factors that must be taken into account. The first is that the immediate context quite clearly does not envisage the coming of a single figure. The phrase "every ruler together" is best understood as a summary of all those who have come forth, namely the keystone, peg and battle bow.[64] This summary expression does not support the view that the three metaphors represent one figure.

Furthermore, in Zech 10:5 this plurality of leadership is referred to as "they" rather than "he," and are likened to "mighty men" (plural) in the

---

59. Mitchell, "Zechariah," 289.
60. Ibid.
61. Mason, "Earlier," 79. While the psalm does not explicitly identify the speaker, Mason believes on the basis of Ps 118:10–13 that the speaker of Ps 118:22 can hardly refer to anyone else but the king.
62. Ibid., 84.
63. Ibid., 34.
64. Cf. Webb, *Zechariah*, 140.

expression וְהָיוּ כְגִבֹּרִים.[65] Moreover, in context, 10:4 is providing a solution to the problem of 10:1–3. In 10:3, Yahweh announces his anger against shepherds who were afflicting Yahweh's flock. In 10:4, Yahweh promises a replacement of these leaders, a leadership that will fight for their people. This balance between problem and solution also points towards the metaphors representing a multiplicity of leaders as Yahweh raises up new leaders to replace those who are under his judgment. Hence the interpretation of these metaphors as referring to a single figure does not adequately account for the text that envisages a plurality of leadership.

Do any of these metaphors convey a hope for a future Davidic king? The keystone or "cornerstone" clearly becomes an image of the future Davidic king in later times (e.g. *Tg. Zech* 10:1;[66] cf. Acts 4:11; 1 Pet 2:6–7), but it is not really clear whether Zechariah drew on earlier biblical material with Davidic associations for this metaphor. Isaiah 28:14–16 speaks of Yahweh having "laid as a foundation in Zion, a stone, a tested stone, a precious cornerstone, of a sure foundation." This is the stone that will stand firm in the coming judgment on Jerusalem and its leadership, but it is not clear in the immediate context of Isaiah what it refers to. The wider context opens the possibility of it being the future Davidic king of Isa 6, 9, and 11; however, scholars think that Isaiah's intent is more general at this point.[67]

The other significant reference to the "cornerstone" is in Ps 118:22: "The stone that the builders rejected has become the cornerstone." Again, it is difficult to know with any certainty whether Zechariah drew his metaphor from this text to convey a hope for a future king beyond the rejection of the Davidic monarchy in the exile. It seems more likely that the keystone metaphor came to Zechariah's mind simply because of its

65. While Zech 10:4 could be taken as an aside, with the referent of "they" being the house of Judah in Zech 10:3, the fact that Ephraim is compared to a mighty one (כְגִבּוֹר—note that the form is singular) in Zech 10:7 seems to suggest that it is not the house of Judah, but the leaders that are on view in Zech 10:5.

66. This reads: "From them will be *their king*, from them *their anointed One*, from them *their strength in* war, from them shall all their *leaders* alike *be appointed*." Quoted from Gordon, *Targum*, 209. Gordon notes that "king" is the translation of MT "cornerstone" and is taken to refer to King David. The "anointed One" is in the place of "tent-peg." Gordon also notes that in the Targum the king and the Messiah may be one and the same.

67. J. N. Oswalt, *The Book of Isaiah: Chapters 1–39* (NICOT; Grand Rapids: Eerdmans, 1986), 518, lists twelve alternatives, which include the temple (Ewald), the archetypal Davidic monarch (Delitzsch), true believers (Eichrodt), Zion (Childs), and the remnant (Donner).

associations with the "house" of Judah and the "house" of Joseph. The keystone would provide support and strength for these houses.

The "peg" is not used elsewhere as a designation for the future Davidic king in the Hebrew Bible, although in Isa 22:22–25 the throne of Eliakim the son of Hilkiah is likened to a "peg" on which is hung the honour of the house of David. In Isaiah's parable, however, the peg will give way and the load that is on it will be cut off and fall down. It is possible that Zechariah had this in mind and spoke of a peg that will not fail to carry the honour of the house of David, as Eliakim had failed. However, once again it seems more likely that the peg metaphor was chosen simply because of the support that it would give to the "house"/ "tent" of Judah and the "house"/"tent" of Joseph.[68]

It has already been noted that the "battle bow" is not used as a metaphor for leadership elsewhere in the Hebrew Bible. Neither is it used with Davidic associations, though it is associated with Joseph in Gen 49:24, and the Ephraimites in Ps 78:9. It is therefore not clear that any of these three metaphors were used because of earlier associations with the house of David.

Having said that, one aspect of these verses that is seldom explored is the description of these leaders in Zech 10:5 "as mighty men" (כגברים).[69] While it is true that in the Hebrew Bible this is often simply a general description of those who are mighty warriors, both Israelite and non-Israelite,[70] it does also refer to a special band of men who supported David in his kingship (e.g. 1 Chr 11:10–12), one that later pledged their allegiance to King Solomon (1 Chr 29:24). David himself is first introduced as a "mighty man" (גבור) in 1 Sam 16:18, and so it is possible that just as Zech 9 drew on the past to paint a picture of the future, so the reference here to "mighty men" invokes the days of David when the "mighty men" subjugated Israel's enemies and in whose time the tribes of the north and south were united.[71] This fits the immediate context (cf. the references to Joseph, Ephraim, and Judah in Zech 10:6–7). Indeed, the image of the leader as a shepherd in the wider biblical context must bring to mind David, the shepherd from Judah.

Hence, while the metaphors of Zech 10:4 envisage a plurality of leadership, in all likelihood the king of 9:9–10 is included within this

68. Note that the Targum translates "peg" as "anointed One." See n. 66, above.

69. This connection is only made, as far as I can tell, by Meyers and Meyers, *Zechariah 9–14*, 204.

70. E.g. Gen 10:8; Josh 6:2; 10:7; Judg 6:12.

71. It must be noted that Chronicles postdates Zechariah and this material is unique to Chronicles, but this does not necessarily mean composition by the Chronicler.

group, being understood from the wider context of ch. 9, as such scholars as C. and E. Meyers have suggested.[72] Many have noted the similarities between chs. 9 and 10: both have a positive tone; they envisage a battle victory; they are concerned for Judah and Ephraim; and they both promote the theme of return from exile.[73] Since the king was the lynchpin of the restoration of land and people in ch. 9, it seems appropriate to understand the king continuing this role in ch. 10—especially since ch. 10 begins by identifying the people's need for their own shepherd-king. The other factor that supports the view that the king of ch. 9 is in view is that the king was the leader of leaders, and if the phrase "every ruler together" is taken on its face value, then we should expect it to include the already identified future Davidic king. Moreover, this is also consistent with Ezek 37:3–6, which speaks of shepherds (plural) being raised up, of which "my shepherd David" is one.

On this interpretation, the picture of the coming king, albeit among other leaders, runs along the same lines as Zech 9. The king will be involved in a victory whereby the enemies of Yahweh will be judged and Yahweh's kingdom will be re-established, reuniting Judah and Ephraim. As in ch. 9, exodus imagery is used to describe the ultimate end of Israel's exile that this will bring (10:8–11), accompanied by blessing (10:7).[74]

6.3.5. *Summary of Shepherd Leadership in Zechariah 10:1–11:3*

There is a great divergence of opinion among scholars on whether the metaphors in Zech 10:4 are to be understood in Davidic terms. A close examination of the text, context, and background of these metaphors reveals that the "keystone," "peg," and "battle bow" refer first and foremost to leaders that Yahweh will raise up to save his people from their affliction, and gather those from both south and north who remain scattered among the nations. From the wider context of Zechariah and the immediate context that sees this action being on behalf of the tribes of Joseph and Judah (cf. Ps 78), it seems almost certain that the Davidic king is to be included among these leaders.[75]

---

72. Meyers and Meyers, *Zechariah 9–14*, 200.

73. M. J. Boda, "Reading Between the Lines: Zechariah 11:4–16 in Its Literary Contexts," in Boda and Floyd, eds., *Bringing out the Treasure*, 277–91 (289).

74. For further treatment of the Exodus themes, see A. F. Schellenberg, "One in the Bond of War: The Unity of Deutero-Zechariah," *Didaskalia* 12 (2001): 101–15.

75. Indeed, Zech 10:4 may have given impetus for later writers to identify the "cornerstone" of Isa 28:14 and Ps 118:22 as the Davidic king, as attested in texts of later Judaism and the New Testament.

6.4. *Two Shepherd Sign-Actions (Zechariah 11:4–17)*

Zechariah 11:4–17 continues the theme of shepherd leadership with the prophet commanded to act the role of two different shepherds in two separate sign-actions. Before investigating the hope expressed for the house of David in these sign-actions, it is necessary to determine the most appropriate approach to this section of Zechariah. Do these sign-actions prophetically portray the future? Do they characterize the contemporary situation and reflect some of the tensions in the post-exilic community? Do they dramatically portray the past? Or are they a combination of these approaches? As shall be seen, the way that the text is approached largely determines the answer that is given to the question of the hope for the house of David seen here. In this section, I shall survey each of the scholarly approaches to this passage, evaluate their strengths and weaknesses, and seek a reading that best coheres with the book of Zechariah as a whole and the wider biblical context. From this position, the implications of this passage for the hope held for the house of David shall be drawn out.

6.4.1. *Structure*

Zechariah 11:4–17 is clearly a separate literary unit comprising two sign-action reports. Butterworth comments: "Despite the acute problems of interpretation, there is no dispute about the fact that vv. 4–17 belong together, and that the section falls into two unequal parts: vv. 4–14, 15–17. The word עוֹד in v. 15 makes the connection explicit."[76] The following thematic structure is also supported by the MT weak paragraph markers at the end of 11:3, 14, 16, and 17:

> *Zech 11:4–17: Two sign-actions*
> | | |
> |---|---|
> | 11:4 | Command to perform the first action |
> | 11:5–6 | Reason for the action |
> | 11:7–14 | Enactment |
> | 11:15 | Command to perform the second action |
> | 11:16 | Reason for the action |
> | 11:17 | Announcement of woe |

6.4.2. *Two Sign-Actions (Zechariah 11:4–17)*

[4] Thus said Yahweh my God, "Shepherd the flock of the slaughter. [5] Those who buy them slaughter them and they are not punished. Those who sell them say, 'Blessed be Yahweh, I am rich!' And their shepherds do not have mercy on them. [6] For I will no longer have mercy on the inhabitants of the

---

76. Butterworth, *Structure*, 77.

land," declares Yahweh. "Behold, I will cause each man to fall into the hand of his neighbour, and into the hand of his king, and they will strike the land, and I will not deliver from their hand."

[7] I shepherded the flock of the slaughter, indeed the afflicted of the flock.[77] And I took to myself two staffs, one I named "favour," and one I named "union," and I shepherded the flock. [8] I got rid of the three shepherds in one month, and I grew impatient with them, and moreover, they loathed me. [9] I said, "I will not shepherd you. The dying one, let die, and the perishing one, let perish, and the remaining ones, let each consume the flesh of its neighbour."

[10] I took my staff 'favour' and I cut it in two to break my covenant that I had made with all the peoples.[11] And it was broken on that day, thus the afflicted of the flock, the ones who had obeyed me, knew that this was the word of Yahweh. [12] And I said to them, "If it is good in your eyes, pay my wage, but if not, cease." And they weighed out my wage—thirty pieces of silver. [13] And Yahweh said to me, "Throw it to the potter"—the handsome price at which I was priced by them. And I took the thirty pieces of silver and I threw them to the potter in the house of Yahweh. [14] And I cut into two my second staff 'union' to break the brotherhood between Judah and Israel.

77. Most scholars propose that the consonantal text should be redivided and repointed by combining לְבֵן with עֲנִיֵּי in Zech 11:7 to give the translation "on behalf of the sheep merchants" (cf. NRSV). They argue that this translation is what lies behind the LXX. For example, T. J. Finley, "The Sheep Merchants of Zechariah 11," *Grace Theological Journal* 3 (1982): 51–65 (60), notes: "The MT is supported by all the other ancient versions and is represented in a fragment of a Qumran commentary on Isaiah (4Q163 21)." Finley, who believes that the more difficult textual variant is to be preferred, argues that the LXX is more difficult because it omits any translation of הַצֹּאן. However, surely it is more likely that the LXX translator has struggled with the two difficult Hebrew phrases, and rendered them inaccurately as εἰς τὴν Χαναανῖτιν (Zech 11:7) and οἱ Χαναναῖοι (Zech 11:11). Further, Finley concludes that the LXX reading makes better sense within the context; however, we shall see that the reverse is the case.

The problem with the translation "on behalf of the sheep merchants" is that it is difficult to understand why or how the prophet would act favourably on the sheep merchants' behalf. To resolve this, other scholars soften the force of ל to "by the sheep traders," but one would normally expect the preposition בּ in this case. It seems best to retain the MT and translate לָבֵן as "hence" (cf. 1 Sam 27:6), with the sense that when the prophet became shepherd of the flock, he also became shepherd of the afflicted of the nation (cf. NASB). The "afflicted of the flock" thereby specifies a class within the nation as a whole, and this becomes an important element in the interpretation of the passage. Scholars who follow the MT reading include Keil, "Zechariah," 361; BDB, 486; A. Caquot, "Brèves Remarques sur l'allegorie des Pasteurs en Zacharie 11," in *Mélanges Bibliques et Orientaux en l'honneur de M. Mathias Delcor* (ed. A. Caquot, S. Légasse, and M. Tardieu; Neukirchen–Vluyn: Neukirchener Verlag, 1985), 45–55 (49); Larkin, *Eschatology*, 110–11; McComiskey, "Zechariah," 3:1194; Webb, *Zechariah*, 148.

[15] Yahweh said to me, "Again, take to yourself an implement of a foolish shepherd. [16] For behold, I am raising up a shepherd in the land. The perishing he will not care for, the young he will not seek, the maimed he will not heal, the standing he will not support, but he will consume the flesh of the fat ones, and tears off their hoofs.

[17] Woe to my worthless shepherd that forsakes the flock! A sword on his arm and his right eye! May his arm be completely withered, his right eye totally blinded! (author's translation)

While the elements of this passage are mostly straightforward, its interpretation is difficult. Many scholars agree with Driver's assessment that this passage is "the most enigmatic in the Old Testament."[78] To begin, there is no consensus on the form of this passage. The four main contenders are: allegory,[79] parable,[80] vision,[81] or report of a prophetic sign-action.[82] While this passage seems to resemble most closely the sign-actions performed by other prophets (e.g. Isa 20:1–4; Jer 13:1–11; Ezek 4–5; Hos 1:2–9; 3:1–5), it is difficult to understand how some of the elements of the first sign-action would have been enacted by the prophet, such as destroying three shepherds (Zech 11:8), or being paid by

78. S. R. Driver, *The Minor Prophets: Nahum, Habakkuk, Zephaniah, Haggai, Zechariah, Malachi* (The Century Bible; Edinburgh: T. C. & E. C. Jack, 1906), 253.

79. E.g. R. C. Dentan, "The Book of Zechariah: Chapters 9–14 (Introduction and Exegesis)," *IB* 6:1089–114 (1091, 1102). L. V. Meyer, "An Allegory Concerning the Monarchy: Zech 11:4–17; 13:7–9," in *Scripture in History and Theology* (ed. A. L. Merrill and T. W. Overholt; Pennsylvania: Pickwick, 1977), 225–40 (226–27), gives three reasons why it is an allegory rather than a symbolic action. First, what is described could not have been carried out by the prophet, especially destroying three shepherds. Second, the passage uses conventional literary images, which weighs against viewing it as an account of a symbolic action. Third, the way that action and meaning are intermixed in this passage is uncharacteristic of symbolic actions.

80. E.g. A. S. van der Woude, "Die Hirtenallegorie von Sacharja XI," *JNSL* 12 (1984): 139–49 (143–44). He believes that the classification of the text as "allegories" does not allow for the view that everything in the text has a figurative meaning. Though the good shepherd is a representative of God, in Zech 11:4–14 he is not a metaphor for the Messiah.

81. E.g. J. Lindblom, *Prophecy in Israel* (Philadelphia: Fortress, 1962), 146.

82. E.g. M. Sæbø, *Sacharja 9–14: Untersuchungen von Text und Form* (WMANT 34; Neukirchen–Vluyn: Neukirchener Verlag, 1969), 245; Floyd, *Minor Prophets*, 490; Curtis, *Steep*, 162. On the terminology of "sign-action," see the work of Friebel, "Sign-Actions," 27–46, who argues that within semiotics and non-verbal communication theory, a "symbol" refers to signs that have no visual or auditory semblance between the sign and referent, whereas a "sign" is a more general term which is inclusive of various types of encoding. While biblical scholars have generally used the terminology of "symbolic action," Friebel argues that a more accurate designation is "sign-action," and so this terminology has been employed here.

the sheep (11:12).[83] Indeed, the second of the sign-actions is never reported as being carried out. Because of this, while the passage contains two reports of sign-actions to be played out by the prophet, it seems best to understand them as a literary device rather than as actual prophetic acts.[84] Whether these sign-actions function as a parable or allegory largely depends on how these terms are defined. Either way, these actions represent a situation or event(s) outside themselves.

Yet, if the form is difficult to define, even more complex is the key issue of what the two sign-actions actually signify. The main issue to resolve here is whether the prophet Zechariah is called: (1) to play out events that were contemporary or future to himself as an enacted prophecy; (2) to characterize the contemporary situation by means of reinterpreting earlier prophet texts; or (3) to represent an event or events in the nation's past. Scholarly treatments of this passage generally fall into one of these approaches. In seeking to establish the meaning and significance of this passage, I shall survey and critique each of these approaches in turn and deal with the various exegetical issues in the passage as they arise.

6.4.2.1. *Enacted prophecy.* The most common approach by scholars to this passage has been to see in it references to events future to the prophet. That is, the prophet is called to act out a representation of the future. Alternatively, some scholars argue that while the text may portray future events, in reality it reflects a past event that the prophet has projected into the future.[85] As to what these events were, there is a vast variety of opinion. Writing in 1912, Mitchell states that there are at least 40 different conjectures as to the identity of the three shepherds who

---

83. Sweeney, *Twelve*, 678, understands Zech 4:4–14 as describing a symbolic act that the prophet was called to play out. He understands "the flock doomed to slaughter" as referring to actual sheep that were used in the temple sacrifice, and therefore that the prophet was called to play the role of a priest involved in the temple sacrifices. Boda, "Reading," 281 n. 17, rightly notes that a priest caring for the temple flocks does not fit with the image of a shepherd who was to protect the flock from slaughter. Further, real sheep do not detest their shepherd (Zech 13:8).

84. So Ackroyd, "Zechariah," 653; Hanson, *Apocalyptic*, 343; Redditt, *Zechariah*, 122–23; Floyd, *Minor Prophets*, 490.

85. So, for instance, Dentan, "Zechariah," 6:1102, when discussing the historical situation that lies behind this passage, favours the Ptolemaic period rather than the time of the Maccabaean wars, because, he argues: "it is hardly likely that the passage can be so late in date." Here again we see how presuppositions come into play in interpretation, particularly the assumption that prophecy must have been written retrospectively.

were removed (Zech 11:8).[86] Mitchell himself believes that this passage is a parable that "requires the prophet to personate a king and illustrate the character of his government."[87] While the author of the parable carefully avoids identifying this king, Mitchell believes it is to be understood as Ptolemy III, king of Egypt from 247 to 222 B.C.E., with the circumstances of the parable paralleling his reign. He argues that the three shepherds are most likely the three Seleucid kings who were removed from power within a year: Seleucus IV, Heliodorus, and Demetrius Soter.[88]

Other examples of this approach include W. O. E. Oesterley, who believes that the shepherds were high priests in the second century B.C.E. The good shepherd was Onias III, and the three who were removed were Jason, Menelaus, and Alcimus.[89] M. Trèves argues that the good shepherd is to be identified as Judas Maccabaeus, who deposed apostate priests and officials loyal to the Greeks when he liberated Jerusalem.[90] He further identifies Alcimus, the high priest appointed by the Seleucids (161–159 B.C.E.), as the worthless shepherd of Zech 11:16.

Another group of scholars, who take the same approach in seeing events future to the prophet being played out here, identifies the good shepherd in this passage as Jesus Christ, and hence the coming king of Zech 9:9–10.[91] Key to this identification is the thirty pieces of silver that

---

86. Mitchell, "Zechariah," 306. Of those suggestions that were future to the prophet, Mitchell cites Maurer (1840), Hitzig (1881), and Ewald (1868), who identify Zechariah, Shallum and perhaps Menahem as the three shepherds; Abarbanel (1508), who identifies Judas Maccabaeus and his brothers Jonathan and Simon; Theodoret (457 C.E.), who identifies kings, priests, and prophets; and Lightfoot (1859), who sees Pharisees, Sadducees, and Essenes.

87. Mitchell, "Zechariah," 303. Later (p. 307), Mitchell argues that Zech 11:6 makes it clear that the term "shepherd" is being used synonymously for "king," but it is not a good shepherd that is on view, much less Yahweh. He argues that it is only a fallible and recreant human ruler who would become impatient with the sheep (11:8).

88. Ibid., 307. One problem with Mitchell's suggestion is that these three Seleucid kings came to power some time after Ptolemy III. Baldwin, *Zechariah*, 182, also cites C. H. H. Wright, *Zechariah and His Prophecies, Considered in Relation to Modern Criticism: With a Critical and Grammatical Commentary and New Translation* (London: Hodder & Stoughton, 1879), 313, who favours Antiochus IV, Antiochus V, and Demetrius.

89. W. O. E. Oesterley, *A History of Israel*, vol. 2 (Oxford: Clarendon, 1932), 258.

90. M. Trèves, "Conjectures Concerning the Date and Authorship of Zechariah IX–XIV," *VT* 13 (1963): 196–207.

91. Baron, *Zechariah*, 382; Keil, "Zechariah," 371; Moore, *Zechariah*, 172–83; Luck, *Zechariah*, 101–2; Boice, *Minor Prophets*, 200–206; McComiskey, "Zechariah," 3:1201.

found its fulfilment in the payment made to Judas to betray Jesus (cf. Matt 27:1–10). Most understand the three shepherds that he cuts off as representative of three classes of leaders in Israel—prophets, priests, and kings.[92] All are agreed that the breaking of the staffs refers to the events immediately preceding the destruction of the second temple by the Romans in 70 C.E. The foolish shepherd of Zech 11:15–16 is identified specifically as Imperial Rome,[93] or more generally as the Antichrist.[94] This interpretation understands 11:4–14 as the rejection of the coming Davidic ruler by his people, as portrayed in 12:10 and 13:7.

A closely related view is simply that the shepherd is to be understood as the coming Davidic king on the basis of earlier prophetic texts.[95] Rudolph argues, for instance, that since the shepherd and Yahweh are intimately related in Zech 11:4–14 (as is seen in 11:10b and 11:13, and in 11:11b where the shepherd speaks the word of Yahweh), and because the same relationship exists between Yahweh and the shepherd in Ezek 34, where the shepherd is the new David (cf. Ezek 34:23; 37:24), then the shepherd of Zech 11:4–14 is to be understood as the future Davidic king.[96]

As is evident from this overview, scholars who attempt to tie the details of this passage into specific historical events that were future or contemporary to the prophet Zechariah have a seemingly endless number of options. This in itself suggests that this approach is largely speculative.[97] Furthermore, the simple identification of the "good shepherd" as

---

92. Baron, *Zechariah*, 399; Moore, *Zechariah*, 176; Luck, *Zechariah*, 102; Boice, *Minor Prophets*, 202. However, Keil, "Zechariah," 363, rejects this identification of the three shepherds that he says was first proposed by Thoedoret, Cyril, and Jerome, and argues that they represent "heathen liege-lords of the covenant nation." He argues that they are not three rulers of one empire, but three rulers of three different empires.

93. So Keil, "Zechariah," 378. Similarly, McComiskey, "Zechariah," 3:1205–7, states that "it is impossible to place this section historically," however, he does suggest it may again be a reference to the emperor Titus in the events of 70 C.E., and the fall of the Roman empire.

94. So Luck, *Zechariah*, 104; Boice, *Minor Prophets*, 204–5. Baron, *Zechariah*, 416–18, makes both identifications.

95. Lamarche, *Zacharie IX–XIV*, 151: "Ce bon pasteur [of Zech 11:4–14] nous a été présenté en 9,9 sous les traits du Roi messianique."

96. Rudolph, *Sacharja*, 205.

97. Referring to the suggestions on the three shepherds, Baldwin, *Zechariah*, 183, makes the apt comment: "In the face of such a diversity of opinions certainty about the identity of the three shepherds is impossible, and, since no one suggestion has proved convincing, further speculation over possible candidates is likely to be unprofitable."

Jesus Christ also raises problems. It is by no means clear who the three shepherds were that Jesus destroyed,[98] how he deserted the flock of his people,[99] or how he annulled any brotherhood between Judah and Israel since during his ministry it never existed.[100] This is not to say that it has no connection with Jesus Christ. Matthew's Gospel certainly sees a fulfilment of this passage in the betrayal of Jesus by Judas for thirty pieces of silver.[101] However, Matthew's usage of this passage is best understood as a typological fulfilment rather than a promise fulfilment.[102] This also means that it is very unlikely that the primary referent of the shepherd image in this passage is the future Davidic king, and hence the argument that uses this identification to equate the "good shepherd" of this passage with the coming Davidic king of Zech 9:9–10 is wanting.

Perhaps the greatest difficulty with the approach that sees references to events future to the prophet in this passage is that it really fails to explain how this passage functions in its context in the book of Zechariah. While the wider context of the book certainly speaks of difficult days ahead for the people of Yahweh, in the wider context, suffering always ends with

98. The view that they refer to the offices of prophet, priest, and king seems to create more problems than it solves. How, for instance, did Jesus abolish the office of king?

99. As the good shepherd, Jesus even goes to his death for his sheep, which is hardly a desertion. Indeed, Jesus makes a *contrast* in John 10:11–12 between his own actions as a shepherd and the shepherd who deserts the flock.

100. We only need to note the way that the Jews despised the Samaritans (e.g. John 4:9; Matt 10:5) to observe something of the division between Judah and Israel in Jesus' day. If anything, rather than breaking the brotherhood between Judah and Israel, Jesus united these groups once more (e.g. John 4:21–26; Acts 8:5–25).

101. For the most recent treatment of why Matthew attributes this passage to Jeremiah, see Ham, *King*, 60–66. Ham concludes (p. 68): "While the citation is primarily from Zech 11:13, Matthew has attributed it to Jeremiah to cite the more notable prophet, to draw attention to allusions to Jeremiah in the passage, and to explain the death of Jesus with reference to Jeremiah as the prophet of rejection. Of the three texts from Jeremiah that may stand behind such allusions, Jer 19:1–13 seems most likely, because it shares with Matt 27:3–10, among other elements, the judgment against those guilty of shedding/betraying 'innocent blood'."

102. For this distinction, see S. Greidanus, *Preaching Christ from the Old Testament: A Contemporary Hermeneutical Method* (Grand Rapids: Eerdmans, 1999), 240–61. So, for instance, Webb, *Zechariah*, 154–55, argues that the shepherd whom the prophet is to portray in this passage is Yahweh, and since the Messiah was Yahweh's representative, Webb suggests it was entirely appropriate for Matthew to "transpose into a higher key" this clash between Yahweh and the false shepherds in this passage in Zechariah as he saw it played out in the person of Jesus the Messiah. Webb, rightly I believe, understands Matthew to use this text of Zechariah typologically.

salvation. Yet here, the first shepherd is rejected, the people are decimated, staffs and what they represent are shattered, and a devouring shepherd is raised up. The only possible ground for optimism is that woe is pronounced on the worthless shepherd in the final verse. The approach that sees references to events future to the prophet in this passage results in a very bleak picture of the future. If this is a picture of the future, it requires a better explanation of how it coheres with the rest of the book. So, for instance, since the wider context sounds the theme of the reunion of Judah and Israel so strongly,[103] how can this be reconciled with this vision of the future where this brotherhood is annulled (Zech 11:14)? How can the book look forward to the remnant being saved (e.g. 8:11) and yet speak of it being destroyed (11:9)? This is also the main problem for such scholars as Rudolph and Lamarche who identify the shepherd of the first sign-action with the coming king of 9:9–10. How is the future destruction of the people of Yahweh that is portrayed in ch. 11 consistent with the salvation and peace that the king is said to bring in the rest of the book? This approach does not adequately explain these difficulties.

6.4.2.2. A characterization of the contemporary tensions in the community. A second approach seems to thrive on the apparent discord within the passage, seeing it as characterizing the contemporary situation, more so than the future, and reflecting different tensions within the community or the changed circumstances of the community. Scholars who take this approach argue that this passage is a reworking of earlier prophetic material to reflect these tensions or changes. This has big implications for the way that the hope held for the house of David is understood.

So, for instance, Hanson argues that Zech 11:4–17 is a commissioning narrative that arose from the struggle between the visionary and hierocratic elements within post-exilic Israel.[104] The spokesman for the visionaries is commissioned to shepherd Yahweh's flock, but in a way that serves as a bitter attack on the nation's hierocratic leaders. The passage then functions as a polemical dialogue with Ezekiel's optimistic vision, which was held by the hierocrats.[105] Rather than an ideal Davidic shepherd being raised up to feed them (as in Ezek 34:23; 37:24), the visionary group contradicts this, instead speaking of an evil shepherd being raised up (Zech 11:15–16). Hence, there are two contradictory views of the future in the background of this passage. The overall

103.   E.g. Zech 8:13; 9:10, 13; 10:6–7; 12:12.
104.   Hanson, *Apocalyptic*, 241–42. For a précis of Hanson's portrayal of the tensions in the early post-exilic community, see Chapter 2, §2.2.1.3.
105.   Ibid., 343–45.

message though, is that the temple and its leaders are responsible for the destruction of the community. In terms of the hope that was held for the house of David, Hanson argues:

> ...there is sufficient grounds tentatively to assume that the Judean governor, at least during part of the fifth century, was of the house of David. If this assumption is correct, the worthless shepherd in verses 15–16 is best interpreted as the Davidic governor... The bitter polemic of this composition thus is directed against the Davidic governor and the hierocratic temple party with which he is associated.[106]

Furthermore,

> If the governors of the part of the fifth century which concerns this study were in fact Davidic, the total absence of a Davidic messianism in the eschatology of the visionary tradition of this period becomes understandable. The future hope crystallizes instead around a vastly different type of figure, one who suffers oppression, even martyrdom (e.g. Is 52:13–53:12; Zech 12:10–14). This figure is comprehensible sociologically only within a matrix of persecution. It was only at a later period, when the Davidic line had ceased and the oppression of the visionaries under a Davidic governor had come to an end, that the idea of a Davidide could again be idealized by the visionary tradition into the conception of a Davidic Messiah.[107]

Hanson's reconstruction has been criticized by Laato, who argues that his view of Zech 11 conveying critical attitudes toward the hierocrats (Zadokites) does not have any support from the text.[108] Laato constructs the sociological background differently. He argues that there were two different religious groups who criticized the same political and religious situation from two different viewpoints. One group, who were responsible for Ezek 40–48, had a critical attitude towards the house of David. The other group, who preserved the earlier Ezekielian traditions, were responsible for Zech 9–14. He believes: "While the Zadokite party modified the Ezekelian vision in Ezek 40–48 by restricting the role of the *nāśîʾ* in the cult, the religious group which is responsible for Zech 9–14 remained loyal to the Zecharianic (i.e. Ezekielian) messianic hopes concerning the coming righteous Messiah as we have seen in 9:9–10."[109]

Laato is not convinced by Hanson's view that the true shepherd refers to the visionaries. He argues that the true shepherd is the eschatological Messiah whom Yahweh would raise up to put into effect the programme

106. Ibid., 350.
107. Ibid., 350 n. 39.
108. Laato, *Josiah*, 280–83.
109. Ibid., 282.

of events outlined in Zech 9:1–11:3.[110] The rejection of the shepherd was the rejection of the religious group's messianic and religious programme. The breaking of the staffs was an indication that it was the people and their leaders who were "responsible for dashing the messianic hopes expressed in the Ezekelian traditions."[111] Zechariah 11:15–17 then presents the consequences of this rejection of "the eschatological group's messianic programme"—they are given a worthless shepherd who will destroy them. Laato suggests that this figure may have been thought to be the governor of Yehud at the time of writing.[112] Hence, in the final form of the book, 11:4–17 reflects a rejection of any messianic hope.

While not reconstructing the social background to the same extent, Mason adopts the same approach when he suggests that what is on view here is a continued reworking of material that reflects a critical attitude to the official leadership of the community. He argues that there is no longer any strong hope for a future Davidic king, as there had been in earlier oracles.[113] He sees a dependence on the prophet Ezekiel, but believes that here the original act of Ezekiel appears to have been completely reversed.[114] The taking of the equipment of a foolish shepherd is directed against the official leadership after the prophet had withdrawn from them. Such leadership is the judgment of Yahweh on his people, and also the target of his judgment.[115]

Redditt believes that this shepherd material is aimed against Judah's leaders. As well as reversing the prophecies of Jeremiah and Ezekiel, he argues:

> the shepherd allegory attacks the key features of 9:1–10 and 9:11–10:1, 10:3b–12: the characteristics of any future king and the reunion of Israel and Judah. Instead of seeing a future David characterized by peacefulness, righteousness, and lowliness, the allegory depicts shepherds who devour their people. Indeed, 11:17 pronounces a woe upon the shepherd. Instead of seeing Judah and Ephraim united as does the second collection, the allegory depicts the breaking of the bond between them.[116]

110. Ibid., 282–83.
111. Ibid., 284.
112. Ibid., 285–86.
113. Mason, "Earlier," 91.
114. Ibid., 106. Cf. Mason, *Zechariah*, 112.
115. Mason, "Earlier," 116. See also R. L. Foster, "Shepherds, Sticks, and Social Destabilization: A Fresh Look at Zechariah 11:4–17," *JBL* 126 (2007): 735–53, who argues that the condemned shepherds are governors of Yehud during the Persian period.
116. P. L. Redditt, "Israel's Shepherds: Hope and Pessimism in Zechariah 9–14," *CBQ* 51 (1989): 631–42 (635).

Elsewhere, Redditt makes similar conclusions to others who adopt this approach:

> Thus, the allegory contradicted the hope for the reunion of north and south. Not only that, the fault lay with the shepherds. Since the term "shepherd" was often a title for a king, the prophet probably meant that no eschatological king would arise out of such a group… Zechariah 11:4–17 reversed the hopes of the post-exilic community for reunion under a Davidic king. The failures of the shepherds precluded the dawning of God's new day.[117]

This second approach has also been adopted by Sweeney, who understands the first sign-action as an analogy of the role of the leaders of the people during the early years of the reign of Darius, a time that he sees well described in Zech 11:6 as a time of conflict between neighbours and king. The three shepherds who were dismissed were three shepherds of the temple flocks over whom the prophet had charge, and these, Sweeney argues, may well have represented the demise of three Persian monarchs: Cyrus, Cambyses, and Darius.[118] The covenant that is broken is a covenant among the nations and reflects a reversal of the scenario portrayed in such passages as Isa 2:2–4; Mic 4:1–5; and Zech 8:18–23. The breaking of the second staff (Zech 11:14) reflects the efforts of the people of Samaria to prevent the rebuilding of the temple in Jerusalem (Ezra 4–6).

Boda believes that the two sign-actions in this passage speak of two different situations that involve two different leaders in the community.[119] Understood against the background of Ezek 34 and 37, he suggests that the good shepherd of Zech 11:4–16 is a Davidic descendant and is probably to be identified with Zerubbabel.[120] In this case, this passage describes the ultimate fate of Zerubbabel.[121] Boda believes that this passage suggests that Zerubbabel resigned from his post due to Persian policies and it was the Persians who paid him off. On the other hand, the foolish shepherd of 11:15–16 is someone outside the Davidic line. Boda summarizes:

> Zech. 11:4–16 represents a prophetic interpretation [of Ezek 34 and 37] designed to explain the waning influence of the Davidic line. The text

---

117. Redditt, *Zechariah*, 127–28. See also the conclusions and implications in P. L. Redditt, "The Two Shepherds in Zechariah 11:4–17," *CBQ* 55 (1993): 676–86 (685–86). Note the criticism by Cook, *Apocalypticism*, 162 n. 50, who believes that the data to support Redditt's argument are limited.
118. Sweeney, *Twelve*, 680.
119. Boda, "Reading," 284.
120. Ibid., 287.
121. See also Boda, *Commentary*, 467.

traces this threat to the people's rejection of the Davidic shepherd and identifies the present inappropriate leadership as judgment from God, giving the people the kind of leadership they deserve.[122]

This second approach to Zech 11:4–17 also has a number of difficulties. Once again, the array of backgrounds that have been reconstructed point to its speculative nature. While the backgrounds are an attempt to explain the apparent tensions or contradictions in the text, scholars who adopt this approach do not adequately explain how it was possible for the author or final editor of the book of Zechariah to leave these tensions in the text unresolved to such an extent. There are obvious difficulties that remain unexplained. For instance, how can the pessimistic view of the future annulment of the brotherhood between Judah and Israel (11:14) be reconciled with the optimistic view of unity presented in the wider context, particularly ch. 10, in which many of the themes of this passage are established? In the end, this approach seems to offer excuses for, rather than an explanation of, the final form of the text.[123]

Furthermore, the question must surely be raised: Why would any prophet who reversed earlier prophecies to such an extent have continued to have an authoritative voice in the community?[124] For scholars who take this approach, the book of Zechariah is not simply reworking the messages of the earlier prophets (particularly Ezekiel), but essentially contradicting their message, and in particular, the hope that they held for

---

122.   Boda, "Reading," 288.

123.   Boda (ibid., 277–91) is an exception to this criticism. He attempts to show how his interpretation of the passage explains elements in the wider context of Zech 9–14 and argues that 11:4–16 functions as a transition between chs. 9–10 and 12–14. The breaking of the first staff explains the focus on the destruction of the nations in chs. 12–14, and the breaking of the second staff explains the absence of references to Israel in chs. 12–14. However, in the end his analysis is not as neat as he claims. Zech 9–10 also speaks of the judgment that is coming on the nations (e.g. 9:1–8, 13), and chs. 12–14 also speaks of their salvation (14:16–19). Further, chs. 12–14 begin with a reference to Israel (12:1) and it is on view in several places (e.g. 13:2, 8; 14:8–10).

124.   The following quote by R. A. Mason, "Why is Second Zechariah so Full of Quotations?," in Tuckett, ed., *The Book of Zechariah and Its Influence*, 21–28 (24), is apt: "This brings us to another important point when we ask the question 'Why?' of the use of earlier material. Not only does its use testify to the belief that the ancients had spoken authentically in the name of God, but it establishes a real sense of continuity between the present speaker and his community and the prophets and their circles of old. And once the note of genuine continuity has been established, then surely the *authority* and *genuineness* of the later speakers are also validated" (emphasis original).

the house of David.[125] If this were the case, then the question must surely be faced as to how the book of Zechariah was ever accepted as authoritative prophetic literature.

Some scholars have responded to the difficulties of the first two approaches by arguing that the historical references or situation behind this passage cannot now be identified. For instance, W. Neil comments: "This passage is doubtless replete with allusions to a historical situation which must have been crystal clear to the readers, but it is impossible now to do more than speculate on the identity of the 'three shepherds' (vs. 8) or the 'worthless shepherd' (vs. 17)."[126] More recently, Conrad states that while the text of Zech 11:4–14 abounds in metaphors and is richly allusive, "the import of the metaphors and also the reference points for the allusions are virtually inaccessible to a contemporary reader."[127] He concludes that there is more in this passage than we can ever understand.[128]

Others, who appreciate the difficulty of tying the details of this passage into contemporary or future historical events, have sought to draw a general message from this passage. For instance, R. C. Dentan believes that this should simply be understood as "an allegory of God's attempt to rule an oppressed but still refractory people."[129] Petersen believes that "any attempt to identify a particular historical figure with the shepherd fundamentally misunderstands the nature of this literature."[130] He thinks it is wrong to treat either of these actions of the prophet as allegories of what was happening in Judah during the Persian period. Instead, Petersen believes that this passage is "perspectival rather than particular."[131] While these are reasonable responses to the difficulties of the first two approaches, there is one further approach, one which has become more popular in recent years, and one that has a lot to offer in terms of making sense of the actual details of this passage and its place in the wider context of the book and Israel's history.

125.   Black, "Messiah," 75, puts it explicitly: "It therefore becomes clear that Zech 9–14 reverses all the promises of Ezekiel."
126.   Neil, "Zechariah," 946.
127.   Conrad, *Zechariah*, 172.
128.   Ibid., 176.
129.   Dentan, "Zechariah," 6:1103, cited in Mason, "Earlier," 93–94. Others cited by Mason who regard it as allegorical, rather than an actual symbolic action, include: Ackroyd, "Zechariah," 653–54; Horst, *Die zwölf*, 251; Elliger, *Die Propheten Nahum, Habakuk, Zephanja, Haggai, Sacharja, Maleachi*, 160; G. Gaide, *Jerusalem, voici ton roi: Commentaire de Zacharie 9–14* (Paris: Cerf, 1968), 111.
130.   Petersen, *Zechariah 9–14*, 91.
131.   Ibid., 100–101.

6.4.2.3. A representation of the past. A third approach sees this passage portraying the past. More specifically, the first sign-action is a dramatic representation of Israel's history under the monarchy to the time of the exile. This was first suggested in very basic terms by Meyer, and then adapted and developed by C. and E. Meyers, E. H. Merrill, and more recently B. G. Webb.[132] Each treatment shall be surveyed and evaluated in turn.

Meyer notes that "shepherd" (רעה) was a title used of kings in both non-Israelite nations, and in Israel.[133] Most significant in Israel was David, who was taken from shepherding sheep to shepherd Israel.[134] The shepherds of Israel had a responsibility to protect the people in the land, and Yahweh would remove those who failed.[135] On the basis of this, Meyer states: "In this allegory the shepherds represent the monarchy in Israel."[136] More specifically:

> The shepherd is a royal figure; his two staffs signify the benefits of his rule; the breaking of these staffs represents judgment on Israel, the flock over which he was appointed by Yahweh. All of this is in the past; it has already taken place. It is not unlikely that the allegory refers to specific historical events and persons. To attempt an identification is, however, unrealistic.[137]

Meyer argues that Zech 11:15–16 is a continuation of the allegory of 11:4–14, but introduces a judgment that lies in the future. He also

---

132. Meyer, "Allegory," 225–40; Meyers and Meyers, *Zechariah 9–14*, 248–304; Merrill, *Zechariah*, 287–301; Webb, *Zechariah*, 147–52. Keil, "Zechariah," 371, cites Hofman, Ebrand, and Kliefoth as supposing (in Keil's view erroneously) that Zech 11:14 refers to the division of the kingdom after Solomon. Laato, *Josiah*, 278, cites Rudolph as believing that the vision refers to the monarchic period and the shepherds as the kings of Judah before the exile. However, Rudolph, *Sacharja*, 205, actually says that the use of the plural for the owners in Zech 11:7 and Zech 11:11 excludes a reference to the monarchy (as in his view this would be singular rather than plural leadership), and therefore it is not pre-exilic in origin or reference. In my view the plural does not exclude the monarchic period, as there was often more than one king reigning at this time (a king in Judah and in Israel), and there were collectively many kings over this period. However, according to Rudolph, the vision refers to the future and not the past.

133. Among the non-Israelite kings called "shepherds," Meyer, "Allegory," 228, lists Gudea of Lagash, Hammurabi of Babylon, and Assurnasirpal II of Assyria.

134. E.g. 2 Sam 5:2; 7:8–16; Ps 78:70–72; Jer 23:4–5; Ezek 34:23–24; 37:24; Mic 5:1–3.

135. E.g. 1 Kgs 22:17–23; Jer 10:21; 23:1–2; Ezek 34:1–10.

136. Meyer, "Allegory," 229.

137. Ibid., 232.

believes that 13:7–9 is to be understood in close relationship with 11:4–17. It also speaks of the future, but shows the final outcome of Yahweh's judgment as a purified remnant. Hence the monarchy still has a role to play as agent and victim of Yahweh's judgment.

While Meyer's treatment orients us in a more favourable direction, it still has several problems. First, Meyer does not convincingly prove that the shepherd whom the prophet is to portray is to be understood as representative of the monarchy.[138] There are indications throughout the first sign-action that the shepherd represents Yahweh. First, both Yahweh and the prophet speak as "I" (11:4; cf. 11:7), and this functions to merge their actions. For instance, when the prophet speaks in 11:10 and says "I cut it to break the covenant that I had made with all the peoples" it seems certain that this is not referring to a covenant between Zechariah and the people, but a covenant that Yahweh has with the people. This indicates that the prophet is acting out Yahweh's role as shepherd, and the actions of the prophet are to be understood as a representation of Yahweh's actions towards his people.[139] Further to this, when Meyer identifies the shepherd as representative of the monarchy, it seems to absolve the monarchy of any responsibility for the people's present state, something that was patently not the case. Third, Meyer's reluctance to make any historical identifications, particularly with the breaking of the staffs, seems overly cautious.

C. and E. Meyers claim to use an approach that "diverges fundamentally from that of virtually all the scholarship that has tackled Zechariah 11."[140] They understand this passage as providing a retrospective view on the devastation that came on Yahweh's people throughout the monarchic era. The fact that the prophets had predicted these events, and they came true, functioned as a legitimation of the prophetic voice.[141] They write:

> Second Zechariah is caught up in the horror of the past events that have brought about the need for the eschatological intervention and restoration depicted in chapters 9 and 10… It is precisely Second Zechariah's retrospective view, looking at the seemingly hopeless dispersion and dissolution of the people over the past centuries, yet subscribing to the idea of a

---

138.   So in Zech 11:10 the prophet, speaking as the shepherd, says that he broke the covenant that he had made with all the peoples. Meyer (ibid., 231) argues that the monarch is here speaking as Yahweh's agent, but this seems strained. The shepherd is better understood as representing Yahweh.

139.   See further, O'Brien, *Zechariah*, 250–51.

140.   Meyers and Meyers, *Zechariah 9–14*, 293. Their approach to this passage has been adopted by Ham, *King*, 51–57.

141.   Meyers and Meyers, *Zechariah 9–14*, 249–50.

new covenant and an eschatological restoration, that allows him to do what no other prophetic figure had dared—to proclaim explicitly the breaking of the historical covenant.[142]

C. and E. Meyers argue that here the prophet is playing the role of the shepherd and in doing so is identifying with the true prophets of the past, whose prophecies had come true. They acknowledge that using shepherd imagery of the prophetic office is unique in the Hebrew Bible, as from David onwards the shepherd motif is attached to political leaders, but see it as evidence that the author of Zechariah is reworking traditional material for his own purposes.[143]

The fact that the first sign-action is reported in the past tense indicates to them that there is no need to find contemporary historical events reflected here.[144] Instead, they understand those who buy the flock of the slaughter to be the leaders of Israel who have violated the covenant.[145] The symbolic action of breaking two sticks completely reverses Ezekiel's portrayal and speaks of termination of unity and covenant.[146] In the breaking of the covenant (Zech 11:10), they state that the prophet "is speaking as if he were God breaking that covenant in historical actuality, which is the way the prophets of the Exile (Jeremiah and Ezekiel), who have great influence on him, have viewed the devastation of the Babylonian conquest."[147] They see the breaking of the second staff as representing the division of the united kingdom after the days of David and Solomon, an event that continued to "represent one of the major traumas in Israel's historical consciousness."[148] They summarize:

> Consequently, if this chapter of Second Zechariah represents a retrospective view of what led to the disruption and dispersal that will come to an end in the glorious future, the two major events that constitute the national trauma are the breaking of the covenant, which is how the events of the sixth century are conceived…and the breaking of the United Monarchy at the end of the tenth century.[149]

142. Ibid., 270.
143. Ibid., 250.
144. Ibid., 251.
145. Ibid., 253–54. On p. 265, they contend that any attempt to identify specific individuals or incidents that lie behind the three-shepherd figure in Zech 11:8 misunderstands the reference. They argue that "three" is the smallest complete number, and probably represents all those in positions of power who are responsible for the present conditions in Israelite society.
146. Ibid., 262.
147. Ibid., 269–70.
148. Ibid., 281.
149. Ibid.

In the second symbolic action where the prophet is to represent a foolish shepherd, C. and E. Meyers believe that the prophet turns to address the fate of the contemporary prophetic figures who abuse their roles. Again, they believe that any attempt to identify this figure with an historical person ignores the way that the shepherd imagery functions in this chapter.[150] They understand this shepherd to represent a prophet who speaks for himself, and not for Yahweh.

There are many positive gains from C. and E. Meyers's treatment of this passage. Seeing the breaking of the two staffs as referring to the breaking of the covenant with Israel that resulted in the exile, and the earlier division of the kingdom after Solomon, gives these prophetic sign-actions the significance that they had in the history of Israel. Furthermore, while they argue that the prophet has modified the prophecies of Jeremiah and Ezekiel, this was not to present an opposing view of the future to these prophets. Since 11:4–14 is presenting a view of Israel's history to the exile, then the prophet is not contradicting these earlier prophets, but creatively using their metaphors to portray the past.

One of main gains of this interpretation is that it explains ch. 11 in the wider context of chs. 9–11. It answers the question, raised by C. and E. Meyers: "Why, after the resoundingly hopeful mood of chapters 9 and 10, does this horrifying picture of strife and destruction present itself?"[151] C. and E. Meyers argue that here the prophet explains why things are as they are in his own day, so as to make his vision of the future (chs. 9 and 10) compelling.[152]

O'Brien finds C. and E. Meyers's approach appealing. However, she believes that it does not account for the judgment theme that continues through the rest of the book, and that "they do not explain why Second Zechariah has been edited in this particular way."[153] In response to O'Brien it can be said that her criticism fails to take into account the literary nature of Zech 9–14. Rather than presenting a strict chronological progression of events, these chapters present different perspectives on Yahweh's eschatological salvation of his people. There is a constant shifting between judgment and salvation throughout these chapters.[154] To claim that C. and E. Meyers do not adequately explain the editing of

---

150. Ibid., 284.
151. Ibid., 293.
152. Ibid., 300–301.
153. O'Brien, *Zechariah*, 254.
154. This shall be dealt with in more detail in the next chapter. Suffice to note the salvation themes in Zech 12:7–9; 13:1, 9; 14:5, 10–11, that run alongside judgment in 13:2–8; 14:1–2, 12–15.

these chapters is to fail to appreciate the very strength of their approach, an approach that provides a coherent explanation of the final form of the text.

However, C. and E. Meyers's argument that the prophet represents the prophetic office in the role of the shepherd is not convincing. As they themselves note, the shepherd image is not associated with the prophet anywhere else in the Hebrew Bible. The weakness of this identification is acutely felt in Zech 11:10, where their explanation of how the prophet can speak of "my covenant" raises the question of whether the prophet should not be understood as playing the role of Yahweh as shepherd.[155] Furthermore, they do not make clear why Yahweh explains the significance of the prophet's actions in the first person (e.g. 11:6), if the shepherd does not represent Yahweh himself.

Merrill, acknowledging the work of Meyer, argues that Zech 11:4–14 is a dramatization of what Yahweh has done in the past, before the exile—a dramatization that probably only occurred in Zechariah's mind.[156] Merrill understands the prophet Zechariah to be playing the role of Yahweh as shepherd (contra Meyer, and C. and E. Meyers).[157] Merrill states that the buyers and sellers of the flock appear to be foreign kings, and that they are set in opposition to the flock's own shepherds (11:5).[158] He identifies the sheep as God's chosen people, Israel and Judah, and the shepherds as the evil kings who abandoned the flock in their times of greatest need, particularly just prior to the Babylonian conquest and deportation.[159] He concludes:

> …it appears best to understand this passage (v. 6) to mean that YHWH will withhold His compassion for His people Israel, delivering them instead to neighboring peoples and their kings who will beat down the land of Israel with no interference from YHWH. This, of course, is precisely what took place in the last decades of Israel's and Judah's history leading up to their respective captivities by the Assyrians and Babylonians, and on into the future as well.[160]

Merrill understands the reference to "the afflicted of the flock" (Zech 11:7, 11) as a reference to the faithful remnant within Israel, and thinks

---

155. Meyers and Meyers, *Zechariah 9–14*, 269–70.
156. Merrill, *Zechariah*, 292: "Zechariah is reliving YHWH's dealings with his people in allegory (if only in his own mind) and is reporting in a fresh way what Israel's history was really all about."
157. Ibid., 287.
158. Ibid., 288–89.
159. Ibid., 302.
160. Ibid., 291.

that the best way of understanding "one month" (11:8) is as a code word for a short time, in which case it may refer to the relatively rapid succession of kings before Judah was taken into exile, the three kings being Jehoiakim, Jehoiachin, and Zedekiah.[161] This is supported by the fact that each of these kings did despise Yahweh and spurn him (2 Kgs 23:37; 24:9, 19–20), and that the covenant curse of cannibalism is reflected in Lam 2:20 and 4:10. Hence the breaking of the covenant was symbolic of the fall of Jerusalem and the exile of Judah.[162] He also understands the breaking of the second staff as a reference to the division of the kingdom under Jeroboam and Rehoboam.[163] Hence: "the shepherd imagery pertained to events of the past, that Zechariah in fact was reliving the history of his own people. That history indeed provided a prototype of future events occasionally (as in vv. 12–13) but essentially was antecedent to the prophet's own time (i.e. was preexilic)."[164]

With the rejection of the good shepherd, Merrill understands that the prophecy turns to speak of a ruler who will utterly disappoint God's people. While Zech 11:4–14 portrayed events of the past, 11:15–17 addresses the future, though the shepherd is probably not to be identified with an individual, but represents "the structure of anti-God leadership that commenced as early as the postexilic days of Zechariah."[165] He argues that the description "in the land" (11:16) means that the shepherd will be the king of Israel. The image that is created here was one that Amos had used to speak of those who would survive the judgment of exile (Amos 3:12).

Merrill's view of Zech 11:4–14 seems to make best sense of the details of the passage itself. Nevertheless, his suggestion that the shepherd of 11:15–17 is a king of Israel seems to ignore the fact that non-Israelites could also be said to shepherd Yahweh's people (e.g. Cyrus in Isa 44:28), and there is no reason that this could not be "in the land," as it was with Darius and his successors. The main criticism of his treatment, however, is that he could do more to explain how this passage fits in its context and contributes to the message of the book.

The most recent advocate of this approach is Webb. He believes that the prophet is to represent Yahweh as shepherd, and in the first symbolic action (Zech 11:4–14) to portray the history of Yahweh's covenant with

161. Ibid., 293–94.
162. Ibid., 294–95.
163. Ibid., 300.
164. Ibid., 303.
165. Ibid.

Israel from the time he made it to the time he revoked it. The revoking is explained: "Historically this happened in stages, from the break-up of Israel into two separate kingdoms after the death of Solomon, to the fall, in turn, of both the northern and southern kingdoms, and the scattering of their citizens."[166]

Webb is hesitant to speculate on the identity of the three shepherds who are removed, but suggests, like Merrill, that it may be an allusion to the last three kings of Judah, namely, Jehoiakim, Jehoiachin, and Zedekiah.[167] He argues that the description of the shepherd deserting the flock is meant to shock, and that the picture in Zech 11:9 of the flock devouring each other's flesh is an allusion to the events of the siege that led to the fall of Jerusalem in 587 B.C.E. (cf. 2 Kgs 25:1–21; Lam 2:20; Ezek 5:10).[168] He follows C. and E. Meyers in understanding the symbolism of breaking the first staff as referring to the breaking of the covenant that Yahweh had made with the nation of Israel, rather than an otherwise unknown covenant with the nations.[169] The section on the payment made to the shepherd (Zech 11:12–13) shows how the people had not really valued Yahweh as their shepherd. Thirty pieces of silver was the amount stipulated as compensation for the death of a slave in the law (Exod 31:22) and could be considered a considerable sum (cf. Neh 5:15). Yet any sum is an insult to Yahweh, since paying him off is a rejection of him as shepherd.[170] The way that the money was thrown into

---

166. Webb, *Zechariah*, 148.

167. Ibid., 149.

168. Ibid., 150.

169. Webb (ibid., 147–48) argues that the expression "all the peoples" is descriptive of all the tribe and people groups that made up the people of Israel. Meyers and Meyers, *Zechariah 9–14*, 270–71, cite Gen 27:29; 48:4; 49:10; 1 Kgs 22:28; Isa 3:13; and Mic 1:2 as precedents for referring to the components of Israel as "peoples." They choose to understand it this way also because there is no evidence of a "covenant with the nations," and a covenant with the people of Israel is understandable in this context. Cf. Redditt, "Shepherds," 683, who cites 1 Kgs 22:28 and Job 36:20 as examples of how the plural form העמים can be used in a singular sense to refer to a single, specific nation. He concludes that in Zech 11:10, "the term probably designates all of the people of Israel, and the covenant was that between the shepherd and the sheep."

170. Webb, *Zechariah*, 151. Cf. K. Luke, "The Thirty Pieces of Silver (Zech 11, 12–13)," *Bible Bhashyam* 30 (2004): 104–22 (118–20), who suggests an ancient oriental background to the phrase "thirty pieces of silver." He notes that in the Sumerian poem, *The Curse of Agade*, Naram-sin is guilty of treating the sanctuary "like thirty shekels," which in context indicates extreme contempt. In the poem, *Lament over the Destruction of Ur*, the destruction of the sanctuary is described:

the temple is probably indicative of the fact that it was in the temple that
the leaders of the nation had shown most contempt for Yahweh as the
true shepherd, particularly by allowing and even promoting idolatrous
worship there (e.g. Ezek 8–11).[171] The breaking of the second staff
depicts the breaking up of the once united Israel.[172]

Webb argues that the tense of מקים in Zech 11:16 is ambiguous, and
therefore, that the foolish shepherd (11:15–16) could be either a past or
future figure. He concludes:

> What is seen as Zechariah performs this act is the *kind* of shepherd God
> gives his people when they have rejected their true shepherd. Understood
> in this way he does not have only one incarnation, so to speak, at one
> point in time. He is Nebuchadnezzar, but he is also the rapacious shep-
> herds of 10:3. He represents all the bad leaders and exploiters Israel has
> had to endure, and will yet endure, because of their contempt for the
> loving care and discipline of God, their true shepherd.[173]

The only difficulty with Webb's analysis is that if Zechariah is portraying the history of Israel's covenant from the time that he made it to the
time that he revoked it, we might expect Zechariah to break his staffs in
the other order, since historically the split between Judah and Israel
(union) happened some three hundred years before the Babylonian exile
(favour). However, it may be that the sign-action conveys these events in
a more general way.

In any case, this approach has significant gains over the approaches
that see it as enacted prophecy or characterizing the tensions in the contemporary community. First, it is consistent with the work of K. Friebel
who has recently been critical of the way that scholars generally understand sign-actions as only predicting future events. Working mainly with
Jeremiah and Ezekiel, he argues that as well as conveying a message in a
non-verbal way, the sign-action also had a persuasive dimension. He
writes: "it must be recognized that some of the sign-acts are not future-
oriented in that what they depicted were not future events. Rather, some
of the sign-acts nonverbally depicted past and present events, which had

"the destroyers made of it thirty shekels." In the poem, *Gilgamesh and the Huluppu
Tree*, Gilgamesh, the hero who cuts down this mighty tree, is said to don heavy
armour weighing fifty minas. The poet says: "He considered the fifty minas (as a
mere) thirty shekels." Similarly, E. Reiner, "Thirty Pieces of Silver," *JAOS* 88
(1968): 186–90.

171.   For a helpful discussion of the text and the significance of the silver being
thrown to "the potter," see Ham, *King*, 55–57.

172.   Webb, *Zechariah*, 151.

173.   Ibid., 152.

already or were currently transpiring."[174] This is consistent with the first sign-action in particular, which depicts past events so as both to explain the present circumstances and provide the backdrop against which to understand the future hope that is presented in the wider context of Zechariah.

Second, while much later, the Targum lends support to this interpretation wherein the elements of the passage are explicitly interpreted in terms of the past experiences of Israel, particularly the division of the kingdom and the Assyrian and Babylonian exiles.[175] The Targum removes the "sign-action" aspect from this passage with the prophet no longer playing the role of a shepherd. Instead, the prophet prophesies against the rulers of the people (*Tg. Zech* 11:4, 15) and Yahweh speaks in the first person throughout. Accordingly, the shepherd's staffs are not mentioned in the Targum. Instead, there is a reference to "dividing…into two parts" in connection with the secession of the house of Israel from the house of Judah:

> And I appointed rulers over the people and they ruled over them as if they were a flock for the slaughter; they impoverished and drove my people astray, and they were divided before me into two parts; the house of Israel seceded from the people of the house of Judah—they loathed the kingdom of the house of David with whom I was well pleased that they should be rulers over my people. (*Tg. Zech* 11:7)[176]

Furthermore, after the division of the kingdom, the Targum explains the exiles of Israel and Judah:

> And I brought the king of Assyria against the king of Israel and I drove him into exile because they changed the *covenant* which was made with them, that they should not serve idols; therefore they went into exile among *the nations*. And because they changed the covenant they went into exile at that time…
>
> And I brought Nebuchadnezzar the king of Babylon against Zedekiah king of the tribe of the house of Judah, and I drove him into exile because the people of the house of Judah also changed the covenant, like their brethren of the house of Israel. (*Tg. Zech* 11:10–11a, 14)[177]

---

174. Friebel, "Sign-Actions," 40. Friebel cites Jer 13:1–2; Ezek 4:4–5; Hos 1:2, and to some extent Ezek 4:12–15 as examples of sign-acts that depicted past history, or some already existent circumstance.

175. For the Targum's treatment of Zech 11:4–17, see Black, "Messiah," 113–16.

176. Gordon, *Targum*, 212–13.

177. Ibid., 214–15.

The Targum therefore demonstrates an early interpretation of Zech 11:4–17 that is in keeping with the approach that understands the sign-actions as a dramatic representation of Israel's history.

Third, the themes in the sign-actions accord well with the wider Hebrew Bible, particularly in the way that the shepherd imagery is utilized. This is to be expected, since Zechariah claims to be well acquainted with the works of what he calls the "former prophets" (cf. Zech 1:4; 7:7, 12). We have seen Ezekiel and Jeremiah both use the shepherd imagery to refer to the unworthy kings of Judah and Israel (e.g. Jer 2:8; 23:1–2; Ezek 34:2–10). The earlier prophets also held the corrupt shepherds responsible for the exile, which is consistent with the view of the exile presented here. Rather than being a contradiction of these earlier prophetic hopes, Zech 11 continues very much in the same vein. It speaks of the judgment on false shepherds that paves the way for the coming king and true shepherd of Yahweh (Zech 11:17; cf. 9:9; 10:4).

Another image that is shared with earlier prophets is found in the reference to the "afflicted of the flock" (Zech 11:7, 11) who are said to obey the prophet (11:11).[178] The image here is of a faithful remnant that endures the judgment (cf. 8:12; 13:9), and this is consistent with Micah and Isaiah where a faithful remnant is said to survive the judgment and affliction of exile and return to the land.[179] Jeremiah also describes the affliction of the faithful remnant who will survive the Babylonian conquest and deportation.[180] In addition, Ps 44 speaks of the faithful among the people of Yahweh whom Yahweh has scattered among the nations in exile as "sheep to be slaughtered" (44:11, 22) as well as being in "affliction and oppression" (44:24).

The way that the first sign-action portrays the failure of the people to value Yahweh truly, as they loathe him (Zech 11:8) and effectively "pay him off" (11:12–13), is also consistent with the earlier prophets. Hosea condemns Israel for using the gifts of grain, wine, oil, silver, and gold that Yahweh had lavished on her on the Baals, and forgetting Yahweh (Hos 2:8, 13). Isaiah speaks of the people of Israel forsaking Yahweh and despising the Holy One of Israel (Isa 1:4). Again, the prophets see this action leading to the exile (Hos 2:23; Isa 3).

Noting again the reference to cannibalism in Zech 11:9, this is consistent with the conditions described by the prophets concerning the fall

---

178.   Conrad, *Zechariah*, 174, helpfully notes the similarities of theme between the beginning of Zech 10 and 11:5, particularly the affliction of the sheep (10:2; cf. 11:7, 11).

179.   E.g. Isa 1:4–9; 4:2–4; 7:3; 10:20–22; 37:21–32; 46:3; 61:1–4.

180.   E.g. Jer 42:1–6; 44:11–14.

of Jerusalem in 587 B.C.E. (cf. Jer 19:9). Furthermore, just as Ezekiel dramatically portrayed the reunion of Judah and Ephraim by joining two sticks (Ezek 37:15–28), if not directly drawing on this imagery, Zech 11:4–14 is certainly consistent with it in explaining how the united nation came to be divided. If there is a new element in this first sign-action that moves further than the earlier prophets, it is, as C. and E. Meyers state, the explicit description of the exile as Yahweh annulling the covenant that he had made with his people.[181] However, there are certainly grounds for this deduction in the way that Jeremiah speaks of Israel breaking the covenant and the need for a new covenant (Jer 31:31–33).

Fourth, perhaps the greatest gain of this approach is the way that it offers a coherent explanation of how this passage functions in the book of Zechariah and complements other aspects of the book's message. There are features of this passage that mirror the explanation of the exile found in Zech 7–8. There the exile is pictured as scattering and desolation (7:14), a time when every man was against his neighbour (8:10; cf. 11:6). Yahweh promises to save the remnant and bring them to dwell in Jerusalem (8:6–8). Furthermore, Yahweh promises to save both the house of Judah, and the house of Israel so that they might be a blessing (8:13); the implication being that the division of the kingdom and the exile were the direct result of Yahweh's judgment on their covenant unfaithfulness (cf. 7:9–10).

Many have observed the way that the shepherd and sheep imagery features in chs. 9 and 10, and this approach to ch. 11 explains the connection. The two sign-actions clarify why things were as they were in the prophet's own day. They explain why the people wandered like sheep, and why they were afflicted for lack of a shepherd (10:2). It is because they had rejected their true shepherd Yahweh.

6.4.3. *Review of Zechariah 11:4–17*

When Yahweh commands Zechariah to perform the sign-action of shepherding his people as they come under his judgment (11:4–6), Zechariah is to represent the events that led up to and included the Assyrian and Babylonian exiles so as to explain these events and show the people Yahweh's perspective on their present circumstances. Continuing the imagery of the people of Yahweh as his flock (9:16) and sheep (10:2), the people are now represented as a "flock of the slaughter" (11:4, 7). The reason for their state is attributed in the first instance to the failure of the leadership of Yahweh's people (11:4–5; cf. 10:2). Whether this

---

181. Meyers and Meyers, *Zechariah 9–14*, 270.

leadership is foreign, Israelite, or a combination of both,[182] these leaders have shepherded for their own gain, without regard for the flock, and they mocked the name of Yahweh: "Blessed be Yahweh, I am rich!" Yahweh's response to this was to hand them over to their neighbours and their foreign kings, with the land being struck (11:6). There is an obvious allusion to exile here.

Acting this out, Zechariah takes up two staffs, "favour" and "union." The significance of these staffs is explained later, when they are broken. The staff "favour" represents the covenant that had been made with all the peoples (11:10). Whether this describes Yahweh's intention to bless the nations through Israel, or, as is more likely, refers to the Mosaic covenant that Yahweh had made with Israel, it symbolizes Yahweh's favourable intentions for his people (and hence the nations). The staff "union" represents the brotherhood between Judah and Israel (11:14). Hence, the meaning of the sign-action as it rehearses Israel's history is that Yahweh sought to shepherd his people for the purpose of favour and union, and even took steps to remove those who opposed this purpose by destroying three shepherds in once month; probably a reference to the removal of Israel's or Judah's kings who had no pity on the flock (cf. 11:5). Yet Yahweh's patience ran thin, and the people's attitude to Yahweh became one of loathing, so Yahweh ceased shepherding his people and handed them over to the destruction of exile (11:9). This indicates that not only were Israel's leaders responsible for the exile, but the people themselves were responsible on account of their despising of Yahweh.

Yahweh's rejection of his people is acted out by Zechariah breaking his two staffs. He first breaks the staff "favour" (Zech 11:10), whereupon those who were afflicted of the flock knew that this was in accordance with Yahweh's word (10:11), presumably because it was entailed in the covenant itself (cf. Deut 28). Zechariah then requests his wages,

---

182.   In Zech 11:5, "their own shepherds" (ורעיהם) has a masculine suffix and elsewhere in this passage the "flock" is regarded as feminine. This seems to indicate that the shepherds are the agents of those who buy and slaughter. Alternatively, if the suggested emendation in *BHS* is followed, which suggests reading it as a feminine suffix (supported by several Syriac manuscripts), "their" then refers to the flock rather than those who buy and slaughter and it does not entail the shepherds being the agents of those who buy and slaughter. The wider context suggests that those who buy and slaughter may be foreign kings and that the kings of Israel and Judah have effectively acted as shepherds for these kings in not pitying the flock and protecting them as they should. This was certainly the case for many of the kings of Judah and Israel who looked for foreign alliances that were detrimental to the flock (e.g. Ahaz in Isa 7).

seemingly from the flock, and is paid thirty pieces of silver (11:12). This sum is an insult to Yahweh and indicates that his people have not valued him at all. The money is not kept, but thrown to the potter in the temple, perhaps as a testimony against the people, and Zechariah breaks his second staff "union" (11:13–14).

In the second sign-action, the prophet demonstrates that the people have received what they deserve for their rejection of Yahweh as shepherd. Zechariah takes up the equipment of a foolish shepherd, who, rather than prospering them, devours their flesh and tears off their hoofs like a lion (11:16).[183] This is a clear reference back to the foreign rulers ("lions") of 11:3. It seems best to understand the reference to the "foolish shepherd" in 11:15 as a veiled reference to the present foreign ruler that had been raised up by Yahweh to rule his people in judgment for their rejection of him.[184] In Zechariah's day this shepherd was the Persian king, but would continue to refer to whoever ruled over the people until the true shepherd of Yahweh's people came. The note of woe on this shepherd on which this passage ends (11:17) connects back to the short oracle at the beginning of the chapter that also looks forward to the elimination of foreign shepherds who have oppressed Yahweh's people (11:1–3; cf. 10:3). Therefore, the overall message of this chapter complements chs. 9–10: Yahweh is coming to save his people, to re-establish them in the land, and in doing so will remove all foreign kings and their agents, just as he had removed false shepherds in the past.

Hence, while the first sign-action speaks of the judgment that has come on the false shepherds which resulted in the experience of exile and judgment of the flock, the second sign-action speaks of the judgment that is coming on the contemporary and future shepherds, a judgment that Zechariah has already explained will usher in the day of Yahweh (10:2–12). On this day, Yahweh will deliver his people, save them from the nations, and install his shepherd-king as ruler over all, as is depicted in the wider context.

6.4.4. *Summary of the Hope Held for the House of David in Zechariah 11:4–14*

The approach to this passage that coheres best with the context of the book of Zechariah and the wider biblical context sees the first sign-action of Zech 11:4–14 as being a dramatic representation of Israel's history

---

183. Clark and Hatton, *Handbook*, 302, note that the participle form of the verb indicates action that is either already in process, or is at the point of being started.

184. Note "*my* worthless shepherd" in Zech 11:17, which indicates an agent of Yahweh.

leading to the exile. It lays the responsibility for the exile on both the people and their kings and explains the post-exilic community's current situation (which is essentially not very different to the setting of chs. 1–8).[185] On this reading, this passage is not directly addressing the issue of the future hope for the house of David. This means, on the one hand, that the shepherd that Zechariah is to portray is not the future king of 9:9–10, as some who treat the first sign-action as predictive prophecy hold. On the other hand, it also means that it is not a rejection of the hopes that the earlier prophets held for a future shepherd/king, as those who treat this passage as reflecting contemporary tensions in the post-exilic community believe.

While this passage is not directly addressing the issue of the future hope for the house of David, it does so indirectly. The judgment that has come on the house of David in the past as portrayed in the first sign-action and the announcement of judgment that is coming on contemporary leaders who continue to ravage the flock as seen in the second sign-action (and 11:1–3), both function to raise the expectation that Yahweh will send the true shepherd of his people, the king of 9:9 and the Shoot of 3:8 and 6:12. This expectation was also reasserted in 10:1–4.

As well as reviewing Israel's past to explain their present circumstances, these sign-actions also suggest that when Yahweh's shepherd comes, he may not be treated favourably. Israel's history was one of rejecting Yahweh as shepherd and there is every indication from these sign-actions that when the future Davidic king comes, he will be treated in exactly the same way.[186] While this is not explicit in this chapter, it is made clear in chs. 12–13, as we shall see.

The approach that sees these sign-actions as a representation of the past results in a reading that is very much in line with the hope of the earlier prophets and the rest of the book of Zechariah. Rather than contradicting the Davidic hope of the earlier prophets, the way in which Yahweh had dealt with false shepherds in the past and the emphatic note of woe on the worthless shepherd and his allies on which this passage is introduced and ends, both serve to raise the hope of a shepherd to come. It is this shepherd who will save the flock, bring them home, and deal with the flock righteously (cf. 9:9, 16; 10:6, 10).

---

185.   I remain unconvinced by Curtis, *Steep*, 279–80, and others that the social setting of chs. 9–14 is radically different to chs. 1–8. Larkin, *Eschatology*, 253, argues that chs. 9–14 are not a product of social conflict.

186.   It seems that this is how this passage is understood in Matt 26:15.

6.5. *The Shepherd of Zechariah 13:7–9*

This short oracle is of far greater significance than its size would suggest. It contains the final "shepherd" reference in Zechariah, and brings together the various strands concerning leadership that have been woven through the book of Zechariah to this point. It continues the theme of the cleansing of the land and also speaks about adversity that lies ahead for Yahweh's people: a refinement that will result in great loss, but also in a renewed relationship with Yahweh for those who survive. It therefore functions as a transition into ch. 14 and brings into clearer perspective a feature of chs. 9–14 that will be explored in the next chapter (Chapter 7), namely, an end-time battle that will usher in Yahweh's kingdom. Zechariah 13:7–9 indicates that this battle will be won at great cost to Yahweh's people.

The key issue in these verses is the identity of the shepherd. Is the description of the shepherd adequate to allow an identification? Do other passages from Zechariah give us clues to his identity? How is he is to be understood in relation to the other shepherds and leaders that have been identified in the book? These are the questions that shall be explored as a conclusion is sought, not only regarding the shepherd's identity, but also concerning the hope for the house of David that is revealed here.

6.5.1. *Structure of Zechariah 13:7–9*
Many scholars, and even a few translations (e.g. NEB), transpose 13:7–9 to follow 11:17 on the basis that "my shepherd" in 13:7 is the same figure as the one mentioned in 11:17.[187] However, there is no manuscript evidence to justify this change, and even if it is the same figure, to switch the text is only to prejudice the interpretation of this passage. It does not help us to understand the final form of the book of Zechariah any more clearly.[188]

---

187. This was first suggested by H. Ewald, *Die Propheten des Alten Bundes*, vol. 1 (Stuttgart: Adolph Krabbe, 1840), 308–24 (cited in S. A. Cook, "The Metamorphosis of a Shepherd: The Tradition History of Zechariah 11:17 + 13:7–9," *CBQ* 55 [1993]: 453–66 [454 n. 3]), and then followed by Wellhausen, "Zechariah," 4:5393; K. Marti, *Das Dodekapropheton* (Tübingen: J. C. B. Mohr/Paul Siebeck, 1904), 442–43; Driver, *Minor Prophets*; Van Hoonacker, *Les Douze Petits Prophètes: traduits et commentés*, 671–80; Mitchell, "Zechariah," 316–18, and later Chary, *Zacharie*; Rudolph, *Sacharja*, 212–15; Mason, *Zechariah*, 110–12; Meyer, "Allegory," 234; Hanson, *Apocalyptic*, 338–39.

188. I am only dealing with the passage directly after Zech 11:4–17 for thematic reasons. It is important that its placement in the wider context of Zechariah is not ignored. For this reason, it will be returned to after dealing with Zech 12.

Clark and Hatton show that 13:7–9 is distinguished from the sections before and after in three ways: (1) this section has a new topic; (2) it is poetry rather than prose; (3) it is marked as a new discourse unit by the vocative noun and imperative verb with which it begins (חרב עורי).[189] The passage can be structured thematically as follows:

Zech 13:7–9: Strike the Shepherd
13:7   The shepherd struck
13:8–9a   The people refined
13:9b   Covenant relationship restored

6.5.2. *Strike the Shepherd (Zechariah 13:7–9)*

[7] "O sword, awake against my shepherd and against the man, my associate," declares Yahweh of hosts. "Strike the shepherd and the sheep will be scattered. I will turn my hand against the little ones."
[8] "And it will be that in all the land," declares Yahweh, "two parts in it shall be cut off and perish, and the third shall remain in it. [9] And I will put the third part into the fire, and I will refine them as refining the silver, and prove them as proving the gold. They will call on my name, and I will answer them. I will say, 'They are my people,' and they will say, Yahweh is my God[190].'" (author's translation)

Before seeking an answer to the question of the identity of the shepherd, there are a number of exegetical issues to address. Yahweh charges a sword to "awake against" his shepherd. This is a unique expression in the Hebrew Bible when used in connection with a sword. The expression "awake against" is used on four other occasions, and in three of these it is used in a negative sense, with Yahweh raising up some agent of judgment against the nations.[191] In Jer 25, Yahweh says that he is "summoning a sword against all the inhabitants of the earth" (25:29), that "he is entering into judgment with all flesh, and the wicked he will put to the sword" (25:31), and that "those pierced by the LORD on that day shall extend from one end of the earth to the other" (25:33). A similar command to a sword is found in Jer 47:6–7 where the sword of Yahweh is

---

189.   Clark and Hatton, *Handbook*, 334.
190.   The third person plural pronouns in the second sentence of v. 9 ("they/them") are masculine singular ("he/it") in the MT. They refer to the group as a singular entity (cf. "sheep" or "remnant").
191.   Isa 10:26 speaks of Yahweh of hosts raising a whip against the Assyrians. In Isa 13:17 and Jer 51:1, Yahweh speaks in the first person to say that he shall raise up a foreign nation against Babylon. In Isa 13, this involves being struck by the sword (Isa 13:15). In a fourth reference (Job 8:6), it is used in a positive sense to speak of Yahweh rousing himself to restore Job.

said to be "against Ashkelon." In this passage, the idea of a sword "being at rest" and "being still" and "being quiet" refers to a sword in its scabbard. It is the opposite state to a sword that has been given a charge by Yahweh. Hence, the charge in Zech 13:7 to "awake" is probably best understood as a charge by Yahweh for a sword to be "drawn," ready to strike the shepherd in judgment.

The expression "my shepherd" (רעי) is the same as in Zech 11:17 (without the adjective "foolish"). As has been noted, this has led many to equate the two, and even to posit that 13:7–9 was earlier attached to ch. 11. The referent of "my shepherd" is a question that shall be returned to. At this stage, it is simply noted that the shepherd metaphor is not limited to 11:4–17. Yahweh's people are described as a flock in 9:16, and then as sheep who are afflicted for lack of a shepherd in 10:2. In 10:3–4, Yahweh's anger burns against the shepherds whom he will punish; he will then raise up an alternative leadership. According to 11:3, when Yahweh brings his people home, shepherds will wail as their glory is ruined. The broader usage of this metaphor in Zechariah should caution us against insisting that the shepherd of 11:17 is the same individual on view in 13:7.[192] The first person suffix "my" seems to indicate a close relationship between the shepherd and Yahweh. This pronoun is also used in the covenant formula at the end of 13:9, where the end result of this action is that Yahweh says, "They are my people," and the people say, "Yahweh is my God."

There are two other descriptions of this shepherd. He is described as a "man" (גבר). This is not the usual word for "man" (איש), but has the nuance of "strength" (cf. Isa 22:17; Jer 17:5).[193] Kosmala claims that it denotes an individual who has a particularly close relationship to God, particularly in Psalms and in Job.[194] Vermes has gone further to suggest that the term "the man" (הגבר) became a symbolic title for a ruler and possibly the Messiah.[195] While it is a term that is appropriate to describe

192. Petersen, *Zechariah 9–14*, 130, is surely right when he says "one need not think that the notion of shepherd functions identically in these various texts."

193. BDB, 150, says it is a term used to distinguish the man from the women, children, and non-combatants whom he is to defend. Cf. H. Kosmala, "The Term *geber* in the Old Testament and in the Scrolls," in *Congress Volume: Rome, 1968* (ed. G. W. Anderson et al.; Leiden: Brill, 1969), 159–69 (160): "Anyway, a *geber* is a male person who distinguishes himself from others by his strength, or courage, or uprightness, or some other quality."

194. H. Kosmala, "*gābhar*," *TDOT* 2:367–82 (377–80).

195. G. Vermes, *Scripture and Tradition in Judaism* (2d ed.; Leiden: Brill, 1973), 56–66. Vermes compares this with the usage in Num. 24:17 (LXX); *T. Jud.* 24:1; *T. Naph.* 4:5, and Zech 13:7. See also Gese, "Anfang," 47.

the future Davidic king and it is used as an adjective (אל גבור) to describe
the future Davidic king in Isa 9:6 (MT 9:5), it is not clear that it is used
here to convey this association.[196] However, reference to the figure in this
way brings to mind a battle context, and this is significant given that the
future Davidic king is probably to be understood as one of the mighty
men (כגברים) who shall restore the fortunes of Israel in 10:5. Furthermore, the one who is pierced in 10:10 is struck in the context of battle.

This "man" is further described as "my associate" (עמיתי), where the
first person possessive pronoun, like that of "my shepherd," refers to
Yahweh of hosts. This is a term that is found elsewhere only in Leviticus, where it denotes an associate or neighbour, and, as Butterworth
helpfully comments, "it always signifies someone who should be treated
rightly."[197] Cook argues that the combination of phrases "my shepherd"
and "the man, my associate" may simply express the thought that the
shepherd is under the control of Yahweh, and not that Yahweh is in a
positive relationship with the shepherd.[198] However, this seems to be
driven by the presupposition that 13:7–9 was originally connected with
11:4–17, rather than taking the phrases at face value. More reasonable is
C. and E. Meyers's belief that the combination of גבר with עמיתי inten-
sifies the sense of close relationship.[199] Similarly, Floyd notes that in
these two descriptions: "Yahweh thus seems to be turning against someone who formerly enjoyed his approval and confidence, or someone who
appeared to do so. This leader enjoyed an at least pro forma designation
as Yahweh's chosen ruler."[200] All this of course raises the question: Why,
if the shepherd is described in such approving terms, does Yahweh command his execution? This question will be addressed in the next chapter.

The command is then given to strike the shepherd. Whereas the command "to awake" was given to the sword (feminine ending), the subject
of the imperative verb "to strike" is masculine, which does not agree
with the sword.[201] This probably indicates that while the call here is for

---

196.   The term is used of David in 2 Sam 23:1 and of Jehoiakim in Jer 22:28.
However, as Vermes, *Scripture and Tradition in Judaism*, 58, notes (regarding 2
Sam 23:1), this may be an "accidental association."
197.   Butterworth, *Structure*, 283.
198.   Cook, "Metamorphosis," 456–57.
199.   Meyers and Meyers, *Zechariah 9–14*, 387.
200.   Floyd, *Minor Prophets*, 539.
201.   See further, Clark and Hatton, *Handbook*, 336–37. They note other attempts
to resolve this, which include (1) assuming a grammatical error with the subject still
being the sword; (2) concluding that it is addressed to an unnamed foe; (3) following a few Greek manuscripts which translate it with a first person verb ("I will
strike").

some unnamed person or party to strike the shepherd, Yahweh stands behind it.[202] The verb "to strike" (נכה) is different from that used in Zech 13:3 of the false prophet who is pierced by his parents, and the one who is pierced in 12:10 (דקר in both instances). In Zechariah, נכה refers to: Tyre's power on the sea and the waves on the sea being struck down (9:4; 10:11); horses being struck with confusion and their riders with madness (12:4); and the inflicting of wounds (13:6). Striking on its own does not necessarily imply death, but the expression "to strike with a sword" does, especially when it is an individual who is struck (e.g. 2 Sam 12:9; Isa 37:38).[203]

The consequence of the shepherd being struck is that the sheep are scattered.[204] This is normally seen as judgment. A similar phrase "sheep without a shepherd" (cf. Zech 10:2) occurs throughout the Hebrew Bible as representing a state of disarray for Yahweh's people that comes from a lack of leadership (e.g. Num. 27:17; Ezek 34:5). In 1 Kgs 22:17, it refers to the scattered state that Israel will become without a king.

This state is further described as Yahweh turning his hand against the little ones. The expression "turn my hand against" occurs on four other occasions in the Hebrew Bible, meaning to destroy in judgment.[205] In Isa 1:24–26 it is used, as here, in conjunction with the idea of refining a remnant.

The term "little ones" is unusual.[206] It most naturally refers to the sheep that are scattered, rather than otherwise unmentioned "shepherd boys" (cf. NEB). If there is a comparison with the expression "little ones of the flock" in Jer 49:20 and 50:45, which seems likely, then it could be referring particularly to the lambs of the flock, highlighting the severity of the coming judgment, where even the lambs will not escape.

---

202. So, for instance, in Isa 13 it says that Yahweh will overthrow the Babylonians (Isa 13:11, 19), and yet it also says that he will use the Medes to accomplish this (Isa 13:17). The Medes are Yahweh's agent, and both can be said to be acting individually while ultimately acting together. Floyd, *Minor Prophets*, 539, notes: "The overall mode of description in v. 7 thus emphasizes Yahweh's direct responsibility not only for the demise of the leader himself but also for the devastating effect of this loss on the rest of the community."

203. The expression occurs over 40 times in the Hebrew Bible, with the object being a city, nation, group or individual that is struck. In each instance of an individual being struck, death ensues (Josh 10:28, 30; 11:10; 2 Sam 12:9; 20:10; 2 Kgs 19:37; Isa 37:38; Jer 26:23; 41:2).

204. Clark and Hatton, *Handbook*, 337, note that the Hebrew does not suggest purpose, but consequence.

205. Ps 81:14 (MT 81:15); Isa 1:24–26; Ezek 38:12; Amos 1:8.

206. It is found only here as a participle in the Hebrew Bible (cf. the imperfects in Job 14:21 and Isa 30:19).

The judgment is further clarified in Zech 13:8–9 as one that will purify a faithful remnant. Yahweh's people will go through a severe refining process where two parts of the people shall be cut off and perish (13:8), and the third part shall then be refined by fire (13:9). The idea of a refined remnant is a common theme among the pre-exilic prophets.[207] The division of the people of Yahweh into thirds for judgment is reminiscent of Ezekiel's sign-action in Ezek 5, which represents a third of the people being burned with fire, a third struck by the sword, and a third scattered to the wind with the sword unsheathed after them (Ezek 5:2). From this final third, a small number are preserved, but even they are further refined (Ezek 5:3–4). For all these prophets, the refining process was that of the exile from which a purified remnant would emerge. Is Zechariah here once again portraying the past exile (cf. Zech 11:4–14), or is this a future refinement that accompanies the battle of "that day," or is this perhaps a way of saying that the exile is not yet over? This question will be addressed shortly.

The people that emerge from this ordeal are pictured as enjoying a fully restored covenant relationship with Yahweh (cf. Exod 3:10; 5:1; 19:5–6), or even a new covenant relationship ("I will be their God and they will be my people," Jer 31:33; cf. Zech 2:11 [MT 2:15]; 8:8; 9:16).[208] The curse of the exile (cf. Hos 1:9) will be reversed. It is a situation that is also reflected in the promise of Zech 10:6: "I will strengthen the house of Judah, and I will save the house of Joseph. I will bring them back because I have compassion on them, and they shall be as though I had not rejected them, for *I am the LORD their God and I will answer them.*"

We are now in a position to reflect on how this passage relates to its immediate and wider contexts and to turn to the key question of the identity of the shepherd, along with the other questions that have been raised. I will begin to do this by reviewing and weighing up the views of scholarship.

As noted, the predominant view among scholars is that the shepherd in this passage is the figure of Zech 11:15–17.[209] There, Yahweh imprecates the worthless shepherd with woe and a sword to strike his arm and his right eye. Apart from the obvious shepherd imagery, the connections with 13:7 include: the desire of Yahweh to strike the shepherd with a sword; the metrical structure that continues through both passages; the

---

207.   E.g. Isa 1:8–9; Amos 3:21; Mic 5:7–8; 7:18.

208.   Cf. Lev 26:12; Deut 26:17–18; Jer 7:23; 24:7; 30:22; 32:38; Ezek 11:20; 14:11; 36:28; 37:23, 27.

209.   For example, Mason, *Zechariah*, 111; Meyer, "Allegory," 234–35; Redditt, *Zechariah*, 136; Mitchell, *Psalter*, 200; Mason, "Earlier," 130.

covenant concepts (11:10; cf. 13:9); and the allusions to smelting.[210] In this case, depending on the approach taken in ch. 11, this figure has been identified as representing Jerusalem's leaders,[211] the king of Egypt,[212] Cyrus, or the present Persian monarch.[213]

There are several problems with these identifications of the shepherd. It is difficult, if not impossible, to see how the cumulative description of the shepherd in 13:7 as "my shepherd" and "the man, my associate" is comparable to the description in 11:16 of the shepherd who "does not care for the perishing, or secure the young, or heal the maimed, or sustain the standing, but consumes the flesh of the fat ones, and tears off their hoofs." Why would this worthless and despotic shepherd be referred to in such elevated terms in 13:7? Mason argues that the description in 13:7 is an ironic reference to the contemporary leadership, but this hardly seems likely.[214] Given that there are at least four different shepherds in chs. 10–11,[215] one would expect a description that made it clear that it was referring to the "foolish shepherd" of 11:17. Furthermore, the shepherd that Zechariah portrayed in 11:15–17 was set up as Yahweh's judgment on his people on account of their rejection of him as their true shepherd, whereas in 13:7b–9 it is the opposite, namely, the removal of the shepherd, which results in judgment falling on Yahweh's people. Similarly, in the wider context of chs. 10–11, the removal of worthless shepherds has a favourable outcome for the flock, but in 13:7b–9 the removal of this shepherd results immediately in the scattering and judgment of the flock. These factors all point to the shepherd of 13:7 being different from that of 11:17.[216]

---

210. Noted by Mason, "Earlier," 129–30. Cf. J. D. Nogalski, "Zechariah 13:7–9 as a Transitional Text: An Appreciation and Re-evaluation of the Work of Rex Mason," in Boda and Floyd, eds., *Bringing out the Treasure*, 292–304 (294). Meyer, "Allegory," 237, also adds the fact that the covenant formula in Zech 13:9 is found in Ezek 37:23, 27 and hence this sequel to the reunification of the two sticks (Ezek 37:15–22) is reflected with a close relationship between Zech 11:4–17 and 13:7–9.

211. Redditt, "Shepherds," 636, argues that Zech 13:7 does not depict a future messianic expectation, but presents a negative view of Jerusalem's leaders so as to explain Yahweh's attack on his people in Zech 14.

212. Mitchell, "Zechariah," 317.

213. Sweeney, *Twelve*, 682–83, 695–96, believes that the oracle in Zech 11:15–17 takes up the language of the prophecy concerning Cyrus in Isa 44:28 to portray a picture of Yahweh's shepherd who will suffer punishment as a result of his neglect for Yahweh's sheep.

214. Mason, *Zechariah*, 111, and "Earlier," 123.

215. The shepherds in Zech 10:3 and 11:3; the three shepherds in 11:8; the shepherd of 11:4–14; and the shepherd of 11:15–17.

216. Most of these criticisms are also made by Larkin, *Eschatology*, 177.

Sweeney argues that the Shepherd in Zech 11:17 and 13:7 is Cyrus, who represents the contemporary Persian king.[217] In Isa 44:24–45:19, Cyrus is spoken of favourably as Yahweh's chosen shepherd who will be Yahweh's instrument in establishing his people in the land and rebuilding the temple. While Cyrus and hence the Persian monarchy was initially viewed favourably, by the time of Zechariah, the Persian monarchy had neglected Yahweh's people and this is reflected in the description of Zech 11:16. Sweeney argues that the oracle of 11:17 which states that a sword will cause the shepherd's right arm to wither and his right eye to be blinded takes up Isaiah's language concerning Cyrus: from Isa 45:1, where it speaks of Yahweh grasping the right hand of Cyrus to subdue nations before him; from Isa 41:2, which speaks of one from the east making kings like dust with his sword; and from Isa 42:4, which also uses the verb "to grow dim, faint" of the shepherd. However, these links to Isaiah seem somewhat tenuous, and are not as precise as Sweeney maintains.[218] Furthermore, Cyrus has already been off the stage for some time and it seems overly subtle to refer to the contemporary Persian monarch in this way.

Ancient Jewish scholars understood the shepherd of Zech 13:7 as a future king. The Targum renders רעי in this verse as מלכא.[219] Mitchell notes several apocalyptic midrashim dating from the early to late first millennium C.E. that cite 13:9 and 14:2 in connection with the death of Messiah ben Joseph.[220] This is not the victorious Messiah ben David, but a second Messiah figure (ben Joseph or ben Ephraim) who dies in a battle against Gog and Magog.[221] When and how this second Messiah figure developed within Judaism is unclear.[222] It may have been an attempt by

217.   Sweeney, *Twelve*, 695–97.

218.   Zech 11:17 does not refer to a right arm but to an arm and a right eye. Isa 41:2 does not explicitly identify this conqueror with Cyrus, and Isa 42:4 speaks of the Servant of the Lord himself and not his eye.

219.   "O sword, *be revealed* against *the king* and against the *prince his* companion *who is his equal, who is like him,* says the Lord of hosts; slay the *king* and the *princes* shall be scattered and I will bring back *a mighty stroke* upon the *underlings*" (Gordon, *Targum*, 221–22).

220.   Mitchell, *Psalter*, 202. These include: *Otot ha-Mashiah* 7:16–19 (cited by ibid., 312) and *Nistarot Rav Shimon ben Yohai* 25–26 (cited by ibid., 331–32).

221.   Horbury, *Messianism*, 33.

222.   See the discussion by R. P. Gordon, "The Ephraimite Messiah and the Targum(s) to Zechariah 12:10," in *Reading from Right to Left: Essays on the Hebrew Bible in Honour of David J. A. Clines* (ed. J. C. Exum and H. G. M. Williamson; JSOTSup 373; London: Sheffield Academic Press, 2003), 184–95 (192–94). Also M. Buttenwieser, "Messiah," in *Jewish Encyclopedia*, vol. 8 (ed. I. Singer; New York: Funk & Wagnalls, 1925), 505–12 (511–12).

Jewish scholars to reconcile the expectations concerning the victorious Messiah ben David who would live forever with Zech 13:7 and other texts from the Hebrew Bible (including 12:10), which they understood to be referring to a Messiah who is killed.

Horbury notes that the death of a Messiah is also envisaged in 2 Esd 7:29 and the cutting off of a rightful ruler called Messiah is also foretold in Dan 9:26.[223] He concludes: "The notion of a slain messiah is then likely to have been current in the Second-Temple period, partly on the basis of Zechariah, although it seems clearly to have been less prominent than the expectation of a great and glorious king."[224] At the least, this demonstrates that ancient Jewish scholars understood the concept of a future king who suffers as existing not only in Zechariah, but also more broadly in the Hebrew Bible.[225]

The interpretation of this passage is difficult. If it is approached as an isolated unit, then it seems right to agree with many scholars, that understanding the shepherd as the future Davidic king may over-read the evidence.[226] Yet, the descriptions of the shepherd are certainly not inconsistent with this. However, the shepherd is not explicitly identified with the future Davidic king, and it may even be that Petersen is correct in saying that the shepherd is not an identifiable individual.[227] However, if

223. Horbury, *Messianism*, 33.

224. Ibid. See also R. B. Crotty, "Suffering in Deutero-Zechariah," *ABR* 20 (1972): 54–56, who believes that while the messianism of Zech 9–14 bypasses the house of David, the figure here is a suffering representative of Yahweh. Contra Collins, *Scepter*, 33, who argues: "there is no parallel for such a notion of messianic martyrdom in Second Temple Judaism."

225. The *Damascus Document* (CD-B) contains a quotation of Zech 13:7 and connects the events of this verse with the coming of the "messiah of Aaron and Israel." However, there is wide disagreement among scholars regarding the identification of the shepherd in this text. For a discussion of the identity of the shepherd in this passage, see Black, "Messiah," 117–20; Mitchell, *Psalter*, 230–31; Ham, *King*, 74–75. On the identity of the "anointed of Aaron and Israel," see C. A. Evans, "The Messiah in the Dead Sea Scrolls," in Hess and Carroll R., eds., *Israel's Messiah in the Bible and the Dead Sea Scrolls*, 85–108 (94–95). There is also controversy over whether 4Q285 5:2–4 refers to a slain Messiah, or a Messiah who slays: "A shoot will emerge from the stump of Jesse [...] 3 [...] the bud of David will go into battle with [...] 4 [...] and the Prince of the Congregation will kill him, the b[ud of David...]" (4Q285 5:2–4; F. G. Martínez, *The Dead Sea Scrolls Translated: The Qumran Texts in English* (Leiden: Brill, 1994), 124). For a discussion, see M. G. Abegg, "Messianic Hope and 4Q285: A Reassessment," *JBL* 113 (1994): 81–91.

226. This point is made also by Lamarche, *Zacharie IX–XIV*, 92–93.

227. Petersen, *Zechariah 9–14*, 132.

Zechariah is not read as disconnected units, but as a piece of carefully crafted literature, written against a background of other literature with which it interacts, then it is reasonable to assume that the reader has already been guided as to how this shepherd figure should be understood. This is essentially the approach of Lamarche, which was groundbreaking for its time in its literary approach to the text. However, while his argument has been accepted by a minority, the majority of scholars have been dismissive.[228] Although the chiastic scheme that he developed for Zech 9–14 may not fit as neatly as he presents it, and I would differ in the interpretation of some of the units (such as 11:4–17), what his thesis demonstrates is that a literary reading of the text naturally highlights the Davidic hope.

I have gone further than Lamarche's thesis and read chs. 9–14 against the background of chs. 1–8 and found that this makes the expectation for the house of David even clearer. Zechariah 9–14 does not present a series of battles that usher in the restored kingdom of Yahweh on earth; rather, there is actually one battle on view that is explored from different perspectives. Throughout these chapters, different aspects of the battle are "telescoped" to focus on different elements. Zechariah 9 establishes the broad outline of the programme: Yahweh is coming to re-establish the kingdom promised to David (9:1–8). Central to this is the coming king (9:9–10), who will save Yahweh's people, as at the exodus, in a great eschatological battle (9:11–15). This will result in the salvation of Yahweh's people, restored covenant relationship, and ensuing blessings (9:16–17). The background of chs. 1–8 has already informed the identity of this king, who is central to this programme; he is the coming Shoot, the eschatological figure who will fulfil Yahweh's promises to David that a house should be built for Yahweh's name and who will establish the throne of David's kingdom forever (cf. 2 Sam 7:13). The descriptions of the king in ch. 9 support this identification.

---

228.   Note the comment of Coggins, *Zechariah*, 64: "Much more problematic is Lamarche's argument relating to the intervening sections [Zech 9:9–13:9], where he claimed to detect recurring references to the king of Israel and to the war and victory of Israel over her enemies, together with the attacks upon idolatry, all set out in an identifiable pattern. Objective proof of theories of this kind is notoriously difficult to achieve; most reviewers and commentators have been reserved in their judgments. Among the most enthusiastic supporters of this view of the structure of Zechariah 9–14 has been Baldwin." For similar criticisms, see D. J. Clark, "Discourse Structure in Zechariah 9–14: Skeleton or Phantom?," in *Issues in Bible Translation* (ed. P. C. Stine; London: United Bible Societies, 1988), 64–80 (77–79); Black, "Messiah," 46–47; Petersen, *Zechariah 9–14*, 28.

In 10:1–11:3, a different perspective is given on this battle. This time the focus is on the leadership of Yahweh's people. Yahweh shall overthrow the false shepherds (10:1–3) by raising up a new leadership for his people, including the eschatological Davidic king (10:4) and his "mighty men," who shall defeat their foe (10:5), unite north and south (10:6–7), and bring back the exiles in a new exodus (10:8–12) that will see the false shepherds overthrown (11:1–3).

The two sign-actions of 11:4–17 explain why false shepherds presently oppress Yahweh's people. The sign-actions make clear that the judgment of exile was a direct response to the rejection of Yahweh by both the people and their kings. The foolish shepherds who rule over them have been put there by Yahweh in judgment (11:15–17). While the two sign-actions do not deal directly with the future Davidic king, they do so indirectly by heightening the expectation of Yahweh's shepherd, who will overturn this present situation, as well as providing an implicit warning not to reject him when he comes.

In ch. 12, a new feature of the battle emerges—the salvation of Jerusalem will not come without cost to Yahweh's own people, and in particular, their king. Once again, the battle that will see the salvation of Jerusalem is pictured (12:1–9). The expectation is raised that the house of David shall once again lead and protect Yahweh's people, like Yahweh himself (12:8). However, where is this coming king? Zechariah 12 shall be closely examined in the next chapter; suffice to say here that 12:10–14 explains that the promised king was pierced in the battle that won salvation; and not only that, but he was pierced by his own people (12:10). However, this piercing has a positive outcome for Yahweh's people. It is accompanied by an outflow of mourning (12:10–14), a fountain being opened to cleanse from sin and uncleanness (13:1), and idolatry and false prophecy being removed from the land (13:2–6).

Given this background, how should the shepherd of 13:7 be identified? Who is the intended referent? A number of possibilities that do not in the end make sense in the overall context of the book have already been examined, namely, the foolish shepherd of 11:17 and the contemporary individuals that he could represent. The same difficulties that were encountered with the foolish shepherd also hold true for the shepherds of 10:3 and 11:3. There are other possible shepherds though. Is it the shepherd of 11:4–14: either the prophet Zechariah or Yahweh himself? The problems with this identification include the fact that the shepherd of the first sign-action is not struck, but resigns from his post (11:9). Further, the prophet is a contemporary figure, whereas the shepherd of 13:7 seems to be an eschatological one, given the outcome of his work.

The fact that it is unusual to describe a prophet as a shepherd also weighs against this identification.[229] The identification of the shepherd with Yahweh himself makes a nonsense of the descriptions that are given of the shepherd in 13:7; while the shepherd is closely associated with Yahweh, they are distinct beings.

O. Plöger and A. Lacoque suggest that the shepherd here may be the high priest, who represented the Jewish community before the Persian king as well as before God.[230] According to Plöger, "this earthly pinnacle of the theocracy is overturned by Yahweh himself."[231] However, this seems to be based on a mistaken reading of the high priest's role in ch. 3.[232] There, the high priest was a different figure to the Shoot.

Conrad argues that the context suggests that the shepherd is one of the prophets of 13:2–6 who deceives and lies and is therefore struck by Yahweh.[233] Comparing this passage with 10:2–3 and 11:17, he argues: "Shepherd passages, then, recur in contexts concerned with those who, rather than speak for the LORD, tell lies and offer empty consolation. The shepherds, therefore, represent leaders who do not speak for the LORD and consequently lead the people astray."[234] However, this does not take account of the fact that Yahweh is also represented as a shepherd in ch. 11 and he is hardly one who tells lies and offers empty consolation. In addition, C. and E. Meyers note that outside Zechariah the shepherd metaphor is never used to represent a prophet apart from Moses.[235] Furthermore, this view also faces the difficulty that the removal of this false prophet results in the immediate scattering and judgment of the flock, whereas one would expect the opposite, especially since Zechariah has already attributed the wandering and affliction of the people to the rule of false shepherds (10:2–3).

By a process of elimination, there is only one referent within Zechariah that makes sense of the designation "my shepherd," namely, the coming king of 9:9, who is also the Shoot of 3:8 and 6:12, and, as we

229.   The only prophet described as a shepherd is Moses.

230.   O. Plöger, *Theocracy and Eschatology* (trans. S. Rudman; Oxford: Blackwell, 1968), 88; A. Lacocque, "Zacharie 9–14," in Amsler, Lacocque, and Vuilleumier, eds., *Aggée, Zacharie, Malachie*, 197. Hinton, *Zechariah*, 116, also suggests the shepherd is the high priest.

231.   Plöger, *Theocracy*, 88.

232.   See also the discussion of the role of the high priest in Cook, "Metamorphosis," 458 n. 14.

233.   Conrad, *Zechariah*, 188–89.

234.   Ibid., 190. Conrad does not strictly identify this shepherd with the shepherd of 11:16

235.   Meyers and Meyers, *Zechariah 9–14*, 250.

shall see, the one who is pierced in the context of a battle in 12:10.[236] This identification fits entirely with the descriptions that are given of the shepherd here ("the man, my associate"), descriptions that we have seen lend themselves to being appropriate descriptions of the future Davidic king, given the background of the Hebrew Bible and 10:4–5.[237] Furthermore, Jeremiah and Ezekiel both depict the future prince of the house of David as a faithful shepherd, unlike the unworthy shepherds who betrayed the flock (Jer 23:1–6; Ezek 34:23–24; 37:24).[238]

As we shall see, in its context, Zech 13:7–9 can be understood as returning to clarify the nature and purpose of the piercing of the king in 12:10, as well as preparing for some of the themes of ch. 14. In the immediate context, the piercing of the prophet (13:3) recalls the pierced one of 12:10, and it may be this that triggers the further explanation of his death.[239] As well as this, the pattern of affliction in 13:7–9 which leads to purification and restoration is also seen in 12:2–13:6 and 14:1–21, and in this way 13:7–9 functions as a transition, highlighting again the suffering that the people of Yahweh will endure before his kingdom is finally established.[240]

There are those who have objected to the identification of the shepherd with the future Davidic king. Mitchell, for instance, argues that the interpretation that identifies the shepherd with the future Davidic king is "forbidden" since the shepherd here is the object of Yahweh's indignation.[241]

236. Cf. Duguid, "Messianic," 276.
237. Cf. Ackroyd, "Zechariah," 654–55: "The description of the shepherd as 'the man who stands next to me'—an associate of God, a suitable term for a royal figure—perhaps suggests a disaster to some messianic personage (should we compare 12:10?), so that the picture is of messianic woes ushering in the final age."
238. The identification the shepherd of this passage with the future Davidic king is also one made by the New Testament writers (e.g. Matt 26:31).
239. Baron, *Zechariah*, 473–74, helpfully observes that Zechariah turns from dealing with the false prophet "to another and altogether different figure, who is now made to pass before his vision, and whose experience, if not foreshadowed, is at least *suggested* by the treatment which had been meted out to the false prophet."
240. Sæbø, *Sacharja 9–14: Untersuchungen von Text und Form*, 279, notes a tripartite pattern of punishment, purification, and restoration that is also seen in Zech 12:2–13:6 and Zech 14. However, while it is certainly affliction, it is not as clear in Zech 12 and 14 that the suffering of Yahweh's people is necessarily punishment. Cf. Cook, "Metamorphosis," 462, who notes that Zech 13:7–9 "not only balances this section [Zech 12] thematically but also has a parallel structure involving a pattern of affliction followed by purification and return."
241. Mitchell, "Zechariah," 318. For a more recent example, see Nogalski, "Zech 13:7–9," 297, who seems opposed to this identification simply because it accords with the New Testament: "Mason's tradition-historical treatment of the shepherd imagery offers a needed corrective to the [*sic*] Cook's retrofitting of 13:7–9

However, it may be that there is an explanation for why the shepherd is struck in judgment by Yahweh. Watts argues that 13:7–9 reflects an anti-monarchical trend where the shepherd is the Davidic king on whom God's judgment falls. He suggests this situation reflects the history of the Davidic house or the final crisis of 587 B.C.E. Zechariah then envisages a restored covenant relationship between God and his people without the Davidic king. He writes: "The entire passage suggests that the problem of the corrupted royal house demands its removal. It recognizes the problems and costs which this will involve (or has involved), but welcomes it as a means toward achieving God's ultimate goal with Israel in making her to be, in the fullest sense, his people."[242]

Watts is right to see exile imagery in these verses, and indeed at one level the exiles would be reminded from these verses that they were part of the people who were being purified, and perhaps even that the exile was not fully over. However, it is clear from the wider context, with the repeated "on that day" formula, and the thematic links that 13:7–9 has with what precedes and follows, that the events portrayed here are future. Once again, this is an occasion when Zechariah draws on the past to paint a picture of the future. C. and E. Meyers, like Watts, note how the shepherd of 13:7, "represents the Davidic line, whose rule comes to a violent end in the sixth century."[243] However, they acknowledge the eschatological note: "This subunit may be anticipating an eschatological catastrophe, but it draws on demographic realities that reflect the events in Judah in the sixth century... Thus the hardships of the remnant in the land are viewed as the mechanism that will rid them of their flaws... These purified survivors become the ones to acknowledge Yahweh's special relationship with Israel."[244]

Merrill takes a similar line when he argues that since 13:1–2a has addressed the corrupt cult and priesthood, and 13:2b–6 has addressed the wicked prophetism, then this passage must be understood in its context to refer to the censure and judgment of the monarchy.[245] He also argues that the innocence of the shepherd is refuted by the fact that it is Yahweh's command that he be slain.[246] For Merrill, this passage calls to mind

with the hermeneutic of the New Testament Gospel writers, a move that becomes explicit in the third portion of Cook's article."

242. Watts, "Zechariah," 359–60.
243. Meyers and Meyers, *Zechariah 9–14*, 386.
244. Ibid., 404–5.
245. That is, censuring prophet, priest, and king. See Merrill, *Zechariah*, 334–35.
246. While he notes that the history of Christian exegesis understands this text as a prophecy concerning the Messiah, Merrill (ibid., 339–40) argues that this was never intended by the original prophet-author.

Ezek 5 and hence: "In an eschatological repetition of exile, then, the shepherd-kings of Israel will suffer the wrath of God (cf. 11:8), the flock-people will endure pestilence and sword (cf. 11:6, 9), and the surviving community will be scattered (cf. 11:16)."[247] Merrill, however, fails to identify these eschatological "shepherd-kings" of Israel who will suffer the wrath of God.[248] These figures are otherwise absent in Zechariah and so it seems incongruous to refer to them. Furthermore, the shepherd of 13:7 naturally refers to an individual, not a group. Therefore, none of the objections to the identification of the shepherd with the future Davidic king can be sustained.

The question remains: Why does this future shepherd fall under Yahweh's judgment? What purpose does it achieve? I shall return to answer this question after dealing with ch. 12 and the one who is pierced.

6.5.3. *Review of Zechariah 13:7–9*

Zechariah 13:7–9 offers a further perspective on the coming day of Yahweh. In keeping with the cleansing of Yahweh's people that will result from the battle in which one close to Yahweh is pierced (12:10), 13:7–9 explains that this piercing will be by Yahweh's own purpose and design. The striking of the shepherd results first in the scattering of the sheep; then, with them scattered, Yahweh will "turn his hand against the little ones." We have seen that similar descriptions in the Hebrew Bible point to this phrase being understood as the direct judgment of Yahweh on his people. The extent of this judgment is portrayed in 13:8, with two parts of the flock being cut off in the land and only a third remaining. It is in this judgment that the land will be cleansed. The devastating extent of the judgment also prepares for ch. 14.

The striking of the coming future king in judgment will bring about a refinement of the third that remains of Yahweh's people. This refinement is pictured as the purification of silver and gold and therefore results in something pure and precious, namely a righteous, faithful Jerusalem (just as in Isa 1:24–26). Reflecting the pattern of Isaiah, it is the refinement of Yahweh's people that will lead to the elevation of Jerusalem and the pilgrimage of the nations (Isa 2:1–4; cf. Zech 14:10, 16).[249]

---

247. Ibid., 338.

248. While in the above quote Merrill refers to the "shepherd kings" of Zech 11:8, when dealing with this passage, Merrill (ibid., 295) suggests that these were the kings at the end of Judah's pre-exilic history and not eschatological figures.

249. K. R. Schaefer, "Zechariah 14: A Study in Allusion," *CBQ* 57 (1995): 66–91 (88), identifies evidence of structural, thematic, and verbal parallels that make it clear that Zech 14 has allusions to and echoes of Isa 2–4; 13; 30, as well as a correspondence of phrase and imagery with other sections of Isaiah.

6.6. *The Shepherd and the Hope for the House of David*

The shepherd imagery in Zech 9–14 provides a rich (and complex!) tapestry that explains the past history, present experience, and future expectations concerning the house of David. The background to this imagery is found in the earlier prophets where unworthy kings of Judah and Israel are condemned as shepherds who feed on the sheep rather than provide for and protect them. In their place, and after the exilic experience, Yahweh promises to raise up one shepherd, a future Davidic king, who will feed and prosper the flock. This shepherd-king will reunite Judah and Ephraim as in the days of David. Rather than transforming and reinterpreting this tradition as many scholars suppose, these chapters of Zechariah re-express this same expectation to hold out hope for the post-exilic community. Zechariah uses the shepherd imagery in exactly the same ways.

This is seen, first, in 10:2–3, with the assessment that the people wander as sheep and are afflicted for lack of a shepherd. This reflects the fact that the post-exilic community had no king of their own on account of the judgment that came in the exile on the kings of Israel and Judah for their sins. Shepherd imagery is also used to speak of foreign kings who have used the flock for their own advantage in 10:3 and 11:3. Nevertheless, Yahweh announces his intention to punish these shepherds and to raise up a new leadership to save his people from their affliction and reunite the houses of Judah and Joseph/Ephraim. The strength and victory that these leaders shall provide is conveyed by their titles: "keystone," "peg," and "battle bow." While none of these metaphors is clearly Davidic, the wider context and background make it almost certain that the Davidic shepherd-king is to be included among these leaders. Furthermore, the way that the passage speaks of the reuniting of the houses of Judah and Joseph/Ephraim, when understood against the background of Ps 78, strongly suggests that a coming Davidic shepherd-king will save them from their present affliction.

The two sign-actions of 11:4–17 also draw on the shepherd imagery of the earlier prophets. In the first sign-action, the shepherd imagery is used to represent Yahweh as the prophet re-enacts Yahweh's dealings with his people. It is also used to represent the kings of Judah and Israel who have had no pity on the flock and who have been removed from office. The prophet plays the role of a shepherd to demonstrate the way that the people had despised Yahweh as their shepherd throughout their history. Yahweh's rejection of the flock is symbolized in the breaking of two staffs that represent the division of the kingdom and the judgment of exile. The first sign-action therefore functions as an historical review and uses the shepherd imagery in the same way as the earlier prophets. In the second sign-action, shepherd imagery is used to represent the contemporary foreign king who ruled Yahweh's people in judgment for their rejection of him. While the future Davidic shepherd-king is not explicitly mentioned in this section, the note of woe on which it ends raises the expectation that Yahweh will send him. At the same time, these sign-actions suggest that when he comes, he may not be treated that favourably. This is confirmed in chs. 12–13.

It has been noted that the identity of the shepherd in 13:7–9 is contested. However, if 13:7–9 is read, not as an isolated unit, but as an integral part of the book of Zechariah, then the referent of the shepherd should be found in what has gone before in the book. While many scholars have identified the shepherd with the foolish shepherd of 11:16–17, the present study has demonstrated how this identification is incongruous and unsatisfactory. It seems that the main reason for making this identification is the presupposition that there was no hope for the house of David (i.e. a future Davidic king) being expressed at this time. Given the expectation of a future king that has been raised to this point in Zechariah (including the Shoot of chs. 1–8, the coming king of 9:9, the rulers of 10:4, and the pierced one of 12:10), it is entirely fitting to identify the shepherd of 13:7 as this king. This also accords with the descriptions of the shepherd that are given in 13:7 ("my shepherd...the man, my associate"), as well as the wider context of the Hebrew Bible.

In terms of the hope that is held for the house of David, Cook believes: "The shepherd of 13:7–9 is now to be interpreted not as the anti-David in 11:15–17, but as a figure within the context of a more positive messianic expectation (as in 3:8; 6:12–14; 9:9–10; 10:4). In contrast to the "anti-shepherd" imprecation, this new context holds out bright hopes for the Davidides."[250] While it seems a little inappropriate to say that the death of the future king is a "bright" hope, Cook is right in his estimate of the robust hope that 13:7–9 presents for the house of David. Once again, there is no evidence that the Davidic hope has diminished in any way. Zechariah continues to exhibit strong expectations for a future king who is central to Yahweh's restoration programme. However, there are still

---

250. Cook, "Metamorphosis," 461. Note also (p. 459): "It should further be emphasized that Deutero-Zechariah's critique of Yehud's civic shepherds cannot be taken as evidence of any movement of the group away from the messianism of Zech 3:8; 4; 6:12; 9:9–10. Deutero-Zechariah's critique of past and present rulers was extended to predict a coming antishepherd, but this development need not have caused the group to abandon their positive messianic hope." However, Cook's belief that Zech 13:7–9 was originally connected with Zech 11 must be questioned.

a few questions outstanding: Can the purpose of the king being struck be clarified against the wider themes of Zechariah and the prophets? Furthermore, if the king has been struck, how can his rule be said to extend from sea to sea, and from the river to the ends of the earth (9:10)? Why is he apparently not mentioned again in ch. 14? Is the hope for a future Davidic king ultimately eclipsed by the hope that Yahweh will be king? These questions shall be addressed in the next chapter.

Chapter 7

THE PIERCED ONE

7.1. *Introduction*

Zechariah 12 returns to the theme of the final victory won by Yahweh for his people with the re-establishment of his kingdom and all of its ensuing blessings. Scholars display a vast diversity of opinion on the hope that is exhibited in this chapter for the house of David and the role of any future king. While the house of David, and indeed David himself, are spoken of in elevated terms (Zech 12:7–8), many scholars are dismissive of this holding out of hope for a future king. Further, 12:10 raises one of the most controversial questions in the book, namely, the identity of the one who is pierced. Does this refer to an historical figure known to the prophet, or is it a future figure? If a future figure, is it to be understood in prophetic or royal terms? Indeed, is it impossible to make any identification? The present chapter will examine these questions.

7.2. *The Pierced One of Zechariah 12*

Before addressing the issue of the identity of the one who is pierced, I shall deal with the immediate context of ch. 12 in which the house of David is highlighted.

7.2.1. *Structure of Zechariah 12:1–13:1*
This unit begins the second oracular section (chs. 12–14), entitled a מַשָּׂא (cf. 9:1).[1] I have followed Lamarche's thematic structuring of 12:2–9.[2] While differing with Butterworth's structure of these verses, he is surely correct to treat 12:10–14 as a unit, beginning with the new element of

---

1. For comments on this term, see the treatment of Zech 9:1 in Chapter 5.
2. Lamarche, *Zacharie IX–XIV*, 74–78. Lamarche groups Zech 12:2–8 into three pairs of what he calls "strophes," each dealing with a similar theme, with an introduction (12:1) and conclusion (12:9).

the pierced figure in 12:10.[3] Regarding 13:1, he writes: "Zech. 13:1 introduces the next new element: a fountain for cleansing from sin of the house of David and the inhabitants of Jerusalem. The verse has more in common with ch. 12 than with 13:2–6 (especially 'house of David', the last occurrence) but 'on that day' also links this latter passage with what has gone before. It is clearly concerned with cleansing."[4]

This section can therefore be structured as follows:

12:1[5]	Introduction
12:2–9	A siege and salvation
12:2, 3	The assault of the nations against Jerusalem repelled
12:4–5, 6	Yahweh acts for Jerusalem through Judah
12:7, 8	Yahweh saves and protects
12:9	Summary
12:10–14	Mourning for the pierced one
13:1	A fountain of cleansing

7.2.2. *A Siege and Salvation (Zechariah 12:1–9)*

[1] An oracle: The word of Yahweh concerning Israel. A declaration of Yahweh, who stretched out the heavens, and founded the earth, and formed the spirit of man within him, [2] "Behold, I am making Jerusalem a cup of staggering to all the surrounding peoples, and it will be against Judah also, in the siege against Jerusalem. [3] And it will be on that day that I will make Jerusalem a burdensome stone to all the peoples. All who carry it will severely cut themselves, and all the nations of the earth will be gathered against her."

[4] "On that day," declares Yahweh, "I will strike every horse with confusion, and its rider with madness. And I will open my eyes upon the house of Judah, and I will strike every horse of the peoples with blindness. [5] And the clans of Judah will say in their hearts: "The inhabitants of Jerusalem are strength to me, on account of Yahweh of hosts, their God."

[6] "On that day I will make the clans of Judah as a pot of fire in wood, as a torch of fire in sheaves. And they will consume to the right and to the left all the surrounding peoples. And Jerusalem will dwell again in its place, in Jerusalem."

[7] And Yahweh will save the tents of Judah first, so that the glory of the house of David and the glory of the inhabitants of Jerusalem will not be promoted over Judah. [8] On that day Yahweh will defend the one who

---

3. Butterworth, *Structure*, 218–19. Butterworth suggests two parallel units: Zech 12:2–5 and 12:6–9.

4. Ibid., 216.

5. I have separated Zech 12:1 from 12:2–9 to show that it forms an introduction for chs. 12–14. For convenience, it will be dealt with along with 12:2–9 in what follows.

dwells in Jerusalem, and the one who stumbles on that day shall be like David. And the house of David shall be like God, like the angel of Yahweh going before them. [9] "And it will be on that day that I will seek to destroy all the nations that come against Jerusalem." (author's translation)

Whereas the oracle in ch. 9 began by indicting cities that circumscribed the ideal land of Israel, this oracle is said to be "the word of Yahweh concerning Israel," and begins with Jerusalem (12:2).[6] Jerusalem, mentioned eleven times in 12:1–13:1, forms the focus of Yahweh's restoration purposes. It is from Jerusalem that salvation will spread to all the nations and families of the earth.[7] Like the earlier prophets, here we see Zechariah drawing on the promises of Yahweh that were associated particularly with Jerusalem and the house of David (cf. 2 Sam 7) to give hope for the future.

Many scholars have noted the way that Zech 9–14 uses battle imagery that closely resembles that found in earlier prophets (e.g. Mic 4–5). Indeed, it is this similarity that led some of these scholars to suggest that Zech 9–14 was pre-exilic. The pre-exilic prophets painted a picture of a future battle that would result in deliverance for the people of Yahweh. In drawing on the themes of the earlier prophets, particularly a future battle, Zechariah is effectively arguing that even though they have returned from exile, the ultimate deliverance still lies in the future.

The significance of what Yahweh will do is highlighted in the threefold description of Yahweh as the one "who stretched out the heavens, and founded the earth, and formed the spirit of man within him." The salvation of Jerusalem with the establishment of the kingdom promised to David (cf. ch. 9) is here understood as an act of new creation.[8] But before the final vindication of Jerusalem, this chapter also spells out the suffering and sorrow that she will have to undergo.

---

6. C. and E. Meyers argue that "concerning Israel" in Zech 12:1 refers to all Israel, as opposed to the view that it is a post-exilic term for Judah, or that it refers to the Southern Kingdom: Judah and Benjamin. Mason, *Zechariah*, 114–15, argues that the use of "Israel" points to the eschatological thrust of the oracle. As Israel was historically a thing of the past, this reference looks forward to the time when the exiled and scattered people will return to become the people of Yahweh once more.

7. Note the concern for the nations who are both judged (e.g. 12:2–6; 14:3, 12, 17, 19) and saved (e.g. 14:16). Hanson, *Apocalyptic*, 355, who believes that the broad international scope of chs. 9–11 has narrowed "to a myopic concern with Judah and Jerusalem" has surely missed the national and international concern here.

8. So Mason, "Earlier," 134; Webb, *Zechariah*, 156. Conrad, *Zechariah*, 180, notes the resonance of these descriptions with the restoration of Jerusalem and the rebuilding of the temple in earlier parts of Zechariah (cf. 1:16; 4:9; 8:9).

The one who made the heavens and earth is said to be making Jerusalem a cup of staggering to all the surrounding peoples (cf. Isa 51:17;
Jer 25:17, 28); that is, to those who have laid siege to Jerusalem (Zech
12:2b).[9] The phrase וגם על־יהודה יהיה במצור על־ירושלם (lit. "and also
against Judah it will be in the siege against Jerusalem") has caused some
difficulty. Some scholars interpret this as Judah opposing Jerusalem,
either by choice or by enemy compulsion, and interpret Zech 14:14 similarly.[10] Others believe that the reference to Judah is simply specifying a
little more broadly whom the siege is against, or that Judah is caught up
in the siege against Jerusalem, but not opposing Jerusalem.[11] They argue
that it is quite clear in the subsequent verses that Judah is fighting for
Jerusalem, and so it would be inappropriate to interpret 12:2 otherwise.
Others seek to maintain the ambiguity.[12]

While it is difficult to be conclusive, it seems best to understand Judah
being initially caught up in the siege against Jerusalem and opposing it.[13]
This makes sense of 12:4 where Yahweh discriminates in favour of
Judah as he strikes those who come against Jerusalem. It also explains
what seems to be a change of heart on the part of the clans of Judah
(12:5) when they see Yahweh protecting Jerusalem, and results in them
turning against the surrounding peoples. Other factors that favour this
interpretation include: (1) the difficulty of envisioning a siege against the
region of Judah since it is normally cities that are sieged; (2) the fact that
14:14 also portrays Judah fighting against Jerusalem.[14]

The phrase "on that day" recurs throughout this section and while it
does not appear to be a structural marker, it does serve to accelerate
the cycle of events, and to heighten the importance of this future day of
battle. On this day, when all the nations of the earth gather against

---

9.   Some scholars have argued that 12:2b is a secondary addition; for instance,
Redditt, *Zechariah*, 129–30, argues that "v. 2b might have been added by a scribe.
Only v. 2b mentioned a siege, while v. 4a spoke of horses and riders, clearly not
needed in a siege. Indeed, nowhere else did 12:1–9 mention a siege." However, it
must be said that the fact of a siege does make sense of the descriptions of "surrounding peoples" (12:2, 6), the nations of the earth who "gather against" Jerusalem
(12:3), and who "come against" her (12:9).

10.   So, Baldwin, *Zechariah*, 189; Clark and Hatton, *Handbook*, 310–11.

11.   Tidiman, *Zacharie*, 258; McComiskey, "Zechariah," 3:1209.

12.   Petersen, *Zechariah 9–14*, 105, 108, 112, proposes an intentionally ambiguous translation: "The siege against Jerusalem will also involve Judah." Also Jones,
Commentary, 158.

13.   This takes the subject of יהיה as referring to the cup of reeling, with Judah
also (וגם) being affected.

14.   See the convincing treatment by Clark and Hatton, *Handbook*, 361.

Jerusalem (12:3), Yahweh will ensure the city's victory. Jerusalem has already been pictured as a "cup of staggering." To this is added further repulsive measures: as one attempts to move a heavy stone and is injured in the process, so will those who come against Jerusalem be severely injured (12:3). The image suggests that Jerusalem will be breached (cf. 14:2), with those attempting to carry off the loot injuring themselves in the process.[15] In addition, the horses that come against Jerusalem will be struck with confusion and blindness, and their riders with madness (12:4). However, for the sake of the house of Judah, Yahweh promises to keep his eyes open, presumably so that they will not be harmed as he acts for Jerusalem.

These clans of Judah,[16] situated outside of Jerusalem, recognize the hand of Yahweh in the ensuing disarray (12:4) and say in their hearts, "The inhabitants of Jerusalem are strength to me, on account of Yahweh

---

15. Cf. Merrill, *Zechariah*, 313.

16. There is some uncertainty as to whether the phrase אַלְפֵי יְהוּדָה (vv. 5–6) should be translated "chiefs" or "rulers" or "leaders of Judah" (so NIV), or whether אַלְּפֵי should be pointed differently (the *BHS* critical apparatus indicates that it should probably be read as אֻלְּפֵי, "clans of Judah," so ESV). There are several arguments advanced for translating it as "leaders." First, this seems to be how it is understood in other contexts (namely, Gen 36:15; Exod 15:15; and 1 Chr 1:51) where it refers to the tribal chiefs of Edom (so Baron, *Zechariah*, 296–97, 432; cf. BDB, 49). Second, the Greek and Latin versions have translated it as "leaders of a thousand" (Meyers and Meyers, *Zechariah 9–14*, 116, 322). A further argument has been put forward from the wider context that these are the leaders "from Judah" promised in Zech 10:4 (so Conrad, *Zechariah*, 181; Webb, *Zechariah*, 158). (There is an obvious parallel between the situation in ch. 12 and that in 10:5, where the leaders trample their foe and shame the riders on horses.) However, there are problems with translating it as "leaders of Judah." While 9:7 is also difficult, the context favours "clan" (note how the NIV is forced to translate the singular form into a plural in 9:7; cf. Petersen, *Zechariah 9–14*, 108, who translates the term as "leader," and states, "Zechariah 9:7 provides no clear guide to the reading here [in ch. 12]," while giving no grounds for this bold conclusion). It seems unusual for the same word to have a significantly different meaning in ch. 12 when it comes in such close proximity. The argument that the expression אַלְפֵי יהודה is referring to the leaders of Judah found in 10:4 also fails. In that context the present study determined that the leaders were more likely not "from Judah" but "from Yahweh" (see Chapter 6, section 2 d. It is clear that the emendation suggested by *BHS* elsewhere refers to the clans into which the tribes were subdivided (cf. Judg 6:15; 1 Sam 10:19; 23:23; Isa 60:22). This meaning makes best sense of the immediate context of ch. 12 where the people of Judah are numbered for battle. It is referring to the same group described as the "house of Judah" in 12:4, but now with military overtones (cf. Num 31:4–6; 1 Sam 29:2). Either אֻלְּפֵי also has this meaning of "clan," or we follow the emendation suggested by the *BHS* and argue that has been wrongly pointed.

of hosts, their God." The initiative of Yahweh in the battle continues with the clans of Judah becoming his agents in the destruction of all the surrounding people, in spectacular fashion, with Jerusalem again being given its rightful place (12:6). The reference to Jerusalem, which "will dwell again in its place, in Jerusalem" implies that the inhabitants were cut off from the city in this battle. This is rather cryptic at this point, especially given the victory that Yahweh has just assured his people. However, as we shall see in chs. 13–14, this victory will not come without a heavy toll on the inhabitants of Jerusalem, and this expression gives a glimpse of that (cf. 14:2, 11).

This military victory is spoken of in terms of "salvation" given to Yahweh's people. There is a clear parallel here with the situation that we have seen in 9:9, 16, and 10:6, 8, where in each case the salvation which Yahweh gives flows directly from the military victory he is said to give his people. Even in these verses there is not a strict chronology, but different perspectives on the activities and outcomes of that day: 12:7 speaks of the salvation that will be granted first to Judah; 12:8 speaks of the protection that will be given the inhabitants of Jerusalem (cf. 12:3, 5); and 12:9 is a summary of all that precedes in 12:2–8, forming an *inclusio* with 12:2–3 with the reference to the nations.

With this victory there is a concern that the tents of Judah should not miss out on the glory that the house of David and the inhabitants of Jerusalem will experience (Zech 12:7). Ollenburger suggests that the "tents of Judah" refers not to an inferior dwelling, but to the homes to which soldiers return after battle (e.g. 2 Sam 20:22).[17] This makes sense in the context here. This day of salvation will be a glorious one for the house of David and the inhabitants of Jerusalem, and, in order that the tents of Judah are not neglected in what will be a great day for Jerusalem, they are given salvation first. Not only will all the people of Yahweh be caught up in the glory of this salvation, but all shall be of equal standing before Yahweh.[18]

Another perspective is provided on this day in Zech 12:8, where Yahweh promises to defend the inhabitants of Jerusalem, with the result that "the one who stumbles on that day will be like David." This most naturally alludes to the might of David, which on many occasions saved Israel by defeating its enemies, not least the mighty Goliath by which he began his career with renown (cf. 1 Sam 17). Yet we also note that David's deliverance was given to him by Yahweh (cf. 1 Sam 17:33–37),

---

17. Ollenburger, "Zechariah," 827.
18. Cf. Unger, *Zechariah*, 212; Merrill, *Zechariah*, 316.

and the weak of the inhabitants of Jerusalem shall also be saved like David, through Yahweh's protection (cf. the "salvation" of the king in Zech 9:9).

Even greater is the promise that "the house of David shall be like God, like the angel of Yahweh going before them." In what sense is this statement to be understood? Petersen, who understands it ontologically, reads it against the background of Ps 2:7 and 2 Sam 14:17, arguing that elsewhere in the Hebrew Bible the king could be addressed in language befitting a deity, and so here it is saying that the house of David will have a divine status.[19] It has already been noted that in Zech 9:9 there is an ambiguity in the relationship between Yahweh and the king, and we shall encounter this again shortly (12:10). However, at this point it seems best to understand the term primarily in functional terms, particularly given the complementary description "like an angel of Yahweh." While some suggest that this is an insertion by a later scribe who sought to protect the sanctity of Yahweh in this text,[20] there is much in the background of this description that makes sense in this context. First, it was the angel of Yahweh who was responsible for leading his people on many occasions and providing protection, particularly in the Exodus (e.g. Exod 13:21; 14:19; 33:2). Second, David himself was likened to the "angel of God," which enabled him to judge for his people between what was good and evil (e.g. 2 Sam 14:17, 20; 19:27 cf. 1 Sam 29:9). Therefore, the addition of "like an angel of Yahweh" more closely defines the way in which the house of David shall be like Yahweh. Namely, the house of David shall once again lead and protect Yahweh's people like Yahweh himself.[21] This verse holds out high hope for the house of David.

With this victory for Yahweh's people, there is a special focus on David and the house of David (the "house of David" being mentioned five times here). As in other passages, there is again a lack of consensus among scholars about the significance of this reference for the role of the house of David and any hope for a future king.[22] So, for instance,

---

19. Petersen, *Zechariah 9–14*, 119. Cf. Meyers and Meyers, *Zechariah 9–14*, 333, who argue that "this seemingly extravagant comparison of the Davidides to the deity has precedent in Scripture."

20. E.g. Sweeney, *Twelve*, 687.

21. So, Webb, *Zechariah*, 159; McComiskey, "Zechariah," 3:1212. A similar idea is expressed in Exod 4:16 where Moses is said to "be as God to him [Aaron]." Moses will function as God to Aaron by giving Aaron the words to say, just as God gave Moses his words. It is a comparison of function.

22. For instance, Hanson, *Apocalyptic*, 365, considers Zech 12:8 "rather garbled." Mason, "Messiah," 356, says that it is "extremely difficult to know what is meant by v. 8."

Sweeney sees a diminishment of the role of the house of David.[23] Mason argues that the "emphasis in these chapters seems to swing more and more to direct, divine leadership, with the human figure fading more and more into the background."[24] Leske believes that there is here again a democratizing of kingship, and that the status of the house of David is not elevated, but brought down to a very human level.[25] Floyd puts forward the view that Jerusalem is now given the role once played by the Davidic king, and that all the inhabitants of Jerusalem will now take the place of David.[26] Petersen argues "it is inappropriate to think that the 'house of David' signifies members of the Davidic lineage or aspirations for a renaissance of kingship associated with them."[27]

Pomykala suggests that the usage of the term "house of David" outside Zechariah may not be helpful in determining its meaning here.[28] His reasoning is that the term here "dates from a time during the post-exilic period when the davidic family did not provide kings for Judah."[29] Drawing on the social analysis of J. P. Weinberg, who identified the "house of the fathers" as being the primary social and economic unit of the post-exilic period, Pomykala concludes that the reference to the house of David "must be interpreted as designating a relatively large social unit consisting of several hundred or even a few thousand members, something like a clan."[30] Pomykala proceeds to argue that the status and function of the house of David "cannot be directly inferred from pre-exilic social arrangements."[31] He believes that if the house of David exercised any form of power in Jerusalem, it was because of its economic status more than its Davidic genealogical connections and concludes:

23. Sweeney, *Twelve*, 685.
24. Mason, "Relation," 237.
25. Leske, "Context," 676.
26. Floyd, *Minor Prophets*, 521–23.
27. Petersen, *Zechariah 9–14*, 118.
28. Pomykala, *Dynasty*, 117–18, notes that the phrase "house of David" occurs 19 times in the Hebrew Bible and determines that: "Apart from references to a building, the phrase refers to the rule, the king or court, or the dynasty of the davidic family."
29. Ibid., 118.
30. Ibid., 119. Cf. J. P. Weinberg, *The Citizen-Temple Community* (trans. D. L. Smith-Christopher; JSOTSup 151; Sheffield: Sheffield Academic Press, 1992). Supporting this is the fact that in Zech 12:8, the house of David is described as a משפחות.
31. Pomykala, *Dynasty*, 120.

the house of David is included not because it represents the royal line, but because it is one of the powerful clans in Jerusalem at the time of this prophecy... Nowhere in the text of Zech 12:2–13:1 is there reference to the terminology and imagery associated with the davidic dynasty tradition. Continuity with or appropriation of a royal ideology is absent; only genealogically [*sic*] continuity with the once royal family is indicated.[32]

One of the planks in Pomykala's argument is that the reference in Zech 12:8 to the glorification of all Jerusalem gives no suggestion of divine, royal, or future kingly status. He contends that there is nothing asserted about an individual here and that any attempt to identify the one who was pierced as the future Davidic king is out of place: "there is no hint that the person himself was from the house of David or was a messianic figure for that matter."[33]

One major stumbling block for this interpretation is that if there is no hope being expressed for a future king, as Pomykala contends, then why is there such a focus here on the house of David and David himself? Why is David referred to in such positive terms? Surely at such a high point in this prophecy of salvation it would be inappropriate even to refer to David and his house if the hopes associated with him had diminished or if the associations were merely social or economic. Further, while the "house of David" may indeed have comprised a large social unit, as Pomykala suggests, if, as we have seen in Zech 1–10, there was a clear hope for a future Davidic king held at the time, then Pomykala is surely wrong to deny that there would have been an interest in the royal line and to hold that there was no royal ideology associated with the "house of David." Pomykala's conclusions rest on the assumption that there was no hope for a future Davidic king, but we have seen that this is unfounded.

Again we see how presuppositions play a major role in the interpretation of these chapters (something we shall see even more clearly in the next section regarding 12:10). If chs. 9–14 are seen as isolated prophecies, brought together by an editor at a later date with no concern for the unity of the final work, then it is easy to see how there is such a lack of consensus among scholars over the role of the house of David and any hope for a future king.[34] If, however, our reading of ch. 12 is influenced

---

32. Ibid., 123.

33. Ibid., 122 n. 231.

34. Note for instance this quote from Crotty, "Suffering," 54: "The prophecy of Deutero-Zechariah is made up of a variety of prophetic utterances from several hands deriving from different times... The block of material in Zechariah ix–xiv differs noticeably from that in i–viii. Whereas Zechariah i–viii centres its interests on the rebuilding of the Temple and the messianic hope that emanates from Jerusalem

by all that we have already seen in the book of Zechariah, and Zech 12 is read against this background rather than isolating it from its wider context, then a very different picture emerges.[35] There are many points of contact in the details of Zech 12 with what has gone before, and what comes after, summarized in the following table:

	Zech 9	Zech 10	Zech 12	Zech 14
Battle against the nations	9:4–7, 13	10:5	12:2–9	14:1–2, 12
Yahweh fights for his people	9:4–7	10:11–12	12:3, 4, 6, 9	14:3–5, 12
Yahweh protects Jerusalem	9:8, 14		12:3, 8	14:11
Future king	9:9–10	10:2, 4	12:10	14:9, 16, 17
Yahweh saves his people	9:9, 16	10:6	12:7	14:5, 10–11
Exiles will return/ be gathered	9:11–12	10:8–11	12:6	14:11, 16–22

These recurring themes strongly suggest that what we are dealing with here is not a collection of disparate prophecies, nor a chronology of separate events, but the same event viewed from different perspectives. In each cycle there is a focus on a different aspect of this final-day battle that will usher in Yahweh's kingdom, but all the time building on and developing what has gone before, rather than negating or modifying it. The oracles of Zech 9 and 12 give the "big picture" of what will happen on that day, each from a different perspective, with chs. 10–11 focusing in on what this day means for the leadership of Yahweh's people, and chs. 13–14 on the cleansing that will come on that day.

Therefore, what is envisaged in Zech 12:1–9 is not a further battle to that of chs. 9–11, but another perspective on the ultimate battle that will bring salvation and abundance to Jerusalem and the world. The fact that there is no explicit mention of a king here does not mean that there is no king on view, nor that earlier hopes had faded. The hope for a coming king has already been firmly established in chs. 1–6, and clearly reiterated in ch. 9; a passage that provides the framework for all that follows. Furthermore, chs. 10–11 has continued to raise the hope of a king to come, and 13:7 will again mention him.

---

and the House of David, Zechariah ix–xiv presupposes the rebuilt Temple and its messianism bypasses the Davidic House."

35. This criticism does not apply to Pomykala and those noted in Chapter 2 who are consistent in denying any evidence for a future Davidic king throughout the whole book of Zechariah.

The fact that the king has already been established as instrumental in this day of salvation makes sense of "glory of the house of David" on that day (12:7). The inhabitants of Jerusalem, who had previously been exhorted to "rejoice greatly" and "shout aloud" with the coming of their king bearing salvation (9:9), now are pictured as glorying in this same salvation as the house of David finally fulfils the role to which it was destined. It is difficult to explain the descriptions of the house of David in these verses if the earlier prophetic hope associated with it had become an embarrassment or had been forgotten.[36]

Furthermore, many scholars acknowledge the prominence of Jerusalem in this chapter, something that is consistent with chs. 1–8. For instance, Mason says: "It does not seem to be too much to say that, not only do the two sections of the book give a similar prominence to the Zion tradition, but that proto-Zechariah has not been without its influence on the way in which this is formulated in deutero-Zechariah."[37] Given the dependence of the Zion tradition on the hope for the house of David, and vice versa, it would be unusual for the Zion tradition to continue so emphatically through the book of Zechariah with the Davidic tradition sidelined. What we see is the continued interplay between them. On this day of Jerusalem's salvation, the house of David will be like God.

This all raises the obvious question, which must be faced: Why is the king not explicitly mentioned here? Zechariah 9:9 has created the expectation that the king will be saved and bring salvation to Jerusalem and rule the whole earth. Where is this king? Why is he not mentioned in Jerusalem's salvation?

Before turning to answer this, there is still the question of whether this is a democratization of the promises regarding the house of David, as Petersen and others suggest, so that the promises for a Davidic king are transferred to the people as a whole. We have already seen that the arguments presenting a democratization of the promises to David in Zech 9 are wanting. Further, Mason has argued with respect to ch. 12 that the way in which the "house of David" is distinguished from the "inhabitants of Jerusalem" speaks against a "total democratization" of the Davidic concept here.[38] The fact that there is still a place for the "house of David" is an argument against a democratizing tendency, as the logical outcome

---

36. McComiskey, "Zechariah," 3:1211, is right to conclude: "The reference to the house of David envisions Israel's future leadership in terms of a restoration of the Davidic monarchy."

37. Mason, "Relation," 231.

38. Mason, "Earlier," 157. This distinction is clearest in Zech 12:8.

of this would surely be the disappearance of the Davidic line.[39] However, the way that the house of David is spoken of here in such elevated terms underscores the hope that was associated with the promise to David that his throne will be established forever.

7.2.3. *Mourning for the Pierced One and a Fountain of Cleansing (Zechariah 12:10–13:1)*

> [12:10] And I will pour out upon the house of David and upon the inhabitants of Jerusalem a spirit of grace and supplications, and they will look to me whom they pierced, and they will wail over him, as a wailing over the only child and grieve[40] over him as grieving over the firstborn.
> [11] On that day the wailing in Jerusalem will become great, as the wailing of Hadad-Rimmon in the plain of Megiddo. [12] And the land will mourn, each family by itself: the family of the house of David by itself, and their wives by themselves, and the family of the house of Nathan by itself, and their wives by themselves, [13] the family of the house of Levi by itself, and their wives by themselves; the family of the Shimeites by itself, and their wives by themselves. [14] Each family that remains, family by family, by itself, and their wives by themselves.
> [13:1] On that day there will be a fountain opened for the house of David and the inhabitants of Jerusalem for sin and uncleanness. (author's translation)

Since the house of David and the inhabitants of Jerusalem are still on view (cf. 12:7), and because the reference to someone being "pierced" suggests the aftermath of a battle, this section should be read in close connection with 12:1–9.[41] Now victory gives way to bitter mourning as the house of David and the inhabitants of Jerusalem look upon the one they have pierced, presumably in the battle itself. They will look and mourn as the result of Yahweh having poured out "a spirit of grace and supplications." The reference to "a spirit" could simply refer to a disposition that Yahweh gives his people.[42] Yet given the background of Isaiah, Ezekiel, and Joel, who all associated the sending of Yahweh's Spirit on the day that Yahweh's kingdom would come (e.g. Isa 32:15; Ezek 39:29; Joel 2:28–32), it seems more likely that this is what is being

---

39. Ibid., 155.

40. Meyers and Meyers, *Zechariah 9–14*, 342, note that וְהָמֵר looks like a singular, but is perfectly acceptable as an infinitive absolute which can have a plural subject.

41. Petersen, *Zechariah 9–14*, 121: "I suggest, tentatively, that this verse be read within the context of the attack on Jerusalem."

42. Note McComiskey, "Zechariah," 3:1214: "The word *rûaḥ* is not marked by references to God as it is in 4:6, 6:8, and 7:12, so we must be cautious about identifying it in this context with God's Spirit."

referred to here, and grace and supplication are the effects of the Spirit's work upon the people of Yahweh.[43] Mason takes this line and helpfully suggests a parallel with Zech 1–8. He recalls that in Zech 4, the completion of the temple by Zerubbabel was a mark of Yahweh's power at work by his Spirit (4:6), and resulted in cries of "grace" (4:7). The completion of the temple was also the means of the continuation of the right cultic relationship between Yahweh and his people. He proposes: "It is possible that in the reference to the gift of חן by virtue of the outpouring of the Spirit here, ideas of Proto-Zechariah are being taken up and re-applied to suggest the restoration of right relationships with Yahweh for the renewed community as a result of the activity of the Spirit of Yahweh."[44]

Whether given directly, or through the agency of Yahweh's Spirit, there is nevertheless a change in disposition by which the people now look upon the one they have pierced and wail for him as one wails for an only child, and grieve as one grieves the death of a firstborn—expressions that convey the depth of anguish and sorrow on this occasion (cf. Jer 6:26; Amos 8:10). While it is not explicit, it is clear that those who have pierced this figure have offended Yahweh, and that they are deserving of his judgment. Yet Yahweh in his grace has moved them to grieve their sin and pray for mercy.[45]

7.2.4. *Scholarly Proposals Concerning the Identity of the Pierced One*

While some would disagree, the key question here is the identity of the one who has been pierced.[46] C. and E. Meyers comment that issues concerning this one who has been pierced provide "surely one of the major interpretative cruxes in Second Zechariah, if not all of prophecy."[47] On the other hand, Sweeney perhaps best captures the concern of most critical scholars:

---

43. Meyer, "Messianic Metaphors," 80–82; Heater, *Zechariah*, 104; Mason, "Earlier," 159–60; Webb, *Zechariah*, 161.

44. Mason, "Earlier," 159.

45. There may also be a contrast here with Zech 11:10 where the staff called חן is broken. The pouring out of a Spirit of חן now reverses the judgment of the exilic experience.

46. For instance, Petersen, *Zechariah 9–14*, 121, supports Plöger, *Theocracy*, 84–85, in "eschewing attempts to identify this individual." Similarly, see Pomykala, *Dynasty*, 122, and Rogerson, "Zechariah," 727.

47. Meyers and Meyers, *Zechariah 9–14*, 337. Cf. Mason, "Earlier," 160, who considers it "a notable *crux interpretum* in Zechariah studies."

Nevertheless, the reader should recognize that interpreters' conceptions of "the one whom they have pierced" may well be overly influenced by theological models that seek to associate the reference with the suffering servant of Isaiah, Josiah, and Zerubbabel in order to provide some analogy with the crucifixion of Jesus or a more general concern with vicarious suffering.[48]

While it is true that the New Testament identifies Jesus as this pierced one,[49] it is also important not to prejudice the interpretation of this passage with the presupposition that Zech 12:10 cannot refer to the future king because this might read later ideas back into the text.[50] As well as the Christian affirmation that the pierced one is Jesus, it is surely significant that a number of Jewish rabbis also interpret this verse in terms of a pierced Messiah—Messiah ben Joseph/Ephraim, who was killed rather than the triumphant Messiah ben David.[51] This indicates that there is an

48.   Sweeney, *Twelve*, 689. Note Petersen, *Zechariah 9–14*, 120: "The latter lines of v. 10, though written in the past tense, have been construed by Christian commentators to reflect the death of Jesus of Nazareth." Also Pomykala, *Dynasty*, 122: "Attempts to see a davidic messiah in the one who was pierced (cf. Lamarche, *Zacharie IX–XIV*, 120–22) are particularly out of place."

49.   Black, "Messiah," 221, summarizes: "There was an early Christian tradition equating Jesus with the pierced one of Zech 12:10. It is found independently in Mark (and expanded in Matthew) and in John."

50.   There is no reason in principle why New Testament authors should not be accurate interpreters of the Old Testament.

51.   Note the Codex Reuchlinianus marginal reading of the Targum: "And they shall look to me and shall inquire of me why the nations pierced the Messiah son of Ephraim." Gordon, *Targum*, 218. See also the helpful discussion on this text and the attempts to account for the introduction of the figure of the Messiah ben Ephraim in Jewish messianism by Gordon, "The Ephraimite Messiah and the Targum(s) to Zechariah 12:10," 184–95. In addition, in the Babylonian Talmud (first century C.E.), *Sukkah* 52a refers to a debate that involved R. Dosa over whether it refers to the slaying of the Messiah son of Joseph. Rashi in his commentary to *Sukkah* 52a says: "The words, 'The land shall mourn', are found in the prophecy of Zechariah, and he prophesies of the future, that they shall mourn on account of Messiah, the son of Joseph, who shall be slain in the war of Gog and Magog." Cited in D. Kimchi, *Rabbi David Kimchi's Commentary upon the Prophecies of Zechariah* (trans. A. M'Caul; London: J. Duncan, 1837), 161. Ibn Ezra: "All the heathen shall look to me to see what I shall do to those who pierced the Messiah, the son of Joseph." Cited in Kimchi, *Commentary*, 158. Abrabanel says: "It is more correct to interpret this passage of Messiah, the son of Joseph, as our rabbis of blessed memory have interpreted in the treatise Succah." Cited in Kimchi, *Commentary*, 159. Moses Alshekh: "I will do yet a third thing, and that is, that 'they shall look unto me', for they shall lift up their eyes unto me in perfect repentance, when they see him whom they pierced, that is Messiah, the son of Joseph; for our rabbis, of blessed memory, have

interpretative tradition outside the New Testament that interprets the pierced one as a future king.

The questions that I am seeking to answer in this chapter are: How would the book of Zechariah have us identify this figure? How is this related to the hope held out for the house of David and what does it reveal about the nature of this hope? There has been a vast array of suggestions as to the identity of the pierced one, and, as Sweeney has highlighted, the presuppositions that are brought to the text often shape the way that the passage is interpreted. I shall begin by surveying these approaches, and the suggestions for the identity of the pierced one that are made.

The first approach is to seek an historical reference behind this figure. The identity of the pierced one is then tied up with the provenance of this section of Zechariah. Mitchell surveys past or contemporary figures that could stand behind this reference to a pierced one. While he does not ultimately adopt any, he considers Zechariah the son of Jehoida (2 Chr 24:20), Uriah (Jer 26:20), Gedaliah (Jer 41:1), the prophet Jeremiah, and Zerubbabel.[52] Conrad also suggests Zerubbabel.[53] Oesterley suggests other historical figures: Onias III, who was assassinated in 170 B.C.E.; or Simon the Maccabee, who was assassinated in 134 B.C.E.[54] While not naming any individual, Andiñach argues that this reference "is without doubt to a contemporary person, probably some leader who had intended a reform in the style of the one initiated by Josiah."[55]

With his sociological approach to the text, Hanson argues that the "house of David" refers to the hierocratic party and the "tents of Judah" to the visionary group, both locked in a struggle for the control of the cult in this post-exilic period.[56] He understands the pierced one as a reference to the visionaries, who, having been defeated and removed

---

said, that he will take upon himself all the guilt of Israel, and shall then be slain in the war to make atonement, in such a manner, that it shall be accounted as if Israel had pierced him, for on account of their sin he has died; and therefore, in order that it may be reckoned to them as a perfect atonement, they will repent, and look to the blessed One, saying that there is none beside Him to forgive those that mourn on account of him who died for their sin: this is the meaning of 'they shall look upon me'." Cited in Kimchi, *Commentary*, 163.

52. Mitchell, "Zechariah," 330, argues, on the basis that the piercing is referred to as a past event, that "the one pierced is not the Messiah, whose advent, all will agree, was still future when these words were written."

53. Conrad, *Zechariah*, 183.

54. Quoted in Baldwin, *Zechariah*, 191. Baldwin states, "no known historical individual quite satisfies, even if it were feasible to date the passage so late."

55. Andiñach, "Zechariah," 1197.

56. Hanson, *Apocalyptic*, 364. Leske, "Context," 676, agrees with Hanson.

from their positions of honour in the cult, will be vindicated in the end-time through an act of Yahweh that makes the hierocrats aware of their sin.[57] Further, Hanson argues that this same visionary group felt an identification with the suffering servant of Isa 40–55, and hence there is a parallel between these two figures.[58]

While not to the same degree, others have also sought to explain this text sociologically. Mason tentatively suggests that the pierced one is a prophet (or prophetic circle) who has been denounced and excluded by the official priesthood in Jerusalem.[59] He believes that what is being spoken of here is a time in the future when Yahweh will graciously pour out his Spirit on the Jerusalem leadership so that "they will suddenly realize that those whom they have all along opposed ('pierced' meta-phorically, or literally 'persecuted') were his true spokesmen keeping alight the flame of genuine faith."[60]

Similarly, C. and E. Meyers put forward the view that the pierced one refers to "the true prophets of Yahweh."[61] While rejecting the view of Hanson that this passage reflects factional tension among leadership groups in post-exilic Yehud, they still argue that the pierced one is a reference to the prophets who were habitually in conflict with nearly all the establishment figures. They support this by contending that the tension between true and false prophecy is a leading issue in much of Zech 9–14 as well as in other prophetic works; in addition, they amass several lines of evidence.[62] First, they note how the prophets suffered physical danger, if not death, for challenging those in power (e.g. Jeremiah in Jer 26:7–8, 11; and Uriah who was killed with a sword in Jer 26:20–23). Second, they suggest on the basis of the prophetic stabbing in Zech 13:3 that the use of the word "stab" may have come to denote all violent acts against prophetic figures, whether mortal or not. Third, they note how the prophet of Zech 9–14 is keenly aware of the historical struggle between prophecy and the ruling establishment (e.g. 10:10; 11:7, 10, 14). The picture of the future age here is of this struggle coming to an end. Fourth, Zech 1–8, particularly 1:4–6, speaks of the refusal of the Judaeans to listen to the prophetic message, and they argue that the prophet of chs. 9–14 "follows his immediate predecessor in this consciousness of

57. Hanson, *Apocalyptic*, 365.
58. Note the critique of Hanson by Coggins, *Zechariah*, 52–59.
59. Mason, "Earlier," 164. Note this suggestion of a prophet also by Crotty, "Suffering," 55.
60. Mason, "Earlier," 164.
61. Meyers and Meyers, *Zechariah 9–14*, 339, and "Fortunes," 218.
62. Meyers and Meyers, *Zechariah 9–14*, 339.

the failure of preexilic society with respect to the prophetic message."[63] They later state, starkly, that "there is not a shred of hard evidence to lend credence to the idea that a Davidide was slain."[64] Similarly, Tigchelaar argues that "exegeses which regard this individual as a leading, perhaps royal, or even messianic figure, are built on shaky grounds."[65] He suggests the singular pronominal suffix be understood as a collective that refers either to those who attacked Jerusalem, referred to in the earlier part of the chapter, or Jerusalem's leaders who shed blood, referred to in Ezek 22.

Meyer argues that this reference to a pierced one is to be understood against the mythology and cultus associated with kingship in the ancient Near East.[66] He proposes that in Israel there was a cultic drama in which the king underwent a ritual of suffering and triumph. In this ritual, the king was pierced to bring about expiation of sin for the community. Meyer believes that 12:10 is therefore a citation or allusion to the liturgy surrounding this ritual. Similarly, Horst believes that the reference may be to a myth that is otherwise unknown to us, one which contains the death of an innocent pierced one, sacrificed for the deliverance from enemies.[67]

Other scholars have sought to explain this passage against the background of other prophetic works without necessarily constructing a social or political milieu. Van Groningren argues that Zechariah does not directly identify the pierced one with the future Davidic king.[68] He says that it is only from previous prophecies that one must conclude this.[69] Delcor believes Zech 12:10 is to be understood against the background of Ezek 36:16–28 which demonstrates that Yahweh has been figuratively pierced by his people.[70] In Ezekiel, Yahweh says that by the action of his people, they have "profaned" (חללוהו) his name among the nations (e.g. Ezek 36:21). His argument is that the root חלל can be understood as "to pierce," and that the author of Zechariah, drawing on this background, has used the word דקר in a metaphorical way to say that Yahweh has been wounded by the sins of his people (cf. Lam 4:9; Prov 12:18).[71]

---

63. Ibid., 340.
64. Ibid., 355.
65. Tigchelaar, *Prophets*, 126.
66. Meyer, "Messianic Metaphors," 79–93.
67. Horst, *Die zwölf*, 256.
68. Van Groningren, *Messianic*, 907.
69. Unfortunately, van Groningen does not explain how this works.
70. Delcor, "Un Problème," 189–99.
71. Delcor also cites Zech 10:5–6, 7–8; 12:6–9 as examples of instances where there is an abrupt transition between the first and third persons, and argues that it is

Many scholars see a connection between the pierced one and the servant of Isa 53, where the servant is understood either as corporate Israel,[72] or a future kingly figure.[73] For instance, Jones argues that the pierced one is a reference to those of Judah who died in the final conflict with the nations.[74] It is by the death of these ones that Jerusalem has been saved, and they represent the cost of salvation. Hence, he says, there is a close relationship with Isa 53, where the servant (righteous Israel) suffers vicariously for the people.[75] The connection between the pierced one and a future kingly figure shall be discussed in detail later in this chapter.

Another group of scholars has attempted to understand the identity of this pierced one in the context of Zech 9–14. Sweeney argues from the immediate context that it is a collective reference to those among the nations who had been destroyed by Yahweh for whom the house of David and the inhabitants of Jerusalem now mourn (cf. 12:9).[76] Watts argues: "The only ones in the context who might merit such concern and prayer would be the Judaean soldiers who had been killed by the attacking peoples in defense of Jerusalem."[77]

Laato presents three lines of evidence for identifying the pierced one with the first shepherd of Zech 11:4–14 and the shepherd of 13:7–9, whom he calls the "good shepherd."[78] First, the good shepherd is killed according to Yahweh's will in 13:7–9—in hindsight, 12:10 might also refer to the death of the shepherd. Second, in 11:4–14 the good shepherd and Yahweh are closely connected—this is also the case in 12:10, where Yahweh stands behind the fate of the pierced one. Third, as the shepherd in 11:4–14 meets with opposition, so it is assumed that the pierced one will be subjected to the assaults of the people and the house of David.

simply a stylistic feature that should not pose any problem. However, in the examples that Delcor cites, the transition happens between sentences, not in the same sentence, as in 12:10.

72. E.g. Lagrange, "Notes," 76; Mitchell, "Zechariah," 331; Dentan, "Zechariah," 6:1108.

73. E.g. Neil, "Zechariah," 4:946; Baldwin, *Zechariah*, 198; Larkin, *Eschatology*, 167–70; Duguid, "Messianic," 275; Mitchell, *Psalter*, 206–9; McComiskey, "Zechariah," 3:1223; Schellenberg, "Unity of Deutero-Zechariah," 115; Mackay, *Zechariah*, 248.

74. Jones, *Commentary*, 161–62.

75. The problem with understanding the one who is pierced corporately, whether or not this is seen with reference to the suffering servant of Isaiah, is as Baldwin, *Zechariah*, 192, points out, the difficulty in seeing any connection between the death of these martyrs, and the cleansing from sin that follows the mourning.

76. Sweeney, *Twelve*, 689.

77. Watts, "Zechariah," 357.

78. Laato, *Josiah*, 290–91, and *Star*, 217.

Laato argues that this gives enough reason to regard the pierced one as the shepherd who is depicted elsewhere in chs. 9–14.[79]

Merrill and Boda believe that the pierced one is Yahweh and that the people have pierced him in a figurative way by disregarding and abandoning him.[80] McComiskey also believes that the text speaks of Yahweh as the pierced one.[81] However, he argues that this description is not to be understood metaphorically; there is an actual figure who is pierced who is closely associated with Yahweh. Like Laato, he believes this figure is the shepherd of 11:4–14, otherwise he can make no sense of how the shepherd of ch. 11 is connected to the flow of the discourse. Similarly, while not holding it himself, Merrill outlines the view that the pierced one is Yahweh in the sense that someone who represented him was pierced.[82] This, he argues, allows the MT to stand as is—the eyes of those who wounded Yahweh are directed towards the one who directly received the mortal blow.

There is therefore a wide range of suggestions by scholars as to the identity of the pierced one. These suggestions not only depend on the approach that is taken to the text, but on conclusions that have been made earlier regarding the hope for the house of David and how the other texts of Zechariah that concern the future Davidic king relate to this passage.

7.2.5. *Exegetical Issues*

Before seeking to assess these various proposals, there are a number of exegetical issues in the passage to address. The first concerns the preposition with the first person pronominal suffix אלי in Zech 12:10. Since Yahweh is the speaker, the suffix identifies Yahweh as the one who is pierced. Because it seems incongruous to speak of Yahweh being pierced, many scholars doubt the integrity of the MT and emend it to fit with the third person reference concerning the one for whom they mourn,

---

79. Laato, *Josiah*, 291.
80. Merrill, *Zechariah*, 320; Boda, *Commentary*, 488.
81. McComiskey, "Zechariah," 3:1214.
82. Merrill, *Zechariah*, 320–21, says that this is the view held by the majority of scholars. However, it is by no means a clear majority! Merrill cites von Orelli, *The Twelve Minor Prophets*, 366–67; A. F. Kirkpatrick, *The Doctrine of the Prophets* (London: Macmillan, 1901), 473; Lamarche, *Zacharie IX–XIV*, 81–83; Chary, *Zacharie*, 202. Mason, "Earlier," 162, notes the objection by J. Knabenbauer, *Commentarius in prophetas minores* (Cursus scripturae sacrae; Commentarii in VT 3:5; Paris: Lethielleux, 1886), 373, that while Yahweh might be wounded in the mistreatment of his representative, he could hardly have been said to have been killed by his death. Similarly Baldwin, *Zechariah*, 191, comments: "But how can two distinct people die in the death of only one?"

mentioned in the next phrase (וספדו עליו). The resulting translations are represented by the NRSV: "When they look upon the one whom they have pierced, they shall mourn for him."[83] However, as several scholars point out, there is overwhelming support in the versions for the MT.[84]

C. and E. Meyers seek to resolve the difficulty of this verse by rendering את אשר as "concerning," which results in the translation, "they will look to me concerning the one they have stabbed."[85] This identifies the pierced one as a separate figure to Yahweh. However, it does strain the usual use of the direct object marker את, which naturally further identifies the one to whom they look.[86] Clearly the Hebrew text is difficult to interpret here.

Regarding the translation of דקרו, C. and E. Meyers establish that the root דקר means "to stab, pierce, wound" with a thrusting weapon (e.g. Lam 4:9; Isa 13:15; 1 Sam 31:4 = 1 Chr 10:4).[87] They point out that this does not necessarily mean that the one stabbed died (e.g. Jer 37:10; 51:4), but this would usually be expected. In the case of the pierced one here, it is almost certain that death ensued, given the subsequent reference to mourning and cleansing, and yet if it refers purely to the piercing of God, this seems inappropriate. Delcor cites two instances where the idea of being pierced by the sword is used in a metaphorical sense.[88] In Lam 4:9, חלל is used to refer to those in Jerusalem who were "pierced," or afflicted by hunger, and in Prov 12:18, the wounds inflicted by reckless words are likened to a "piercing" (root דקר) sword. It may have this metaphorical sense here.

The mourning that the piercing occasions is likened to the mourning of Hadad-Rimmon in the plain of Megiddo (Zech 12:11). Hadad was the Syrian storm god, otherwise called Baal, and Rimmon was also a deity (cf. 2 Kgs 5:18); accordingly, many scholars argue that this is therefore a reference to a pagan mourning ritual.[89] However, others consider that the

---

83. Cf. "They will look upon him whom they stabbed." Petersen, *Zechariah 9–14*, 106.

84. Meyers and Meyers, *Zechariah 9–14*, 337; Merrill, *Zechariah*, 320; McComiskey, "Zechariah," 3:1214; Mason, "Earlier," 162; Webb, *Zechariah*, 160, n. 74.

85. Meyers and Meyers, *Zechariah 9–14*, 307, 337.

86. Keil, "Zechariah," 387–88, notes that את אשר marks אשר more clearly as an accusative. The simple אשר might also be rendered "who pierced (me)."

87. Meyers and Meyers, *Zechariah 9–14*, 338. Cf. McComiskey, "Zechariah," 3:1214–15.

88. Delcor, "Un Problème," 193–95.

89. E.g. T. Jansma, "Inquiry into the Hebrew Text and the Ancient Versions of Zech 9–14," *Oudtestamentische Studiën* 7 (1950): 1–142 (118); Watts, "Zechariah," 358; Smith, *Micah–Malachi*, 278–79; Stuhlmueller, *Rebuilding*, 149–50.

reference here is geographical and that Hadad-Rimmon refers to a place in the plain of Megiddo.[90] One of the difficulties is that there is no place otherwise known as Hadad-Rimmon. However, Merrill notes greater problems with the view that it refers to a cult-mourning ritual:

> the major objection to this is the lack of any evidence for a Hadad-Rimmon shrine at Megiddo where such lamentation might have taken place at such an exaggerated level as to make it a point of comparison. Moreover, the fact that deep sorrow for sin in Judah should be compared to the lament of pagans over a catastrophe that had befallen one of their mystic deities seems most unlikely.[91]

Looking more closely at the text, Laato notes that the phrase כמספד הדד־רמון (Zech 12:11) differs from the similar phrase כמספד על־היחיד ("as one mourns for an only [child]") (12:10) and the lack of the preposition על indicates that 12:11 does not refer to weeping for Hadad-Rimmon, but weeping of/in Hadad-Rimmon.[92] Furthermore, he reasonably proposes that the preposition ב may simply have been dropped so as to avoid repetition with the phrase בבקעת מגדון.

Additional support for the view that Hadad-Rimmon is a place name is the fact that Rimmon is a place name in various passages and is associated with different regions.[93] Zechariah 14:10 refers to a Rimmon which is south of Jerusalem. It is likely that since there was more than one Rimmon, Hadad functions to further identify it. Furthermore, it seems that the passage is comparing the mourning *in* Jerusalem with the mourning *in* this other location in the plain of Megiddo.

Hence, the statement could be a way of saying that on this day the whole of the land will mourn, not only in Jerusalem, but in the outlying regions like Hadad-Rimmon. Just as the tents of Judah have been saved along with the inhabitants of Jerusalem (12:7), so the mourning in regions such as Hadad-Rimmon in the plain of Megiddo will be as great as in Jerusalem.

It is also possible that this location is intended to bring to mind the death of Josiah, as a number of scholars suggest.[94] 2 Kings 23:29 states that King Josiah was killed at Megiddo by Pharaoh Neco. The mourning

---

90. Luck, *Zechariah*, 109; Achtemeier, *Nahum–Malachi*, 162; Rosenberg, "The Slain Messiah in the Old Testament," 260; Merrill, *Zechariah*, 323–24; Ollenburger, "Zechariah," 7:828; McComiskey, "Zechariah," 3:1215; Mackay, *Zechariah*, 238.
91. See further, Merrill, *Zechariah*, 324.
92. Laato, *Josiah*, 289.
93. E.g. Josh 15:32; 19:7, 13; Judg 20:45, 47; 21:13; 1 Chr 4:32.
94. McComiskey, "Zechariah," 3:1215.

on this day is described in 2 Chr 35:24–25. Significantly, the Targum explicitly interprets the mourning in this way: "At that *time* the mourning in Jerusalem will be as great as the mourning for *Ahab son of Omri whom* Hadadrimmon *son of Tabrimmon killed, and as the mourning for Josiah son of Amon whom Pharoah the Lame killed* in the valley of Megiddon" (*Tg. Zech* 12:11).[95]

While the Targum's interpretation of Hadad-Rimmon as a person is unlikely, it does provide support for understanding the mourning at Hadad-Rimmon in the plain of Megiddo as a reference to the mourning at the death of Josiah. Laato goes further to argue that Zech 12:10 provides a description of the death of the future Davidic king patterned on the death of Josiah at Megiddo. Both were pierced and the people mourn both.[96]

The mourning in the land is described in some detail in Zech 12:12–14 with a pattern repeated for the house of David, the house of Nathan, the house of Levi, the Shimeites, and all who are left. Some scholars limit the reference to "the land" (הארץ) in 12:12 to the inhabitants of Jerusalem,[97] and others see a reference to entire earth.[98] In the rest of the book of Zechariah, this term is used to refer either to the whole earth,[99] or perhaps to the land of Judah,[100] but is never limited to Jerusalem.[101] Given that it is the "families" of Israel that are on view, the claim seems to be that not only will Jerusalem mourn (12:11), but the whole nation shall mourn. Ollenburger contends that the extent of the mourning in 12:12–14 also supports the suggestion that the victim is of royal status.[102]

Baldwin argues that the repetition of "the family by itself and the wives by themselves" stresses that the repentance is genuine: "None is merely being influenced by the tears of others, nor acting hypocritically, as the professional mourners did."[103] More likely is Merrill's contention that it shows that corporate repentance is not sufficient, but that each member of the community is individually culpable before God, with

---

95.   Gordon, *Targum*, 219.

96.   Laato, *Josiah*, 293.

97.   E.g. Redditt, *Zechariah*, 134.

98.   Petersen, *Zechariah 9–14*, 122–23.

99.   E.g. Zech 1:10–11; 4:14; 6:5; 12:1, 3; 14:9.

100. E.g. Zech 7:14; 11:6; 13:2, 8.

101. Note the reference to the "whole land" from Geba to Rimmon in Zech 14:10. This is not saying that this region comprised the whole land, but that the whole land between these points will become a plain, with Jerusalem aloft.

102. Ollenburger, "Zechariah," 7:828.

103. Baldwin, *Zechariah*, 194.

even wives responsible for their own sin, rather than being covered by their husbands (cf. Ezek 18:4).[104]

The names that are mentioned seem significant. The "house of David" has already been mentioned (Zech 12:7, 8, 10; cf. 13:1). However, the "house of Nathan" occurs nowhere else in the Hebrew Bible, and there are seven or eight individuals who go by the name Nathan.[105] While the most prominent Nathan is the prophet (2 Sam 12), C. and E. Meyers rightly note that prophets have no dynastic significance, in contrast to kings and priests. Another Nathan was a member of the "thirty" that comprised David's mighty men (2 Sam 23:36; 1 Chr 11:38), and given the references that we have seen to the leaders whom Yahweh will raise up in Zech 10:4, this may be a possibility. More likely, however, is C. and E. Meyers's third suggestion that it refers to the Nathan who was one of David's sons (2 Sam 5:14; 1 Chr 3:5; 14:4).

Merrill takes this suggestion further and, following Chary, argues that what we have here is evidence that, after the exile, royal descent was traced through Nathan, rather than through Solomon. There is evidence for this in the New Testament with Luke's genealogy of Jesus going through Nathan (Luke 3:31), and also with Zerubbabel, who was of royal blood, but not in the line of Solomon.[106] All this is further evidence that the "house of David" did have genealogical significance, if not associations with a royal ideology (contra Pomykala).[107]

The "house of Levi" seems to be an equivalent term to the "tribe of Levi," who served among all the tribes (e.g. Josh 18:7; Deut 18:1). While strictly speaking it was the descendants of Aaron who were priests, the other Levites were to keep charge of the tent of meeting and the sanctuary and assist the sons of Aaron in their service of the house of Yahweh (e.g. 1 Chr 23:28–32).[108] While Shimei refers to at least 15 individuals in the Hebrew Bible, including the brother of Zerubbabel (1 Chr 3:19), the "house of Shimei" occurs once in Num 3:21 to refer to the

---

104. Merrill, *Zechariah*, 325. Cf. Webb, *Zechariah*, 162: "In other words, there is no pointing the finger at others; each individual and group accepts its own responsibility for what has been done, and owns the sin."

105. Meyers and Meyers, *Zechariah 9–14*, 346.

106. Merrill, *Zechariah*, 325; cf. Chary, *Zacharie*, 205.

107. Note R. H. Kennett, "Zechariah 12–13:1," *JTS* 28 (1926–27): 1–9 (6), who, although he dates this passage at around 141 B.C., concludes, "it is at any rate clear that there were at this time descendants of David, recognized as such, with whom hopes for the restoration of the line of David would naturally be connected."

108. On the distinction between the priests and the Levites, see Alexander, *Paradise*, 238–39.

grandson of Levi through Gershom.[109] If this is whom the reference is to, then the family of the Shimeites represents a subsidiary Levitical lineage in the same way that the house of Nathan represents a subsidiary Davidic line. This gives a balanced arrangement among the mourning families, with David and Nathan representing royal and dynastic families, and Levi and Shimei representing priestly families.[110]

The significance of combining references to the mourning of the royal and priestly lines should not be lost. In doing so, it indicates that there was still a strong connection between the temple and the throne at this time. Just as the rebuilding of the temple under Zerubbabel in Zech 4 raised the hope for the re-establishment of the other house of David, namely, for the Shoot to take up David's throne, so here, the mourning of the Davidic line along with the priestly line raises the hope for its restoration with a coming king. Just as Jeremiah connected the covenant with David with the covenant made with the Levitical priests to provide hope for their future restoration (Jer 33:20–22), their connection here indicates a similar hope.[111]

The scene of the whole community mourning for the one whom has been pierced dramatically shifts in Zech 13:1 to one of hope, with a fountain opened for the cleansing of those who pierced him. The reference to water cleansing from sin and uncleanness finds a precedent in the Torah, where water was used to purify and consecrate the Levites, thereby setting them apart for Yahweh (Num 8:5–14). The image of the fountain suggests an abundant supply of water; all that is needed to cleanse from sin and uncleanness. Zechariah 13:1 refers specifically to the cleansing that comes to the house of David and the inhabitants of Jerusalem, to those who had pierced the king (cf. Zech 12:10). However, in 13:2, the rest of the community is also on view with cleansing flowing out to the rest of the land (i.e. the inhabitants of the land; cf. 12:12).

---

109. Meyers and Meyers, *Zechariah 9–14*, 348.

110. Ibid., 347.

111. In a passing comment, Larkin, "Zechariah," 614, notes that there was a Shimei involved in Absalom's rebellion against David. There are some tantalizing allusions here to the account in 2 Sam 12–19. It is a rebellion in which the prophet Nathan and the priests are also mentioned and David's son Absalom is eventually pierced. It is difficult to draw any direct lines from Zechariah back to these events, and the interpretation outlined above seems more likely. However, if it is the descendants of these individuals who mourn, then Zechariah may once again be drawing on the past events surrounding the life of David to offer hope for the future restoration of the Davidic house with a Davidic king.

7.2.6. *The Identity of the Pierced One*

Having surveyed the variety of approaches and suggestions for the identity of the pierced one, let us now turn to weigh them up in the light of the exegesis of the passage and the themes of the book of Zechariah as a whole. It has already been established that the events of Zech 9–14 are not to be read in a strictly chronological way, or in isolation from each other, or in isolation from the expectation created in chs. 1–8. Zechariah 9–14 offers different perspectives on the ultimate battle that will see the defeat of the nations, the salvation of Yahweh's people including a remnant from the nations, the final return from exile, and the re-establishment of Jerusalem as the throne of the king. If ch. 9 is understood as building on the perspective of chs. 1–8, and establishing the programme for this "day," then what has already been firmly established is that a future Davidic king is central to the salvation of this day (cf. 9:9–10). Given this, the absence of the king in 12:1–9 is all the more pointed. As the events are laid out and the battle advances, the expectation has been raised that the king will be instrumental in this campaign, and yet when the victory is won and salvation comes (12:7), the king seems conspicuous by his absence.

As has been observed, scholars often take the apparent lack of any explicit reference to the king in ch. 12 as evidence of the decline in the fortunes of the house of David, or the expectations associated with Zerubbabel not being fulfilled.[112] However, it has already been seen that David and his house are spoken of in very favourable terms in 12:7–9, and that this fact does not support these views. How, then, can the absence of the king be explained? Is he the one who has been pierced?

The interplay of the themes of the coming Shoot, king, and shepherd that have already been established in the book of Zechariah strongly suggests that the one who is pierced in Zech 12:10 is to be associated with the coming Davidic king. Zechariah 3 established that in the coming of the Shoot, the iniquity of the land would be removed in a single day (3:8–9). This same cleansing from sin is envisaged here in connection with the pierced one (13:1).[113] Zechariah 6 identified the coming Shoot as

---

112. Meyers and Meyers, *Zechariah 9–14*, 356, are forced to the somewhat contradictory notion that "this emphasis on the house of David...[arose] from a historical situation in which just the opposite condition—the deemphasis of Davidic potential—obtained."

113. Note Laato, *Josiah*, 292: "In 13:1 an idea already presented in Zech 3:8–10 is developed further. We noted...that Zech 3:8–10 should be interpreted as referring to the idea that YHWH will finally remove all sin and guilt from the people through the reestablishment of the Davidic dynasty. In 12:10–13:1 this same idea is visible even though in a more developed way." I would agree with this, except to say that

a priest who would rebuild the temple and thereby re-establish Yahweh's rule in Jerusalem (6:13). Here the salvation and restoration of Jerusalem along with the people's forgiveness are key parallel themes that connect with the pierced one. In 9:9 and ch. 10, the future Davidic king is central to the salvation of Jerusalem, Judah, and Ephraim. Similarly, the salvation of Judah and Jerusalem are connected with the pierced one in ch. 12. Perhaps the strongest line of identification comes from 13:7, where the shepherd, who was shown to be the coming Davidic king, is struck by the sword. This naturally connects with the pierced one of 12:10.[114] The death of the royal figure in 13:7 has tragic consequences for the flock, and this seems an appropriate cause for the intense mourning of 12:10–14, particularly if the description here is patterned on the death of the Davidic king Josiah. The great irony is that the death of the king comes at the hands of his own people. Yet this in itself is not surprising given the history of the people in rejecting Yahweh as their shepherd, as enacted in 11:4–17. All this is evidence from the immediate and wider context that the pierced one is to be understood in connection with the coming Davidic king. The various sociological and mythological reconstructions that have been reviewed do not adequately account for the strong hope for a Davidic king that I have established in the book. Nor do they account for the immediate context that speaks so favourably of the house of David and of David himself.

In addition, the association of the pierced one with the future Davidic king provides a reasonable explanation for the abrupt shift in the same verse of the MT from the first to third person in referring to the pierced one (Zech 12:10). It is only the king who could be said to represent Yahweh, so that to pierce the king is to pierce Yahweh.[115] Kingship in Israel, rightly understood, saw the king as Yahweh's agent on earth (e.g. Ps 72).

Zechariah envisages sin and guilt being removed more specifically through the coming of the Davidic Shoot, rather than the re-establishment of the Davidic dynasty per se.

114.   While C. and E. Meyers suggest that the pierced one represents the true prophets of the past, Duguid, "Messianic," 276, rightly questions whether this does justice to the royal overtones of the figure of the pierced one. Duguid argues that if a prophet is intended, it is difficult to explain why the imagery surrounding the death of Josiah is referred to. He believes it makes better sense to see the death of Josiah as in some sense typological of the death of the future royal figure. Furthermore, since דקר usually refers to a wound inflicted by a sword, Duguid believes that it makes more sense to identify the pierced one with the shepherd of Zech 13:7–9, a figure against whom God's sword is coming. Larkin, *Eschatology*, 162–65, has also noted the kingly and divine overtones present here.

115.   I agree with Laato, *Josiah*, 291, though for different reasons, that 12:10 reveals the intimate relationship between Yahweh and the promised future king.

While, as Mowinckel maintains, this status of the king in no way threatens "the exclusive dominion of Yahweh or the monotheism of the Old Testament,"[116] there is a real sense in which Yahweh and his king are inseparable. The close relationship between Yahweh and the Davidic king is seen in a number of passages. So, for instance, while Brueggemann argues that the notion of the king as "son of God," as in Ps 2:7, does not concern any ontological linkage to Yahweh, he does concede: "Perhaps an important exception is Ps 45:6, which appears to address the king as 'Elohim'."[117] Other passages include Isa 9:6, where the coming king who will sit on the throne of David is given the name: "Wonderful Counselor, Mighty God [אל גבור; cf. Zech 13:7], Everlasting Father, Prince of Peace."[118] In addition, Jer 23:5–6 (cf. Jer 33:16) speaks of the future Davidic Shoot who will save Judah and Israel and reign as king with justice and righteousness. This king will be named, "Yahweh our righteousness." While it is possible to see nothing more than the name of the king as "Yahweh is our righteousness," it is also possible that the giving of Yahweh's name to the coming Davidic Shoot indicates that they essentially act together. Ezekiel 34 also blends the activity of Yahweh and "my servant David," both of whom will shepherd and feed Yahweh's people.[119] This background offers an explanation of how the action against the Davidic king can at the same time be against Yahweh. The identification of the pierced one with the future Davidic king allows the MT to be explained without emendation. Keil captures the sense of this: "Thus the transition from the first person (אֵלַי) to the third (עָלָיו) points to the fact that the person slain, although essentially one with Jehovah, is personally distinct from the Supreme God."[120]

The absence of an explicit reference to the king in Zech 12 can be explained if, in the bringing of this salvation, the king was pierced and killed by his own countrymen, even members of his own house. This is such an unspeakable act that it is described in the way that it is, namely, as piercing Yahweh.

---

116. Mowinckel, *Cometh*, 171–72.

117. W. Brueggemann, *Theology of the Old Testament: Testimony, Dispute, Advocacy* (Minneapolis: Fortress, 1997), 606 n. 12.

118. Motyer, *The Prophecy of Isaiah*, 85, explains the background for understanding such a description: "Stemming from 2 Samuel 7 (especially verses 14–16), rich expectations were treasured in the house of David. Psalm 2, probably a coronation psalm greeting the new Davidic king at his enthronement, speaks of him as 'son of God' and Psalm 45:6<7> ascribes deity to the king. The case for the expectation of a divine Messiah is strong in the Old Testament."

119. E.g. Ezek 34:11–16; cf. 34:23–24.

120. Keil, "Zechariah," 388.

7.3. *The Pierced One and the Suffering Servant of Isaiah*

The question remains: Why is the king pierced (Zech 12:10)? In seeking to answer this question, it will be useful to recall our treatment of 13:7–9 in the previous chapter where the shepherd falls under Yahweh's judgment by being struck by the sword (13:7). Furthermore, the certainty with which an answer can be given depends to some degree on the extent to which Zechariah drew on Isaiah's presentation of the suffering servant. This is a controversial question and worthy of future research. It must be noted that scholars are just as divided on the identity of the suffering servant as the pierced one.[121] Limitations of space permit only a brief response.

Many scholars conclude that the differences between Isaiah's suffering servant and the figure of Zechariah are greater than the similarities, and that the comparison is of little use. For instance, Petersen states:

> The differences remain important. In Isa 53, the suffering of an individual results from Yahweh's intent. Moreover, the suffering and death have some sort of vicarious effect on the people. In Zechariah, the people have killed the individual, and the effect is one of lamentation—which is not present in Isa 53—and then, there is an outpouring of divine spirit.[122]

On the other hand, there are many similarities between the two figures, especially if the pierced one is connected with the future king of Zech 9:9 and the struck shepherd of 13:7.[123] Both are represented as humble and gentle (Zech 9:9; Isa 42:2). Both bring blessing to the nations (Zech 9:10; Isa 42:1, 4, 6; 49:6). Both release captives from the pit or dungeon (Zech 9:11–12; Isa 42:7; 61:1). Both gather those who have been scattered from Israel (Zech 9:12; Isa 49:5–6). Significantly, both are struck (Zech 13:7; Isa 53:4)[124] and pierced (Zech 12:10; Isa 53:5).[125] Both are associated with shepherd imagery (Zech 13:7–9; Isa 53:6–7), though

---

121.   I am convinced by the arguments of Motyer, *The Prophecy of Isaiah*, 13–16; Schultz, "The King in the Book of Isaiah," 141–65; Webb, *Isaiah*, 233–34, that the suffering servant is the future Davidic king promised elsewhere in Isaiah.

122.   Petersen, *Zechariah 9–14*, 121. Scholars who take a similar line include Mason, "Earlier," 164; Boda, *Commentary*, 488.

123.   Many of the following similarities are taken from Mitchell, *Psalter*, 208–9. I have excluded some of the similarities that he makes that I do not think are valid, particularly concerning Zech 11, which I interpret differently. Note also Curtis, *Steep*, 218: "in Zech 13:7–9, the influence of the earlier Isa 53 is likely."

124.   The same word "strike" (נכה) appears in Isa 50:6; 53:4 and Zech 13:7.

125.   The vocabulary is different in each instance. In Zech 12:10 it is דקר and in Isa 53:5 it is חלל.

the servant is likened to a sheep rather than a shepherd. Both suffer on account of a scattered flock (Zech 10:2; Isa 53:6).[126] Both are rejected by the people (Zech 12:10; 13:7; Isa 53:3). Both figures are connected with the pouring out of the Spirit upon people (Zech 12:10; Isa 44:3–5).[127] Contrary to Petersen's assessment, both are said to suffer by Yahweh's intent (Zech 13:7; Isa 53:6, 10), and their deaths result in forgiveness for the sins of the people (Zech 13:1; Isa 53:5–6).[128] Furthermore, the people later mourn over both figures (Zech 12:10; Isa 53:4–12).[129] These similarities seem too numerous to be coincidental.

Lamarche's monograph devotes a whole chapter to comparing Zech 9–14 with Isa 40–55 and his conclusion is valid: "Whatever the differences between our two authors, whatever the obscurities that still surround the suffering servant, through and perhaps beyond the part played by contemporary communities or persons, it is finally the same prophetic current, heralding a humble and suffering Messiah, which traverses these two books."[130] Hence, it seems reasonable to conclude that Zechariah is not saying any more than Isaiah did before him. Zechariah expresses it differently, but the underlying concepts are the same. In the battle that wins victory for Yahweh's people, a victory that brings cleansing and a restored covenant relationship with all of its blessings, the death of Yahweh's king plays a pivotal role in the purification and cleansing of the people.[131]

If the piercing of the future Davidic king and the striking of the shepherd in Zechariah are read against the wider background of Isaiah, then this clearly suggests a vicarious purpose in this figure's death.[132]

126. Black, "Messiah," 130, notes that the Targum of Isa 53:6 draws on the scattering of the sheep in Zech 13:7, and comments: "It is quite possible, however, that an identification of the smitten shepherd with the servant or even the messiah is somewhere in the exegetical history upon which the targumist is drawing."

127. For this connection, see Meyer, "Messianic Metaphors," 80–81.

128. Note Webb, *Zechariah*, 169–70: "like the great prophet Isaiah before him, Zechariah understood that the Messiah would have to suffer if sin were to be atoned for and Israel's relationship with God were to be restored. Furthermore, this suffering would be expressly brought about by God."

129. The mourning over the servant is implicit in Isaiah.

130. Lamarche, *Zacharie IX–XIV*, 147 (author's translation).

131. Note also the echo of Isa 53:12 in Zech 14:1 with the spoil that is divided as a result of the servant's death.

132. R. B. Crotty, "The Suffering Moses of Deutero-Zechariah," *Colloquium* 14 (1982): 43–50 (47), also believes the pierced one is a figure that is similar to the suffering servant of Isaiah: "The Pierced One is an essential part of a project of YHWH—the final forgiveness of the people."

Indeed, when 12:10 and 13:7–9 are read in this way against the rest of the book of Zechariah, it makes sense of the way in which the coming Davidic king would be instrumental in dealing with sin. Zechariah 3:9 spoke of the coming of the Shoot as coinciding with the removal of the iniquity of the land in a single day and 6:12–13 spoke of the coming Shoot as building the eschatological temple and re-establishing the rule of Yahweh in Jerusalem. The possibility that 6:13 be translated "he will be a priest on his throne" was also considered. In 12:10–13:9, the case for seeing the future Davidic king functioning as a priest is strengthened further: it is through the death of the king (12:10; 13:7) that purification and cleansing shall come to the people of Yahweh and to the land (13:1–6). It is by this cleansing that a new covenant relationship will be established (13:9). In this way the coming king will function as a priest for Yahweh's people and bring the earlier themes of the book into resolution. While not drawing out the priestly associations, Larkin's conclusion on this matter is apt:

> Zechariah has applied his study to the problem of how to remove human guilt, something promised by Proto Zechariah (3:9), but not accounted for. His solution is to portray a figure strongly identified with God, perhaps a kingly/divine figure, who seeks no attention at all but focuses both the hostility and the repentance of the people. In this way, the fact of human guilt is taken up into the promise of the outpouring of the spirit of grace and supplication. The writer has done more than either Ezekiel or Second Isaiah to illuminate those who stand around the kingly figure, widening the circle imperceptibly from the house of David and the inhabitants of Jerusalem (12:10) to "all the families that are left" (12:14) and perhaps beyond (13:8).[133]

Hence, it seems that Zechariah is announcing to those in his day that the judgment and purification that Isaiah prophesied, along with the suffering of Yahweh's servant, still lies in the future for Yahweh's people with the work of a coming Davidic king. This king will be killed, and the people will be judged, but the final outcome of the judgment of Yahweh on his shepherd and his sheep will be glorious. Those who emerge shall enter into a restored covenant, or even a new covenant relationship with Yahweh (cf. 13:9). The same pattern of suffering, refinement, and restoration is seen in 12:1–13:6 and 13:7–9 and prepares for the presentation in ch. 14.

---

133.   Larkin, *Eschatology*, 170.

7.4. *Zechariah 14 and the Hope for the House of David*

The majority view of scholarship is that Zech 14 demonstrates that any hope for the house of David and a future king has been eclipsed by the hope that Yahweh alone will reign in Jerusalem.[134] So, for instance, K. R. Schaefer in his study on ch. 14 is representative when he says, "The king of 9:9–10 is eclipsed in chap. 14 where all authority is subsumed under Yhwh."[135] Space does not permit a detailed treatment of ch. 14; suffice to say that Horbury has traced this view of a reduced hope for the house of David in the early post-exilic period back to the work of Gunkel, Gressman, and Mowinckel, particularly in their work on the Psalms.[136]

The interpretation of ch. 14 that sees a reversal of any hope for the house of David and a coming future king is driven largely by external factors rather than the book of Zechariah itself. Conjectures such as the failure of Zerubbabel to take the throne, disappointment with contemporary leadership, political fears, or power struggles within the post-exilic community do not present themselves as adequate reasons for controlling the way that ch. 14, in the context of the final form of the book, should be read. If ch. 14 is read as an integral part of the book, which is justified in the light of the way it continues many of the earlier themes of the book, then the view of the majority of scholars that sets the kingship of Yahweh against the kingship of the future Davidic king loses its force. Indeed, there is considerable evidence from later Jewish literature that ch. 14 was interpreted as holding out hope for a future Davidic king.[137]

---

134. A more detailed treatment of Zech 14 can be found in A. R. Petterson, "Behold Your King: The Hope for the House of David in the Book of Zechariah" (Ph.D. diss., The Queen's University, 2006).

135. K. R. Schaefer, "Zechariah 14 and the Composition of the Book of Zechariah," *RB* 100 (1993): 368–98 (372). Also Mason, *Zechariah*, 133: "there is no reference to human leadership, not even the muted hope attached to the Davidic line in 12:7–13:1" (cf. Mason, "Relation," 237). Similar comments are made by Jones, *Commentary*, 171, 176; Watts, "Zechariah," 359–60; Stuhlmueller, *Rebuilding*, 157; Hartle, "The Literary Unity of Zechariah," 155; Larkin, *Eschatology*, 180; Meyers and Meyers, "Fortunes," 220; Pomykala, *Dynasty*, 125; Ollenburger, "Zechariah," 7:743; Leske, "Context," 677.

136. Horbury, *Messianism*, 15–20. The relevant works are H. Gressmann, *Der Ursprung der israelitisch-jüdischen Eschatologie* (FRLANT 6; Göttingen: Vandenhoeck & Ruprecht, 1905); H. Gunkel, *Ausgewählte Psalmen* (Göttingen: Vandenhoeck & Ruprecht, 1905); S. Mowinckel, *Psalmensudien: Das Thronbesteigungsfest Jahwäs und der Ursprung der Eschatologie*, vol. 2 (Amsterdam: Schippers, 1961).

137. Mitchell, *Psalter*, 212–13.

In the final form of the book of Zechariah, the coming of the future king, and the coming of Yahweh are not pitted against each other, but are intimately related. Indeed, the future hope is not dissimilar to what happened when David became king and established Jerusalem as his capital. One of David's key tasks in this endeavour was bringing the ark to Jerusalem (2 Sam 6). The ark was later brought into the temple in Solomon's reign (1 Kgs 8). The co-existence of the Davidic king and Yahweh in Jerusalem had been a reality in the past. There is no reason to exclude it from being a reality in Zechariah's prophecy.

7.5. *Conclusion and Implications for the Hope Held for the House of David*

Zechariah 12 has again highlighted the diversity of opinion among scholars on the question of the hope that Zechariah held for the house of David, particularly in relation to the significance of the references to the house of David (12:7, 8, 10, 12; 13:1), the identity of the pierced one (12:10), and the absence of any explicit reference to a coming Davidic king in ch. 14. We have seen that the presuppositions that are brought to the text shape the background against which the text is interpreted and in many cases actually presuppose the conclusions.

The approach of this present study has been to read these chapters against the immediate background of chs. 9–14, and the wider background of chs. 1–8, which has firmly established the expectation for a coming Davidic and eschatological king, through whom the iniquity of the land would be removed in a single day (ch. 3), who would rebuild the eschatological temple and thereby establish Yahweh's rule in Jerusalem (ch. 6). Furthermore, this king would be instrumental in Yahweh's salvation (9:9–10), ushering in the day of peace and prosperity (3:10; 9:16–17).

Against this background, it is possible to make sense of the issues in ch. 12 that have long puzzled scholars. It enables us to understand why the reference to David and his house in 12:8 is so favourable, because there was a continued hope for a king from the house of David to rule once again from Jerusalem. It explains the focus on the priestly and Davidic lines among those who mourn in 12:12–14. It also explains why this king is not directly mentioned in the salvation of 12:1–9, namely, because this promised king has been pierced in the battle that won salvation, and worse still, he was pierced by his own people (12:10) as part of Yahweh's plan, as 13:7–9 goes on to make clear. Not only can this passage be understood in the light of the wider context, but this reading also makes sense of many of the details in the immediate context: the transition from first to third persons in the MT at 12:10; the nature and extent of the mourning, particularly the comparison with the mourning in Megiddo; and the cleansing that comes to the community as a result of the coming of this king. The many similarities that this presentation has with Isaiah suggests that Zechariah drew on Isaiah's presentation of the suffering servant to explain how the coming Davidic king would deal with the sins of the people. This explains how the coming king would act as a priest (cf. 3:9 and possibly 6:13). Hence, there is no evidence in ch. 12 that the hope associated with the house of David that we have seen expressed in the book up to this point has diminished in any way.[138]

Rather than reducing any hope for a future Davidic king, ch. 14 pictures the outcome of the advent and work of this king that climaxed in 13:7–9, namely, the introduction of the rule of Yahweh as king as he dwells among his people. Rather than seeing the hope for a coming Davidic king being eclipsed by the hope for Yahweh to be king, ch. 14 continues to hold out a strong hope for a future king in the line of David by portraying the outcome and fruit of his death.

138. I concur with the conclusion of Cook, *Apocalypticism*, 138, "[My] analysis does not support the view that Zechariah 1–8 and Zechariah 9–14 represent two diametrically opposite traditions, the former espousing a realized eschatology, the latter an apocalyptic eschatology. Instead, the evidence points to one Zechariah tradition that was messianic from the beginning."

Chapter 8

CONCLUSION

This monograph has been a study of the nature of the Davidic hope in the final form of the book of Zechariah. The need for this study was threefold: (1) the present lack of scholarly consensus on the nature of the Davidic hope in the book of Zechariah; (2) the fact that Wellhausen's assessment of the post-exilic period continues to influence heavily the way in which the Davidic hope is read, even though his historical-critical framework has largely been rejected; and (3) the lack of a major study that has sought to address specifically the nature of the Davidic hope in the whole book of Zechariah. While the recent monographs of Rose and Pola have addressed the nature of the Davidic hope in relation to Zech 1–6, this study has sought to critique their work and to advance their broad thesis that Zechariah looked to a future king who would restore the fortunes of the people of Yahweh, in relation to the whole book.

The method that has been followed has been to read the final form of the book of Zechariah against the wider background of the Davidic dynasty tradition in the Hebrew Bible, particularly those whom Zechariah calls the "former prophets." At the same time, there has been an attempt to interact with the wide diversity of scholarly interpretations. Since critical scholarship from the middle of the nineteenth century has generally divided Zech 9–14 from chs. 1–8 and understood it to be reflecting the hopes of a different author (or authors) from a different period, it has been common to read the nature of the Davidic hope in the two parts of the book, and even within the parts themselves, as set against each other. In doing this, not enough weight has been given to the fact that the editor responsible for the final form of the book and those responsible for its incorporation into the Hebrew canon considered it to be a distinct prophetic work and attributed the whole book to the prophet Zechariah. Assuming that the final redactor sought to produce a coherent presentation throughout the work, I have sought to determine the nature of the Davidic hope as it is presented in the whole book.

After reviewing the literature on the Davidic hope in Zechariah, the key themes that emerged and that have subsequently been dealt with in depth in this study are: the role of Joshua and Zerubbabel in Zech 3–4; the nature and identity of the Shoot in 3:8 and 6:12; the king in 9:9; the shepherd imagery in chs. 10–13; and the one who is pierced in 12:10. In each of these passages, a strong hope for a future king from the house of David has been demonstrated, and taken together the case is strengthened still more. At the same time, there is a complexity to the picture of the Davidic hope that emerges, with many of the above themes interacting with each other as they develop throughout the book.

Beginning with the role of Joshua and Zerubbabel, it was noted that the continued influence of Wellhausen has meant that many have mistakenly interpreted the relationship between the high priesthood and the monarchy in Zechariah in terms of what is known from the Hellenistic period. However, the text of Zechariah provides no evidence that the high priest was given the responsibilities of the pre-exilic monarch, nor that the Davidic hope was transferred to the priesthood. Instead, 3:1–7 is a vision of Joshua being cleansed and commissioned to serve, along with his priestly associates, in the reconstructed temple. As well as anticipating the reconstruction of the temple, the vision of ch. 3 points to the re-establishment of the temple cult by which cleansing and forgiveness could be mediated to the community, which had been defiled by the exilic experience.

In Zech 4:1–10, Zerubbabel is given the key role of rebuilding the temple. Zerubbabel was the Persian-appointed governor and was of Davidic ancestry. The reconstruction of the temple in Jerusalem would naturally raise the hope of a king to be reinstated on the throne of David on the basis of the covenant with David in 2 Sam 7 and the close connection between the temple and the throne (i.e. house of Yahweh and house of David). While there is not adequate evidence to be definitive, it seems unlikely that Zechariah ever identified Zerubbabel as this king (the "Shoot"). Regardless of this, it is clear that in the final form of the book of Zechariah the Shoot cannot refer to Zerubbabel. The Shoot refers to a future king from the house of David, beyond Zerubbabel, who will restore the fortunes of Yahweh's people after the devastation of the exile. Zechariah uses the term "Shoot" in a manner that is consistent with the way that this arboreal imagery is used by those whom Zechariah calls "former prophets" (i.e. Isaiah, Jeremiah, and Ezekiel), to offer hope once again to the nation.

In both Zech 3 and 6, the coming of the Shoot is set in a time following after Zerubbabel. In ch. 3, this is seen particularly in the forgiveness, prosperity, and abundance that will accompany the coming of the Shoot (vv. 9–10). In ch. 6, the symbolic action of crowning the high priest Joshua and then having the crown deposited in the temple points to a time beyond him when the Shoot will come. While this interpretation is supported by the recent work of Rose and Pola, we have seen that Rose neglects the element of continuity for the house of David contained in this imagery and Pola has over-realized expectations for the Shoot in seeing him already present in the temple and in the priesthood in a mystical sense.

The Shoot is a future Davidic king who will "shoot up" from the stump of the judged house of David. In drawing on the Shoot imagery of the earlier prophets (Jer 23:5; 33:15; cf. Isa 11:1 and Ezek 17), there is also a tacit acknowledgment of the failure of the house of David in history and the fact that the fulfilment of the hope for a coming king ultimately lies with Yahweh (in Zech 3:8 it is Yahweh who will "bring" the Shoot). While the great tree of the Davidic monarchy had been cut down in the judgment of the exile, Yahweh would cause a future king to shoot up from this stump to mediate forgiveness and usher in the age of prosperity and abundance (cf. 3:9–10). However, the house of David still has a contribution to make in the contemporary situation. As a Davidide, Zerubbabel has a key role in reconstructing the temple in Jerusalem. In addition, the house of David will provide the lineage from which the future king, as promised in 2 Sam 7, will come (Zech 6:12). Rose's interpretation of the Shoot imagery in Zechariah, in which he offers a false dichotomy between the action of Yahweh and the input of the house of David, ultimately distorts the connotations of this term.

Zechariah 9–14 presents and explores different perspectives on the one end-time battle that will usher in the restored kingdom of Yahweh on earth. Zechariah 9 establishes the broad outline of this programme, in which the Davidic king is central. Zechariah 10–14 then "telescopes" different aspects of the battle to focus on various themes. While the Shoot terminology is not used in chs. 9–14, the ideas contained in this term continue to be seen in these chapters. These ideas include: (1) past judgment on the house of David; (2) continuity between the old and the new (i.e. the new king will come from the house and line of David); and (3) the new king will have humble beginnings but will grow to produce magnificent fruit. In addition, the past failure of the house of David and the need for forgiveness for both the house of David and the community become significant features of the presentation of the Davidic hope in chs. 9–14, as does the development of the idea that the Shoot is a priest (6:13), which will be discussed shortly.

It has been demonstrated that the past judgment on the house of David is a significant feature of the presentation of chs. 10–11. In these chapters Zechariah draws on the Davidic dynasty tradition and the shepherd imagery of the earlier prophets to explain the present circumstances of the people and to offer hope for the future. Zechariah 10:2 attributes the current wandering and affliction of the post-exilic community to the fact that they have no shepherd of their own. The reason that they do not have their own shepherd is explained in the two shepherd sign-actions of ch. 11. The first sign-action, understood as a dramatic representation of Israel's history to the exile, places the responsibility for the division of the kingdom and the exilic experience on self-serving and self-aggrandizing leaders and on a people who failed to value Yahweh as their shepherd. The second sign-action shows that the people have received what they deserve for their rejection of Yahweh as shepherd. A foreign shepherd who has no concern for their welfare is presently ruling them (cf. 7:1). In this way, the past judgment on the house of David is highlighted, and the need for cleansing from sin for the house of David and the inhabitants of Jerusalem becomes obvious (cf. 3:9; 13:1).

The hope for a righteous Davidic king is made clear in many ways in chs. 9–14. Zechariah 9 begins by proclaiming that Yahweh is coming to re-establish the kingdom promised to David, with the cities mentioned in this section marking the extent of the kingdom at the time of David (9:1–8). The king who will come will be the lynchpin of a restored land and people (9:9–10). Yahweh will use his people to defeat their enemies and establish them in the land under the heir of David's throne (9:11–17). This king will rule over all the earth, over a kingdom that encompasses all the nations (9:10). This same pattern is reflected in ch. 10, where the king is probably to be understood as one of the leaders (10:4) whom Yahweh will use to defeat the enemies of his people and re-establish them in the land, reuniting Judah and Ephraim as he had done in the days of David (10:6–9).

While the two shepherd sign-actions of Zech 11 do not directly speak of a future Davidic king, the emphatic note of woe on the worthless shepherd and his allies on which this section begins and ends (11:3, 17) serves to raise the expectation of a shepherd king to come; a shepherd who will save the flock, bring them home, and deal with them righteously. The hope for a future Davidic king is also seen in 12:8, where, upon the victory and deliverance of the inhabitants of Jerusalem and Judah, the house of David is said to be like God. That is, the house of David will once again lead and protect Yahweh's people like Yahweh himself, presumably through the agency of the future Davidic king. The house of David will be returned to glory (12:7).

These aspects of the Davidic hope in Zechariah are clear. More controversial is whether the coming Davidic king is to be identified with the shepherd who is struck in 13:7 and the pierced one of 12:10. In my treatment of these passages it was shown that if they are treated as units isolated from the wider context of the book of Zechariah, then it is not clear that that either of them refers to a future Davidic king. This has been the approach of many critical scholars. However, if these passages are read as an integral part of the book of Zechariah, then the only identification that makes sense of the shepherd who is struck (13:7) and who is described by Yahweh as 'the man, my associate' is that this shepherd is the coming Davidic king, who is central to Yahweh's restoration programme. The striking of the shepherd results in a refining and purification of Yahweh's people with those who emerge enjoying a fully restored relationship with Yahweh (13:9; cf. 2:11 [MT 2:15]; 8:8; 9:16). Similarly, when 12:10 is read in the wider context of Zechariah and against the background of Isaiah's presentation of the suffering servant, several features of this passage suggest that the piercing of the future Davidic king is on view. These include the abrupt shift from the first to third person in referring to the one who is pierced; the nature and extent of the mourning that highlights the priestly and Davidic lines and also alludes to the death of king Josiah at Megiddo; and the cleansing that comes to the community as a result of this event through the fountain that it opens for cleansing from sin and uncleanness (13:1).

Reading these passages in this way serves to explain earlier features of Zechariah, namely how the coming of the Shoot will result in the cleansing of the land from sin in a single day (3:8–9) and the likely description of the Shoot as a priest (6:13). As well as acting as a king who will be instrumental in overthrowing the nations who troubled Yahweh's people (chs. 9–10), Zechariah holds out the hope that the coming king will also provide cleansing and purification for the people and the land (chs. 12–13). Like the suffering servant of Isaiah, Zechariah suggests that the death of the shepherd-king will have a vicarious function and result in a restored or even a new covenant relationship between Yahweh and his people (cf. Zech 13:9). In this way the coming king will function as a priest (like David; cf. 2 Sam 24:18–25) and the sin that culminated in the experience of exile will finally be undone.

Treating the book of Zechariah as a whole, it is clear that there is no abandonment or democratization of the Davidic hope as many suppose. Neither does the hope shift onto the priesthood, nor is it subsumed by the hope that Yahweh alone will be king. Rather, just as earlier prophets held out the hope for a future Davidic king who would reunite the people of Israel and Judah and bring cleansing, restoration, and blessing (e.g. Isa 9:6–7; 11:1–10; 16:5; Jer 23:3–6; 33:14–22; Ezek 37:21–25; Hos 3:5; Amos 9:11–15; Mic 4:8–5:5 [MT 4:8–5:6]), Zechariah draws on the Davidic dynasty tradition to hold out the hope for a future king to his contemporaries. Were he to be contradicting these earlier prophets, it is hard to understand how his work would ever have been accepted as authoritative prophetic literature.

Even though Zechariah draws on the hopes of the earlier prophets and often paints a picture of the future in terms of the past history of Yahweh's dealings with his people, the hope for the house of David in Zechariah is not a simple return to the past. We have seen that the sins of the house of David are acknowledged tacitly. Furthermore, the king when he comes will not be self-aggrandizing and self-serving, but righteous and saved, humble and riding on a donkey (9:9). Indeed, the house of David will be delivered itself when Yahweh sends the king (12:8; 13:1). Yet, the outcome of the work of the Shoot is robust and glorious. Through being struck, the coming Davidic shepherd-king will restore the covenant relationship between Yahweh and his people (13:9) and mediate the rule of Yahweh to the whole earth. This is consistent with the third aspect of the Shoot imagery noted above, where the king, through humble beginnings, grows and produces something robust and magnificent.

The fruit of the coming king is pictured in ch. 14. This chapter also brings to completion many of the other themes of the book, including: the judgment and salvation of the nations; Yahweh saving and gathering his people; the coming of Yahweh to dwell in the midst of his people in the eschatological temple in Jerusalem; and the holiness that will spread throughout the land. In this way, the coming Davidic king will usher in the untrammelled rule of Yahweh with "a counsel of peace between the two" (i.e. between Yahweh and his Davidic king; cf. 6:13).

In the light of this overview, this study of the hope for the house of David in the book of Zechariah makes a positive contribution to a number of current issues in Zechariah studies. It elucidates the nature of the expectations found in the book regarding the house of David in the post-exilic period and provides a comprehensive survey and assessment of the present state of scholarship on this issue. It demonstrates that the "house of David" was more than simply a social unit in the early post-exilic period; it had genealogical significance that was associated with the dynastic promise to David.

This study also challenges the scholarly consensus, going back to Wellhausen, that the high priest took over the role and prerogatives of the pre-exilic monarch in the early post-exilic period. Instead, it has been demonstrated that ch. 3 pictures Joshua the high priest being reinstated along with the priesthood to the temple duties that the priesthood exercised before the exile. This reinstatement heightens the expectation for a coming king from the house of David (the Shoot), especially given the close connection that has been seen between the temple and the throne.

Related to this, the present study also suggests that the priestly character of the future Davidic king may be more significant than has otherwise been acknowledged in the study of Zechariah. This ties into a wider tradition of the Hebrew Bible that sees Adam acting as a priest and king in the Garden of Eden, and the nation of Israel as a kingdom of priests (or "priestly kings"). The hope for the coming priest-king was central to Israel's hope for restoration and blessing that would encompass the world and was connected with the earlier prophetic hope of an eschatological temple beyond any physical structure in Jerusalem. This study also highlights a neglected theme—the role of the priest-king in bringing cleansing to the land.

Finally, this study confirms that the book of Zechariah, read as a whole, provides a strong impetus for later messianic hope in the post-exilic period. Recent studies in Chronicles and the Psalter (compiled in the post-exilic period) also demonstrate an enduring Davidic hope.[1] It is not insignificant that when the New Testament Gospel writers seek to explain the significance of the death of Jesus Christ, the Old Testament prophet cited more than any other in the passion narratives is Zechariah.

---

1. For instance, on Chronicles: S. Romerowski, "L'esperance messianique dans les Chroniques," *Hokhma* 34 (1987): 37–63; J. L. Townsend, "The Purpose of 1 & 2 Chronicles," *BibSac* 144 (1987): 277–92; B. E. Kelly, "Messianic Elements in the Chronicler's Work," in Satterthwaite, Hess, and Wenham, eds., *The Lord's Anointed*, 249–64; G. N. Knoppers, "The Davidic Genealogy: Some Contextual Considerations from the Ancient Mediterranean World," *Transeuptratène* 22 (2001): 35–50. On the Psalter: Mitchell, *Psalter*, 214–16; D. I. Starling, "The Messianic Hope in the Psalms," *RTR* 58 (1999): 121–34.

BIBLIOGRAPHY

Abegg, M. G. "Messianic Hope and 4Q285: A Reassessment." *JBL* 113 (1994): 81–91.

Achtemeier, E. *Nahum–Malachi*. Atlanta: John Knox Press, 1986.

Ackroyd, P. R. *Exile and Restoration: A Study of Hebrew Thought of the Sixth Century B.C.* London: SCM Press, 1968.

———. "Zechariah." Pages 646–55 in *Peake's Commentary on the Bible*. Edited by M. Black and H. H. Rowley. London: Thomas Nelson, 1962.

Albertz, R. "The Thwarted Restoration." Pages 1–17 in Albertz and Becking, eds., *Yahwism After the Exile*.

Albertz, R., and B. Becking, eds. *Yahwism After the Exile: Perspectives on Israelite Religion in the Persian Era*. Studies in Theology and Religion 5. Assen: Royal Van Gorcum, 2003.

Alexander, T. D. *From Paradise to the Promised Land: An Introduction to the Pentateuch*. 2d ed. Carlisle: Paternoster, 2002.

Alexander, T. D., and S. Gathercole, eds. *Heaven on Earth: The Temple in Biblical Theology*. Carlisle: Paternoster, 2004.

Alexander, T. D., and B. S. Rosner, eds. *New Dictionary of Biblical Theology*. Nottingham: IVP, 2000.

Amsler, S. "Aggée, Zacharie 1–8." Pages 11–126 in Amsler, Lacocque, and Vuilleumier, eds., *Aggée, Zacharie, Malachie*.

———. *David, Roi et Messie: La Tradition Davidique dans l'Ancien Testament*. Neuchâtel: Delachaux & Niestlé, 1963.

Amsler, S., A. Lacocque, and R. Vuilleumier, eds. *Aggée, Zacharie, Malachie*. 2d ed. Genève: Labor et Fides, 1988.

Andersen, F. I. "Reading the Book of Zechariah: A Review Essay." *ANES* 37 (2000): 229–40.

Andiñach, P. R. "Zechariah." Pages 1186–98 in *The International Bible Commentary*. Edited by W. R. Farmer. Collegeville: Liturgical, 1998.

Armerding, C. E. "Were David's Sons Really Priests?" Pages 75–86 in *Current Issues in Biblical and Patristic Interpretation*. Edited by G. F. Hawthorne. Grand Rapids: Zondervan, 1975.

Bailey, J. W. "The Usage in the Post Restoration Period of Terms Descriptive of the Priest and High Priest." *JBL* 70 (1951): 217–25.

Baldwin, J. G. *Haggai, Zechariah, Malachi: An Introduction and Commentary*. TOTC. Leicester: IVP, 1972.

———. "ṣemaḥ as a Technical Term in the Prophets." *VT* 14 (1964): 93–97.

Barker, M. "The Two Figures in Zechariah." *HeyJ* 18 (1977): 38–46.

Baron, D. *The Visions & Prophecies of Zechariah: An Exposition*. London: Morgan & Scott, 1918.

Barton, J. *Reading the Old Testament: Method in Biblical Study*. Philadelphia: Westminster, 1984.

Beale, G. K. "The Final Vision of the Apocalypse and Its Implications for a Biblical Theology of the Temple." Pages 191–209 in Alexander and Gathercole, eds., *Heaven on Earth*.

———. *The Temple and the Church's Mission: A Biblical Theology of the Dwelling Place of God*. NSBT 17. Leicester: Apollos, 2004.

Beatty, B. "Who Wears the Crown(s)? A Rationale for Editing Forwards." *Downside Review* 113 (1995): 1–19.

Becker, J. *Messianic Expectation in the Old Testament*. Edinburgh: T. & T. Clark, 1980.

Beckwith, R. T. "The Temple Restored." Pages 71–79 in Alexander and Gathercole, eds., *Heaven on Earth*.

Bedford, P. R. *Temple Restoration in Early Achaemenid Judah*. Leiden: Brill, 2001.

Ben Zvi, E. "Twelve Prophetic Books or "The Twelve": A Few Preliminary Considerations." Pages 125–56 in *Forming Prophetic Literature: Essays on Isaiah and the Twelve in Honour of John D. W. Watts*. Edited by J. W. Watts and P. R. House. Sheffield: Sheffield Academic Press, 1996.

Bentley, M. *Building for God's Glory: Haggai and Zechariah Simply Explained*. Welwyn Commentary Series. Darlington: Evangelical, 1989.

Bentzen, A. "Quelques remarques sur le mouvement messianique parmi les Juifs aux environs de l'an 520 avant Jésus-Christ." *RHPR* 10 (1930): 493–503.

Berquist, J. L. *Judaism in Persia's Shadow: A Social and Historical Approach*. Minneapolis: Fortress, 1995.

Beuken, W. *Haggai–Sacharja 1–8: Studien zur Überlieferungsgeschichte der frühnachexilischen Prophetie*. Studia Semitica Neerlandica 10. Assen: Van Gorcum, 1967.

Beyreuther, E. "Shepherd." Pages 3:564–69 in *The New International Dictionary of New Testament Theology*. Edited by C. Brown. Rev. ed. Carlisle: Paternoster, 1992.

Beyse, K.-M. *Serubbabel und die Königserwartungen der Propheten Haggai und Sacharja: Eine historische und traditionsgeschichtliche Untersuchung*. Stuttgart: Calwer, 1972.

Bianchi, F. "Le rôle de Zorobabel et de la dynastie davidique en Judée du VI siècle au II siècle av. J.-C." *Transeuphratène* 7 (1994): 153–65.

Bič, M. *Das Buch Sacharja*. Berlin: Evangelische Verlagsanstalt, 1962.

———. *Die Nachtgesichte des Sacharja: Eine Auslegung von Sacharja 1–6*. Biblische Studien 42. Neukirchen–Vluyn: Neukirchener Verlag, 1964.

Bimson, J. "Old Testament History and Sociology." Pages 125–55 in *Interpreting the Old Testament: A Guide for Exegesis*. Edited by C. C. Broyles. Grand Rapids: Baker Academic, 2001.

Black, M. C. "The Rejected and Slain Messiah who is Coming with His Angels: The Messianic Exegesis of Zechariah 9–14 in the Passion Narratives." Ph.D. diss., Emory University, 1990.

Block, D. I. "Bringing Back David: Ezekiel's Messianic Hope." Pages 167–88 in Satterthwaite, Hess, and Wenham, eds., *The Lord's Anointed*.

———. "My Servant David: Ancient Israel's Vision of the Messiah." Pages 17–56 in Hess and Carroll R., eds., *Israel's Messiah in the Bible and the Dead Sea Scrolls*.

Boda, M. J. "Figuring the Future: The Prophets and the Messiah." Pages 35–74 in *The Messiah in the Old and New Testaments*. Edited by S. E. Porter. Grand Rapids: Eerdmans, 2007.

————. "Freeing the Burden of Prophecy: *Maśśāʾ* and the Legitimacy of Prophecy in Zech 9–14." *Biblica* 87 (2006): 338–57.

————. "From Fasts to Feasts: The Literary Function of Zechariah 7–8." *CBQ* 65 (2003): 390–407.

————. "Messengers of Hope in Haggai–Malachi." *JSOT* 32 (2007): 113–31.

————. *The NIV Application Commentary: Haggai, Zechariah*. Grand Rapids: Zondervan, 2004.

————. "Oil, Crowns and Thrones: Prophet, Priest and King in Zechariah 1:7–6:15." *Journal of Hebrew Scriptures* 3 (2001): Article 10.

————. "Reading Between the Lines: Zechariah 11.4–16 in Its Literary Contexts." Pages 277–91 in Boda and Floyd, eds., *Bringing Out the Treasure*.

Boda, M. J., and M. H. Floyd, eds. *Bringing Out the Treasure: Inner Biblical Allusion in Zechariah 9–14*. JSOTSup 370. London: Sheffield Academic Press, 2003.

Boer, P. A. H. de. "An Inquiry into the Meaning of the Term אשׂמ." Pages 197–214 in *Oudtestamentische Studiën*. Edited by P. A. H. de Boer. Leiden: Brill, 1948.

Boice, J. M. *The Minor Prophets*. Vol. 2, *Micah–Malachi*. Grand Rapids: Zondervan, 1986.

Briggs, C. A. *Messianic Prophecy: The Prediction of the Fulfilment of Redemption Through the Messiah*. Peabody. Mass.: Hendrickson, 1988.

Bright, J. *A History of Israel*. 3d ed. London: SCM Press, 1981.

Brueggemann, W. *Theology of the Old Testament: Testimony, Dispute, Advocacy*. Minneapolis: Fortress, 1997.

Buhl, M.-L. "Hamath." *ABD* 3:33–36.

Buttenwieser, M. "Messiah." Pages 8:505–12 in I. Singer, ed., *Jewish Encyclopedia*. New York: Funk & Wagnalls, 1925.

Butterworth, M. *Structure and the Book of Zechariah*. Sheffield: JSOT, 1992.

Calvin, J. "Zechariah & Malachi." In *A Commentary on the Twelve Minor Prophets*, vol. 5. Edinburgh: Banner of Truth Trust, 1986.

Caquot, A. "Brèves Remarques sur l'allegorie des Pasteurs en Zacharie 11." Pages 45–55 in *Mélanges Bibliques et Orientaux en l'honneur de M. Mathias Delcor*. Edited by A. Caquot, S. Légasse, and M. Tardieu. Neukirchen–Vluyn: Neukirchener Verlag, 1985.

Carroll, R. P. *Jeremiah: A Commentary*. London: SCM Press, 1986.

————. *When Prophecy Failed: Reactions and Responses to Failure in the Old Testament Prophetic Traditions*. London: SCM Press, 1979.

Charlesworth, J. H., ed. *The Messiah*. Minneapolis: Fortress, 1992.

Chary, T. *Aggée–Zacharie, Malachie*. Sources Bibliques. Paris: Librairie Lecoffre, 1969.

Childs, B. S. *Introduction to the Old Testament as Scripture*. London: SCM Press, 1979.

Clark, D. J. "Discourse Structure in Zechariah 9–14: Skeleton or Phantom?" Pages 64–80 in *Issues in Bible Translation*. Edited by P. C. Stine. London: United Bible Societies, 1988.

Clark, D. J., and H. A. Hatton. *A Handbook on Haggai, Zechariah, and Malachi*. United Bible Societies Handbook Series. New York: United Bible Societies, 2002.

Clements, R. E. "The Messianic Hope in the Old Testament." *JSOT* 43 (1989): 3–19.

Coggins, R. J. *Haggai, Zechariah, Malachi*. OTG. Sheffield: JSOT, 1987.

Collins, J. J. "The Eschatology of Zechariah." Pages 74–84 in *Knowing the End from the Beginning: The Prophetic, the Apocalyptic and Their Relationships*. Edited by L. L. Grabbe and R. D. Haak. JSPSup 46. London: T&T Clark International, 2003.

────. *The Scepter and the Star: The Messiahs of the Dead Sea Scrolls and Other Ancient Literature*. Anchor Bible Reference Library. New York: Doubleday, 1995.

Conrad, E. W. *Zechariah*. A New Biblical Commentary. Sheffield: Sheffield Academic Press, 1999.

Cook, S. A. "The Metamorphosis of a Shepherd: The Tradition History of Zechariah 11.17 + 13.7–9." *CBQ* 55 (1993): 453–66.

Cook, S. L. *Prophecy & Apocalypticism: The Post-Exilic Social Setting*. Minneapolis: Fortress, 1995.

Cooke, G. A. *The Book of Ezekiel*. 2 vols. ICC. New York: Scribners, 1936.

Craigie, P. C. *The Twelve Prophets*. Daily Study Bible. Philadelphia: Westminster, 1984.

Cross, F. M. "The Council of Yahweh in Second Isaiah." *JNES* 12 (1953): 274–77.

Crotty, R. B. "The Suffering Moses of Deutero-Zechariah." *Colloquium* 14 (1982): 43–50.

────. "Suffering in Deutero-Zechariah." *ABR* 20 (1972): 54–56.

Curtis, B. G. *Up the Steep and Stony Road: The Book of Zechariah in Social Location Trajectory Analysis*. Academia Biblica 25. Atlanta: SBL, 2006.

Davidson, S. *An Introduction to the Old Testament*, vol. 3. Covent Garden: Williams & Norgate, 1863.

Davis, J. D. "The Reclothing and Coronation of Joshua. Zechariah iii and vi." *Princeton Theological Review* 18 (1920): 256–68.

Day, J., ed. *King and Messiah in Israel and the Ancient Near East: Proceedings of the Oxford Old Testament Seminar*. Sheffield: Sheffield Academic Press, 1998.

Delcor, M. "Un Problème de Critique Textuelle et d'Exégèse." *RB* 58 (1951): 189–99.

Dempster, S. G. *Dominion and Dynasty*. Leicester: IVP, 2003.

Demsky, A. "The Temple Steward Josiah ben Zephaniah." *IEJ* 31 (1981): 100–102.

Dentan, R. C. "The Book of Zechariah: Chapters 9–14 (Introduction and Exegesis)." *IB* 6:1089–114.

Dods, M. *The Post-Exilian Prophets: Haggai, Zechariah, Malachi*. Handbooks for Bible Classes. Edinburgh: T. & T. Clark, 1879.

Dothan, M. "Ashdod." *ABD* 1:477–82.

Dothan, T., and S. Gitin. "Ekron." *ABD* 4:415–22.

Douglas, J. D. et al., eds. *New Bible Dictionary*. 2d ed. Leicester: IVP, 1982.

Driver, S. R. *The Minor Prophets: Nahum, Habakkuk, Zephaniah, Haggai, Zechariah, Malachi*. The Century Bible. Edinburgh: T. C. & E. C. Jack, 1906.

Duguid, I. M. *Ezekiel and the Leaders of Israel*. VTSup 56. Leiden: Brill, 1994.

────. "Messianic Themes in Zechariah 9–14." Pages 265–80 in Satterthwaite, Hess, and Wenham, eds., *The Lord's Anointed*.

Dumbrell, W. J. *The Faith of Israel*. Leicester: IVP, 1989.

────. "Kingship and Temple in the Post-exilic Period." *RTR* 37 (1978): 33–42.

────. *The Search for Order*. Grand Rapids: Baker, 1994.

Eichrodt, W. *Theology of the Old Testament*, vol. 1. Translated by J. Baker. London: SCM Press, 1961.

────. *Theology of the Old Testament*, vol. 2. Translated by J. Baker. London: SCM Press, 1967.

Eissfeldt, O. *The Old Testament: An Introduction*. Translated by P. R. Ackroyd. Oxford: Blackwell, 1965.

Elliger, K. *Das Buch der zwölf kleinen Propheten*. ATD 25. Göttingen: Vandenhoeck & Ruprecht, 1982.

————. *Die Propheten Nahum, Habakuk, Zephanja, Haggai, Sacharja, Maleachi.* ATD. 6th ed. Göttingen: Vandenhoeck & Ruprecht, 1967.

Emmerson, G. *Nahum to Malachi.* The People's Bible Commentary. Oxford: The Bible Reading Fellowship, 1998.

Esse, D. L. "Ashkelon." *ABD* 1:487–90.

Evans, C. A. "The Messiah in the Dead Sea Scrolls." Pages 85–108 in Hess and Carroll R., eds., *Israel's Messiah in the Bible and the Dead Sea Scrolls.*

Ewald, H. *Die Propheten des Alten Bundes*, vol. 1. Stuttgart: Verlag von Adolph Krabbe, 1840.

Feinberg, C. L. "Exegetical Studies in Zechariah." *BibSac* 100 (1943): 513–23.

————. "Exegetical Studies in Zechariah." *BibSac* 101 (1944): 434–45.

————. "Exegetical Studies in Zechariah." *BibSac* 103 (1946): 161–75.

Finley, T. J. "The Sheep Merchants of Zechariah 11." *Grace Theological Journal* 3 (1982): 51–65.

Floyd, M. H. "The מַשָּׂא (*MAŚŚĀʾ*) as a Type of Prophetic Book." *JBL* 121 (2002): 401–22.

————. "Cosmos and History in Zechariah's View of the Restoration (Zechariah 1:7–6:15." Pages 125–44 in *Problems in Biblical Theology.* Edited by H. T. C. Sun and K. L. Eades. Grand Rapids: Eerdmans, 1997.

————. *Minor Prophets: Part 2.* The Forms of the Old Testament Literature 22. Grand Rapids: Eerdmans, 2000.

————. "Zechariah and Changing Views of Second Temple Judaism in Recent Commentaries." *Religious Studies Review* 25 (1999): 257–63.

Foster, R. L. "Shepherds, Sticks, and Social Destabilization: A Fresh Look at Zechariah 11:4–17." *JBL* 126 (2007): 735–53.

Friebel, K. G. "A Hermeneutical Paradigm for Interpreting Prophetic Sign-Actions." *Didaskalia* (2001): 27–46.

————. *Jeremiah's and Ezekiel's Sign-Acts.* JSOTSup 283. Sheffield: Sheffield Academic Press, 1999.

Frolov, S. "Is the Narrator also Among the Prophets? Reading Zechariah Without Presuppositions." *BibInt* 13 (2005): 13–40.

Fuggian, H. J. "The Messianic Teachings of Zechariah 9–14." Ph.D. diss., Southern Baptist Theological Seminary, 1951.

Gaide, G. *Jerusalem, voici ton roi: Commentaire de Zacharie 9–14.* Paris: Cerf, 1968.

Galling, K. "Die Exilswende in der Sicht des Propheten Sacharja." *VT* 2 (1952): 18–36.

Gese, H. "Anfang und Ende der Apokalyptik, dargestellt am Sacharjabuch." *Zeitschrift für Theologie und Kirche* 70 (1973): 20–49.

Gordon, R. P. "The Ephraimite Messiah and the Targum(s) to Zechariah 12.10." Pages 184–95 in *Reading from Right to Left: Essays on the Hebrew Bible in Honour of David J. A. Clines.* Edited by J. C. Exum and H. G. M. Williamson. London: Sheffield Academic Press, 2003.

————. *The Targum of the Minor Prophets.* Edited by K. J. Cathcart, M. McNamara, and M. Maker. The Aramaic Bible 14. Edinburgh: T. & T. Clark, 1989.

Green, W. S. "Introduction: Messiah in Judaism: Rethinking the Question." Pages 1–13 in *Judaisms and Their Messiahs at the Turn of the Christian Era.* Edited by J. Neusner, W. S. Green, and E. S. Frerichs. Cambridge: Cambridge University Press, 1987.

Greidanus, S. *Preaching Christ from the Old Testament: A Contemporary Hermeneutical Method.* Grand Rapids: Eerdmans, 1999.

Gressmann, H. *Der Ursprung der israelitisch-jüdischen Eschatologie*. FRLANT 6. Göttingen: Vandenhoeck & Ruprecht, 1905.

Groningren, G. van. *Messianic Revelation in the Old Testament*. Grand Rapids: Baker, 1990.

Gunkel, H. *Ausgewählte Psalmen*. Göttingen: Vandenhoeck & Ruprecht, 1905.

Halpern, B. "The Ritual Background of Zechariah's Temple Song." *CBQ* 40 (1978): 167–80.

Ham, C. A. *The Coming King and the Rejected Shepherd: Matthew's Reading of Zechariah's Messianic Hope*. New Testament Monographs 4. Sheffield: Sheffield Phoenix, 2005.

Hamilton, V. P. "Satan." *ABD* 5:985–89.

Hanhart, R. *Sacharja 1–8*. Biblisher Kommentar Altes Testament. Neukirchen–Vluyn: Neukirchner Verlag, 1998.

Hanson, P. D. *The Dawn of Apocalyptic: The Historical and Sociological Roots of Jewish Apocalyptic Eschatology*. Rev. ed. Philadelphia: Fortress, 1979.

———. "Messiahs and Messianic Figures in Proto-Apocalypticism." Pages 67–75 in Charlesworth, ed., *The Messiah*.

Harrelson, W. "The Trial of the High Priest Joshua: Zechariah 3." *Eretz-Israel* 16 (1982): 116–24.

Hartle, A. "The Literary Unity of Zechariah." *JETS* 35 (1992): 145–57.

Heater Jr., H. *Zechariah*. Grand Rapids: Zondervan, 1987.

Hengstenberg, E. W. *Christology of the Old Testament*, vol. 2. Translated by Anon. Florida: Macdonald, 1854.

———. *Christology of the Old Testament*. Translated by R. Keith. Grand Rapids: Kregel, 1970.

Herrick, G. "Conceptions of Davidic Hope in Ezekiel, Zechariah, Haggai, and the Chronicles." (1998) No pages. Cited 2008. Online: http://www.bible.org/page.asp?page_id=1565.

Hess, R. S., and M. D. Carroll R., eds. *Israel's Messiah in the Bible and the Dead Sea Scrolls*. Grand Rapids: Baker Academic, 2003.

Higginson, R. E. "Zechariah." Pages 786–803 in *The New Bible Commentary Revised*. Edited by D. Guthrie and J. A. Motyer. London: IVP, 1970.

Hill, A. E. "Dating Second Zechariah: A Linguistic Reexamination." *HAR* 6 (1982): 105–34.

Hinton, L. B. *Micah, Nahum, Habakkuk, Zephaniah, Haggai, Zechariah, and Malachi*. Basic Bible Commentary 16. Nashville: Abingdon, 1988.

Hitzig, F. *Die zwölf kleinen Propheten erklärt*. Leipzig: Hirzel, 1881.

Hobbs, T. R. "The Language of Warfare in Zechariah 9–14." Pages 103–28 in *After the Exile: Essays in Honour of Rex Mason*. Edited by J. Barton and D. J. Reimer. Macon: Mercer University Press, 1996.

Horbury, W. *Jewish Messianism and the Cult of Christ*. London: SCM Press, 1998.

Horst, F. *Die zwölf kleinen Propheten: Nahum bis Maleachi*. Handkommentar zum Alten Testament. Tübingen: Mohr, 1964.

Jansma, T. "Inquiry into the Hebrew Text and the Ancient Versions of Zech. 9–14." *Oudtestamentische Studiën* 7 (1950): 1–142.

Japhet, S. "Sheshbazzar and Zerubbabel." *ZAW* 94 (1982): 66–98.

Jauhiainen, V. M. "'Behold, I Am Coming': The Use of Zechariah in Revelation." Ph.D. diss., University of Cambridge, 2003.

————. "Turban and Crown Lost and Regained: Ezekiel 21:29–32 and Zechariah's Zemah." *JBL* 127 (2008): 501–11.

Jenson, P. P. "The Levitical Sacrificial System." Pages 25–40 in *Sacrifice in the Bible*. Edited by R. T. Beckwith and M. J. Selman. Carlisle: Paternoster, 1995.

Jeremias, C. *Die Nachtgesichte des Sacharja. Untershuchungen zu ihrer Stellung im Zusammenhang der Visionsberichte im Alten Testament und zu ihrem Bildmaterial*. FRLANT 117. Göttingen: Vandenhoeck & Ruprecht, 1977.

Jones, D. R. "A Fresh Interpretation of Zechariah IX–XI." *VT* 12 (1962): 241–59.

————. *Haggai, Zechariah, and Malachi: Introduction and Commentary*. Torch Bible Commentaries. London: SCM Press, 1962.

Jonker, L. "*rᶜh*." *NIDOTTE* 3:1138–43.

Kaiser Jr., W. C. *The Messiah in the Old Testament*. Grand Rapids: Zondervan, 1995.

————. *Micah–Malachi*. The Preacher's Commentary 23. Nashville: Thomas Nelson, 1992.

Katzenstein, H. J. "Gaza: Prehellenistic." *ABD* 2:912–15.

————. "Philistines." *ABD* 5:326–28.

Keil, C. F. "Zechariah." Pages 217–421 in *Biblical Commentary on the Old Testament: The Twelve Minor Prophets*, vol. 2. Edited by C. F. Keil and F. Delitzsch. Grand Rapids: Eerdmans, 1949.

Kelly, B. E. "Messianic Elements in the Chronicler's Work." Pages 249–64 in Satterthwaite, Hess, and Wenham, eds., *The Lord's Anointed*.

Kennett, R. H. "Zechariah 12–13.1." *JTS* 28 (1926–27): 1–9.

Kimchi, D. *Rabbi David Kimchi's Commentary upon the Prophecies of Zechariah*. Translated by A. M'Caul. London: J. Duncan, 1837.

Kirkpatrick, A. F. *The Doctrine of the Prophets*. London: Macmillan, 1901.

Kitchen, K. A. "Gilead." Page 421 in Douglas et al., eds., *New Bible Dictionary*.

————. "Tent." Page 1175 in J. D. Douglas et al., eds., *New Bible Dictionary*.

Klausner, J. *The Messianic Idea in Israel from Its Beginnings to the Completion of the Mishnah*. London: George Allen & Unwin, 1956.

Kleven, T. "The Use of ṣnr in Ugaritic and 2 Samuel V 8: Hebrew Usage and Comparative Philology." *VT* 44 (1994): 195–204.

Kline, M. G. *Glory in Our Midst: A Biblical-Theological Reading of Zechariah's Night Visions*. Eugene: Wipf & Stock, 2001.

————. *Images of the Spirit*. Grand Rapids: Baker, 1980.

————. "The Structure of the Book of Zechariah." *JETS* 34 (1991): 179–93.

Knabenbauer, J. *Commentarius in prophetas minores*. Cursus scripturae sacrae. Commentarii in VT 3.5. Paris: Lethielleux, 1886.

Knoppers, G. N. *1 Chronicles 1–9: A New Translation with Introduction and Commentary*. Anchor Bible 12. New York: Doubleday, 2003.

————. "The Davidic Genealogy: Some Contextual Considerations from the Ancient Mediterranean World." *Transeuptratène* 22 (2001): 35–50.

Köhler, L. "Eine archaistische Wortgruppe." *ZAW* 46 (1928): 218–20.

Kosmala, H. "*gābhar*." *TDOT* 2:367–82.

————. "The Term *geber* in the Old Testament and in the Scrolls." Pages 159–69 in *Congress Volume, Rome 1968*. Edited by G. W. Anderson et al. VTSup 17. Leiden: Brill, 1969.

Kraus, H.-J. *Theology of the Psalms*. Minneapolis: Augsburg, 1986.

Kronholm, T. "*qešet̠, qaššāt̠*." *TDOT* 13: 201–8.

Laato, A. *Josiah and David Redivivus: The Historical Josiah and the Messianic Expectations of Exilic and Postexilic Times.* ConBOT 33. Stockholm: Almqvist & Wiksell, 1992.

―――. *A Star is Rising: The Historical Development of the Old Testament Royal Ideology and the Rise of the Jewish Messianic Expectations.* Atlanta: Scholars Press, 1997.

―――. "Zechariah 4:6b–10a and the Akkadian Royal Building Inscriptions." *ZAW* 106 (1994): 53–69.

Lacocque, A. "Zacharie 9–14." Pages 127–215 in Amsler, Lacocque, and Vuilleumier, eds., *Aggée, Zacharie, Malachie.*

Lagrange, M. J. "Notes sur les prophéties messianiques des derniers prophètes." *RB* 15 (1906): 67–83.

Lamarche, P. *Zacharie IX–XIV: Structure Littéraire et Messianisme.* Études Bibliques. Paris: Librairie Lecoffre, 1961.

Larkin, K. J. A. *The Eschatology of Second Zechariah: A Study of the Formation of a Mantological Wisdom Anthology.* Contributions to Biblical Exegesis and Theology 6. Kampen: Kok Pharos, 1994.

―――. "Zechariah." Pages 610–15 in *The Oxford Bible Commentary.* Edited by J. Barton and J. Muddiman. Oxford: Oxford University Press, 2001.

Laubscher, F. d. T. "The King's Humbleness in Zechariah 9:9. A Paradox?" *JNSL* 18 (1992): 125–34.

Leske, A. M. "Context and Meaning of Zechariah 9:9." *CBQ* 62 (2000): 663–78.

Lindblom, J. *Prophecy in Israel.* Philadelphia: Fortress, 1962.

Long, V. P. "The Art of Biblical History." Pages 281–429 in *Foundations of Contemporary Interpretation.* Edited by M. Silva. Grand Rapids: Zondervan, 1996.

―――. "Historiography of the Old Testament." Pages 145–75 in *The Face of Old Testament Studies: A Survey of Contemporary Approaches.* Edited by D. W. Baker and B. T. Arnold. Grand Rapids: Baker, 1999.

Longman III, T. *Immanuel in Our Place.* Phillipsburg: P & R Publishing, 2001.

Love, M. C. *The Evasive Text: Zechariah 1–8 and the Frustrated Reader.* JSOTSup 296. Sheffield: Sheffield Academic Press, 1999.

Luck, G. C. *Zechariah: A Study of the Prophetic Visions of Zechariah.* Chicago: Moody, 1969.

Luke, K. "The Thirty Pieces of Silver (Zech 11, 12–13)." *Bible Bhashyam* 30 (2004): 104–22.

Luther, M. *Lectures on the Minor Prophets III: Zechariah.* Translated by H. C. Oswald. Luther's Works 20. Saint Louis: Concordia, 1973.

Mackay, J. L. *Haggai, Zechariah & Malachi.* Focus on the Bible. Fearn: Christian Focus, 2003.

Malamat, A. "The Secret Council and Prophetic Involvement in Mari and Israel." Pages 231–36 in *Prophetie und geschichtliche Wiklichkeit im alten Israel.* Edited by R. Liwak and S. Wagner. Stuttgart: W. Kohlhammer, 1991.

Marinkovic, P. "What Does Zechariah 1–8 Tell us about the Second Temple?" Pages 88–103 in *Second Temple Studies.* Vol 2, *Temple Community in the Persian Period.* Edited by T. C. Eskenazi and K. H. Richards. Sheffield: JSOT, 1994.

Marti, K. *Das Dodekapropheton.* Tübingen: J. C. B. Mohr/Paul Siebeck, 1904.

Martínez, F. G. *The Dead Sea Scrolls Translated: The Qumran Texts in English.* Leiden: Brill, 1994.

Mason, R. A. *The Books of Haggai, Zechariah, and Malachi*. Cambridge Bible Commentary. Cambridge: Cambridge University Press, 1977.

———. "The Messiah in the Postexilic Old Testament Literature." Pages 338–64 in Day, ed., *King and Messiah in Israel*.

———. "The Prophets of the Restoration." Pages 137–54 in *Israel's Prophetic Tradition*. Edited by R. Coggins, A. Phillips, and M. Knibb. Cambridge: Cambridge University Press, 1982.

———. *Preaching the Tradition: Homily and Hermeneutics After the Exile*. Cambridge: Cambridge University Press, 1990.

———. "The Relation of Zech 9–14 to Proto-Zechariah." *ZAW* 88 (1976): 227–39.

———. "The Use of Earlier Biblical Material in Zechariah 9–14: A Study in Inner Biblical Exegesis." Pages 1–208 in Boda and Floyd, eds., *Bringing out the Treasure*.

———. "Why is Second Zechariah so Full of Quotations?" Pages 21–28 in Tuckett, ed., *The Book of Zechariah and Its Influence*.

Matties, G. H., and J. Walton, "pinnā." *NIDOTTE* 3:640.

May, H. G. "A Key to the Interpretation of Zechariah's Visions." *JBL* 57 (1938): 173–84.

McComiskey, T. E. "Zechariah." Pages 1003–1244 in vol. 3 of *The Minor Prophets: An Exegetical and Expository Commentary*. Edited by T. E. McComiskey. 3 vols. Grand Rapids: Baker, 2000.

McConville, J. G. *Law and Theology in Deuteronomy*. Sheffield: JSOT, 1984.

McCready, W. O. "The 'Day of Small Things' vs. the Latter Days: Historical Fulfillment or Eschatological Hope?" Pages 223–36 in *Israel's Apostasy and Restoration*. Edited by A. Gileadi. Grand Rapids: Baker, 1988.

McEvenue, S. E. "The Political Structure in Judah from Cyrus to Nehemiah." *CBQ* 43 (1981): 353–64.

McKane, W. *Jeremiah 1–25*. ICC. Edinburgh: T. & T. Clark, 1986.

McKelvey, R. J. "Temple." Pages 806–11 in Alexander and Rosner, eds., *New Dictionary of Biblical Theology*.

Merrill, E. H. *An Exegetical Commentary: Haggai, Zechariah, Malachi*. Chicago: Moody, 1994.

———. "Royal Priesthood: An Old Testament Messianic Motif." *BibSac* 150 (1993): 50–61.

Meyer, L. V. "An Allegory Concerning the Monarchy: Zech 11:4–17. 13:7–9." Pages 225–40 in *Scripture in History and Theology*. Edited by A. L. Merrill and T. W. Overholt. Pennsylvania: Pickwick, 1977.

———. "The Messianic Metaphors in Deutero-Zechariah." Ph.D. diss., University of Chicago, 1972.

Meyers, C. L., and E. M. Meyers. "The Future Fortunes of the House of David: The Evidence of Second Zechariah." Pages 207–22 in *Fortunate the Eyes That See*. Edited by A. B. Beck et al. Grand Rapids: Eerdmans, 1995.

———. *Haggai, Zechariah 1–8: A New Translation with Introduction and Commentary*. New York: Doubleday, 1987.

———. *Zechariah 9–14: A New Translation with Introduction and Commentary*. New York: Doubleday, 1993.

———. "Zechariah, Book of (Zechariah 1–8)." *ABD* 6:1061–65.

Meyers, E. M. "Messianism in First and Second Zechariah and the 'End' of Biblical Prophecy." Pages 127–42 in *"Go to the Land I Will Show You."* Edited by J. E. Coleson and V. H. Matthews. Winona Lake, Ind.: Eisenbrauns, 1996.

Millar, J. G. *Now Choose Life: Theology and Ethics in Deuteronomy*. NSBT 6. Leicester: IVP, 1998.

Mitchell, D. C. *The Message of the Psalter: An Eschatological Programme in the Book of Psalms*. JSOTSup 252. Sheffield: Sheffield Academic Press, 1997.

Mitchell, H. G. "A Commentary on Haggai and Zechariah." Pages 1–357 in *A Critical and Exegetical Commentary on Haggai, Zechariah, Malachi and Jonah*. Edited by S. R. Driver, A. Plummer, and C. A. Briggs. The International Critical Commentary on the Holy Scriptures of the Old and New Testaments. Edinburgh: T. & T. Clark, 1912.

Moore, T. V. *A Commentary on Zechariah*. Edinburgh: The Banner of Truth Trust, 1958.

Moseman, R. D. "Reading the Two Zechariahs as One." *Review and Expositor* 97 (2000): 487–98.

Motyer, J. A. *The Prophecy of Isaiah*. Leicester: IVP, 1993.

Mowinckel, S. *He That Cometh*. Translated by G. W. Anderson. Oxford: Blackwell, 1956.

———. *Psalmensudien: Das Thronbesteigungsfest Jahwäs und der Ursprung der Eschatologie*, vol. 2. Amsterdam: Schippers, 1961.

Mullen, E. T. *The Divine Council in Canaanite and Early Hebrew Literature*. Atlanta: Scholars Press, 1980.

Neil, W. "Zechariah, Book of." *IDB* 4:943–47.

Newcome, W. *An Attempt Towards an Improved Version, a Metrical Arrangement, and an Explanation of the Twelve Minor Prophets*. Dublin: Robert Marchbank, 1785.

Nogalski, J. D. "Zechariah 13.7–9 as a Transitional Text: An Appreciation and Re-evaluation of the Work of Rex Mason." Pages 292–304 in Boda and Floyd, eds., *Bringing out the Treasure*.

Nogalski, J. D., and M. A. Sweeney, eds. *Reading and Hearing the Book of the Twelve*. SBL Symposium Series 15. Atlanta: SBL, 2000.

North, R. "Zechariah's Seven-Sprout Lampstand." *Biblica* 51 (1970): 183–206.

Nurmela, R. *Prophets in Dialogue: Inner-Biblical Allusions in Zechariah 1–8 and 9–14*. Åbo: Åbo Akademi University Press, 1996.

O'Brien, J. M. *Nahum, Habakkuk, Zephaniah, Haggai, Zechariah, Malachi*. AOTC. Nashville: Abingdon, 2004.

O'Kennedy, D. F. "The Theological Portrayal of Forgiveness in Zechariah 1–8." *Scriptura* 84 (2003): 410–22.

Oeming, M. "*pinnâ*." *TDOT* 11:586–89.

Oesterley, W. O. E. *A History of Israel*, vol. 2. Oxford: Clarendon, 1932.

Ollenburger, B. C. "The Book of Zechariah." Pages 7:733–840 in *The New Interpreter's Bible*. Edited by L. E. Keck et al. Nashville: Abingdon, 1996.

Orelli, C. von. *The Twelve Minor Prophets*. Translated by J. S. Banks. Edinburgh: T. & T. Clark, 1893.

Oswalt, J. N. *The Book of Isaiah: Chapters 1–39*. NICOT. Grand Rapids: Eerdmans, 1986.

Petersen, D. L. "The Book of the Twelve/The Minor Prophets (Hosea, Joel, Amos, Obadiah, Jonah, Micah, Nahum, Habakkuk, Zephaniah, Haggai, Zechariah, Malachi." Pages 95–126 in *The Hebrew Bible Today: An Introduction to Critical Issues*. Edited by S. L. McKenzie and M. P. Graham. Louisville: John Knox, 1998.

———. *Haggai and Zechariah 1–8: A Commentary*. OTL. London: SCM Press, 1985.

———. *Zechariah 9–14 and Malachi: A Commentary*. OTL. London: SCM Press, 1995.

———. "Zechariah, Book of (Zechariah 9–14)." *ABD* 6:1065–68.

Petitjean, A. "La Mission de Zorobabel et la Reconstruction du Temple. Zach., III:8–10." *Ephemerides Theologicae Lovanienses* 42 (1966): 40–71.

———. *Les oracles du proto-Zacharie. Un programme de restauration pour la communauté juive après l'exil.* Études bibliques. Paris: J. Gabalda, 1969.

Petterson, A. R. "Behold Your King: The Hope for the House of David in the Book of Zechariah." Ph.D. diss., The Queen's University, 2006.

Pitard, W. T. "Damascus: Pre-Hellenistic History." *ABD* 2:5–7.

Plöger, O. *Theocracy and Eschatology.* Translated by S. Rudman. Oxford: Blackwell, 1968.

Pola, T. *Das Priestertum bei Sacharja.* FAT 35. Tübingen: Mohr Siebeck, 2003.

———. "Form and Meaning in Zechariah 3." Pages 156–67 in Albertz and Becking, eds., *Yahwism After the Exile.*

Pomykala, K. E. *The Davidic Dynasty Tradition in Early Judaism: Its History and Significance for Messianism.* Atlanta: Scholars Press, 1995.

Portnoy, S. L., and D. L. Petersen. "Biblical Texts and Statistical Analysis: Zechariah and Beyond." *JBL* 103 (1984): 11–21.

Provan, I. W., V. P. Long, and T. Longman III. *A Biblical History of Israel.* London: Westminster John Knox, 2003.

Pusey, E. B. *Zechariah.* The Minor Prophets 8. London: James Nisbet & Co., 1907.

Pyper, H. S. "Reading in the Dark: Zechariah, Daniel and the Difficulty of Scripture." *JSOT* 29 (2005): 485–504.

Radday, Y. T., and D. Wickmann, "The Unity of Zechariah Examined in the Light of Statistical Linguistics." *ZAW* 87 (1975): 30–55.

Redditt, P. L. *Haggai, Zechariah and Malachi.* NCBC. London: Marshall Pickering, 1995.

———. "Israel's Shepherds: Hope and Pessimism in Zechariah 9–14." *CBQ* 51 (1989): 631–42.

———. "The Two Shepherds in Zechariah 11:4–17." *CBQ* 55 (1993): 676–86.

———. "Zerubbabel, Joshua, and the Night Visions of Zechariah." *CBQ* 54 (1992): 249–59.

Redditt, P. L., and A. Schart, eds. *Thematic Threads in the Book of the Twelve.* BZAW 25. Berlin: de Gruyter, 2003.

Reed, S. A. "Jebus." *ABD* 3:652–53.

Reiner, E. "Thirty Pieces of Silver." *JAOS* 88 (1968): 186–90.

Rendtorff, R. *The Old Testament: An Introduction.* Translated by J. Bowden. Philadelphia: Fortress, 1986.

Renz, T. "Review: W. H. Rose, Zemah and Zerubbabel: Messianic Expectations in the Early Postexilic Period." *VT* 53 (2003): 136.

Reventlow, H. G. *Die Propheten Haggai, Sacharja und Maleachi.* Göttingen: Vandenhoeck & Ruprecht, 1993.

Rignell, L. G. *Die Nachtgesichte des Sacharja.* Lund: Gleerup, 1950.

Roberts, J. J. M. "The Old Testament's Contribution to Messianic Expectations." Pages 39–51 in Charlesworth, ed., *The Messiah.*

Robinson, T. H., and F. Horst, *Die zwölf kleinen Propheten: Hosea bis Micha. Nahum bis Maleachi.* Handbuch zum Alten Testament 14. Tübingen: J. C. B. Mohr (Paul Siebeck), 1964.

Rogerson, J. W. "Zechariah." Pages 721–29 in *Eerdmans Commentary on the Bible.* Edited by J. D. G. Dunn and J. W. Rogerson. Grand Rapids: Eerdmans, 2003.

Romerowski, S. "L'esperance messianique dans les Chroniques." *Hokhma* 34 (1987): 37–63.

Rooke, D. W. "Kingship as Priesthood: The Relationship between the High Priesthood and the Monarchy." Pages 187–208 in Day, ed., *King and Messiah in Israel*.

———. *Zadok's Heirs: The Role and Development of the High Priesthood in Ancient Israel*. Oxford: Oxford University Press, 2000.

Rose, W. H. "Messianic Expectations in the Early Postexilic Period." Pages 168–85 in Albertz and Becking, eds., *Yahwism After the Exile*.

———. *Zemah and Zerubbabel: Messianic Expectations in the Early Postexilic Period*. JSOTSup 304. Sheffield: Sheffield Academic Press, 2000.

Rosenberg, R. A. "The Slain Messiah in the Old Testament." *ZAW* 99 (1987): 259–61.

Rothstein, J. W. *Die nachtgeschichte des Sacharja. Studien zur sacharjaprophetie und zur jüdischen geschichte im ersten nachexilischen jahrhundert*. Leipzig: J. C. Hinrichs, 1910.

Rudolph, W. *Haggai–Sacharja 1–8 –Sacharja 9–14–Maleachi*. Kommentar Zum Alten Testament. Gütersloh: Gerd Mohn, 1976.

Ryken, L., J. C. Wilhoit, and T. Longman III. "Sheep, Shepherd." Pages 782–85 in *Dictionary of Biblical Imagery*. Downers Grove: IVP, 1998.

Sæbø, M. *On the Way to Canon: Creative Tradition History in the Old Testament*. JSOTSup 191. Sheffield: Sheffield Academic Press, 1998.

———. *Sacharja 9–14: Untersuchungen von Text und Form*. WMANT 34. Neukirchen–Vluyn: Neukirchener Verlag, 1969.

Sailhamer, J. H. "The Messiah and the Hebrew Bible." *JETS* 44 (2001): 5–23.

Samaan, P. G. *Portraits of the Messiah in Zechariah*. Washington: Review & Herald Publishing, 1989.

Satterthwaite, P. E., R. S. Hess, and G. J. Wenham, eds. *The Lord's Anointed: Interpretation of Old Testament Messianic Texts*. Carlisle: Paternoster, 1995.

Schaefer, K. R. "Zechariah 14: A Study in Allusion." *CBQ* 57 (1995): 66–91.

———. "Zechariah 14 and the Composition of the Book of Zechariah." *RB* 100 (1993): 368–98.

Schellenberg, A. F. "One in the Bond of War: The Unity of Deutero-Zechariah." *Didaskalia* 12 (2001): 101–15.

Schmitz, P. C. "Sidon (Place)." *ABD* 6:17–18.

Schöttler, H.-G. *Gott inmitten seines Volkes: Die Neuordnung des Gottesvolkes nack Sacharja 1–6*. Trierer theologische Studien 43. Trier: Paulinus, 1987.

Schultz, R. "The King in the Book of Isaiah." Pages 141–65 in Satterthwaite, Hess, and Wenham, eds., *The Lord's Anointed*.

Scott, R. B. Y. "The Meaning of *Maśśā'* as an Oracle Title." *JBL* 67 (1948): v–vi.

Segal, M. "The Responsibilities and Rewards of Joshua the High Priest According to Zechariah 3:7." *JBL* 126 (2007): 717–34.

Seitz, C. R. *Prophecy and Hermeneutics: Toward a New Introduction to the Prophets*. Grand Rapids: Baker Academic, 2007.

———. *Word Without End: The Old Testament as Abiding Theological Witness*. Grand Rapids: Eerdmans, 1998.

Selman, M. J. "Zechariah: Theology of." *NIDOTTE* 4:1303–7.

Seybold, K. *Bilder zum Tempelbau: Die Visionen des Propheten Sacharja*. SBS 70. Stuttgart: KBW, 1974.

———. "Die Königserwartung bei den Propheten Haggai und Sacharja." *Judaica* 28 (1972): 69–78.

Siebeneck, R. T. "Messianism of Aggeus and Proto-Zacharias." *CBQ* 19 (1957): 312–28.

Slayton, J. C. "Bashan." *ABD* 1:623–24.

Smith, R. L. *Micah–Malachi*. WBC 32. Waco: Word, 1984.

Stacey, W. D. *Prophetic Drama in the Old Testament*. London: Epworth, 1990.

Starling, D. I. "The Messianic Hope in the Psalms." *RTR* 58 (1999): 121–34.

Stead, M. R. *The Intertextuality of Zechariah 1–8*. LHBOTS 506. New York: T&T Clark International, 2009.

———. "Zechariah and the 'Former Prophets': An Intertextual Examination of the Re-use of the Prophetic Tradition in Zechariah 1–8." Ph.D. diss., University of Gloucestershire, 2007.

Stuhlmueller, C. *Rebuilding with Hope*. ITC. Grand Rapids: Eerdmans, 1988.

Sweeney, M. A. *The Twelve Prophets*. Vol. 2, *Micah, Nahum, Habakkuk, Zephaniah, Haggai, Zechariah, Malachi*. Berit Olam: Studies in Hebrew Narrative & Poetry. Collegeville: Liturgical, 2000.

Sykes, S. *Time and Space in Haggai–Zechariah 1–8: A Bakhtinian Analysis of a Prophetic Chronicle*. Studies in Biblical Literature 24. New York: Peter Lang, 2002.

Thomas, D. W. "The Book of Zechariah: Chapters 1–8 (Introduction and Exegesis)." *IB* 6:1053–113.

———. "A Note on מחלצות in Zechariah 3.4." *JTS* 33 (1932): 279–80.

Thompson, H. O. "Jordan, Jungle of." *ABD* 3:960–61.

———. "Jordan River." *ABD* 3:953–58.

Thompson, J. A. *The Book of Jeremiah*. NICOT. Grand Rapids: Eerdmans, 1980.

———. *Deuteronomy*. TOTC. Leicester: IVP, 1974.

Thomson, J. G. S. S. "The Shepherd-Ruler Concept in the OT and Its Application in the NT." *SJT* 8 (1955): 406–18.

Tidiman, B. *Le Livre de Zacharie*. Vaux-sur-Seine: Édifac, 1996.

Tidwell, N. L. A. "*waʾōmar* (Zech 3:5) and the Genre of Zechariah's Fourth Vision." *JBL* 94 (1975): 343–55.

Tiemeyer, L.-S. "The Guilty Priesthood (Zech 3)." Pages 1–19 in Tuckett, ed., *The Book of Zechariah and Its Influence*.

———. *Priestly Rites and Prophetic Rage: Post-Exilic Prophetic Critique of the Priesthood*. Tübingen: Mohr Siebeck, 2006.

Tigchelaar, E. J. C. *Prophets of Old and the Day of the End: Zechariah, the Book of Watchers, and Apocalyptic*. Oudtestamentische Studiën 35. Leiden: Brill, 1996.

Tollington, J. E. *Tradition and Innovation in Haggai and Zechariah 1–8*. JSOTSup 150. Sheffield: JSOT, 1993.

Tomasino, A. "*yātēd.*" *NIDOTTE* 2:568–70.

Townsend, J. L. "The Purpose of 1 & 2 Chronicles." *BibSac* 144 (1987): 277–92.

Trèves, M. "Conjectures Concerning the Date and Authorship of Zechariah IX–XIV." *VT* 13 (1963): 196–207.

Tromp, J. "Bad Divination in Zechariah 10:1–2." Pages 41–52 in Tuckett, ed., *The Book of Zechariah and Its Influence*.

Tuckett, C., ed. *The Book of Zechariah and Its Influence*. Aldershot: Ashgate, 2003.

Turner, M. "Holy Spirit." Pages 551–58 in Alexander and Rosner, eds., *New Dictionary of Biblical Theology*.

Uffenheimer, B. "Zerubbabel: The Messianic Hope of the Returnees." *JBQ* 24 (1996): 221–28.

Unger, M. F. *Unger's Bible Commentary: Zechariah*. Amsterdam: Drukkerij Holland, 1963.

Van Hoonacker, A. *Les Douze Petits Prophètes: traduits et commentés*. Paris: J. Gabalda, 1906.

VanderKam, J. C. *From Joshua to Caiaphas: High Priests after the Exile*. Minneapolis: Fortress, 2004.

———. "Joshua the High Priest and the Interpretation of Zechariah 3." *CBQ* 53 (1991): 553–70.

Vermes, G. *Scripture and Tradition in Judaism*. 2d ed. Leiden: Brill, 1973.

Vincent, J. M. "L'apport de la recherche historique et ses limites pour la compréhension des visions nocturnes de Zacharie." *Biblica* 87 (2006): 22–41.

Wanke, G. "Prophecy and Psalms in the Persian Period." Pages 162–88 in *The Cambridge History of Judaism*, vol. 1. Edited by W. D. Davies and L. Finkelstein. Cambridge: Cambridge University Press, 1984.

Waterman, L. "The Camouflaged Purge of Three Messianic Conspirators." *JNES* 13 (1954): 73–78.

Watts, J. D. W. "Zechariah." Pages 308–65 in *The Broadman Bible Commentary*. Vol. 7, *Hosea–Malachi*. Edited by C. J. Allen. London: Marshall, Morgan & Scott, 1972.

Webb, B. G. *The Message of Isaiah: On Eagle's Wings*. The Bible Speaks Today. Leicester: IVP, 1996.

———. *The Message of Zechariah: Your Kingdom Come*. The Bible Speaks Today. Leicester: IVP, 2003.

Weinberg, J. P. *The Citizen-Temple Community*. Translated by D. L. Smith-Christopher. Sheffield: Sheffield Academic Press, 1992.

Weis, R. D. "Oracle." *ABD* 5:28–29.

Wellhausen, J. *Die Kleinen Propheten*. Berlin: de Gruyter, 1963.

———. *Sketch of the History of Israel and Judah*. 3d ed. London: A. & C. Black, 1891.

———. "Zechariah, Book of." Pages 4: 5390–95 in *Encyclopaedia Biblica*. Edited by T. K. Cheyne and J. Sutherland Black. London: A. & C. Black, 1903.

Westermann, C. *Isaiah 40–66: A Commentary*. Translated by D. M. G. Stalker. OTL. London: SCM Press, 1969.

Whybray, R. N. *Isaiah 40–66*. NCBC. Grand Rapids: Eerdmans, 1975.

Wifall, W. "David: Prototype of Israel's Future?" *BTB* 4 (1974): 94–107.

Williamson, H. G. M. *Variations on a Theme: King, Messiah and Servant in the Book of Isaiah*. Carlisle: Paternoster, 1998.

Williamson, P. R. *Sealed with an Oath: Covenant in God's unfolding purpose*. NSBT 23. Nottingham: Apollos, 2007.

Wolters, A. "Confessional Criticism and the Night Visions of Zechariah." Pages 90–117 in *Renewing Biblical Interpretation*. Edited by C. Bartholomew, C. Greene, and K. Möller. Grand Rapids: Zondervan, 2000.

Woude, A. S. van der. "Die beiden Söhne des Öls (Sach. 4:14): Messianische Gestalten?" Pages 262–70 in *Travels in the World of the Old Testament*. Edited by M. Heerma van Voss. Assen: Van Gorcum, 1974.

———. "Die Hirtenallegorie von Sacharja XI." *JNSL* 12 (1984): 139–49.

————. "Serubbabel und die messianischen Erwarungen des Propheten Sacharja." Pages 138–56 in *Lebendige Forschung im Alten Testament*. Edited by O. Kaiser. Berlin: de Gruyter, 1988.

————. "Zion as Primeval Stone in Zechariah 3 and 4." Pages 237–48 in *Text and Context*. Edited by W. T. Claassen. Sheffield: JSOT, 1988.

Wright, C. H. H. *Zechariah and His Prophecies, Considered in Relation to Modern Criticism: With a Critical and Grammatical Commentary and New Translation*. London: Hodder & Stoughton, 1879.

Wright, C. J. H. *The Message of Ezekiel*. The Bible Speaks Today. Leicester: IVP, 2001.

INDEXES

INDEX OF REFERENCES

7:14	150		155–94,	2:10	52, 75,
7:18	200		211, 223,		76, 135,
			225, 228,		138
Nahum			237, 244–	2:11	72, 75,
1:5	70, 161		46		103, 113,
1:6	161	1–6	2, 4, 23,		134, 136,
3:18	158		33, 37,		200, 250
			39, 41,	2:12	51, 52
Habakkuk			45, 125,	2:13	52, 76
3:10	70		126, 129,	2:14 MT	52, 76,
			222		135, 138
Zephaniah		1–3	52	2:14–15	141, 142
1:16	161	1–2	83	2:15 MT	113, 134,
3:6	161	1:1–6:15	2		200, 250
3:9	138	1:1–6	2, 50	2:16 MT	51, 52
3:12	140	1:1	2, 86,	2:17 MT	52, 76
			102, 159	3–6	32
Haggai		1:3	75, 113	3–4	247
1:1	63	1:4	87, 147,	3	26, 46,
1:6	83		190		47, 59,
1:14	63, 83	1:7–6:15	2		78, 80,
2:1	63	1:7–6:8	2, 100		83, 85,
2:3	72	1:7	2, 86,		86, 98,
2:6–9	113		102, 159		99, 107,
2:7–9	118	1:9	49		112, 114,
2:14	99	1:10–11	234		116, 120,
2:20–23	65, 85	1:14	49		121, 126–
2:21	63	1:16–17	113		28, 142,
2:23	18, 63–	1:16	50, 52,		206, 244,
	65, 137		55, 72,		247, 252
			75, 76,	3:1–8	136
Zechariah			113, 118,	3:1–7	46–48,
1–10	221		215		62, 93,
1–9	22, 32	1:17	51, 75		247
1–8	2, 3, 8,	1:18	105	3:1–5	48, 97
	11, 13–	1:20	49, 105	3:1–3	49
	16, 18–	2:3 MT	49	3:1	49, 53
	21, 23,	2:5	52, 75, 76	3:2	51, 113
	25, 27–	2:6–7	52	3:3	52
	31, 33–	2:8–9	136	3:4–7	49, 52
	36, 38,	2:9	72, 103,	3:4–5	53
	40–44,		113	3:4	47, 53
	87, 129,	2:9 MT	52, 76	3:5	48, 53, 61
	131, 136,	2:10–11 MT	52		
	141, 142,			3:6–10	48
	146, 147,			3:6–7	53

INDEX OF AUTHORS